BURIED DREAMS

BURIED DREAMS

Inside the Mind of a
Serial Killer

Tim Cahill
based on the investigative reporting of Russ Ewing

BANTAM BOOKS
TORONTO · NEW YORK · LONDON · SYDNEY · AUCKLAND

BURIED DREAMS
A Bantam Book / March 1986

Library of Congress Cataloging in Publication Data

Cahill, Tim.
  Buried dreams.

  1. Gacy, John Wayne.   2. Crime and criminals—
Illinois—Chicago—Biography.   3. Mass murder—
Illinois—Chicago—Case studies.   I. Title.
HV6248.G24C34   1986   364.1'523'0924   [B]   85-47793
ISBN 0-553-05115-6

Published simultaneously in the United States and Canada

PRINTED IN THE UNITED STATES OF AMERICA

BP   0   9   8   7   6   5   4   3   2   1

INTRODUCTION

A HOT SEPTEMBER MORNING on the north side of Chicago. Russ Ewing and I were crouched over double, working with trenching tools under a three foot high ceiling and sweating heavily: two men digging in the mud of a crawl space under the porch of a north side home, hoping that we wouldn't find what we half expected to uncover. Russ and I had reason to believe the body of a murdered boy was buried there in the hard-packed, yellow-brown mud.

We were partners, the two of us, working together on the story of John Wayne Gacy, America's most prolific convicted mass murderer. Ewing is a reporter for WLS-TV in Chicago: a tough soft spoken man whose collegiate degree—unusual for a newsman—is in psychology.

In 1977, Ewing had done a report on missing children in Chicago. It seemed there were a disproportionate amount of young men, teenagers for the most part, reported missing from a neighborhood called Uptown. Russ Ewing didn't know it then, but he was working on the story of John Wayne Gacy. A year later, Gacy was arrested, and charged with the murders of 33 young men. He had buried most of the victims in the crawl space under his house. Russ Ewing, who had done stories about several of the

missing boys whose bodies were found in the wet mud under
Gacy's house, felt as if he knew those boys, and the Gacy story
became a very personal one for him.

Reporting on the early stages of the murder trial, Ewing
said, on camera, that "John Wayne Gacy must be considered
innocent until proven guilty." Mr. Gacy, who collected clippings
about himself and monitored news reports compulsively, apparently began to believe, on the strength of that statement, that the
newsman was somehow "on my side." He phoned Russ Ewing.
The first contact led to prison interviews, protracted correspon-
dence, and hundreds of dollars worth of collect calls from Gacy to
Ewing.

In 1981, after working on the Gacy story, on and off, for
four years, Ewing agreed to turn his information and the names of
his contacts over to me for the purpose of writing a book. Russ
would function as a consultant, providing information I might be
unable to develop for myself. The actual writing was, by agreement, entirely my own.

A reporter is interested in facts. Early on, I discovered
that, in addition to factual truth, I would be dealing with complex
emotional and psychological nuances—information not easily reported
in a two-minute news segment. During the next three and a half
years, Russ and I worked together on the project, developing
precisely this sort of information, retracing steps in his four year
long investigation, speaking to people who had known Gacy both
as a free man and a convict.

Mr. Gacy, for his part, provided information, dates, places,
and the names of people we might contact. His motivation was
muddy, at best, and he professed confusion concerning "the crimes."
At one point, Mr. Gacy suggested that there may have been more
victims than the police knew about. Maybe, Mr. Gacy said, he
didn't actually commit any murders: perhaps they had been done
by young employees of his contracting company. He recalled
some of those employees working on his north side home, in the
crawl space under a porch. The young men had dug a hole too
deep for the work they were doing, and Gacy had seen it. Perhaps
this was a grave. Perhaps there was a body buried there.

Mr. Gacy recalled the address—he has an extraordinary
memory for such details—and described the house. Russ Ewing
and I obtained permission from the owner to dig up the crawl space

under his porch. Sometime during the third hour of work, we uncovered something ominous. It looked, in the dust, like the back of a man's head. There was an odor of death that drove us from the crawl space.

Russ had three important telephone numbers in his notebook. They were written down in the precise order: Coroner, cops, camera crew.

"Do we call?" I asked Russ.

"Let's be sure," he said.

We put on painting masks to mute the smell. Kneeling by the hole, we brushed away the dust, careful not to destroy evidence. The hair didn't seem to be human. It had a strange, coarse texture, and its color was odd: orange with streaks of black. I cleared away a bit more of the dirt with my shovel. We had uncovered a calico cat.

"Thank God," I said. Only a cat.

Later Ewing told me he'd felt the same emotions that I had. There was horror at the core of it, of course, and revulsion, all of this mixed in with a sense that we'd been had, that we'd been blatantly manipulated. It was a combination of emotions I became entirely familiar with in the next few years.

"You could almost hear him laughing down in that crawl space," I told Ewing.

"I know," he said.

The reader should be aware at the outset that John Wayne Gacy has not and will not profit monetarily from this book. Nevertheless, Mr. Gacy has continued to talk with Russ Ewing and with other people who provided information to me. The latter sources are, by agreement, confidential. Why Mr. Gacy chose to cooperate with them, and with Russ Ewing, is a question I believe is fully answered in the narrative.

If the reader senses some uncertainty regarding motive here, it is because Mr. Gacy often contradicts himself, presents alternative explanations, or simply denies that he said something. Some psychologists and psychiatrists who have studied him think this tendency mirrors Mr. Gacy's confusion, his underlying mental illness. Others state flatly that it is an attempt to "obfuscate," to manipulate the listener, to "feign insanity."

Whatever the case, John Gacy is a tireless talker. Sometimes he prefers to speak like a lout, and will litter the conversation with conscious double negatives, repetitive curses, and various tough-guy locutions. At other times, Mr. Gacy is positively pretentious in describing his own idealism. Almost simultaneously, he can play the sensitive "victim," courageous enough to cry.

In analyzing what amounted to over 100 hours of interviews with Mr. Gacy, I concentrated on answering three questions. First, what did he actually do—as opposed to what he said he did? How did he choreograph the killings, the central events of his life: was there significant ritual involved in the terrible danse macabre of death? Secondly, what was the facade that allowed him to literally get away with murder for almost six years? Finally, and most important, what was going on in his mind? How can such a man live with himself?

In constructing this book, I originally sought to find "the real John Gacy." The idea was to subtract the lies, the misrepresentations, the false idealism. With the material available to me, I intended to identify internal contradictions, and work my way down into a solid core of truth. I was looking for a simple explanation. And yet . . . the more I studied Mr. Gacy, the more I came to realize that the apparent complexity of his personality defined him more accurately than any single theory I might formulate or propose. The "real John Gacy" is a creature composed of lies, internal contradictions, misrepresentations, and false idealism.

Buried Dreams, then, mirrors my research method. In understanding the crimes committed by John Wayne Gacy, I found it was necessary to learn to think like John Wayne Gacy. This is neither pleasant nor entirely healthy. We are diving into some dark and chilly psychic waters here. The reader may feel claustrophobic, may feel trapped inside the killer's mind, as I did in writing this book. Even so, it is the mind of the murderer—not murder itself—that ought to concern us.

In the three and a half years I spent writing and researching this book, I held one statistic in mind: the FBI estimates that there are at least 35 other serial killers at large in the United States today. In reviewing the literature on such multiple murderers I was struck by certain terrifying similarities. Among men like Jack the Ripper, Ted Bundy, and John Wayne Gacy there is a pattern that seems to repeat itself, a pattern, most professionals agree, that is too little studied and imperfectly understood. *Buried Dreams* is an attempt to isolate that pattern.

For this reason, I have tried to present a picture of a man's mind, in his own style of speech, often in his own words. I wanted to put the reader inside that mind—the mind of the murderer—and that is why this book is written, for the most part, from Mr. Gacy's point of view. I have endeavored to make his best case for him, as he would have done. The reader might imagine himself or herself sitting across from Mr. Gacy in a prison conference room or a psychiatrist's office.

John Gacy himself believes that "no one can tell when you're lying and when you're not," at least in regard to such intangibles as motive. I am not so certain that this is true and *Buried Dreams* has been written in full confidence that the reader, like a smart cop or a good psychiatrist, will be able to see through the shifting ambiguities, to sweep away the "rationalizations" and "suppositions" until the soul of John Wayne Gacy lies bare.

From time to time, I have seen fit to intrude in order to set the record straight, to prevent libeling certain persons Mr. Gacy clearly wished to defame, and to provide information that he may have forgotten or purposely omitted. In some few cases, names have been changed to insure privacy, but all incidents are as Mr. Gacy related them, or as they were reported in the public record.

Some members of Chicago's homosexual community have expressed fear that a book about John Wayne Gacy could result in a new wave of repression against gays. This is a legitimate concern, and one that compels me to state the perfectly obvious: for every serial killer who has preyed on men or boys, there is one who has stalked women and whose crimes have been essentially sexual in nature. Should heterosexuals be condemned because Ted Bundy is thought to have killed over 30 young women?

I suspect that the majority of readers—those whose lives never touched John Wayne Gacy's—share, at the outset, my original belief that anyone committing such incomprehensibly cruel crimes must necessarily be insane. But if John Gacy is sane, as those who prosecuted him argued—if the pattern is not symptomatic of mental disease but is rather a rational criminal's "method of operation"—we are confronted with an intensely disturbing moral and philosophical concept. It is not something we ordinarily care to examine too closely, this idea that evil exists in our world.

Confronted with the crimes committed by John Wayne Gacy, decent people cling to the cold conceptual comfort of insanity. One psychologist I spoke with about Mr. Gacy stated this position best: "Evil is a medieval superstition." Then again, that man never personally examined John Wayne Gacy, as the reader of this book is about to do.

TIM CAHILL

CHAPTER

1

ONE OF THE NEIGHBORS was wakened from her sleep by screams in the night: faint, high-pitched screams that drifted across the neatly mowed lawns and seemed to come from the house beyond a hedge she could see from her back door. It was hard to tell, on that humid summer night, when the air was still and thick as cotton, exactly where they were coming from, or even if they were nothing more than a remnant of troubled sleep, some dim, half-remembered nightmare. But no, fully awake now, she could hear them through the open window. They sounded like the cries of a boy, a fifteen-, sixteen-, seventeen-year-old boy: a young man about the same age as her son. The muffled screams went on and on, reaching a tormented crescendo that lasted for half an hour or more. "Drugs," the woman thought. Maybe the boy was taking drugs, and maybe the drugs made him scream. Could drugs make boys scream like that?

She called the police and reported the disturbance, which, as near as she could tell, seemed to be coming from the house behind hers out in Norwood Park, an unincorporated area north and west of Chicago. Officers visited the house at 8213 Summerdale, where they talked with the owner, a contractor named John Gacy. Nothing seemed to be amiss.

There were other nights, almost always weekend nights, when the woman woke to screams across the lawn in the still of the night, but the police had investigated, and there was never anything on the radio or television about foul play in Norwood Park.

Several months later, on the night of December 11, 1978, a fifteen-year-old boy was reported missing by his worried parents. Rob Piest was an A student, a standout gymnast, an ambitious, intelligent boy who was very close to his family—not at all the sort of kid who runs away from home. Certainly not at nine o'clock in the evening, after putting in four hours on his part-time job; certainly not on the night of his mother's forty-sixth-birthday party, a party that had been postponed until Rob finished work. The boy was last seen on his way to talk to a contractor about a summer job. The contractor's name was John Gacy. That night, Rob Piest simply disappeared.

Suburban Des Plaines police, investigating the case, put a tracer on John Wayne Gacy, Jr., and found that he had been convicted of sodomy, in Iowa, ten years previous. That offense had involved a fifteen-year-old boy.

Ten days later, after an intensive investigation, John Gacy was arrested. He insisted that he knew nothing about the Piest boy's disappearance. The interrogation was cut short when the suspect complained of severe chest pains and said that he had a history of heart trouble. Officers rushed Gacy to Holy Family Hospital in Des Plaines.

Meanwhile, a search warrant was obtained for Gacy's house. Officers and evidence technicians—representatives of the Des Plaines police department, the Cook County sheriff's police, and the state's attorney's detail—began arriving at the brick ranch house about seven that night. They were looking for evidence of a kidnapping; they feared they might find evidence of a murder.

The front room of the house at 8213 Summerdale was choked with plants, and there were several pictures of sad-faced clowns on the wall. In a business office just off the living room, officers found several sets of meticulous records detailing Gacy's business, as well as photos showing the chunky contractor shaking hands with the mayor of Chicago and with the wife of the President of the United States. In a rec room, hidden near the pool table, officers found a large vibrating dildo crusted with disagreeable evidence that it had been used in some recent anal penetration. There were a number of books and magazines about homosexuality, and several of them featured older men in congress with young boys. Ominously, in the attic, investigators found some wallets, and the information inside proved that they belonged to young men, teenagers.

Toward the front of the house, in a living-room closet, police found a trapdoor leading down into a dark, dirt-floored crawl space, which seemed to be flooded. The beam of a floodlight pointed into the open hatchway was reflected on the surface of the dank water that stood a foot deep below. Cook County evidence technician Daniel Genty saw a cord just under the hatchway door; he plugged the cord into a nearby socket. There was a rumble of machinery, and a sump pump, somewhere in the murky depths, began pumping water out of the darkness. A dank, putrid smell emanated from the crawl space: the smell of sewage and something worse, something officers recognized as the odor of a morgue.

It took about fifteen minutes for the crawl space to drain, and in that time, evidence technicians searching the garage and workshed found a number of wallets containing IDs belonging to several young men, as well as some items of personal jewelry a teenage boy might wear. It didn't seem possible that all these boys had just happened to leave their clothes, their jewelry, and their wallets at John Gacy's house.

Daniel Genty now had an idea of what he might find in the crawl space. When the water had been flushed away, Genty dropped through the hatchway, into the mud. There was no ladder: the crawl space was only about two and a half feet deep. Genty dragged a small shovel and fire department floodlight with him. He crawled, on his hands and knees, toward the south wall, dropping to his belly to get under the center-support beam that ran the length of the house. In the southeast corner of the house, up against the foundation, Genty could see two long depressions, parallel to the wall. They were about six feet long and a foot and a half wide: the size of graves.

Genty crawled to the northwest corner of the crawl space, then moved to the southwest, where he noted three small puddles, about the size of ashtrays. One of the puddles was a dark, murky, purple color. The other two were filled with hundreds of thin red worms, about two inches long, and when Genty shone the flood-light on them, they burrowed into the soft mud.

It was there, in the southwest corner of the crawl space, that Genty decided to make his first excavation. He knelt, nearly doubled over, and plunged his trenching tool into the mud. An unbearably putrid odor burst up out of the earth and filled the crawl space. The second shovelful of earth contained a clot of adipocere: white, soapy, rotting flesh, almost like lard. A product of decomposition, adipocere takes twelve months or more to form. The body could not be Rob Piest's.

Gacy, it seemed, could possibly be guilty of more than one murder. Genty took one last scoop of mud, hit something hard, and pried up what looked like a human arm bone. Skeletal remains: definitely not the body of a boy last seen alive eleven days ago.

Genty shouted to Lieutenant Joseph Kozenczak of the Des Plaines Police Department upstairs: "Charge him! Murder!"

Kozenczak yelled, "Repeat that!"

"I found one."

"Is it Piest?"

"No. I don't think so. It's been here too long."

Another evidence technician and an investigator dropped into the crawl space.

The odor, in that damp and confined area, was almost as unbearable as the thought of what the crawl space contained. "I think this place is full of kids," Genty said.

In the northeast corner of the crawl space under John Gacy's house, the officers found more puddles, all swarming with thin red worms. There, two feet from the north wall, they uncovered what appeared to be a knee bone. The flesh was so desiccated that at first they thought it was blue-jean material.

South of that dig, Genty uncovered some human hair in the soil. The second evidence technician dug along the south wall and found two long bones, human leg bones, both very blackened. Rather than disturb any more remains that might complicate identification procedures or destroy evidence, the officers decided to quit the crawl space and call the coroner.

At about the same time, John Gacy was being released from Holy Family Hospital. He had been thoroughly examined, and doctors could find no evidence of a heart attack. Gacy's pulse was a little high, that was all. Under heavy guard—detectives had been told what the search uncovered—Gacy was returned to the Des Plaines police station, where he was arrested and charged with murder.

Gacy signed a card waiving his Miranda rights, then spoke to detectives David Hachmeister and Michael Albrecht.

"My house," Gacy said. "Did you go into the crawl space?"

"Yeah," Albrecht said, "we did."

"I used lime," Gacy said. "That's what it was for."

"What was it for, John?" Albrecht asked.

"For the sewage, the dampness . . . for . . . what you found there."

A mug shot, taken at the time, shows a stuporous, uncomprehending man. Gacy's puffy face and undistinguished features look slack, as if the bones of his skull have no substance to them. He stares into the camera, and his eyes are glassy, dull, and dead. He looks like a man insane. Or on drugs.

"There are four Johns," Gacy told Albrecht. "I don't know all of them." One of the four, Gacy explained later, was called "Jack." Jack didn't like homosexuality, and he detested homosexuals. The bodies in the crawl space? You'd have to ask Jack how they died. John did the dirty work. John, it seemed, had been forced to cover for Jack, to bury the bodies, to live with the stench, to spread the lime.

In a second voluntary statement, given about three-thirty the next morning, Gacy said there were "twenty-five to thirty bodies." Detectives found that number hard to comprehend, and they questioned Gacy closely. The suspect said he couldn't answer every question. Some things, he said, he just honestly didn't know. "You'd have to ask Jack that," he explained.

Piest's body, Gacy said, had been thrown from a bridge on I-55 into the Des Plaines River. Jack was working too fast for John to keep up. The crawl space was full, and John, with his worsening heart condition, couldn't dig any more graves.

The killer was named Jack: Jack Hanley.

John could tell the police that much.

The next morning, a fleet of police vehicles and nearly three dozen officers, including representatives from three different law-enforcement agencies, invaded Norwood Park. They were closely followed by about as many reporters.

The media were hungry and the suspect was in custody, unavailable. As is usual in such cases, the neighbors were interviewed about the accused killer who had lived in their midst. No one could believe it, not at first. The man had a heart condition, after all: how could he have dug those graves, doubled over in that cramped crawl space? He was 5 feet 8 and weighed over 230 pounds.

There was an odd sense of *déjà vu* about these postarrest interviews with the accused killer's friends and neighbors. It was a scene that had been played in 1971 in Yuba City, California, when Juan Corona was arrested and charged with the murders of twenty-five young farm workers, all males; a scene that had its run in Houston, when Elmer Wayne Henley was charged with the sex-torture murders of twenty-seven young men. It was a scene that would play in Atlanta in 1981, when Wayne B. Williams was arrested and charged with the murders of two young blacks. Prosecutors insisted they could link Williams with the murders of twenty-eight young men. Eighty young men dead in all: Eighty murders, all of them, so it seemed, committed in some insane sexual frenzy or in a calculated effort to conceal evidence of homosexual activity.

These were not mass murders, journalists pointed out. It was a problem of semantics, as well as a difference in method. Richard Speck—who invaded the Chicago living quarters of eight nurses in 1966 and murdered seven—was a mass murderer. The slaughter had been accomplished in a matter of hours, all at once. Charles Whitman, who climbed a tower at the University of Texas and shot twelve in 1966, was a mass murderer. Henley, Corona, and later Williams were not mass murderers in that sense; they were serial killers. All three seemed to lead normal lives, and they killed their victims one at a time, as the mood struck them, over a period of years. The serial killer was a colder, more calculating animal than the mass murderer. Part of the serial killer's method was façade, the ability to live an apparently normal life between, and in spite of, the accumulating murderous episodes. The serial killer is everyone's next-door neighbor.

Serial murderers survive and kill, and get away with the killings, in part because life does not emulate art. It is not the way we expect it to be, not as it is on TV or in the movies, where discordant music hints at some character's frightening psychological problems, where low camera angles and shadowed lighting can suggest an impending homicide. The serial murderers lived next door, or across the street, or down the block. They talked and walked and laughed like any other man, but they killed, and killed again—and again, and again after that—until they were caught.

Normal-enough guys; pretty good neighbors; bright, friendly fellows. And when they were caught, their neighbors found themselves squinting into bright television lights, feeling defensive, as if they had to justify themselves; feeling angry or confused; feeling somehow betrayed. The killer, in his frenzy, had destroyed something soul deep in those who lived around him. The viewer sensed it in the troubled glance off camera; the facial tic; the odd, inappropriate gesture: these were innocent people destined to live with a sickly sad, unearned guilt the rest of their lives.

No, the neighbors and friends said in California, there didn't seem to be anything troubling Juan. I never thought he might have homosexual tendencies. Never had an inkling. In Atlanta, they would say that Wayne was a bright young man, destined to go places. Elmer Henley was a hard worker, they said in Texas. The neighbors were numb in Texas, stunned in California, staggered in Georgia.

It was no different in Chicago. The day the story broke, there were shots, broadcast live, of the brick ranch house with the outdoor Christmas lights mysteriously blinking (the owner, after all, was in jail), and the neighbors, in voice-over—or on the radio, or in newspaper columns—described the man who had lived there as gregarious, community-minded, generous. When the snow piled up on the streets, they said, John Gacy hooked up a snowplow and cleared the driveways up and down his block. He had worked long and hard to get streetlights installed in unincorporated Norwood Park. He was a man said to have important political connections, and some neighbors had seen, in the office in his home, those pictures of John Gacy shaking hands with the mayor of Chicago, with the wife of the President of the United States. He was a man who gave an annual summer lawn party for four hundred or more people, at his own expense; a man who organized Chicago's Polish Day parade and saw that it ran like clockwork. And this—on his own time, and at no pay, John Gacy went to hospitals where he entertained sick children, dressed as a clown. Pogo the clown.

Even as the neighbors spoke, John Gacy was giving another voluntary statement. At four o'clock on the afternoon of December 22, one day after his arrest, Gacy asked to talk with Larry Finder, of the state's attorney's office. In the course of the conversation, Gacy began describing where some of the bodies were buried, and Finder said he was having difficulty picturing the graves in his mind. Gacy asked for a sheet of paper and a pen. Resting the paper on the metal part of the bunk in his cell, Gacy drew a rectangle and began filling it with smaller rectangles he said represented graves, or trenches, where the bodies were buried. There could be as many as thirty of them.

And while Gacy was drawing his map, the neighbors were being grilled by reporters. No, they said, the man never seemed insane. He drank now and again, no more than anyone else, and if he had one too many, which happened infrequently, he simply became a little louder, a little more friendly. He was proud of himself and his business, maybe even a bit of a braggart, and, sure, sometimes he bullied the teenage boys who worked for him, but the man himself regularly put in twelve- and sixteen-hour days. He pushed himself hard and obviously felt he had a right to revel in his accomplishments, to expect from his employees the same perfection he demanded of himself.

The crawl-space map was the work of a perfectionist: very neat, very precise, everything neatly squared off on a thin sheet of pink paper. When he finished the work, the suspect's head dropped to his chest in a sudden, poleaxed bow. His fists were clenched tightly at his sides, but he remained motionless, as if suddenly frozen, unconscious. There was no sound in the room. After about a minute, Gacy raised his head and stared at the rectangles within rectangles on the pink sheet. "What's going on?" he asked, and there was a grogginess in his voice. "Did Jack . . . I see Jack . . . drew a diagram of the crawl space."

The people who lived on Summerdale, of course, did not know then of the map Jack drew, and when they talked of John Gacy, they were, in a sense, defending themselves. The monster of Summerdale? None of the neighbors had met that John Gacy. No one could believe it; no one wanted to believe it. The crimes, if indeed Gacy was guilty, would diminish them, haunt them the rest of their lives. It couldn't be true. They would wait and see.

Evidence, the most grisly and final evidence, was being

collected and catalogued from the moment Daniel Genty found the first body. On December 23, 1978, two days after the arrest of John Wayne Gacy, the first two bodies were exhumed from the crawl space under the house, and police were driven from the house by methane gas, a product of putrefaction, which caused nausea and a kind of physical dizziness altogether separate from simple moral revulsion. The bodies were taken to the Cook County Forensic Institute, the morgue, for autopsy and identification.

Several of the bodies had lain for years in the crawl space and had been partially converted to adipocere. The lardlike product of decomposition has a stench so all-pervading that clothes, once exposed to it, must be destroyed; it was a stench that floated, faintly, over the lawns of Norwood Park and lacerated minds like the sounds of screams in the night.

Some evidence technicians, investigators, police, and coroner's deputies working in the crawl space below the house wore disposable paper jumpsuits to save their clothes, and gas masks with charcoal filters to mute the smell. The newer bodies, those buried less than a year, had distended, the cavities had ruptured, and noxious gases—methane, hydrogen sulfide, half a dozen others—erupted from the graves as they were uncovered. Putrid fluids escaping from the bodies permeated the soil, and a particularly virulent form of streptococci bred there, so that the danger of working in the crawl space was very great. A cut, even the smallest nick, could lead to gas gangrene. The men who worked in the crawl space under John Gacy's home shaved after work, at night, and they were careful with their razors.

Such details weren't fit for the evening news, and reporters concentrated on official statements. Sheriff Richard Elrod told the assembled journalists that the remains were all those of young males, boys, and that there might be as many as twenty more buried under the house. Investigators still weren't willing to take John's count—or perhaps it was Jack's—at face value. The search was suspended on December 24 and 25, but ten more bodies were recovered from the crawl space when the digging resumed two days after Christmas. There were shots, on the evening news, of investigators carrying body bags out of the house on Summerdale. Some of them seemed much too small to contain the remains of an entire human being.

The next day, December 28, Cook County medical examiner Robert J. Stein stood in front of John Gacy's house and said, "I have horrible news. Six more bodies were exhumed today."

Morbidity, like a magnet, drew hundreds of people from Chicago and nearby suburbs to Norwood Park. They stood outside the death house, hunched against the cold and shifting from foot to foot. Ropes strung to stakes served as police lines and kept the crowds off Gacy's property and that of his two adjacent neighbors. When more bodies were carried out of the house and into the glare of the television lights, the crowd reacted as one, surging forward, and their voices, from a slight distance, sounded like the rumbling of a single great beast.

There were those in the crowd who felt that the stench of death clung to Gacy's neighbors, that the good people who lived on Summerdale and Berwyn were, in part, responsible for the unthinkable nightly parade of horror. John Gacy had lived among them, killing, killing, killing. Some of those who stood watching knew, for a stone-cold fact, that they could spot a killer on sight. They would have put a stop to it.

Gacy's neighbors lived as if under siege. Most of them had stopped talking to reporters. Every day, over the Christmas holidays, the crowd stood out in front of their homes like an angry accusation. "How could you let this happen?"

Inside the house, investigators found Jack's map of his own private boneyard uncannily accurate. Bodies had been buried parallel to the foundations on all four sides with the exception of a narrow section between a strip of concrete and the main floor support, where one victim was laid perpendicular to the wall. One body was buried under a slab of concrete. Along the southeast wall, Jack, or John, had worked his way in from the foundation and buried two bodies on a diagonal. Two more, farther in toward the center of the house, lay perpendicular to the foundation. It was, the medical examiner noted, an extremely orderly arrangement, one that made full and efficient use of the space available. The work of a perfectionist.

None of the victims had been mutilated, but some of the bodies exhumed had been buried in plastic garbage bags. Several of the bodies were found with what appeared to be their own underwear lodged deeply in their throats; other bodies were found with a length of rope wrapped tightly around their necks. Some of the bodies had been buried in common graves and were in a similar state of decomposition, indicating that they had been killed at about the same time, perhaps on the same day. Bodies exhumed along the southeast wall had been buried one on top of the other—one victim lay face down, his head to the west, and below him, a second body lay face up, head to the east—in positions that suggested sexual activities, as if the killer wished to humiliate his victims, even in death.

Gacy had, evidence technicians discovered, repeatedly spread the crawl space with layers of lime, apparently in an effort to stanch any odors and to hasten decomposition. Lime, ordinary calcium oxide, forms a caustic fluid, calcium hydroxide, when combined with water. The death house had been built over re-claimed swampland, and the crawl space periodically flooded. When that happened, calcium hydroxide seeped into the graves, macerating the bodies and sometimes dissolving organic matter altogether. In some cases, John—or Jack—had doused the bodies with muriatic acid to speed decomposition.

Water continued to seep into the crawl space during a late-December thaw. Evidence technicians sloshed knee deep through the putrid chemical muck of death. To facilitate the search effort, portions of the main floor had been removed so that the gases could escape and lights could be focused on the crawl space, where the remains of the victims were catalogued with archaeological precision.

When the excavations were finally complete, when the last of twenty-nine bodies had been removed from the property, when police were finally satisfied that there were no more victims to be found there, the house was little more than a shell.

Bernard Carey, the state's attorney general, claiming the house unsafe and a public nuisance, filed suit to have it torn down. That spring, a wrecking crew demolished what was left of Gacy's house and hauled the scrap to a dump. All that remained was a flat, excavated plain of yellow-brown mud, slowly reverting to swamp.

By September of that year, grass had begun to grow again on the mud flat that was once 8213 Summerdale. Once every few weeks that summer, an unfamiliar car—another "tourist"—drifted down the street, coasting past the manicured lawns and formal gardens, past the house with the flowering crabapple trees on the lawn, past the house where a statue of the Virgin stands in its own little shrine. The cars would pull to a stop next to the only empty lot in dozens of square blocks. The tourists seldom got out of their cars. Instead, they sat and stared.

There was nothing to see that summer, and there is nothing now: nothing of interest in that empty lot. A few steel girders, five or six feet long, lay twisted in the ocher mud, in a place where the grass will not grow. It is a very small lot, actually—too small, it would seem, to accommodate twenty-nine graves. A pair of mourning doves pick in the gravel at the foot of one of the girders. These birds—named for the male's soft, melancholy call—are common to suburbs throughout the Midwest. Still, the fact that mourning doves should feed here, in this place, where so many died: it is a poetry too rich for the mind's appetite. The tourists—there are still tourists—never stay long. They drive back up Summerdale, back past the manicured lawns, past the gardens, past the shrine of the Virgin, past the people of Norwood Park watching from their windows.

Behind those windows, there are Poles and Germans, Lithuanians and Italians: Americans all. Most everyone is Catholic; most families attend church on Sunday. It is a blue-collar suburb composed of frugal, hardworking people whose homes, in many cases, are the embodiment of a lifelong dream. Very few of John Gacy's former neighbors have moved out of Norwood Park. Property values aren't what they once were on Summerdale.

Most of the people who live on Summerdale, in constant sight of that empty lot, don't care to discuss their former neighbor and become angry at the very mention of his name.

"What he did was carefully, thoroughly planned. John Gacy is Satan."

There are those among his former neighbors—a very small minority—who are more generous of spirit. "He slept six years in that house with all those people buried there? That's not normal. That's insane." Comparing the man they knew to the one they didn't has led some to suppose that Gacy might be schizophrenic, "some kind of split personality."

He was evil.

He was insane.

At twilight, on a late summer's evening, when the air is as

still and thick as cotton, the mourning dove's call drifts across the neatly mowed lawns of Norwood Park.

As the summer of 1979 gave way to winter, four more bodies—four more victims, including Rob Piest—were recovered from the Des Plaines River. Thirty-three bodies in all. John Gacy was now accused of committing more murders than anyone in American history; John Gacy was also undergoing one of the most intense psychological and psychiatric evaluations in American criminal history.

CHAPTER

2

CAST BACK FAR ENOUGH, and there is a shining time, at the dawn of memory, that the mind's eye sees bathed in a misty, golden light. Fragmented incidents emerge out of the mist, and sometimes we can't truly recall if we actually remember these things, or if our parents, or brothers and sisters, told us this story about ourselves and our minds have manufactured fond images to suit the tale. We recall trivial tragedies—a lost toy, a skinned knee—with bemused nostalgia. It is a time when the worst that could happen—the worst that did happen—is stripped, within minutes, of its pain. It is a time of innocence, before the age of reason, at the dawn of memory.

Images of Opal Street, almost rural in the 1940s: six houses set on a single block, the prairie grasses lush and green in the spring, stretching out forever, in all directions. A ragman with a horse-drawn cart who collected discarded clothes. The railroad thumping through, screaming south and east toward nearby Chicago. Houses with large yards and big vegetable gardens; a cinder alley that split the block. Streetlights but no sidewalks. Summer evenings and Ma's rule: "Be home when the streetlights come on."

Fragmented images: caught picking corn in the neighbor's garden and Mrs. Kranz—was that her name?—dragging the kids home to the Old Man. Wasn't she the one with the pigeon coop? And the Polack—you could call him the Polack if you were Polish, too—the Polack with his chickens and turkeys. The turkeys so dumb you could put their heads under their wings, rock them in your hands, and put them to sleep in the middle of the day; just standing by the fence, you could set them all to gobbling, that strange, strangled sound of outraged poultry, and the Polack would come bursting out the back door and you could hardly hear him hollering for the sound of the angry turkeys. The Greek whose goats ran free, always in the backyard, raiding the grapes that grew there.

A big fort the kids built in the prairie, half underground, all scrap lumber and tar paper. Summer evenings catching fireflies in a bottle—all the kids screaming and laughing—so there would be lights in the clubhouse.

A first train ride to Springfield, to visit an aunt and uncle. John was four and the train is one of his first coherent memories. But later there is a story told about him walking out the front door and wandering down a city street, naked as a jaybird, innocent as only a very young child can be. All the adults running and laughing, catching up to him, carrying him back to the house, dressing him. A funny incident: but did he really remember it, or had his mother just told him the story? John couldn't be sure.

There was some joke the adults had about his birthday: the boy a middle child, between JoAnne, twenty-eight months older, and Karen, twenty-eight months younger. He was born in Chicago's Edgewater Hospital, the only son of a Polish father, himself the son of immigrants; and the boy, John Wayne Gacy, Jr., was born on St. Patrick's Day, March 17, 1942. A bright green Polack, his father's son, anxious to please, hungry for praise, but never quite good enough for the Old Man.

Dad worked all day, coming home to fix anything in the house—the wiring, the plastering, everything—a perfectionist who made his own tools and was never satisfied, not with his work, not with the kids, especially not with his son. John Stanley Gacy was heavy on the razor strop he kept hanging on a nail, as an educational device:

"I'll teach you to steal corn."

JoAnne, the eldest, an idol, collecting all those garden snakes from under the front porch and bringing them in the house, the snakes slithering under the stove and the icebox, under the sofas and chairs. Dad taking the razor strop to JoAnne. "I'll teach you to bring snakes into the house."

Karen, the tag-along little sister, toddling after John and JoAnne. Good times. All three of the kids sharing John's model train set: a circular track, a big model gas station in the middle that pumped water instead of gas into the model cars, the Packards and the Buicks and the Hudsons.

A tree house built in an empty lot, and that summer the trucks and grading equipment coming in, the workers looking up at the tree house and the little boy sitting on a limb with tears in his eyes. The tree would have to come down, but the workmen saved that job for last. John coming every day to his house, sitting alone in the tree, waiting stoically for the tragedy that would destroy his entire life. The whole story funny now, but in a bittersweet sort of way.

So much interest in building: the fort in the prairie, another by the coalyard, another in the backyard, this one right over the septic tank, built with a brick foundation and everything. The Old Man finally putting his foot down: "One house on one lot is enough." The razor strop hanging on the nail, and the Old Man ready to teach him about the symmetry of houses and lots.

"I'll teach you . . ."

Another playhouse, this one under the front porch, hidden from the street and not such an eyesore. The Old Man allowed that one to stand. The neighbors said the Gacys had a house under a house. It was a secret place where a quiet, polite boy could be alone, a boy who had been sick, frail as long as he could remember. In the damp darkness under the porch—garden snakes and salamanders there—John could think about flowers, about landscaping and building: the things he liked. The other boys were playing baseball or football or basketball, but John never had any interest in sports. A loner, sickly and weak, uncoordinated, flabby even as a child.

All the memories swirling in a golden mist: sudden bright images, incomplete stories, everything coming together at a point where memory becomes linear and a certain kind of innocence dies: a point when the child realized he was not like other little boys. He was a "loner," an "ugly duckling"; he was "not good enough," he was "different."

*   *   *

All the docs wanted a piece of his youth. John up there under heavy guard in 3 North, the isolation wing, the criminal psychiatric section of Cermak Hospital in Chicago. A literal madhouse, with all these screaming nuts, all the guys trying to hang themselves, "swingers" around every corner, and the gospel music blasting him awake at six in the morning when he never could get to sleep until four. John was supposed to talk with Dr. Rogers and Dr. Rappaport, with Dr. Freedman and Dr. Morrison, with Dr. Brocher and Dr. Cavanaugh, all of them trying to crack the shell and pick away at his guts with their shining, sharp-pointed questions.

Rogers was almost funny. John could see the guy was "scared," didn't like to be alone with him. Rogers was supposed to take "a sexual history" from John, and then—John supposed—the doc would bend all the information around, fit some pieces in here, some in there, and come up with a theory about all those bodies in the crawl space. Something to do with jagging off in the eighth grade.

John figured Rogers purposely acted dumb, always asking him to define terms, explain things, like a doc who's been studying this shit all his life didn't know. Rogers, the way John saw it, got a kick out of asking questions. Not because he didn't know the answers. The guy liked hearing other people talk about their sex hang-ups. He got his rocks off that way, and that was Dr. Rogers' sex hang-up. Pervert questions, John thought.

Still, John talked and talked and talked, elaborating on every detail, answering the questions as fully and honestly as he could, because, in a way, Rogers and all the other doctors were helping. The cross God gave John Wayne Gacy to bear was a heavy one: bad enough to be accused, but John told the docs he truly and honestly did not know if he committed the crimes. He could recall some parts leading up to just five of them, and it was as if he were a witness to what was happening, like he was another person in another body, watching. And then it all faded out and there was nothing until morning, and he found another body with a rope wrapped around its neck, some little present Jack had left for John to bury.

If he did the crime—if the docs could prove to him that he did—then John would save Illinois the expense of a trial. There were twenty ways to commit suicide, even under heavy guard in 3 North. No one has the almighty right to take another life—the Bible says, "Thou shalt not kill"—and if the docs could show him, in his own mind, that he was a killer . . . well, a man like that, thirty-three bodies, he "didn't deserve to live."

So he gave Rogers the sexual history, casting back into the golden time. The first memory, the first thing he could recall and be sure was his and not pieces of a story told to him, was a sexual event.

1946. John was four and she took him out to the prairie where the grasses were high and they were hidden from the houses on Opal Street. A fifteen-year-old girl, some Norwegian girl, stringy blond hair and a slack expression on her face: a neighbor's mildly retarded daughter. She took his pants down and played with him there in the prairie grass, and when he told Ma, there was some commotion in the house, Ma and the Old Man yelling and angry about something.

1949. John, a neighbor boy, and the boy's little sister, all of them naked, John and the boy "messing" with the little girl. When the Old Man found out, he took the razor strop off its nail.

"I'll teach you . . ."

And the same year, a contractor friend of the Old Man was always taking John, the little builder, for rides in his truck. Real friendly, always "horsing around," tickling him, "wrestling" with the seven-year-old boy, whose head always seemed to end up between the man's legs, pressed hard to the crotch of his rough work pants. John, aware even then that the contractor was "messing" with him, just the way he himself had "messed" with the neighbor girl. He never told the Old Man about these rides, and he was never punished for what the contractor had done to him. John remembered that he dreaded the man, his truck, the little drives. He hated being messed with.

Strange, then, that he should have become a contractor. What could Rogers make out of that one?

Then, in the sex history, there was the panty thing that Dr. Helen Morrison thought was important. A nice lady with a good mind: John found her attractive and sympathetic. Some of the victims were found with what appeared to be their own underwear—queeny silk stuff that women wear—lodged deeply in their throats. So maybe the panty thing was important.

The first time it surfaced, John was six, maybe seven: call it 1949, the year too many people were getting messed over. Ma and the Old Man were getting dressed on their way somewhere, and Ma couldn't find any underwear in her drawer. Every piece missing. They found it, all of it, in a brown paper bag, under the front porch, in the sandbox Dad built where John played.

John never knew why he took his mother's underwear—it couldn't be a sex thing at that age—but he told his parents that he liked the feel of it. The Old Man took down the razor strop and taught him what he would like and what he wouldn't like. And the strop wasn't enough for John Stanley Gacy: for the rest of John's life—and maybe it started right there—he felt that the Old Man never "accepted" him.

The next time the panty thing surfaced, John was twelve or thirteen. It was almost as if he wanted to block it out of his mind, the underwear thing, because he couldn't recall if it was then or later (the next time he was fifteen and Karen found panties while making his bed) that Ma told him she'd make him wear the underwear he seemed to like so much. For punishment. Maybe she did make him wear it, once. It was all hazy in there, and he couldn't clearly recall exactly what had happened.

Ma didn't tell the Old Man, though. There came a time when Ma just stopped talking about her only son's problems. The Old Man picked on the boy, swung on him for nothing, hollered at him because he wasn't perfect. Ma kept John's transgressions to herself, punished him herself, and then—whatever John had done—it was over and no one had to talk about it again.

But the Old Man wasn't dumb. Maybe he never got any further than the eighth grade, but he read a lot, and there wasn't anything he couldn't do with tools. A jack-of-all-trades, very intelligent. The night of the second panty thing, John was up in his room, sitting out Ma's punishment, dreading the moment when the Old Man, finally home from work, stepped in the door. Because he would know. John lay on his back in his bed. Over in one corner were the bookcases he had made out of orange crates and painted so they looked like fine furniture. The bed was made, his clothes were all folded in drawers or neatly hung. John's bedroom: the cleanest place in the whole Gacy house. You could eat off the floor. He tried so hard.

When the Old Man got home, Ma would just say, "John's being punished."

"How come?"

"Just something. It's all taken care of now."

And the Old Man would know. The Old Man wasn't dumb.

One of his very first memories: four-year-old John watching the Old Man fix the car. He wanted to help, hand him something, and suddenly there was his father, terrifying in anger, hollering: Dad's huge red face, his eyes . . .

Four years old, how was he supposed to know that when you take something apart—a carburetor, a water pump—you laid down all the parts in order, so that when you put the thing back together, everything would be right there, in its place?

A first memory: "being whipped for messing up car parts."

"I'll teach you . . ."

The Old Man thought punishment was teaching. So how come John Gacy, as an adult, how come John could build anything but he didn't know anything about cars? Pay someone else to do it. John couldn't even begin to tell you what was under the hood of a car.

Just like, after that, he went around afraid of things that had never scared him before. Fire engines scared him. The first one he remembered, he was maybe five, and he couldn't say why it frightened him. Just a vague image of a red truck speeding by the house, and men wearing strange shiny black suits, holding on to the front and the back. You couldn't see their faces, and there was this loud constant screaming that hurt your ears and a sense of something huge and dangerous, careening out of control. Like it was coming to get you.

Then later, he didn't even have to see the truck. When John Gacy heard the sirens, he hid under the porch.

Even the other kids could scare him. While John was in the second grade there was some madman, a slasher, who struck out on Opal Street: some guy who waited for women on their way home from work. John guessed that what he did was to threaten them with a knife and take their paychecks. Except maybe one time he cut one of them, or killed her in an alley or something. It seemed silly to John, looking back, that he was afraid of the

Slasher, who went after women only, and only for money. Back then, though, he thought the Slasher wanted little John. All the kids knew it, all of them making wet, sloshy sounds with their tongues against their teeth and telling him, "The Slaaa-aaaasher is coming" in wavery little-kid ghost voices.

They had some kind of game then, he couldn't even remember if it was about the Slasher, just that at the end there was a part where the black hand would get you. Kids could just put a palm in his face—"Oooooooo, the black hand is after Johnny" —and it was like all those black figures on the fire truck, something dark you couldn't understand, coming after you. For no reason.

The docs—Rappaport and Freedman for the defense, Cavanaugh for the prosecution—were all interested in the Old Man. "I loved my dad," John told them. "Just like I love Ma." It was as if the docs didn't believe him, and they kept poking away at his feelings toward the Old Man. One of the docs—later John couldn't even remember which one—asked him if, maybe, deep down, he actually hated his father. John wouldn't accept that—the Bible says, "Honor thy father and thy mother"—but the more he thought about it, the more he came to understand that it was possible. There was, he decided, a fine line between love and hate, and in certain situations you could love someone and hate that person at the same time.

His whole adult life, John had always been too busy to think about himself, but now his life depended on finally seeing things whole. Up to the time he was arrested in December 1978, when John thought about the Old Man, he made excuses for all the yelling, the frightening bursts of violence. "I was never good enough for him," John knew, and he imagined that the Old Man did what he did for a reason. "To make me better. To teach me with punishment."

The first time there was real violence John was only a baby, too young to remember. Ma never talked about it at home. She was the soul of the family, always smoothing things over, inclined to forgive and forget. But after John got into trouble and people dug the incident out of old court files, after Ma understood that John's relationship with his father might have warped him in some incomprehensible manner, she explained what had happened.

A hot summer night in 1944: Ma was just home from the hospital with three-week-old Karen. John, almost two and a half years old, and JoAnne, nearly five, were sitting at the dinner table when John Stanley Gacy exploded. Ma, Marion Gacy, never knew why.

"I don't know what triggered it," she said.

The Old Man picked up some food and threw it in his wife's face, then he came up over the table and "he hit me square in the face and knocked my bridge out. I was all blood. I ran out. I got away." John and JoAnne started to scream. Marion Gacy, covered with blood, ran into the street, where she stumbled and fell. The Old Man was running after her, and a neighbor yelled, "Don't hit her again! I'm calling the police!"

The Old Man went back into the house, bulled his way past the screaming children, got a gun he kept hidden somewhere, and left. The police arrived and advised Marion Gacy to take the children and leave the house "in case he came back."

Ma had to borrow two dollars from a neighbor for a cab. She went to a sister-in-law's house for a few days, then went to Domestic Relations Court. Of this court she said, "They couldn't do anything, only tell him he would have to pay for my support and the children."

Ma's brother told her, "I can't afford to keep two families."

A few days later, "after I had calmed down," Ma took the children back to the house at 3536 North Opal. Everything was just as she had left it. There was still food on the table and broken dishes on the floor. Ma cleaned up the kitchen, then cooked her husband's favorite meal of boiled meat and potatoes.

"When he came home," Marion Gacy recalled, "he had supper there. Nothing was said, but he ate and everything." It was like the whole incident never happened: a make-believe happy family. "We resumed our normal life," Marion Gacy recalled.

The docs would really fasten on the bad stuff like that, make the Old Man a real monster. They wanted John to talk about his father, but he couldn't—he absolutely would not—come out and say he hated the Old Man. You had to do it like a theory or something, a supposition. Talk about yourself in the third person, like someone else, a whole other guy, who actually hated his dad.

That way—in the third person, as supposition—John could let it all out. From the beginning.

Just like the incident with the enamel. Little John helping the Old Man paint window trim. The enamel goes on hard, doesn't spread easy, and John thinks, Well, if I put more on the brush, it'll spread easier. Except that he had never painted before and didn't know that enamel runs.

"Goddamn it," the Old Man hollered, "now look at what you've done!" John Stanley Gacy, the almighty white wonder who never made a mistake in his life.

John Gacy tried to tell his father that it was the paint, and the Old Man said that these are things a man knows, that you'd have to be stupid, "dumb and stupid" to mess up windows like that. And then John turned to get something, and his brush hit the windowpane.

"Holy shit," John recalled. "You'd think I busted the whole window. I said, 'Can't we let it dry, scrape it off with a razor blade?' "

"You don't want to listen!" the Old Man shouted. "You do something, you don't make mistakes you have to fix. Because then it's never right. You're dumb and stupid, you don't know that. You don't want to learn."

And Ma standing there, toe to toe with the Old Man, hollering right back. "What are you, perfect personified? Were you perfect when you started?"

The Old Man wouldn't stand for that: Ma "conniving" with her son, the two of them so dumb and stupid they thought they could "outsmart" him.

Dr. Rappaport was interested in the Old Man's secret spot, the basement, and John could tell by his questions that he saw some correlation between that and the crawl space under the house on Summerdale.

In 1952, when John was ten, the Gacy family moved to a bigger house, closer to Chicago proper, at 4505 North Marmora. The new house had a basement, and it was almost as though the Old Man lived down there, underground, in a sunless, subterranean world of his own. John thought of the basement as his dad's vault, a secret hiding place, a sacred area. There were locks on the door leading down there, and no one but the Old Man had the key, so that when a fuse blew, the family had to wait for John Stanley Gacy to come home from work to change it. "And then," John recalled, "we got our asses chewed out for overloading a circuit and blowing the fuse."

The Old Man had other secret places. John remembered a dresser in his parents' bedroom. John Stanley put a padlock on the top drawer, just drilled a couple of holes in it, completely ruined a good piece of furniture.

But the basement was his sacred spot. He'd come home from work—hardly even say hello—and go right downstairs into the cellar. John knew, even as a kid, that the Old Man drank down there and that his sudden rages had something to do with alcohol. Ma and the kids could hear him in the basement, some- times shouting, sometimes talking to himself in different voices. The family had to wait, upstairs, with the beef and potatoes boiling away into mushy slop. You couldn't eat before the Old Man, and you couldn't call down and say that dinner was ready. Not if you didn't want the Old Man to fly into a rage.

Then, later, you could hear him stumbling up the stairs, drunk, ready now for dinner. And always an argument. "If my father said the sun wouldn't rise tomorrow," John recalled, "you couldn't disagree with him. He'd argue you into the ground. But when I was young, I didn't know. I argued with him, and he'd holler at me. Tell me I was dumb and stupid. Arguing with little kids, and every time he had to win. Never wrong."

The Old Man always thought people were sneaking into the basement, violating the secret spot, stealing his tools. There was a big barrel of nuts and bolts down there, and he accused John of stealing and selling them—as if the man knew exactly how many bolts were in a barrel. And once, when he had a vat of tar in the basement, he said John had stolen some and sold it. Like a little kid is going to take a sand bucket, fill it with tar, walk down the street, and try to sell it to some adult.

"Do you think I'm dumb and stupid?" the Old Man hol- lered. "I know who took it. You're dumb and stupid, think you can get away with stealing from me."

If the Old Man misplaced a tool, John stole it. Even Ma's brother, John's uncle, after he helped move the family from Opal to Marmora, John Stanley said he stole some shit. And then when he found it later, he never apologized to Uncle Harold. Because he was never wrong. He'd find the hammer or the wrench he said

John stole and just ignore the fact that he had misplaced it and blamed his son for stealing.

Ma tried to smooth things over, always excusing John's behavior to the Old Man, the Old Man's behavior to John. She said the drinking was a physical problem: John Stanley Gacy had a blood clot, a tumor on the brain. When he drank, the blood vessels swelled up and pressed on the tumor. Back then, John had a vision of some little dark thing, swollen with alcohol, pumping like a little black heart, pressing against his dad's brain.

"So why doesn't he go to the doctor to have it taken out?" John asked, and Ma said that the operation would be too danger- ous. What John had to do, Ma explained, was to "pacify" the Old Man, agree with him. She said some little argument didn't matter, not even if John was being accused of something he didn't do, not even if his father was dead wrong. What mattered was the Old Man's physical condition: you didn't want to argue with him, didn't want to make him mad. The tumor could burst or some- thing. You could kill the Old Man, arguing with him. It would be like an explosion inside his head, the little black thing bursting apart in an eruption of pus.

Subsequently, John had a theory about why his father drank alone in the basement every night. The Old Man was a master control assembler, a machinist. They have a master control board where you pour in all the ingredients. And in those days it wasn't done by computer, so you had to know exactly how long to leave the valves open or you could ruin everything. Thirty years in the same job with all that pressure; a job where measurements had to be absolutely precise; a job where the technology was getting ahead of the workers, everything changing all the time, young guys coming in to train the Old Man: smart-ass college boys with their time-and-motion studies, telling him how to do his work.

John Stanley Gacy had to quit school to work at twelve, to help feed the family. At seventeen, he went into the First World War. So even though he read, the Old Man never had much of an education. Maybe by the time the kids got to high school, he thought they were passing him up, outsmarting him with education.

Because at work, young guys were coming in, getting promoted over him. So whatta you do? John Gacy's father drank like a fish and took it all out on his son. Nobody was going to outsmart John Stanley Gacy in his own home.

That's how John explained his father's drinking when the docs asked him. As an adult, John could see clear reasons for the Old Man's raging temper, but when he was young, he never understood. It was like (he could almost laugh about it after nearly thirty years) some dumb horror film. Little John sitting at the dinner table hears clumping feet coming up the stairs—fear on the boy's face—and then, wham, the cellar door bursts open and there he stands, the Old Man, swaying back and forth, frowning, bleary-eyed, ready for battle. And right above the Old Man's head, arching over like a rainbow, there's one of those blood-dripping monster-movie titles: *The Creature That Came Up Out of the Basement.*

Doc Rappaport was working on the basement/crawl space correlation, but when John tried to express his feelings, the psychology of putting the two things together seemed murky, imprecise. What John remembered from those days was anger. And fear: like being afraid of the black hand, or afraid of the faceless men in black suits on the fire engine, only it was all jumbled together with fear of something in the basement, something dark, coming to get him, for no reason.

CHAPTER
3

IsoLATION, Cermak Hospital:

John up there in the jail complex with a private room in 3 North, separated from the main population of criminal patients, where he wouldn't have lasted a day. All the rapists and killers, the assault artists and thieves in agreement, child molesters are scum below scum. Niggers standing on the other side of the barred gate separating 3 North from the main population, all of them yelling for Gacy.

John would stand bravely behind the locked gate, saying, "Jump up, froggy. One more don't make no difference to me." Give the sons-of-bitches something to think about.

The next day, he'd look through the gate and see some nigger trying to hang himself out in the hall, pants all wet at the crotch where he lost control of his bladder, tongue sticking out of his mouth. John calling for Officer Pocious or one of them to save the guy.

"We got another swinger down the hall."

One of John's closest friends in 3 North was also accused of killing young boys. The guy used to cruise around picking young hustlers, and he had the car set up so the seat belt locked down on them once they snapped it on. "Buckle up for safety" was the joke. A schoolteacher, the guy told John he resigned

when he realized that he was looking at his students, teenage
boys, and thinking now much he'd like to kill them, and how
killing them would be a way of actually helping them. John
remembered the Old Man then, how his father thought punishment was teaching.

It kept getting back to the Old Man.

This guy with the seat belt, he had an inverted dick or
something—always crouched over in the shower, ashamed of what
he had between his legs—and John was sympathetic; he understood the guy's problem. Something like that, it's right out on the
surface, and you didn't have to tear a whole life apart to get to the
meaning of murder.

John had to see the docs every day, every one of them
poking and stabbing into a different area. Just like Morrison: she
was trying to make something of his stealing. John could see her
constructing a neat little theory, making correlations between
petty theft and serial murder. When John looked back on it, he
had been stealing all his life. Mostly just little shit, and half the
time he gave it away. Maybe he wanted to be a big man, generous
guy, something, John didn't know.

The first time, when he was about six, walking home from
the store with Ma, with a little truck that he had stolen while no
one was looking. She turned him around and marched him right
back to the store. "It was the longest walk of my life," John
recalled. And he had to tell the man he stole the truck, giving it
back and apologizing. That night Ma told John Stanley, and the
Old Man took the razor strop down from the nail.

"I'll teach you to steal."

Always swiping little shit. But once, when he was a teenager working at some discount store, Ma found a roll of bills
wrapped up in a rubber band in her son's dresser drawer. John
didn't make that kind of money. The same day, they called from
the store asking about some stolen money, and Ma made John take
it back even though she knew he'd be fired. She never told the
Old Man about that one; she just made John do the right thing
and then "it was over and nobody had to talk about it again."

That was Ma's way. She was fair, so trusting she was
almost naïve.

Dr. Morrison seemed to think you could draw some kind
of psychological line through the stealing, extending it right into

the killings. Maybe John stole shit because he got away with it most of the time. So if you take the first murder—one of the five John vaguely remembered: an accident, self-defense—you could put it on a kind of graph.

First murder: January 1972.

Second murder: August 1975.

After that, the graph just kept going up, getting steeper and steeper, the dead line shooting right up off the paper. Of course, John couldn't recall the murders and had to rely on bullshit newspaper stories. The rest of the victims: the way the state's attorney's office was working, they were matching up bodies the coroner was able to identify with names and asking around about the last time the kid was seen alive. By that count, 1978, the year John was arrested in December, Jack was killing some kid right there in the house about once every two or three weeks.

So Morrison asked him if maybe, subconsciously or something, he figured he got away with the first one after three and a half years. And when nobody came around asking about that kid, maybe he did another. Then another. Like it got easier after each one, just the way stealing gets easier when you aren't caught.

That kind of thing burned in John's brain every night up there in 3 North. He'd play dominoes with the seat-belt guy, watch TV, or play cards with other inmates. The docs couldn't figure out why he never had nightmares, or remorse. He explained it to them over and over: you can't have remorse if you don't know whether you committed the crime. And yet, he could be sitting there watching *The Lou Gehrig Story* on TV and feel tears in his eyes. Never even heard of Lou Gehrig, and he starts to cry.

Just like, some of the inmates would be sitting around playing cards, talking about their trials, how they were going to "walk," and it was sad. John felt compassion for them, because they didn't know how the system worked, or because they were really crazy, or because everything was stacked against them. Allan Washington, a black guy, had it tough from the start. Accused of his second child killing, he'd already served a term for the murder of his two-year-old daughter. The little girl wouldn't stop crying. Washington was feeding her and she wouldn't stop. This time they said he beat his three-year-old stepson to death, dumped the body in a field, doused it with gasoline, and set it on fire.

Washington wasn't going to "walk," not without John's help. The black guy was grateful—John offered money and help finding a lawyer—and Allan called John "big brother."

The thing of it was: how could you think about yourself when everyone had another sad story to tell? Heartbreakers whizzing by at a mile a minute up there in 3 North.

John spent a lot of time in his room working on jigsaw puzzles: those eighty-six-cent Tuco dime store puzzles, twenty-one inches by twenty-one inches, with a thousand interlocking pieces. He liked outdoor scenes, horses. There was one of a cabin in the woods, a river running by, the trees an autumn gold, snowcapped mountains rising in the distance. It didn't take much to figure out why an inmate liked outdoor scenes. You didn't have to be a hotshot psychiatrist to realize that what John knew of his life was scattered about in little pieces, like the parts of a puzzle. He was honestly working, working hard, to put them all together so he could see the picture whole, so he could finally and truly understand John Wayne Gacy, Jr.

The puzzles were like therapy. He had to start at the periphery, get the sky first, which was easy because all those pieces were blue, then work his way down into the guts of the picture, matching one piece against the other until the mind went blank and fuzzy. Then, suddenly, when he wasn't even thinking about it, bam, a big revelation, a couple of pieces of his life slipping together, fitting perfectly, one against the other, just like parts of a perfect puzzle.

He could be fitting in one of the pieces—part blue, part white: the top of the mountain—and suddenly, in his mind's eye, he could see Allan Washington. And at the same time, he could hear the Old Man going on about niggers, about how they all ought to be sent back to Africa, which was too good for them, anyway. Kill the sons-of-bitches was the best deal.

The Old Man was "racial." John, sitting there with part of a mountain in his hand, would wonder why he hadn't become a racist, growing up with John Stanley. Oh, sure, John Gacy, as an adult, would use the word "nigger," but the way he meant it, a nigger was lowlife, scum. There were white niggers just as there were black niggers. In fact, John thought he was more likely to give a black guy a chance, a man like Allan Washington, just because he had had it so tough in America: putting up with all that intolerance and shit.

But the Old Man, the way he thought, the South Side of Chicago would be one big pile of dead niggers. And John was just the opposite. It was like—and a couple of the pieces slid together right here—everything the Old Man did or said, everything he stood for, his son was just the opposite. John suddenly saw that it was a way to analyze his whole life, this idea of himself as the Old Man turned inside out, the two of them polar opposites.

Just like the summer John was eleven when the Old Man finally took him fishing. Fishing was one of the important things in life to the Old Man.

He liked fishing so much, it was a sort of affectionate joke around the house on Marmora. Ma even wrote a joke poem about it. It went something like this:

F is for the fish he always catches,
A is for the angling that he does,
T is for the tales he tells about them,
H is for how he hopes for big ones,
E is for . . . some shit, John forgot,
R is for the rowing out to get there,
Put them all together they spell father,
And something something ratta tat tat.

No, wait, E is for his eyes with fishlight shining. Eyes with fishlight shining. John Stanley kept his rods and reels, his tackle box, in the basement under lock and key. Like somebody might want to steal them.

Two weeks a year, on his vacation, the Old Man could go up to Wisconsin to fish. And in 1953, they went fishing together, man and boy. In the Catholic church that John attended, they had a sacrament called confirmation where you became a "soldier of Christ." It was like officially becoming a man, and you were confirmed at about the age of eleven or twelve. In the Gacy family, being confirmed, becoming a màn, meant that the Old Man asked you to go fishing with him.

The women went on their own separate vacation: they took

the train down to Springfield to visit John's aunt and uncle. The menfolk went fishing.

Except that there was a lot of rain that year, heavy midwestern squalls rolling across the lake; rivers and streams dark with runoff making the water muddy; the rain like something out of the Bible, the water pounding down in sheets, driving the fish deep, where they lay indifferent to bait or spoon. The fish waiting out a two-week spate of bad weather that just happened to coincide with the Old Man's yearly vacation.

"So," John recalled, "he drank. And the more he drank, the more he figured the rain was my fault. And then, when it was nice, we still didn't catch fish, and that was my fault. What the hell, an eleven-year-old kid, he doesn't have the same attention span. If I started to fidget, I was making waves, scaring the fish. And you couldn't talk. You just had to sit there. And everything was your fault."

The next year, when John was twelve, the Old Man went fishing alone. John went to Springfield with his mother and sisters. He wasn't man enough to fish. He would never be man enough to fish with his father.

"Consequently," John recalled, "one thing I always hated, I always hated fishing."

Looking back, John could see that Ma's encouragement, her uncritical acceptance—her mother's love for an only son—was often expressed in clichés. A young boy doesn't know these sayings are supposed to be corny. He's never heard them before, and they settle in his mind and inspire him. "No matter how hard it seems," Ma said, "you just gotta keep working at it."

For Ma, things were always darkest just before the dawn. She knew that God worked in mysterious ways but that he helps those who help themselves. Love conquers all. Winners never quit, quitters never win.

While the Old Man was harsh and smart and violent, Ma was fair and accepting but maybe just a little too trusting. Naïve. She thought everybody was basically good; the Old Man figured people would fuck you any way they could. You had to stay one step ahead of them, you had to outsmart them. Trust was weakness.

After the panties incident, there seemed to be no pleasing the Old Man. Go out to the quarry with a wagon, bring back over nine hundred pounds of limestone, make a walkway to the house on Marmora, and the Old Man said it wasn't straight. The Old Man, who spent an hour with a tape measure before he'd hang a picture. "I was never good enough for him," John recalled. "Never accepted."

"You tried," Ma said, "that's the important thing."

He was eight when John learned from Ma that he moved his bowels when he was born and almost died. His health problems started at birth. He had never been a strong child, and it wasn't his fault. Ma said there was a physical explanation for it, just as there was a physical reason for the Old Man's rages. John had been born with an enlarged bottleneck heart, a serious condition. Baseball, football, any kind of sport at all could kill him just as surely as an argument could pop the Old Man's tumor.

"So I was a disappointment to my dad," John said, "because I was weak and he was strong. He hated the weak person. Even in emotions. We'd go to funerals for someone in the family, and he'd never get tears in his eyes. At a party, he'd never laugh. A strong, somber individual. Emotion was a weakness. Physical illness, even when it couldn't be helped, was a weakness. I remember once he was so sick he couldn't get out of bed, and Ma finally called a doctor. The doctor said, 'How long have you been like this?'

"My dad said, 'Ten days.'

"The doctor said, 'Why didn't you wait another day and just call the undertaker?' And it turned out my dad had pneumonia."

By contrast, John was sick as long as he could remember. A heart problem from birth; then, at the age of ten, something seriously wrong with the brain. He began passing out for no reason at all.

The Old Man tried to connect it to school. Early on, John attended St. Francis Borgia Grade School, and he feels he truly became a Catholic there, at the age of eight. When the family moved to Marmora Street, John transferred to the public school. That school was different, the teachers assholes, and John began getting failing grades. He couldn't bring himself to attend classes: he'd walk his sister Karen home for the lunch he was supposed to make while Ma and the Old Man were at work.

Karen and John would take a vote, very democratic, and

decide that the afternoon would be better spent eating puddings and Twinkies that they bought on their lunch money.

John's parents were called in for conferences, and Ma thought it might be a health problem. The boy sometimes just fell over, passed out for ten minutes at a time. They took him to the hospital a dozen times, and no one could ever tell them just exactly what the physical problem was. Maybe psychomotor epilepsy. Recurrent syncope. Nothing definite, though, no way to explain the symptoms.

The Old Man knew, though: the kid was skipping school when he was healthy, so he was probably pretending to pass out so he wouldn't have to attend classes. Drawing sympathy to himself. Faking.

"I'd pass out for ten minutes at a time when it started," John remembered, "then later I'd be out for, oh, half an hour. Even longer. Sometimes they'd find me and no one would know how long I'd been out." John figured that he spent over a year, all told, in the hospital between the ages of fourteen and eighteen.

"My dad," John said, "thought it was an attention-getter."

If it was an attention-getter, why would you pass out when no one's there? Richard Dalke, a boyhood friend of John's, remembers looking for him at school one day. Both boys were fourteen. "I went into the office," Dalke said, "and I asked one of the secretaries, 'Where's John?' She said, 'He's in the next office.' And I went in there and I didn't see him. I came back into the office and she said, 'He just went in there five minutes ago.' So I went back into the office and there was this big desk and he was on the other side, passed out on the floor."

The fire department was called, and John was revived by paramedics, who took him to the hospital. The Old Man stood in the hospital, telling John to his face that he was faking.

John's friends—Barry and Ken and John and Richard—never had any doubts about John's physical problems. "I always thought he was sick," Richard Dalke recalls. "He had heart problems, and more or less we were around to protect him in case anybody wanted a conflict with him."

There was no protecting John from the Old Man, though. When the boys were fifteen and sixteen, Dalke saw John Stanley Gacy swing at his son on several occasions. "I can remember once being at the house when his dad came up from the basement, started swinging and yelling at him, and his mother stepped in, tried to protect him. John would never strike his father. He always just put up his hands and tried to protect himself."

Dalke recalled that there was no provocation at all. When it happened, he said, "We were usually sitting around talking or just coming into the house."

It was like a contest of wills between John and his father. Was the boy really sick, or was he looking for sympathy? In 1957, at the age of fifteen, John had his tonsils out. You couldn't argue with that one. But when he complained of a severe stomach ache and the doctors could find nothing wrong, the Old Man thought he'd scored a point for his side. Except that John's appendix was placed oddly, back behind the spleen or something. The doctors made a mistake, and when John was in so much pain that Ma finally took him back to the hospital, the appendix had burst and the boy very nearly died. Because the Old Man thought he was faking.

That was one John won.

A year later, in August, the Old Man scored big.

John's sister Karen thinks it started when "he and dad had an argument. It was something over the car. John walked out. Dad held back the car on him. It was like a punishment. If you don't do things my way, I'll take the keys."

Later that night, John was playing cards with Richard Dalke and Ken Dunkle in Bill Lambert's basement. The boys had each drunk a beer or two. Richard Dalke remembers that John passed out, fell on the floor. "We called the fire department again and they came to take care of him. We thought he was having a severe heart attack, and somebody called one of the priests from the nearby church."

Marion Gacy was notified, and she arrived just as the priest was giving her son the last rites. "I wanted to get him to the hospital," Marion Gacy recalled, "so I took an ambulance over to Northwest Hospital." John was there for three weeks until the Old Man came to sign him out.

Back at home, John passed out again. "I found him laying on the floor, in the bedroom," Marion Gacy said, "and when the doctor came he was going to give him a shot to bring him to. He said that John had like an epileptic fit. And John began fighting and kicked him. Fighting and kicking just like a madman. My husband came in and held him down, and the doctor gave John a shot. Then they put him—we had to get him to a hospital and put him in a straitjacket."

At Norwegian American Hospital, extensive tests were administered. The Old Man would visit once in a while, just sit in the bedside chair, silent, suspicious. After a month in the hospital, a doctor took Marion Gacy aside and suggested that her son be sent to Cook County Hospital for psychiatric evaluation.

The Old Man loved that. It was a kind of proof to him that John was never sick at all, that it was all in his head. And John begged his mother, "Don't send me to the psychiatrist ward, I'll be good." Like you can promise not to pass out.

Those were a few of the bigger battles in what amounted to a six-year war. As John got older, the issues at stake expanded. Years later, John would say that the Old Man had a way of looking at him, a cold, dark glare beyond disappointment or even disgust, a way of staring at his son as if the boy was beneath contempt. As if he could see into John's soul and there were crawling, slimy things in there; as if he knew something about his son that John himself didn't know.

John had another seizure, a kind of epileptic fit in a bowling alley called the Fireside Lanes. He kicked one of his friends in the neck and broke the boy's glasses. The paramedics had to strap John down to a stretcher.

But it was a physical problem, not his fault.

The Old Man continued to drink, and the tumor Ma said was there throbbed inside his skull, pressed into his brain, pushed him to violence. "I thought one time he was going to kill me," John remembered years later. "He was swinging on my mother and I yelled something at him. He told me to mind my own business or he'd take care of me, too. I hollered right back and he came for me, swung on me right there. But he was drunk and he hit the refrigerator. He turned and came at me again. I pinned his arms to his sides and pressed him up against the wall. I couldn't hit him. I just couldn't hit him. But if I let him go, he'd swing on me again. So we struggled like that. And I must have held him with his arms pinned for ten minutes."

Father and son stood face to face in a sort of rough embrace. John said, "I can still picture that: my dad's face looking right at me. The glare in his eyes. Through his eyes I thought he was going to kill me. And I was crying and upset . . . you know, thinking, he can't kill you, he loves you. It was such a mixed-up feeling. . . ."

John remembers the Old Man's breath coming ragged in his throat, recalls smelling the alcohol there. He was looking into those spinning eyes and seeing a rage like murder, seeing the Old Man's special knowledge burning like fire. John was sobbing, pressing his father's back into the wall, hugging him in a confusion of love and murder.

Something else. John felt it in his groin. Just a faint stirring down there.

CHAPTER

4

FIVE FEET EIGHT AND already bloating up toward two hundred pounds. An eighteen-year-old should be hard, muscular. He shouldn't have a body like a sack of flour. And just look in the mirror: a face like Mr. Potato Head, that toy for kids, a bunch of goddamn plastic mouths and eyes and shit that you could stick into a lumpy old spud and make it just as fucking ugly and funny-looking as John Wayne Gacy, Jr., himself.

No wonder he didn't care that much for dating; no wonder he didn't "have much of a sex drive."

Instead, he worked. John was a worker as long as he could remember. He had a paper route, some lawn-mowing jobs; then, at fourteen, he nailed down his first real job: delivering groceries for the local IGA store. He also helped Ma around the house, moving furniture, painting rooms.

And there was the stuff he did free, volunteer stuff, like yardwork for an elderly neighbor. Once, when John was twelve, a big storm knocked down some power lines over a neighbor's garage. John took it on himself to warn the woman who lived there that stepping in a puddle out behind the house could kill her. "I didn't know that," this neighbor said years later. "I might have gone out there to look. He might have saved my life. And

John stood by the garage all day, waving traffic away, making sure no one got hurt."

When John transferred from the public grammar school—where he was skipping classes and failing—to the vocational school, he got so far out ahead of his class in science that the teacher said he didn't need to attend that class; he could work in the office. John ran errands for the teachers—"call me a teacher's pet, I enjoyed it, I got along with all the administrators"—and worked as an assistant to the truant officer. It was a big switch from being a truant to becoming a truant officer. "I wasn't any snitch," John said. "I just had to call parents and see if kids were really sick at home."

In high school, John was a Civil Defense captain. A boyhood friend remembers, "He pretty much organized the whole thing. Like for fire drills, where each fire marshal had to stand to make sure everyone got out." Civil Defense captains got a portable flashing blue light they could put on the dashboard of their cars to use on official business.

Years later, Ray Kasper, who eventually married John's elder sister, JoAnne, said that Gacy, as a teenager, had "a hang-up" about uniforms. In later years, John always referred to Ray as "my asshole brother-in-law." John thought Ray "could find something wrong with anything I ever did." Still, even John's sisters, Karen and JoAnne, said he got a little excessive, playing cop, speeding off to any fire or accident with blue light flashing.

At eighteen, John began to get involved in Chicago politics. He worked as an assistant precinct captain on behalf of the Democratic candidate for alderman in the Forty-fifth Ward. "My dad," John recalled, "said I was a fool. He said, 'all those politicians are crooks and phonies.' But, son-of-a-bitch, I worked my ass off on that campaign. Because a politician doesn't always have to be a phony; sometimes a politician can help the little people; sometimes he can show compassion and do good."

When John looked back on it, he could see some other reasons why he got into politics. "Maybe it was a way to antagonize my dad. In part. And maybe it was a way to get acceptance. I was always looking for acceptance because my dad made me feel that I was never good enough."

John sought acceptance in volunteer work, in politics, in

just helping people because it made him feel good. The Old Man thought John was "stupid," "softhearted," "an asshole." Why would you go out of your way to do something for someone else when you know that person will turn around and fuck over you the first chance he gets? Because it's dog eat dog, and everyone's looking to outsmart the other guy. Only an "asshole" is gullible enough to do something for nothing.

Even at his best, even when John was giving of himself, giving out of the fullness of his heart, the Old Man could find a way to make him feel "dumb and stupid."

Maybe if he was just a little better-looking. John knew he was "an ugly duckling." And there were strange thoughts, little compulsions that shamed him. He was "different," "the odd man out." The things he saw in lazy daydreams, all those unwanted desires, they were "feelings." Having feelings made him "weak." And the Old Man: nothing was ever said, but John felt the Old Man knew. He had that way of looking at you.

"Consequently," John remembered, "from about the age of sixteen, I was thinking of death." Not suicide. John was a devout Catholic, and suicide was a mortal sin. No, death, like the shameful daydreams, should arrive unbidden, a faceless figure that emerged out of the dark, a shadow blacker than the night itself. Death had to come from outside of himself, like a favor from God Himself. Death was the Lord's ultimate blessing.

With all the odd pressure—the lack of acceptance, the fear of his father, the strange compulsions—John Gacy thought for a time about becoming a priest. Make a life for himself helping others.

The priesthood, John imagined, would provide the kind of clean, caring life that would fill him with clean, caring thoughts, that would keep him holy, eliminate the bad daydreams, and finally earn him a measure of respect: how could anyone have certain suspicions about a priest? Priests exert a sort of unassailable moral authority—you could think of them as God's cops—that puts them above suspicion.

John began thinking this way while he was "rolling" with St. John Berchman's parish Holy Name Society bowling team. John wasn't a half-bad bowler, and that was good because at least he could get some small amount of respect—some reduction of suspicion—from such important team members as Ray Kasper and his father. His mother bowled with them, but John knew he had her trust, even if she was "naïve."

Bowling led to work within the parish organization and some involvement in its politics. John became a member of the Holy Name Society. Immediately, at eighteen, he could see the parish wasn't properly serving people in his age group. Few of the young men he knew were active in the Church. John felt older teenagers were under so much outside pressure—sex, new jobs, social responsibilities—that they just fell away from the Church. It was like a syndrome, and it lasted about four years. Between the age of eighteen, when people graduated from high school, until the time they married, at about age twenty-two, there was little in the Church for them to do.

St. John Berchman's had a problem, and John Wayne Gacy had a solution. He organized a young adults club, the Chi Ro Club, that would stop the drift away from the Church he had seen in eighteen- through twenty-two-year-olds. One of his coorganizers—John remembers to this day—was an alderman's daughter. It was an important concept and an important club supported by important people.

When the young adults club held their formal winter dance, the "Snowtillion," John organized the event in military style. It was all white crepe paper, demure romance, and no goddamn sloppy pageantry, not with John in charge.

The club was a minor success, a step toward solving one of the Catholic Church's perennial problems. Still, it was something conceptual, and even as an eighteen-year-old, John understood that success and improvement are seen in practical things, pragmatic improvements a guy could point to with pride. He helped build booths for the carnival, helped with the organization of that event, and he was also on the parish building committee. When the church needed repainting, John figured they could save the cost of professional painters if they did it themselves. All they needed was a man with the knowledge of a professional painter to head the job. And young John had learned well from his father about painting. John volunteered to "work his ass off" and get the church painted properly, perfectly. The church looked great when John and his crew finished with it.

He spent so much time at the church, so much energy doing good works, that it could sometimes be embarrassing. You'd go into the confessional, and it would already be a little weird, because how many eighteen-year-old males do you see there, anyway? Most guys saved up their sins and came in to make their yearly Easter duty—the one confession a year—and that was it. But John confessed regularly: he liked the clean feeling, the knowledge that he was, at that moment, beloved of God. It was a warm sensation that started in your chest and made you feel good from the inside out.

Each time John went to confession, the other people scattered sparsely about the church were very devout older women. They always wore wraps around their necks: some ratty animal with little beady eyes biting its own tail.

John would wait his turn and then go into the dark confessional with its odor of leather and wood, only the opaque screen between him and eternal salvation. "Bless me, Father, for I have sinned." John confessed to the few little lies he might have told that week—a series of the most venial sins—and the priest would give him about three Hail Marys as a penance. But sometimes, just as he was ready to leave, the priest, who knew him like a son and recognized his voice, would say, "Uh, John, as long as I got you here, you know anything about weather stripping? I only ask because the wind just whips through the sacristy door in the morning."

And John'd end up talking about weather stripping in the confessional. Spend twenty minutes discussing the cost of materials, the amount of labor and time necessary to do the job, the best day of the week to do it. By the time he got out of the box, some of those older women would give him a strange look and glance at their watches. John imagined they were thinking, Half an hour with Father, oh, my, what could he possibly have done? What a dirty, dirty sinner that boy must be.

It pleased John to start the Hail Marys on the way back to the pew, kneel for about fifteen seconds, and then be gone, lickety-split, just like that: a man of mystery as far as sin was concerned, and a wonder to the devout elderly of St. John Berchman's.

Sunday nights, John usually was at the rectory, playing cards with the parish priests. And both of them—perfect Chicago

Irish priests—would talk to the teenager about a possible vocation. "John," one or the other of them would argue, "you're around the church six, seven days a week as it is. Maybe God is speaking to you in a very special way." John'd play a card and really consider. it. Doing things for people made him happy, helping poor people made him feel warm inside. The respect sanctity brought scoured a soul like steel wool cleans a soiled pot.

There wouldn't be any problem with the chastity thing: "Oh, sure," John explained later, "I was dating broads and getting laid, but there wasn't anything serious. And why would you wanna get married? Why take on the burden of having some stupid broad around you day and night?" Being a priest was a natural, John felt, because he was different from the other boys. "I was sickly, and I certainly wasn't no physically built individual, and I didn't have no sex drive, so being a priest seemed perfect, a natural thing to do for a kid like me."

He would wear the robes with dignity; he would be compassionate and help the poor and the homeless and the bereaved. People could come to him for advice, and one thing he'd know is that every problem, everything in life, has two sides. Nothing is just one way. As a priest, Father Gacy would use that knowledge to help others. When people came to see him, he would be understanding and liberal, very different from the way his father was.

He'd be a good priest.

"You're going to be queer just like your friend Barry," the Old Man said.

A bookish boy who collected antiques, Barry was one of John's few close friends. Barry was interested in Illinois history and landscaping. He and John talked about flowers, shit like that. Neither of them liked to repair cars, neither liked sports or, especially, fishing. "The kid's a fairy," the Old Man said.

John never remembered the Old Man telling him he was going to turn out "queer," but his sister Karen recalled it clearly. "Dad had an attitude about John and was hard on him because of it. He thought John was a mama's boy just because Ma was a buffer between the Old Man and John. Just because John could talk to Ma."

"My dad," John said, "I don't think he ever mentioned homosexuals in the house. Never said anything about them. Just like, there was this lesbian couple, they lived down the block, and I remember he made fun of them. They sold brushes and one came to the door dressed like a man. Dad called her a he-she. But he never came right out and called them homosexuals. You just knew they were bad people." So bad, in fact, the subject wasn't fit to discuss. "Nothing had to be said." If you weren't dumb and stupid, you just knew.

There was some spectacular murder case with homosexual overtones in Chicago at about that time, and the Old Man kept harping on how it happened early in the morning. "It's what comes of being out after midnight," he said. Anytime you were out after midnight, the Old Man knew you were up to no good. That's when they all came out, like some dark flower that bloomed only at night: the fairies and the he-shes, perverts up to no good, killers. You got what you deserved after midnight.

Strange, then, that it should be late at night, after midnight, when troubling thoughts invaded John's mind. In the dark, when it was lonely and quiet in his room, or in the hospital, John would wonder how it would be to hug one of his friends, hold him tight, just for a moment. No sex thing. It was a kind of compassion, all tangled up with a desire to help people, like being a priest, except that you could get an erection thinking that way, and John didn't like to talk about it. Nearly twenty-five years later, the idea still bothered him.

Bad dreams, and who could you go to? Where could you talk about the thing that bothered you the most? Whine to your buddies and let it get around that you're about half queer? Wouldn't the Old Man love that. Ask the priest? Sure, right in the middle of confession when Father so-and-so's getting a bid on weather stripping the sacristy. "We could do it for less than eighty-five dollars, and what does it mean when you want to hug your best friend and he's a boy?" No, those thoughts were little secrets, something best kept to John Gacy and no one else.

Except the Old Man knew!

He never said anything, but he had a way of looking at you like he could see right through you. Come home from a date, the Old Man's still up. Sit down and tell him how you scored with some broad. No smile, no wink. The Old Man just looked at you.

Because he knew you didn't score at all. So you'd make up some details talking to your father man to man, and he'd just stare, no emotion, cold as ice.

John figured that sexually he was a late bloomer because he was all of eighteen before he really did "score with some broad."

Just like there was this one time he was parked with a broad: they were necking in John's car, really getting somewhere, and John got her blouse off, then her skirt, and she was naked right there in the car, and it was all going to happen.

The next thing John knew, she was all dressed again, and his head ached because he'd passed out, just slumped over on the seat, unconscious for he didn't know how long, with this naked broad probably getting all hysterical next to him.

And the Old Man thought he was lying for some reason. "You don't just pass out," he said. "You hadda be doing something, wrestling, horsing around."

John told him exactly what he was doing, because they were arguing again, hollering at one another. The Old Man screamed that John wasn't really sick, that he "faked" passing out, that he "faked" heart problems so that he could skip school, draw attention to himself, avoid situations that scared him. But John had learned to argue from a master, and he turned the whole thing around on his father. "If I pass out to get attention, why would I pass out when something good is going on?" Reversing the Old Man right there. "Why would I fake passing out when I'm just about to score with this broad? Go on, answer that."

The Old Man just stared at him, disappointed, the bleary, drinker's eyes icy with unvoiced suspicions.

Years later, after John was charged with the murder of thirty-three boys and young men, Marion Gacy told police that her husband absolutely despised homosexuals. If John Stanley Gacy thought his son was a homosexual, Ma said, "I think he would have killed him."

It was his fourth high school in as many years, another vocational school, where he had to work with machines. The administration was worried about John's health. What if he passed out, fell into the teeth of some grinding machine? Ma couldn't get him into any other high school, and the military took one look at his medical records and classified him 4F.

John was nineteen, unable to finish high school, and all he had was his car. The car and Civil Defense work with the flashing blue light.

It wasn't even his car. The year before, the Old Man had bought it for him. John had enough money of his own to buy a used vehicle, but the Old Man wouldn't hear of it. "Why buy someone else's problems? Get a new car, you know it'll be right."

So the car was in his Old Man's name. John was paying him off monthly. This was, John came to realize, pretty dumb and stupid, because the Old Man had the final say about how "his" car was to be used. John Stanley would just take away the keys, refuse to let John drive anywhere until the boy did as he was told. The Old Man had outsmarted John, with money.

John Stanley was a good provider, but he was careful with the money he made. The kids never had more than one pair of shoes. "You can only wear one pair at a time," John Stanley said. "Why would you need two pairs?"

It made hard sense, but as John got older, he saw how the Old Man used money as a club. His mother hadn't left the Opal Street house when the Old Man busted her in the face because she couldn't support herself and the three kids.

In the late 1940s, the Old Man gave Ma thirty dollars a week for household expenses. She was supposed to buy food and clothes for the kids out of that. Thirty dollars might have been enough then, but in the late 1950s, the weekly allowance wouldn't cover both food and clothes. The Old Man saw no reason to shell out any more. They could get by on thirty dollars, just as they always had. John remembered Ma buying good, clean clothes at the thrift shops. She was incredible at making the money last, and the Gacy family was never in debt. Finally, Ma had to take a job herself to make ends meet.

Of course, there were no luxuries, no meals out, none of that. Ma said restaurants were "a foolish waste. You can eat for a week on what you spend in one night at a restaurant." Half the fights at the dinner table, if they weren't about being sick, were about money. Having your own money meant you didn't have to take so much shit off the Old Man. "Consequently," John said, "my sisters and I are real skinflints to this day."

John bought himself an extra set of keys after some argument and drove the car even though the Old Man had denied it to him. He thought he had outsmarted the Old Man, but the next time, John Stanley just went under the hood and pulled the distributor cap, outsmarting John, who was so dumb and stupid he didn't even know you could go down to the auto parts store and buy a new one.

John was twenty then, and the Old Man kept the distributor cap for three days. It made John sick, physically sick, affecting his heart in such a way that he had to stay home from work, too ill to take a bus. That day, the day the Old Man put the distributor cap back, Ma called John from her job. She felt nauseous and wanted to know if John was well enough to drive down and pick her up. John could have been dying, he would have gone to get Ma. When they arrived at the house on Marmora, John said, "Ma, I better get some air in the tires."

Marion Gacy waited for her son, but "he never came back. He was gone for three months. I had them looking for his car and the police called me at work and nobody knew where he was until I got a medical bill from the White Cross Insurance Company."

The bill was from Las Vegas, Nevada. Marion Gacy called the hospital, to find her son was paying off the balance of his medical bill by working at the Palm Mortuary. He had started with the mortuary's ambulance service, but when they found that he wasn't yet twenty-one—not yet eligible for that sort of work in Clark County—he was transferred to the mortuary proper, where he worked as an attendant. John told Marion Gacy that he was living in the mortuary, sleeping on a cot behind the embalming room.

Years later, George Wycoski, manager of the Palm Mortuary, told police that John Gacy helped unload the ambulances but that he couldn't have had much contact with the bodies.

"I always say I ran away from home," John said, "but I was twenty at the time, old enough to be out on my own." Still, it seemed like running away, it sure felt like running away, and the reason it did, John theorized, was that he still owed the Old Man money on the car. He had outsmarted John Stanley with distance.

Working with the ambulance service, speeding through traffic with the lights flashing and the siren blaring, had almost been fun. And it was enlightening. You could learn shit. Like people lose control of their sphincters, sometimes even their bowels, when they die. Some poor guy has a heart attack in his room at some hotel on the Strip, you walk in to an awful smell.

When John had to move over to the mortuary because of his age, it was like a demotion. Not as much excitement, no sirens, no flashing lights. In the mortuary there aren't a whole bunch of people gathering around all the time and you never get to say, "Stand back, please. Will you please stand back."

Mortuary attendant: it's a transient's job, a job for somebody dumb and stupid, somebody who'd never amount to anything. Working there was proof that he hadn't outsmarted the Old Man at all.

Just like the time he passed out in the car with that naked broad. Even while he was working on the buttons of her blouse, John had a feeling that he was doing something that was expected of him. Like it was a duty to go ahead and bang this broad. And all the time he was getting her blouse off and unsnapping her bra, he was thinking about how he had to be gentle and that what he was about to do was beautiful, one of God's miracles.

Because it was Ma who taught him about sex. The Old Man never said jackshit about it. For all John knew, John Stanley didn't even have a dick. Except that he had three kids, so he must have gotten it on once in a while. Maybe the Old Man jagged off in the basement. Maybe he had some dirty magazines locked up down there or something.

Ma was in charge of John's sex education. She was not ashamed to tell her son the things he needed to know, and the way she described the act, it was almost like a sacrament of the Church. Ma said the act took two people, in communion, in one effort. Sex is not just for the enjoyment of one individual; it was not for quick animal gratification. The sexual act is a way to communicate feelings and emotions, to express love. The beauty in it is in the sharing, in mutual satisfaction. If you could satisfy your partner, then you would satisfy yourself. You had to satisfy your partner first.

John thought about all this satisfaction and shit when that broad was naked, ready for him. He liked looking at her body: he liked the beauty of it, the swell of her breasts, the smoothness of her skin, the tautness of her nipples. Looking at her was fine. But the thought of actually banging her, right there in the Old Man's fucking car, was suddenly repulsive. It was supposed to be beautiful and emotional, but all John felt was a kind of vague disgust. It was his duty to satisfy her, and he passed out.

There was an actual blackness or something that John felt slumped there in the seat. But yes, he knew the broad was trying to revive him; and yes, he knew when she started putting her clothes back on; and yes, he managed to come to when she was fully dressed. So you could say that he faked it and the Old Man was right, except how do you explain the feelings that brought on the blackness? Wasn't there something wrong, physically wrong, when you felt like that?

And in the mortuary, when they brought in the bodies: some of them were young men, teenagers, hard and muscular in a way that he'd never been. In the mortuary John would look at those bodies and have compassion. It was as if he should be the dead one—John Gacy, sick all his life—and not these smooth young men.

Still, it was fascinating to watch the morticians, their professional detachment, as they worked with the dead. John memorized the embalming process, studied the steps until he thought he could do it himself. The thing about bodies, once they were embalmed, you could do anything with them. Cut one, it wouldn't bleed. You had to be professional about dealing with corpses: the bodies were just dead things. The soul had left the flesh. It didn't matter what you did to them.

Later, up in 3 North, in Cermak Hospital, John told the psychiatrists that he had conducted some experiments at the Palm Mortuary. Little experiments to satisfy his curiosity. He didn't care to be any more specific than that. Dr. Freedman, who pushed harder than most of the others, wanted to know more.

John would say only that he was alone and it was dark. The lights were off, and it was after midnight, in the secret time, when the dark flower blooms. And there was a coffin, silver-gray, with a white interior.

Bodies all around: dead things, they didn't care. A silver-gray coffin with white interior, open. John got inside with the body. He wanted to feel death, in the darkness. And there was a fear, a terrible fear, like someone coming who would discover him there, only there was no sound at all, no one to find him, and he was still afraid.

Later, when it was light, and the light would not burn away his fear, John called Ma in Illinois.

"Mother," he said, "do you think Dad would let me come home?"

CHAPTER
5

IT WAS THE FEAR, the crushing weight of darkness he felt inside the coffin that set John Gacy on the road back home. Back to a familiar place, where he wouldn't be so goddamn lonely, where he didn't have to feel like such a nothing. In Las Vegas he wasn't much more than a transient, a failure, a nobody: the living embodiment of his father's expectations. An asshole. Dumb and stupid.

Gacy's family must have thought the three-month stint on his own was good medicine for the boy. Despite his lack of a high-school diploma, Gacy soon talked his way into Northwestern Business College, where he took the standard year-long course. This time he did well, graduating with good grades and enough recommendations to secure a job as a "management trainee" for Nunn-Bush Shoes. Gacy was twenty-one, and when he later described the job, he systematically forgot the "trainee" designation. "In 1963, I traveled for Nunn-Bush, as a manager," at sixty-five dollars a week.

Even at that salary, John had more drive than any four shoe salesmen combined. "The son-of-a-bitch could really sell shoes," an acquaintance of the time remembered. The company transferred Gacy to Springfield, where he handled the Nunn-

Bush line at Roberts, one of the larger department stores in town. It was a big promotion.

Gacy moved in with his aunt and uncle, and—finally free of his father's constant disapproval, all those unvoiced suspicions—he set out to prove the Old Man wrong.

He dated frequently and, to replace the Chi Ro Club, he joined the Springfield Junior Chamber of Commerce. His life was coming together, and the realization filled him with energy. The man was a dynamo, a prodigious worker on the job and a volunteer for any of the ongoing myriad of projects the Jaycees sponsor every year. In 1964, Gacy was chosen the Jaycees' Key Man for April. He had been in town less than two months. In September, he married Marlynn Myers, another employee at Roberts.

That was the year that John helped promote the sale of savings bonds with Jaycees, that he organized the club's annual boss's night, that he ran the "largest Christmas parade in central Illinois." Fellow Jaycees thought the ambitious young shoe salesman enjoyed working the parade so much because he got to drive around with a flashing red light on the dashboard of his car, just like detectives on TV. There was some sniggering about that—the guy was a "police freak"—but everyone had to admit, goddamn, not only could the son-of-a-bitch sell shoes, he also ran a hell of a parade. John Gacy just loved being in charge.

The next year, 1965, John was elected the Jaycees' first vice president, named the outstanding first-year Jaycee and the third outstanding member statewide.

John reveled in the recognition. All he had to do was look at the plaques on the wall to see how wrong the Old Man had been about him. Marlynn was pregnant. He was the outstanding man. His father was an asshole.

They may have been the best years of John's life: 1962, 1963, 1964, 1965. Both his sisters were married then, and he was happy for them. His parents had their twenty-fifth wedding anniversary in 1964, and the Old Man spent most of the party treating his son like an actual human being.

The Jaycee work was almost like therapy, and John would be the first to admit that he needed the recognition that came along with it. "I like being in the limelight."

Even his health improved, though he was hospitalized in 1965 for what he said was "nerves" or "a mild stroke."

Given his medical history, the sickness could almost be expected. There was only one truly bad thing that happened in Springfield during the good years: one mark on an otherwise unblemished life. "Just like I had my first sexual experience with a woman when I was eighteen," John recalls, "I had my first sexual experience with a male in 1964, in Springfield, when I was twenty-two."

John said it all happened before he got married that year. He was out drinking with an older fellow, a guy named Richard Stuart,* and they were looking to pick up women. After several hours and more than enough drinks, they decided to give up on it for that night. Stuart invited John to his house for coffee. "But instead," John said, "we had more drinks. Or I did. And Richard was telling me, he said, 'You know, you go out looking for women, you strike out, you probably go home and play with yourself. Me, I don't give a shit who blows me. A mouth is a mouth. So if I strike out with women, I pick up a guy. Which means on any given night, I got twice the chance to score that you do.' "

Looking back on it, John realized he should have just said what he believed: that it would be all right for Richard Stuart— John Wayne Gacy doesn't sit in judgment on anybody—but that he himself didn't go for that shit. Unfortunately, the drinks Stuart poured were stiff, and John was young and gullible. Naïve.

"I passed out," John said, "and when I woke up, I was nude and Richard Stuart was blowing me. What are you going to do? You're nude, you're in a guy's house, he's going down on you?"

John said he wouldn't lie about it, either. "It felt good, which, I suppose, is one of the reasons I didn't stop him."

When it was over there was the postejaculation sadness, and the hangover, and a depression so abysmal, so lasting, that John remembers the next months as one of the lowest periods of his life.

"I said to myself," John recalls, "watch out for Richard Stuart. Go drinking with him, go to public places, but don't go to his house. Because he outsmarted you."

Being outsmarted in precisely that manner, it changed a person, killed a little part of him. Living with it, as a victim, was as lonely as constant illness, as castrating as a father's rage; it was

*Name changed.

as dark and wrong and foul as the inside of a coffin; it was a dying that came before death.

That's the way John said he felt about it.

The breaks began rolling John Gacy's way. Marlynn's father, Fred Myers, owned three Kentucky Fried Chicken restaurants in Waterloo, Iowa, where business was booming, and he needed a manager. Myers never liked Gacy, but Marlynn was his only daughter, and he wanted her close to home. John could manage the restaurants. Myers said he would provide a home for the newlyweds and he paid his son-in-law fifteen thousand dollars a year plus 20 percent of the profits. Good money.

Gacy did the obligatory stretch at Kentucky Fried University, then brought his pregnant wife to Waterloo and began learning the business from the bottom up. He regularly worked ten- and fourteen-hour days, but he still found time to join the Waterloo Jaycees.

Gacy's fellow Jaycees considered him their hardest-working member. He put in long hours managing the three Kentucky Fried Chicken outlets, but when the club needed someone to donate his time or skills on any of the forty to fifty community or fund-raising projects the Waterloo Jaycees undertake in any given year, Gacy would volunteer. When club members discovered one Thursday afternoon that the ramp for that Sunday's soapbox derby was in shoddy shape, Gacy said he'd fix it. He worked late in the evenings, frequently until well past midnight, but he was up early in the morning, already doing business at ninety miles an hour. On Sunday morning, Jaycee organizers were delighted to see the ramp not only repaired but also newly painted.

Gacy put in tireless hours for the Jaycees. That was the word everyone used to describe him: tireless. He worked on as many as forty Jaycee projects a year. He could be overbearing, arrogant, and a braggart—"He had a hell of a big-man complex," Steve Pottinger, a fellow Jaycee, recalls—but the "big man" was an invaluable member of the club. He was absolutely inexhaustible.

Once, in 1967, visiting his good friend Jaycee president Charles Hill, at the Clayton House Motel lounge, Gacy learned that the Jaycees were twenty-three members short of reaching their membership quota and that the deadline was fast approaching. Gacy went out that afternoon and personally recruited twenty new members. "John was a heck of a promoter," Hill remembers, "and I would say you could classify him as a great con artist. He had a lot of con about him, he could manipulate people and get them to do things, both for the Jaycees and for himself, too." And he was tireless. "The club," Hill recalls, "was his whole life."

Gacy often provided the Jaycees working on various projects with free chicken from his restaurants, and he insisted that his employees and friends call him "Colonel." People who worked for him or ate his fried chicken were inclined to comply. The colonel explained to his friend Hill that he was "a real colonel," though not in the Marines, where he said he had served with some distinction. No, he had actually been commissioned an honorary colonel in the Governor's Brigade of Illinois. Years later, Gacy would say, "I don't know where he got that story. I'm an honorary colonel for the state of Kentucky. I have a certificate to prove it." One can apply for this honor and certificate through the mail.

Gacy seemed to have a knack for club politics, though his machinations were sometimes baldly transparent to those who found his personality grating. Occasionally, even his friends and supporters saw a bizarre manipulative streak in the colonel, and there was talk about the time he offered his wife to the president of the club.

The two men and their wives had just finished dinner at Hill's house, and while the women were in the kitchen, Gacy asked his friend if he liked the dress Marlynn had on.

"Yes," Hill said. "It's very attractive. . . ."

"Do you like her?" Gacy asked.

Hill said that he liked Marlynn. He had always liked Marlynn.

Gacy was happy to hear it. "She likes you, too." He leaned closer to Hill and whispered, "Do you want her?"

Hill didn't quite know how to respond. "Uh, John," he said, "we're friends, you know?"

And that was the end of it. Gacy treated his offer as a joke, and that's how Hill took it.

In spite of this episode, Gacy rose rapidly through the ranks of the Jaycees. He served on the Board of Directors in 1967. In the next two years, Gacy turned the ordinarily nondescript office of chaplain into an influential and even powerful position. The boy who once thought he might become a priest conducted all the club's religious activities. In 1967 he scored a coup of impressive proportions by bringing Bill Brownfield, the author of the Jaycee creed and perhaps the most influential Jaycee nation- wide, to Waterloo for a prayer breakfast. Representatives from most every Iowa chapter attended the breakfast. Gacy, as chair- man, organized the entire affair, which drew more than 225 people. It was one of the most successful club functions of the year.

Because he put in so much time working for the Jaycees, almost all of Gacy's friends were club members, though he was a lot friendlier to some than to others. A persistent rumor had it, for instance, that a few of the younger Jaycees were involved in a bit of infrequent, old-fashioned, straight-ahead wife swapping. The club's chaplain, the rumor held, was right in the middle of that clique. It seemed a bit naughty, not much more, just a case of praise the Lord and pass your wife. Nobody's business, really. Gacy had, after all, been named best Jaycee club chaplain in the state of Iowa.

In addition to the long hours in the restaurants and the never-ending Jaycee projects, Gacy also put in time on the Mer- chant Patrol, a sort of auxiliary police force manned by ordinary citizens, designed to supplement police protection of various busi- nesses. The patrol would look for suspicious activities around closed businesses, check doors, and provide a deterrent presence. Gacy, his friends noted, liked playing the cop. He carried a gun on patrol and explained that he needed protection because of carrying sums of money from the restaurants to the bank. He also had a flashing red light that could be placed on the hood of the car.

"We went to the Jaycee convention in Phoenix," John remembers, "and one time we were late getting from the motel to the convention center: tied up in traffic, all the lanes full, creeping along at about twenty miles an hour. Charley Hill, Jaycee presi- dent at the time, says, 'Goddamn it, I got business, I gotta be there!' So I take and reach under the seat for the red light we used on the Merchant Patrol, just lean out the window and put the light on the hood. Then I pulled out around all the traffic, crossed the double yellow line, and took off like a bat. Lights flashing, the whole works. Went right through every intersection.

"We got to the convention center about two minutes early. As we pulled up, the governor was walking in. So we walked in right behind the goddamn governor, and everyone treats us like we're with him, part of the party." And people thought the light was part of some psychological cop thing he had.

John made no secret of the fact he was fascinated by police and police work. His cheap-ass father-in-law—who was becoming just like the Old Man: Freddy shoveling a shitpile of constant disapproval and suspicion every day—couldn't understand it. John would take free buckets of chicken to the cops, and Asshole would complain about the expense. He couldn't see that these gifts were good public relations and that it paid to have the cops on your side.

There were other reasons, "nice little secrets" John wasn't anxious to share with Freddy. The prostitution, for instance: John was pals with the fellow who ran the operation. In that business you want to buddy up to the right cop, provide the right girl, and keep your mouth shut. It's like having a "get out of jail free" card in your wallet.

A thing like that, a guy gets a little drunk at some bar, he doesn't have to worry about driving home so much. Someone shows a few dirty films in his home or over at Clayton House, there aren't going to be any raids coming down. Have a stag party with a stripper/prostitute, how do you suppose a cop who screwed that same girl is going to bust you? When he knows that you know?

The way John saw it, he couldn't pay to get arrested in Waterloo, Iowa. He was bulletproof.

Perfect. It was the perfect American family. John and Marlynn lived in a bungalow on Fairlane Street, where he was forever fixing the driveway and remodeling the basement. The colonel relaxed in his woodworking shop or in the garden. Marlynn had given birth to a perfect son in 1966, and a year later presented her husband with a perfect baby girl. John took the children with him when he checked the restaurants. He took them to Clayton House after work, putting them on display, proud. Everyone said he was great with the kids.

The Old Man even came out from Chicago to visit and he went to work with John, riding with him in the car, talking all the way, treating his son as he would treat any man, holding a regular conversation and not yelling or making accusations. They'd float from one fried-chicken store to another in the new Olds Vista Cruiser, having a real father-and-son conversation while John's young son fussed in the backseat. They talked like two adults, man to man. It was almost as if the Old Man were making an apology—"I was wrong about you, John"—and when he left, the two looked one another in the eye as they shook hands. The Old Man smiled.

John had friends in the government and on the police force. He was the best Jaycee chaplain in the state; he was named the club's outstanding member for 1967; and in 1968, he looked like a shoo-in for president. "Back then," John remembers, "I was thinking of running for alderman. After that I wanted to go for mayor, and if that worked, I was going to run for the state Senate. I didn't see any limits."

He was twenty-six years old and ready to take on the world. Then, on the night of May 10, 1968, the police came to the bungalow on Fairlane Street and arrested John Wayne Gacy, Jr., for the crime of sodomy.

It wasn't fair, what happened with Voorhees. John's only crime was he was naïve, gullible. He was the victim, outsmarted by a fifteen-year-old blackmailer.

He hadn't even been drinking the day he picked him up. Ask anyone in Waterloo. John wasn't the sort of businessman who went around picking up hitchhikers. He was driving fast along the highway in his car with the Kentucky Fried Chicken stickers on the door. It was a late summer evening in 1967, and the window was open. Standing by the side of the highway, there was this kid and he yelled, "Hey, Mr. Gacy!"

John stopped and backed up right away when he saw that the kid was Donald Voorhees, the son of a Jaycee colleague. The boy was short, had blue eyes, blond hair, and a muscular build. Marlynn was out of town, and John had the house to himself. Was that his fault?

John knew that the kid had been having some trouble with his father, and the first thing he asked him was, "How you getting along with your old man these days."

The Voorhees kid said, "All right," like he didn't want to

discuss it: exactly the kind of sulky comment that brought out the father in a man like John Wayne Gacy, who had had so much trouble with his own father, and he said, "You ever think your dad might have a point of view here? You ever stop to look at it from his side?"

"I looked at it—"

"My dad, we never got along when I was your age," John said. "I could never do anything right. Even ran away from home, but that's not the way you solve anything. We get along okay now, and I see where he gave me my drive and shit. If I didn't have drive, I wouldn't have my degree in accounting and my degree in business administration. I wouldn't have a nice house. Wouldn't own three restaurants. It's part of growing up, feeling that way about your dad, I think. Then, later on, you see it from another perspective."

"I suppose," the kid said, and John felt a little twinge of anger. Get to feeling a little fatherly, try to help someone out, and they act like you're boring them to death.

"So what the hell you doing out here, anyway?" he asked, changing the subject.

The Voorhees kid brightened up some. "I was at my girlfriend's house. I was walking home. I don't get my license until next year."

"Yeah, well . . ." And somehow the conversation switched around to girls, and John thinks he might have asked Voorhees if he laid a broad yet. Something like that, because pretty soon they were talking about the stag films some of the Jaycees had been showing in their homes. The way John remembers it, it wasn't him, it was the damn Voorhees kid who brought up the subject.

"My dad said something about a stag party at the Jaycees."

The kid honest to God said that. Something like that. Anyway, John replied, "Yeah, we showed some films. I still got 'em over at my house."

"I didn't know you had films or anything," the kid said. "My dad just said they had a stag party. He never mentioned about films."

John swears, with God as his witness, that he made the offer purely out of compassion, that he invited the kid over to his house to watch the films because "you're getting to an age where you can get a good educational experience out of something like that."

"Well," the boy said, "I've heard about those kind of films. Never seen one, though."

"You ever talk about that kind of stuff with your father?"

Voorhees laughed aloud. "Shit, no," he said, relaxing a little bit.

"Well, come on back to the house. I'll set up the projector and we'll watch a couple of them."

Marlynn wouldn't be back that night, and John set up the projector in the basement rec room. He wasn't much interested in watching the film himself, and while the Voorhees kid was transfixed in front of the screen—furthering his education, really—John went upstairs and grabbed a beer. Maybe he made a sandwich. He didn't watch the films. Not for a time, anyway. What he did, he had something to eat. Which shows that he really wasn't thinking about inducing what happened next.

Later on, John wandered back downstairs, where the kid was watching the end of a thing where some broad was going down on a guy. When it was over, John asked Voorhees if he liked the films and the kid said, "Yeah, they opened my eyes about sex and that. Really."

Maybe it was the film, or the conversation, but John started feeling a little horny, and he began asking the kid questions.

"Good-looking kid like you, I bet you're fucking some broad regular?"

John said he just kept asking questions like that; it was like he couldn't stop himself. "You ever get into it like that, have one of 'em go down on ya?"

Strange thing about it: just talking dirty, John realized he was getting an erection. Here he was, just being a little fatherly, helping the kid where his real father didn't even talk about this kind of shit, and suddenly he felt that familiar swelling in his pants. The kid was sort of good-looking—the long blond hair, short muscular build, blue eyes, real innocent look—and Marlynn was gone for the night. They were sitting in the basement, and the kid, Chrissake, fifteen years old, watching a film like that, the kid was probably feeling pretty horny himself.

There wasn't anything they could do about it, the two of them sitting there in the empty house. Then John remembered

Springfield and the first time. He remembered the last few drinks at Richard Stuart's house—when he woke up, nude, and Richard was on it. That was the first time. Shit, there hadn't even been any suggestion of it—well, maybe a little talk—and John was nude and half drunk in a guy's house. Whatta you gonna do, tell him to knock it off? "Hey, stop blowing me, you shithead."

Later in his life, John could see how he brought the Stuart affair on himself. He had been naïve; he had been dumb and stupid. Stuart had victimized him, he had outsmarted John Gacy. John was the victim in that one, just as he would eventually become the victim in the Voorhees affair. But that night, standing there talking to the kid, John couldn't help but remember that he'd done it once before. And it had felt good.

"You hard?" John asked. The kid seemed a little embarrassed, and John started to explain, in a fatherly way, that stag films are supposed to make you horny. It's natural. You'd have to be queer, films like that, you didn't spring one. John knew that "the kid had to be interested in getting his rocks off, too."

"The thing of it is," he says, "read the Kinsey Report and it shows how most guys your age sometimes go down on a guy. Or have a guy go down on them. It don't mean you're queer; it's part of growing up, becoming a man. You have to have sex with a man before you start having sex with women. Nobody tells you this shit, but it's scientific, and you could read it in reports. So what happens, if you get two guys who are horny and there's no one else around, then you got to take care of each other. You have to help each other out. It's only natural to calm your emotional feelings, or you can actually get sick."

John heard himself going on and on about the fucking Kinsey Report, the biggest load of horseshit he'd ever heard in his life, but the way he was saying it, Christ, he could almost believe it himself.

Pretty soon he was right down to it with the kid, arguing about who would go first. John figures, "Since I was the one who brought it up, I probably went first."

When John finished, the kid was still scared, a little reluctant. "Doesn't it taste sorta, you know . . ."

"Whatta you think?" John said, and he saw that his hands were shaking and knew that he was angry. He took a breath, then let it out slowly. "It don't have no taste." Jesus Christ! John took another deep breath, and then, calmly, rationally, and with the utmost sincerity, he said, "It's like sucking on your thumb or something. You want to see what it tastes like, go ahead and put your thumb in your mouth."

Dumb and stupid kid: sitting there with his fucking thumb in his mouth. John knew he had him then, and he said, "See, it don't have no taste." And then solemnly, using his chaplain's voice, John explained to the kid about morality. "There's nothing wrong with anything," he said, "unless you make it wrong in your own mind." Kid sitting there with his thumb in his mouth and his eyes as big as pie plates. It was all John could do to keep from laughing aloud.

That would have been the end of it then, just a one-night stand, an aberration in one man's otherwise exemplary life, but the way John remembered it, the fucking kid showed up at the door a couple of more times. Kid wanted money, and somehow the two of them got into it each of those times. Later, John could see how the kid victimized him, how Voorhees used the sexual approach to "borrow" money. You want to know how dumb and stupid John was: he didn't even realize he was being blackmailed.

"Each time," John explained, "I thought, well, I'll just give him a little more money, help him get straightened out, and that'll be the last time I see him."

There was no way to tell, really, whether the kid actually enjoyed the things he did with John, and John, for his part, wants to be fair on that one point. "Let's just say he did what he did. Whether he was really into it would just be supposition on my part. But he kept coming back, and whether it was for the money or the sex, I'd have to conclude that it was a willing thing on his part."

The kid was like a bad penny, the way John remembered it. Voorhees never told anyone, but every time he turned up at the door, John felt a jolt of fear in his belly. What could he do; tell the kid he wasn't really into it, yell at him? Up to this time, it had just been one of those nice little secrets between John and the kid. But now the thing was beginning to cost money, and John had a family to feed. The kid was actually taking food off the Gacy family table, out of the children's mouths, for Christ's sake, and John knew he had to put a stop to it.

When he came to think about it later on, John realized that

it wasn't the money so much. Not really. With his salary and his cut of the profits, he was knocking down nearly thirty thousand dollars a year. A five here, a ten there wouldn't break him.

What bothered John about the Voorhees affair, he theorized later, wasn't so much the amounts involved, it was the principle of the thing. He was being fucked over every time the kid showed up at the door. Try to help the kid, get him straightened out, be a little fatherly even, and some fifteen-year-old "fucks over" you, makes you feel dumb and stupid.

That's what bothered John the most: being "outsmarted." Every dollar out of his pocket that went to Voorhees proved that the kid was smarter than John. It was a quantitative thing. You could measure what an asshole you were with each five-dollar bill.

The way John recalls it, Voorhees came by his house sometime around the Christmas holidays of 1967. The kid played in some asswipe band and wanted to "borrow" enough money to buy an amplifier so he could play at a big New Year's Eve party.

"My dad won't lend me the money," the kid whined, "so I thought maybe you could."

Voorhees was talking "a hundred and some bucks," an amount that was clearly out of the question. "I'll pay you back," Voorhees said. "You'll get the whole amount right after we get paid." It was as if the kid thought John couldn't add.

Still, there was that little secret to consider, and John sat down with the kid to negotiate. They finally compromised on a plan where John would give the kid enough money to rent the amplifier.

"You don't even have to pay me back," John said. The way he figured it, the kid could use the money he made from playing at the dance to rent the amplifier the next time his band got a job. "That way," John explained later, "I thought he could keep making money and that he wouldn't come to me for it anymore. I told him, this is the last time: I don't want to see you around here anymore. I says, 'You think you can go tell about us, but I'll just deny everything. Who do you think they're going to believe? Asshole!' And that was the last I heard of Voorhees until May of the next year."

In March 1968, Voorhees told his father a story about the outstanding Jaycee chaplain in the state of Iowa. The little secret went to a Black Hawk County grand jury, and the world exploded in John Wayne Gacy's face.

CHAPTER

6

LOOKING BACK ON IT years later, John could see how his father was right about politicians. They're all phonies and liars. Just like the sodomy charge: the whole thing was a frame constructed by his political enemies. "How it came down," John explained, "is that the Voorhees kid is sitting at the table with his old man. Well, the night before, I had had Voorhees, Sr., at my house, and I told him I was going to run for Jaycee president and I wanted him to be my campaign manager."

The way John tells it, Voorhees, Sr., agreed to manage John's campaign that night. "And the next day, the kid spills the little secret. This is just supposition, but I suppose Voorhees, Sr., is sitting at the table and he mentions this to his family, and the kid tells him he shouldn't get involved with me. Something like that." John imitates the way the kid must have said it: he lets his voice go slack and dumb and weepy. "Please don't help Mr. Gacy," he says, sounding like a moron at the point of tears, "he molested me."

These days, John's pretty sure someone had been working on the frame for some time. "What happened, one of the Jaycees had borrowed some of the stag films from me, and he brings them back: actually carried them right downstairs to my office." The next day, the police knocked on John's door. "If they were looking for personal items and shit," John argued, "how come they didn't go into the bedroom, which is where you'd think a guy'd keep stuff like that? Instead, they go right downstairs and pick up the films. They're still in the same envelope from when the guy brought them over the night before."

Up to this point, it was just as John said it would be: his word against the kid's. But now the cops had evidence. Never mind that the films had been planted there by a political enemy who opposed John for the presidency of the Jaycees. The films had been found in John's house. He couldn't very well deny knowledge of them. "So, in accordance with Iowa State law, they indicted me for the sodomy. The definition then was very broad, and the films showed oral sex, which was sodomy. So I was indicted for the sodomy of the films."

The charge, in fact, was sodomy committed with a teenage boy. The Black Hawk County grand jury acted not only on the testimony of young Voorhees, who said that Gacy had forced him to perform oral sex and had attempted anal sex with him, but also on Edward Lynch, sixteen, a clean-up boy and occasional cook at the Kentucky Fried Chicken outlet on the corner of Broadway and Park Road. One day in late August of that year, when Lynch had finished his work at the restaurant, Gacy offered to give him a ride home but said he had to stop at one of the other restaurants on the way. Somewhere along the way, Gacy suggested another stop, at his house. According to Lynch, Gacy said, "I have some stag films. We can have a couple of drinks at my place and watch the films."

Gacy drove the boy to his house and led him to the downstairs rec room, where they had a drink and played several games of pool. Marlynn Gacy was in the hospital, where she was about to give birth to the couple's second child, the perfect baby girl.

Lynch remembered that Gacy said something about being involved in an important scientific study of sex. The boy was making eighty-five cents an hour, and Gacy had proposed a bet of fifty cents on each game of pool. Lynch won every game, and Gacy upped the bet to a dollar. After losing another game, Gacy said:

"Well, let's make it interesting."

"What do you mean?"

"Well, let's play for a blow job."

The boy said he wasn't at all interested, and Gacy redefined the bet in a way that confused Lynch. It wouldn't be a blow job exactly, it could be whatever amount of money a guy named if he won, but there was a sexual option—just an option—thrown in there somewhere. Lynch wasn't real sure about the terms of the bet, but he wasn't worried. He hadn't lost a single game.

When Lynch won again, Gacy asked, "What would you like?"

"You can pay me," Lynch said.

"I'd rather give you a blow job," Gacy replied.

"No," Lynch said. This was getting a little sticky, but the man was his boss. "That's okay, just forget it."

Gacy seemed unconcerned. He mentioned the stag films again and brought out a projector and screen. The first film showed sex between men and women; the second showed women coupling with animals. When the films were over, Gacy suggested they go back upstairs. Lynch stood at the head of the stairs, while Gacy went into the kitchen. He came back with a carving knife in his hand.

"Do you see this?" he asked.

Gacy was holding the knife in a threatening manner, and Lynch said, "Yes, I see it."

"Well, get in the bedroom," Gacy said. He advanced on the boy, holding the knife in front of him. Lynch backed up, staying out of Gacy's reach. He was moving down a narrow hallway, and the man kept coming at him, brandishing the knife. Lynch backed through a doorway into a small bedroom. There was no way out for him. As Gacy moved within reach, the boy grabbed at and caught Gacy's knife arm at the wrist. The man's forward momentum carried Lynch backward, and he felt himself toppling onto a bed behind him. Lynch kept hold of Gacy's wrist. He could see the blade, pointing down, could feel Gacy flexing his wrist, trying to cut at his arm with the knife. Lynch couldn't hold him, and he saw the point of the knife puncture the skin of his arm.

Gacy was ten years older than the boy and about 50 pounds heavier, but Lynch, who stood six feet and weighed 160 pounds, was strong for his age, and there was blood running down his arm. He forced Gacy off his body, turned him over onto his back, and hit him twice, hard. Gacy dropped the knife.

The boy had disarmed the man. Gacy, breathing hard, asked Lynch to turn on the light. He seemed very apologetic.

"Did I cut you?"

"Yes." In the light, Lynch could see that it wasn't really a bad cut, just a little puncture wound, without much blood. Gacy got up and got a Band-Aid. As Lynch peeled the Band-Aid and put in on his arm, Gacy continued to apologize, saying he was sorry about the incident. Lynch believed him. It was just a bit of harmless horseplay that had gotten out of hand. Lynch may have even been made to feel that he brought it on himself, that he had overreacted to what amounted to a little joke.

Gacy couldn't stop apologizing. He was, Lynch knew, a man under a lot of stress. He worked long hours in the restaurants, where things were never quite right, never satisfactory. He was always working on community projects, burning himself out, and on top of everything else, his wife was in the hospital, having a baby.

Still, Lynch wanted to get out of the house, and when Gacy said, as part of his continuing apology, "Come on, let's go back downstairs. Let's watch this other film," the boy declined.

"I better get going. It's kind of late."

Gacy insisted, as if watching the last film was a way for Lynch to show that he had accepted the apology. John Wayne Gacy was the boss on the first job the boy had ever had. Lynch followed him downstairs. During the film, Gacy went into another room in the basement and returned with a length of chain and a padlock. The film was over in about ten minutes, and Gacy said:

"Stand up a minute. Just let me try something here."

Lynch looked at the chain and padlock. He felt very hesitant but may have actually believed he had overreacted to the earlier horseplay. He wanted to keep his job, and Gacy's tone was reassuring. "I ain't going to do nothing," the man said.

"I don't think I'm interested," Lynch said.

"Come on, just let me try something. Put your hands behind your back."

"No."

"Ah, come on," Gacy said. "I ain't going to hurt you."

Recalling the incident a dozen years later, Lynch said, "I had just turned sixteen. He reassured me. I was very gullible. I believed him."

Lynch put his hands behind his back, one crossed over on the other, and Gacy wrapped the chain around them once and secured it with the padlock.

"Is it secure?" Gacy asked. "Can you get loose?"

"No, I can't," Lynch said, and when he sat back down in his chair, Gacy sat on his lap in a suggestive, straddle-legged posture. It took Lynch less than five seconds to realize he had made a bad mistake. He gave Gacy a head butt to the face and stood up, toppling the man off him.

Gacy struggled up off the floor and disappeared into the room where he had gotten the chain. In less than half a minute, Gacy came back into the rec room pushing a fold-up cot on wheels. Lynch stood watching, his hands locked behind his back, as Gacy unfolded the bed between the screen and the projector. Then he began walking toward the boy.

"Don't come near me," Lynch said. "I want this chain off."

"It's okay," Gacy said. All at once he was apologetic again, very reassuring. "Here," Gacy said, "I'll take it off." He walked around behind Lynch as if to remove the chain, then shoved him, savagely, face first down onto the bed. Gacy had both his big hands around the boy's neck and he began to choke, bearing down hard. Lynch felt his throat being closed off: he couldn't call out, he couldn't even breathe. He struggled, but Gacy kept his full weight on the boy's back, and it was no contest.

After about a minute, Lynch felt "consciousness teetering" and realized, with a shock of horror, that Gacy might actually kill him. He stopped struggling, and the man relaxed his grip somewhat but then continued to choke the boy for a period of time Lynch was never able to determine.

The boy felt himself falling off into a whirling darkness. There was a "dizziness," a "blackness," and in some remote corner of his mind, Lynch felt himself lose control of his bladder and urinate in his pants. He was dying. He knew he was dying.

Lynch never could say whether he was absolutely conscious at all times. He only knows that he was lying still, his soul falling into some dark, spinning void, when he felt himself being rolled over onto his side. Then his hands were free and he was gasping for breath, trying to swallow. It took some time before he was able to stand.

"Are you okay?" Gacy asked. It seemed a question of little significance, and there was no apology in the man's tone.

Lynch swallowed, unsteady on his feet, and said, "Well, yeah." Then, with the blackness receding and the breath back in his body, he advanced on the man, his fists clenched. Gacy backed up, staying out of reach. "I'm sorry," he said, and his tone was now one of abject apology.

"I think you just better take me home," Lynch said, threateningly.

"Sure," Gacy said. "Okay, okay, I'll take you home. I mean, I'm sorry. Are you okay? I didn't mean to do that. I'm sorry." Years later, Lynch would tell an Illinois jury that Gacy didn't apologize until "after I threatened him."

"I really didn't mean to do that," Gacy said. "I'm very sorry."

A few days later, Edward Lynch was fired from his job at the Park and Broadway Kentucky Fried Chicken restaurant.

At first, Gacy denied all the accusations, insisting that he be given a lie-detector test. People in Waterloo—his colleagues in the Jaycees, his family and friends—must have been reassured by this request. Generally, guilty men do not demand lie-detector tests.

On May 2, 1968, John Wayne Gacy was given a polygraph test in nearby Cedar Rapids. He was asked a series of gentle warm-up questions so that the operator could measure his responses. The examiner read the lines on the graph, noted the readings on emotionally neutral questions, then asked Gacy if he had ever indulged in homosexual activities of any kind with Donald Voorhees. Gacy insisted that he had not. The polygraph noted increases in his blood pressure, respiration, and pulse as well as an aberration in his psychogalvanic skin response. The official results say flatly that Gacy's answers were "indicative of deception," which is to say that he failed the test.

A week later, on May 10, the grand jury indicted John Wayne Gacy on a charge of sodomy.

*   *   *

Even after failing the lie-detector test, John loudly and publicly maintained that he was innocent of all charges. The Lynch kid's testimony was a joke. "He says I attacked him with a knife," John said later, laughing at the absurdity of it. "Then he says he sat down and watched more films with me. Then, get this, then he says he let me chain his hands behind his back. That's real believable, after I just supposedly attacked him with the knife. What happened is he got fired and wanted to get back at me."

According to John, there was a transparent conspiracy in the works, a blatant frame. Ask anyone in Waterloo: John was going to be the next president of the Waterloo, Iowa, Jaycees.

The truth is he had never really gotten along with Voorhees, Sr.—there had been some public friction—and Voorhees probably had been backing his opponent for Jaycee president all along. John blamed himself for being too naïve to see this. At the time, however, Voorhees was running for statewide Jaycee office, and he was influential. John was willing to let bygones be bygones. Voorhees was the best man for the job he had in mind. How dumb. How dumb and stupid.

Those who opposed John for the presidency could see he had a lock on it, and they had to stop him somehow. The Lynch kid and the Voorhees kid were good friends, by their own admission. Anyone with a nose could smell a frame-up.

There were people who believed John without question, influential people such as the Jaycee president, Charles Hill. Many people thought the charges absurd on the face of them: Christ, the colonel had been a marine, and if he wasn't making jokes about "fruits" and "queers," he was bragging about how many women he had laid last week. "Listen to John," one Jaycee said, "and you'd think he slept with a hundred women a month." The guy went to strip shows, for Chrissake. No way the colonel was queer for boys.

John's friends gathered around him in his time of need; they believed him. He could see it in their eyes as he talked. And talked. And talked. John could wear you down, just blow right over you with sheer verbal energy. People got tired of listening to an innocent man defend himself against the manufactured charges. It was less exhausting to capitulate completely, to believe him.

However, John's political enemies made the most of the

charges. The Jaycees were now split pretty evenly among those who bought John's story and those who didn't. The colonel had been indicted on May 10, 1968. The charges, he thought, would surely be dropped before he was nominated for the presidency in late May. John thinks he was naïve back then. He was just a young man, barely twenty-six years old, and so dumb and stupid he really believed he could beat the frame-up.

Unfortunately, a young assistant county attorney named David Dutton had been named to prosecute the case. The guy was politically ambitious, looking to run for office himself. John could see it all very clearly. A prominent businessman indicted on charges of sodomy: it was a headline-grabber, a reputation-maker. "The charges weren't dropped," John explained later, "because Dutton turned me into a political football." The sodomy charge was still pending when the Jaycees met to nominate their choices for office.

It was a very tense gathering, and John could see the continuing controversy was harming the image of the Jaycees and of Waterloo, Iowa. There was no point in running if his candidacy would just rip apart everything he was trying to build. He made up his mind to do the Right Thing. He waited until he was nominated—no use not to accept that honor at the very least—and then, with all the considerable courage at his disposal, he stood and declared that he was withdrawing from the race for the good of "the organization and my family." It was a very emotional speech, a speech tinged with a certain sad nobility.

Thinking about it later, John remembered that he had never been very worried about what the Lynch kid had to say. The story sounded idiotic, and even if it was true—which, of course, it wasn't—anyone could see how it could have been a kind of practical joke that got out of hand. Edward Lynch never said he was raped. He was just a kid who got fired for sloppy work and had a gripe.

No, it was the lying little fuck Voorhees who landed John in the shit. It was Voorhees whose testimony led to the one charge he could never ride out. It was Voorhees who accused him of sodomy; it was Voorhees the blackmailer who cost him what would have been his highest honor, the presidency of the Waterloo, Iowa, Jaycees; it was Voorhees whose testimony before the grand jury generated all those reputation-shattering headlines in the *Waterloo Courier*. Because of Voorhees, half the people in town thought he was some kind of goddamn fruit picker.

Because of Voorhees, he lost everything he had ever worked for: his reputation, his standing in the community, everything. Because of Voorhees, he would never be president of the Jaycees. Refusing the nomination had been a sacrifice John Gacy felt honorbound to make. Because of Voorhees.

Voorhees!

Despite the indictment and the results of the polygraph test, Gacy continued to proclaim his complete innocence. In July, a month after the total collapse of his presidential campaign, he was one of four Waterloo Jaycees to receive Key Man awards. When you are facing a trial where it's going to be your word against someone else's, the heft of an award like that adds weight to your testimony.

Apparently encouraged by this evidence of acceptance, Gacy agreed to take a second polygraph test. The lines on the graph showed Gacy's responses rising from the flat land of neutral questions to a mountain range of "emotional disturbances indicative of deception" each time he answered "no" to questions about having either oral or anal sex with Donald Voorhees.

At the county attorney's office, investigators were astounded by the results of the two tests. The man had insisted that the first be administered, had readily agreed to the second, and he had failed more miserably than anyone in recent memory. "The only thing Gacy got right," the joke in the county attorney's office went, "was his name."

At this point, the colonel began to change his story. First of all, he wanted investigators to know that what had happened was really just a matter of curiosity on his part. It wasn't as if he was "queer," but, yes, he said, he had picked up the Voorhees boy that summer night in 1967. Gacy had heard that the boy hustled blow jobs for cash and had simply asked the kid if this was true. Voorhees, in this version of Gacy's story, not only admitted that he engaged in acts of prostitution for money, he also made a proposition. The price for oral sex was forty dollars.

There were some negotiations then, and the price dropped to five dollars. Voorhees, according to Gacy's postpolygraph story, attempted to consummate the act right there in the car. Gacy said that he couldn't even maintain an erection. It was all just curiosity on his part, and he didn't find the act all that exciting. He said the Voorhees boy offered to try again, some other time, but he wanted to be paid another five dollars. It was Voorhees who kept coming on to him.

A few days later, Voorhees stopped by the Gacy house. It was a Saturday morning and, in his own house, for some reason, Gacy was more successful. A month or so later, in this version of the story, Voorhees dropped by to ask for a loan. Gacy worked for his money, and he expected others to do the same. He told the boy that he already knew how to earn five dollars. It was more a fatherly gesture, a lesson in economics, than a desire for sex on his part.

That was it, according to Gacy: three acts spread out over a month-long period, all of them initiated by Voorhees for financial gain, and committed, on John's part, entirely out of curiosity about homosexual relations, a type of sex he had never indulged in before. He didn't like homosexuals, but he was liberal-minded and didn't condemn them. With that sort of attitude, was it any wonder that, when the opportunity presented itself, he would try a little experiment? A man should know what he's talking about. Voorhees provided the opportunity. For a price.

Gacy's second story still didn't mesh with testimony the grand jury had heard. Donald Voorhees, testifying under oath, said that he had been working for Gacy, spreading gravel on the driveway, when the man invited him to take a break in the downstairs rec room. There the two of them engaged in oral sex, and Gacy had attempted and failed to perform anal sex. He said the acts had been forced upon him. He was then sixteen years old, a sophomore in high school, and he seemed very troubled.

It was still a question of the word of a man—a Key Man—against a boy's, but the fact that Gacy had amended his statement to the police and had made limited admissions did not look good. And the results of the two separate lie-detector tests were damning.

Gacy may have been working behind the scenes, applying leverage in the places where it would do the most good. There was a feeling in the county attorney's office that there was a certain amount of foot-dragging involved in the case, that certain individuals who had pledged to uphold the law weren't particularly interested in seeing John Wayne Gacy go to trial. Gacy, the prosecutors knew, had not only been involved in wife-swapping, he also was neck deep into the prostitution and gambling rackets at a local motel. What if he had a list of names, a nice little secret list showing who did what with whom? It would explain why the case was being allowed to drift into a kind of limbo.

Gacy, however, didn't know of the prosecutors' frustration, and it is likely that he saw only one way out of his troubles. If Donald Voorhees were to recant his testimony, or refuse to appear at the upcoming trial, Gacy was home free. There had to be a way to scare the kid away from court. On August 30, 1968, the colonel set his plan in motion.

Russell Schroeder, an eighteen-year-old West High School senior, had been employed for two years as a night cook at one of the restaurants Gacy managed. On the night of August 30, Gacy, after work, invited Schroeder to ride with him on the Merchant Patrol route. At each stop, Schroeder helped check doors to see if they were securely locked. Brown's Lumber Company, for one, was locked up tighter than a drum, but it was there that Gacy took an iron bar from under the seat of his car.

"You can get into any place with one of these," Gacy told the boy. He seemed very proud of the iron bar, and it took only seconds to break into Brown's. Once inside, Gacy gave Schroeder the bar, then told him to open the Coke machine and take what money was there—three dollars. Gacy insisted the boy keep the money. Schroeder had never stolen anything in his life, but he did as his boss said, putting the coins in his pocket. The colonel stole an extension cord and a can of paint.

Gacy and the boy drove around for six hours, checking some businesses and burglarizing one other. At the Oldsmobile lot in downtown Waterloo, Gacy asked the boy to get out and pop the hubcaps off a few of the cars. The colonel would monitor his police radio, checking to see that there were no police patrols in the neighborhood. Once again, Schroeder did as he was told. It was the first time he had ever ridden with Gacy on the patrol route, and within about two hours, he had committed two crimes. It changed his relationship with the boss. Now there was a nice little secret just between the two of them.

The boy didn't have any experience at theft, and he wasn't

particularly good at it. "Don't make so much noise," Gacy counseled. "Quiet, quiet."

After stealing the hubcaps, Gacy and the boy drove around listening to the police radio and talking.

"You want to steal anything else?" Gacy asked, as he would to a confederate, a partner in crime.

"No," Schroeder replied.

Gacy began to coax the boy. "It's so easy with the police radio," he said. "I know where they are at all times."

"No," Schroeder said. "I want to go home."

Gacy shrugged, driving around some more, protecting the businesses of Waterloo from thieves. The colonel carried a gun and a badge. He was about as proud of his police gear as he was of his burglary tools.

Schroeder had read about the charges against Gacy in local papers, and sometime during their six hours of burglaries and police work, Gacy mentioned Donald Voorhees.

"I want him beaten up," Gacy said. "So he won't testify."

Schroeder stood six feet tall and played football for the West High team. He had never met Voorhees, but Gacy described him as nearly half a foot shorter than Schroeder and a good deal lighter. The kid was a sophomore, almost three years younger than Schroeder. It would be easy.

Schroeder said he wasn't interested. They were thieves together, buddies now, but Schroeder wasn't mad at the Voorhees kid. He had never even met him. Gacy dropped Schroeder off at about six in the morning.

The next night, Gacy picked Schroeder up and drove him to a local quarry known as the Sand Pits. Sitting there in the darkness, Gacy once again brought up the subject of Voorhees and his testimony at the expected trial.

"I want him taken care of," Gacy said. "I want him persuaded not to testify. I want him beaten."

Once again Schroeder declined, but he was under a great deal of pressure. Not only was Gacy his boss, but now the colonel could also implicate the boy in two burglaries. If the matter of the burglaries were put before the police, it would be Schroeder's word against the state's outstanding Jaycee chaplain.

Five days later, on a Thursday afternoon, Gacy picked Schroeder up at work, and they went driving around. Gacy was rattling on about the conspiracy against him and about how the Voorhees kid had blackmailed him. At one point, they stopped at a car lot. Schroeder couldn't afford a new car. He told Gacy he still had three hundred dollars to pay on his four-year-old Pontiac.

"Tell you what," Gacy said. "I don't want Voorhees to testify. You want to pay off your car. If you beat up Voorhees, tell him not to testify, I'll pay off the loan on your car."

This time Schroeder agreed to the plan. He had never seen Voorhees, so Gacy showed him a picture in the East High yearbook. The kid had recently transferred to West, Schroeder's school, so it would be easy to nail him. Just to be sure there were no problems, Gacy gave the husky football player a spray can of the tear gas Mace. A few squirts of Mace in the face will temporarily blind a man, Gacy explained. It hurts like hell. A faceful of Mace would scare the shit out of Voorhees.

"Look," Gacy said, "the kid likes to drink. I know that. Just tell him you got some booze stashed somewhere. Take him there, then Mace him and beat the shit out of him. Tell him not to testify."

Schroeder was on a school-work program, and he was scheduled to attend school in the mornings and work in the afternoons, but that Thursday afternoon he returned to West High, went to the attendance office, and asked where Voorhees would be at the end of the day. When school let out, Schroeder met Voorhees, introduced himself, and said that he had recently stolen twenty cases of liquor. The stuff was stashed at Access Acre, a lonely wooded county park about five miles out of town.

The two students drove out to the park in the Pontiac Schroeder believed he would soon own free and clear. They parked in an isolated spot, and Schroeder led Voorhees deep into the woods, secretly pulling Gacy's can of Mace out of his clothes and positioning his fingers on the spray device. Suddenly he spun around and sprayed the younger boy full in the face. Voorhees thrashed around, suddenly blind, his face streaming with tears and his eyes burning like fire and sudden death.

Voorhees lurched like a man aflame, then fell, more than jumped, into a nearby creek. Schroeder watched him as he splashed water into his face, trying to cool the burning in his eyes. And when Voorhees finally managed to crawl, weakly, out of the water, Schroeder sprayed him again. Then he began to beat the boy.

"Don't testify against John Gacy!" Schroeder shouted, hammering away at Voorhees, telling him all the time exactly why he was doing it. Eventually the younger boy, battered and in tears, escaped through the woods and hid in a cornfield.

Schroeder drove home thinking he had just made the final payment on his car. That night, Schroeder returned the Mace to Gacy, saying he'd done the little job they had talked about. "Don't tell me about it," his boss said, "I don't want to know anything about it. I don't want to be involved." Somehow, Schroeder didn't get his three hundred dollars from Gacy that night.

The next day, Friday, September 6, county sheriff's deputies picked Schroeder up at his parents' house. Voorhees had been able to identify him. The kid had come into the police department, covered with angry bruises, and put the finger on Schroeder. The deputies dragged Schroeder to the station and grilled him. They said they knew the whole story; they knew that he had beaten the kid to prevent him from testifying.

"Gacy put you up to it, didn't he?" the cops said.

Schroeder tried his best to stand up against the curses, the shouted accusations. He said that he had never talked to Gacy about Voorhees. Someone else had put him up to it.

"Who?"

A guy named Jim. Schroeder couldn't remember his last name, but it was an older guy named Jim, who thought Voorhees had stolen his tires. Jim had given Schroeder ten dollars to teach Voorhees a lesson. Jim was behind the whole thing, an older guy who had no last name.

The boy could see the cops didn't believe him, not even a little bit. They told him they'd get the story out of him. "You'll crack," one of the cops said. "You can't stand the pressure."

That night, at work, Schroeder talked with Gacy about his interview with the police.

"I didn't mention your name," Schroeder said.

"Good," Gacy replied. "Don't get me involved. Don't tell them anything. It's your word against Voorhees'. They can't prove anything." Somehow, in all the excitement, all the counseling he had to do, Gacy forgot to give the boy his three hundred dollars.

The next day, Gacy again instructed the boy not to say

anything. "Just don't get me involved," Gacy said. He was understanding, though. He said he knew it had to be tough on the boy and asked him how he was holding up. Schroeder shrugged and said he guessed he was holding up all right. In fact, it was just like the cop said: Schroeder found "I couldn't stand the pressure." Over the weekend, he met with his parents and a lawyer, who urged him to go the police and tell the truth.

On Monday, September 9, Schroeder met with Gacy at about noon. The colonel went through the same litany and added one further inducement. "Get yourself a good lawyer," he said, "and don't worry about the fee. I'll take care of the fee."

Gacy's offer was several hours late. That morning Schroeder had voluntarily gone to the police, told them Gacy had offered him three hundred dollars to beat Voorhees and "persuade" him not to testify. He confessed to the burglaries at the lumber company and the car lot, and he implicated John Wayne Gacy in those thefts.

That Monday night Gacy was arrested and charged with attempting to suborn perjury and malicious threats to extort in connection with the beating. He went free on a one-thousand-dollar bond. On Thursday, the colonel was again arrested, this time on a charge of burglarizing Brown's Lumber. He could not raise ten thousand dollars for bail and was immediately jailed.

Appearing that day before Judge George Heath, Gacy, in an emotional statement, proclaimed his complete innocence in the Voorhees beating affair. "I am guilty of none of these," he said, "except for making a verbal threat to Voorhees in December of 1967, when he wanted me to give an amplifier or else he would tell his father. . . ."

Judge Heath ordered a pretrial psychiatric evaluation. Until that could be arranged, the colonel would remain in jail. Several hours later, Gacy met with the county attorney and five law-enforcement officers. While the officers took notes, Gacy drew a detailed verbal map of Waterloo's seamy underbelly.

He talked about the wife-swapping, and he named names.

He talked about the gambling, and he named names.

He talked about the prostitution ring, and he named names.

The colonel talked well into the night. Guards, he might have reasoned, tend to coddle cooperative and informative prisoners. In any case, it is not at all unpleasant to sit in the limelight and talk while important men hang on your every word. His first day in the slam and he was already a Very Important Prisoner.

Several people Gacy named were fellow Jaycees, a small group compared to the total membership, but they were some of the very men who had stood behind the colonel during his troubles. They were men who believed in him, supported him in his abortive bid at the presidency. Now they were being fingered by their own Key Man, the best Jaycee chaplain in the state of Iowa.

On November 2, Gacy entered an institution where he would submit to psychiatric evaluation, an institution with a quaintly archaic name: the Psychopathic Hospital, at the State University of Iowa, in Iowa City.

Schroeder never got his three hundred dollars.

CHAPTER

7

WHILE GACY WAS IN jail awaiting trial, investigators were now working overtime on the Gacy case, determined to convict him on the sodomy charge. The colonel, it seemed, was a master of manipulation. One incident involved another East High School senior, Richard Westphal, a seventeen-year-old who had been employed at the Park and Broadway restaurant for two years. Westphal was helping remodel the basement rec room and building a bar in the Gacy house. He worked at the house a couple of times a week for almost two years.

Occasionally, Gacy and Westphal would break off to play a game of pool. Sometimes other boys were present, and several times, Gacy suggested they play pool "for a blow job." When the boys declined the proposition, Gacy laughed. Just one of his jokes.

Another of Gacy's odd jokes was his habit of offering Westphal Marlynn's sexual favors. Once in a while, Gacy turned the joke into a kind of humorous threat: "If I ever catch you in bed with my wife, you'll owe me a blow job." One night in January 1967, Westphal would later testify, he and Gacy were working on the basement bar. It was late and cold, and Gacy told Westphal he was welcome to sleep in the guest room. Shortly after Westphal got into bed, the door opened. Marlynn Gacy walked into the room and got into bed with Westphal. It was Westphal's first time, and it likely remains one of the oddest such experiences of his life. As soon as Westphal and Marlynn were done, Gacy stepped into the room and switched on the light. It was almost as if he had been waiting outside the door for just the right moment. The colonel did not seem to be in the least upset. He was, in fact, triumphant.

"See, I caught you," he said. "Now you owe me a blow job."

Gacy and his wife left Westphal alone and confused in the room. The boy had been making pretty good money at the two jobs he worked for Gacy. But now he had been caught screwing the man's wife. Days later, Westphal said, he was "more or less coerced" into paying Gacy what he owed.

Another boy who worked for Gacy at the same restaurant told police that his boss drove him up to the Sand Pits quarry one night after work where they talked for some time, and the colonel urged the boy to drink as much beer as he liked. The boy drank more than enough, began feeling ill, got out of the car, and vomited.

The youth wiped his mouth and looked up, bleary-eyed. Gacy was standing there, holding a pistol. It was a six-shot revolver, and the colonel opened the chamber and removed five shells.

"Let's play Russian roulette," he said.

The boy was drunk, but it sure didn't sound like fun to him. "Are you kidding?" he said. "I could get killed."

"That's exactly what I had in mind," Gacy said. "You know too much."

"Hey, no," the boy said, and Gacy—very professionally, just as they do on the cop shows—pointed the gun at the boy's face and said, "Run."

"Don't—"

"Get down on your fucking knees."

"No."

Gacy pulled the trigger, and the hammer clicked down on an empty chamber. The boy stood his ground. The hammer snicked down a second time and hit another empty chamber. It was a pretty one-sided game of Russian roulette.

Gacy pulled the trigger five times and hit five empty chambers. He thumbed back the hammer one last time. This was the Big One, the death shot, right in the face. The boy stared into the barrel of the gun. He was eighteen years old. No one dies when he's eighteen. When you're eighteen, you know that you're going to live forever. Why would someone want to kill you? It had to be a joke, some kind of weird practical joke.

Gacy pulled the trigger. The hammer clicked down on the last empty chamber.

The boy concluded that his boss sure had one strange sense of humor. Jokes about killing you, for Chrissake.

Whatever Gacy meant about the boy "knowing too much," it struck police as a legitimate worry. In addition to Gacy's involvement in prostitution, gambling, and wife-swapping, the police discovered that the Voorhees affair was not, by any means, an isolated incident. The colonel, it seemed, had formed a little club, a sort of junior Jaycee chapter, consisting of his employees and other teenage boys. There was an open bar, and the boys were encouraged to drink as much as they liked. John was a real joker when he entertained his club, always making humorous propositions about playing pool for blow jobs.

Sometimes he was more serious, though. When he was alone with a boy he might tell him about the book he once wrote. It was all about sex, so, besides owning the Kentucky Fried Chicken stores and being the Jaycee "Man of the Year" and a colonel in the Illinois Governor's Brigade, Gacy was also a distinguished scientific sex researcher. He had some kind of certificate attesting to his expertise in the field. Most of his research had been done when he was in Illinois. That's why the governor of that state had appointed him to conduct an ongoing series of scientific experiments, the results of which would be used to "revise the antiquated sex laws" there. Most of the research was of a heterosexual nature, but—purely in the interests of science and in the bold spirit of true research and because the law applies to everyone, no matter what his or her sexual orientation—some of the experiments had to be of a homosexual nature. This was the governor's wish.

The experiments, however, were to be conducted in the strictest secrecy. At that particular time, it was not politically feasible for the governor to declare publicly his intention to revise the sex laws. The colonel was dutybound to compile his research in the utmost privacy. He was a sort of sexual secret agent.

Incredibly, at least one of the members of Gacy's little club bought this story. In the summer and fall of 1967, Gacy conducted a series of "experiments" with a fifteen-year-old boy. Science was served in Gacy's rec room, though they sometimes met at a motel. Almost every time they met, Gacy encouraged the boy to get good and drunk. The man, however, had to remain clearheaded—proper research methods—and he seldom had more than one or two drinks. Such are the sacrifices of science.

The colonel was thorough in his methods, and when they had completed whatever experiments were on that day's research schedule—when the boy had been paid his five dollars out of the governor's secret fund—Gacy usually asked a detailed series of questions about responses and feelings before, during, and after the acts performed. Just some things the governor would want to know.

The police asked the boy the very same questions, though in a different context. Just some things the prosecuting attorney would want to know. The boy said he felt guilty, all the time, every day. He seemed confused and was not entirely coherent: a fifteen-year-old-boy already moving on a slick slide toward alcoholism.

David Dutton, spearheading the prosecution for the county attorney's office, wanted a sodomy conviction very badly. The boys who met in the rec room paid Gacy monthly dues for the privilege. Monthly dues!

Hygiene is important in a place like the Psychopathic Hospital, where so many people are forced to live in such close proximity. That's why John told the night crew there that he'd be forced to put them on report if they didn't do a better job mopping the floor. He did not have to live like an animal in some filthy cave. His papers specifically said that he had joined the court in requesting a psychiatric evaluation, which meant that he should be considered in the category of a private patient. He had voluntarily sought out help for his problem. His goddamn taxes were paying salaries, and he wanted his money's worth. That meant clean floors at the very fucking least.

Not that he didn't treat people with the respect he expected to receive in return. It was just a matter of sanitation and common courtesy. On the whole, he got along perfectly with everyone.

John knew the nurses liked him. He was always joking around them, making them laugh. And when somebody got out of line, John was prompt in letting the proper authorities know.

There were, of course, bad days for John in the hospital. He remembered that he broke down in tears once, but the nurses were there and they helped comfort him. Just by talking. Because they could see that "instead of being a perpetrator, I was really a victim."

One or two of the attendants were very good at their jobs, really efficient, and John was shocked when he found out how little they made. He told one fellow that after this whole nightmare was over, after John got out and was back in business, there'd be a job waiting at "twice your salary here."

Some of the nurses, however, were very poor workers. They slacked off, didn't give it 100 percent, and often weren't around when they were needed. When that happened, John felt obligated to step into their shoes. A few of the patients, for instance, were complete slobs. They'd leave stuff lying around their beds or in the dayroom where people could stumble over it and break their necks. With that kind of safety infraction, a clear and present danger, you couldn't wait for a nurse to decide it was time to make the rounds. In a very nice way, John told the patients to pick up after themselves. It was a way of showing compassion for people. Sometimes, yes, he had to bark at them, but only as a last recourse. He couldn't understand why he had to do what others should have done, what he was actually paying them to do. Just like that old saying about how you have to do something yourself if you want it done right.

Sometimes he felt as if he was "running the whole place by myself."

During his seventeen days at the Psychopathic Hospital, Gacy underwent both mental and physical examinations. Given the results of the physical exam, which included an electroencephalographic test, it seemed highly unlikely that Gacy had actually had "a mild stroke" in Springfield in 1965. Whatever he was hospitalized for, it wasn't a stroke.

Gacy told the doctors he had constant health problems

throughout his life. At the age of nine he learned from his family doctor that he had been born with a "bottled heart." Doctors at the Psychopathic Hospital knew of no such medical condition.

Still, his records showed that he had been hospitalized for what he said were "heart problems" once at the age of thirteen and several times between the ages of sixteen and nineteen. He told the doctors that he never finished high school because of these problems—administrators had felt that attendance at class would endanger his health—and when the military saw his medical records, he said he was immediately classified 4F. The most painful memories of his childhood and teenage years were those long, dreary weeks of hospitalization, weeks and years of suffering made almost unbearable by his father's angry insistence that John was "faking." Once, when John had a bellyache and was certain there was something terribly wrong, the Old Man refused for the longest time to take him to the hospital. When he finally did go, they found that his appendix had burst and they had to work fast to save his life. That was one time John almost didn't mind the pain and the long stay in the hospital. It was worth it to see his father proved wrong in front of everyone. The thing of it is, John almost had to die to prove that he wasn't a phony. It was like death was some kind of goddamn ultimate argument: death was the one thing that would prove something to the Old Man.

Bad enough to be sick all the time—to have to give up football and basketball, to restrict your physical activities at all times, to be rejected by the military—but to live in the shadow of constant accusation from your father, that was mentally painful, nearly unbearable. It was, in John's opinion, a kind of rejection that could scar a kid for life.

Doctors at the Psychopathic Hospital who examined Gacy could find no evidence of heart disease. X rays of his chest, his heart, and other internal organs showed that aside from being overweight, John Wayne Gacy was in robust good health.

While he was in the hospital, he was examined by two psychiatrists and a psychologist. Years later, John said that he very carefully explained how each and every accusation against him had come about.

The doctors listened intently to John's stories. They had, in their possession, the statements of Schroeder, Voorhees, Lynch, and four others. The colonel's version of the events were wildly out of synch with everyone else's. The more the doctors compared John's stories to the police reports, the sharper the contrasts became. Someone was lying.

In making their evaluation, the doctors also used patient notes compiled by their nurses, who felt that Gacy was a "con man," even something of a bully. He was pleasant and ingratiating with those in positions of authority, but he behaved in a domineering fashion toward those he perceived to be weak or submissive. When caught in a lie, he became "overly defensive."

Dr. Eugene F. Gauron conducted the psychological testing on Gacy. In the behavioral-impressions sections of his report, Dr. Gauron wrote:

"John Gacy was very pleasant, friendly, highly talkable in the interview. He prided himself on being a good talker and felt this was a desirable quality which pays off in sales work. There was an element of control in his garrulousness, and he talked extensively only about what he wanted to talk about. It was apparent that John would twist the truth in such a way that he would not be made to look bad. He would admit to socially unacceptable actions only when directly confronted. My general impression was that he was both a smooth talker and an obscurer who was trying to whitewash himself of all wrongdoing."

Dr. Gauron administered the Wechsler intelligence test, on which Gacy scored a full-scale IQ of 118—placing him in the "bright normal" category—though low scores on the math skills subtest pulled down the average. His verbal subtest scores were high, and the highest of these was in comprehension. Dr. Gauron felt that Gacy's "high degree of social intelligence" made him aware of "the proper way to behave in order to influence people." Another doctor who examined Gacy described him as "extremely intelligent."

The psychological testing showed no motor damage, no organic damage, nothing physically wrong with John Gacy's brain. Although such tests yield some information about how the brain functions and can be indicative of possible brain damage, this is not their primary function. To be certain that Gacy was not suffering from brain damage of any kind—possibly incurred when he was hit in the head with a swing at the age of fifteen, or when he fell from the second floor of a building at the age of eighteen—an electroencephalogram was taken. The EEG showed some "asymmetrical eye movement artifacts," a common problem in an EEG, which often picks up artifacts such as the contraction of the heart or the movement of the eye muscles. Other than the eye movement artifacts, the EEG was completely normal. Doctors concluded that Gacy was not suffering from organic brain damage, and the results of the psychological testing confirmed this diagnosis.

In addition to the EEG and just to make certain, Gacy's skull was X-rayed. The film showed no abnormalities.

What Dr. Gauron found "most striking" about his interviews with Gacy and the results of the tests—which included Minnesota Multiphasic Personality Inventory—was the man's "total denial of responsibility for anything that has happened to him. He can produce an 'alibi' for everything. He alternately blames the environment while presenting himself as a victim of circumstances and blames other people while presenting himself as the victim of others who are out to get him. Although this could be construed as paranoid, I do not regard it this way. Rather the patient attempts to assure a sympathetic response by depicting himself as being at the mercy of a hostile environment. To his way of thinking, a major objective is to outwit the other fellow and take advantage of him before being taken advantage of himself."

Dr. Gauron's diagnostic impression was that "the test results do not provide any support for the presence of unusual thought processes. Rather, everything points to a diagnosis of sociopathic personality disturbance, antisocial reaction."

This diagnosis—sociopath or psychopath or antisocial personality—is a problematic one for psychiatrists and psychologists in that it defines a person whose problems are not primarily emotional or psychological in nature. The sociopath may steal or rape or murder, but the crimes are committed—and repeatedly committed—as a matter of free will and not as the result of any mental illness these doctors are trained to treat.

Sociopaths make up the great majority of criminal elements in every society. Because sociopaths' activities are not generated out of emotional or psychological illness, the condition is defined as a "personality disorder" or "character disorder."

A psychiatrist or psychologist can define the symptoms of the disorder, but because the sociopath is propelled by choice rather than illness, the concept becomes almost philosophical, even theological. In discussing sociopathic personalities, one is forced to deal with such abstractions as the idea of free will; in extreme cases, the sociopath brings some of the people he meets face to face with the very nature of evil itself.

The two psychiatrists who examined Gacy found him competent to stand trial and concurred with Dr. Gauron. Dr. L. D. Amick noted that Gacy seemed "to have no remorse over the admitted deeds. . . ." In their report to the court, Dr. Amick and Dr. Leonard Heston wrote: "We regard Mr. Gacy as an antisocial personality, a diagnostic term for individuals who are basically unsocialized and whose behavior pattern brings them repeatedly into conflict with society. Persons with this personality structure do not learn from experience and are unlikely to benefit from known medical treatment."

Three weeks after leaving the state Psychopathic Hospital, Gacy appeared before Judge Peter Van Metre in the Tenth Judicial District Court and pled guilty to sodomy. Prosecuting attorney David Dutton, who had been committed to convicting Gacy on the sodomy charge from the first, struck a plea bargain with the colonel's attorney: If Gacy pled guilty to sodomy, the other charges—burglary, going armed with intent, attempting to suborn perjury, and malicious threats to extort—would be dropped.

Judge Van Metre asked for a presentence report from Drs. Heston and Amick. The psychiatrists seemed to take Gacy at his word on one point at least: The incident with Voorhees was really just a matter of curiosity. Gacy, they wrote, was apparently bisexual, and his behavior, based on what they understood about his personality structure, was more a matter of "thrill-seeking," a kind of explorative foray into sodomy, than "an absolute fixation on abnormal sex objects."

Even more encouraging for Gacy, the psychiatrists said that sociopathic individuals like Gacy tend to do best when there are "firm, consistent, external controls on their behavior" and that "intensive parole supervision" might accomplish this goal as well as prison.

Probation officer Jack Harker had also made a presentence investigation and reported to the court. Gacy had told him that the admitted acts were mere "curiosity," that should he receive probation he would relocate to Illinois, accept his old job selling shoes, and seek psychiatric help. Harker noted that Gacy was only twenty-six, that he had never been in trouble before, that he was known as a hard worker and a community-minded man. Back in Illinois, Gacy would be in constant contact with his family: respectable, law-abiding people, a family where the father was known as "a strict disciplinarian but fair."

Harker's report recommended probation.

Judge Van Metre was a man who had been criticized for handing out what some prosecutors and police thought were excessively lenient sentences.

"I was confident," John said years later, "that I'd get probation and go to Illinois."

It wasn't any new thing, John's decision to return to his home state. He couldn't stand his father-in-law and had been thinking of quitting the chicken business and starting something of his own even before the sodomy charge came down. He sure wasn't being driven out of Iowa: it was a matter of free choice, and it had been a long time coming. John certainly wasn't going home because, as one of his former Jaycee buddies put it, "two years in town and everything Gacy touched turned to shit." He could stand the stink if people could stand the truth.

No, going back home on probation would finally yank him out from under Freddie's thumb, it would get the old colonel started on a business of his own.

They had dropped the other charges—the suborning and extorting, all that happy horseshit—because they knew they couldn't prove anything. It just wasn't true. Now all he had to worry about was Voorhees and the sodomy charge.

Even the doctors were on his side: he wasn't fixated on that shit. He wasn't a thrill-seeker, just curious, really. The doctors liked him and knew he'd do well on probation. The probation officer agreed. And he had met Judge Van Metre when he was working on some potential legislation for the Jaycees. He knew the man personally.

The only problem was Dutton, eloquent in his ambition. The prosecuting attorney said that the defendant "gained the confidence of many young people and abused their trust to gratify his desires." Dutton argued that there was a pattern of repeated offenses and that John would be a threat to society even under the strictest supervision. The guy got his sodomy conviction, but that wasn't enough for him. Now he wanted the judge to hand down the maximum sentence. Then he could say, "Yeah, I'm the guy who put Gacy away."

Judge Van Metre reviewed the arguments on both sides, looked down at the defendant, and, as John recalls, "just raked me over the coals."

"The particular pattern you have chosen is to seek out teenage boys and get them involved in sexual misbehavior." John couldn't believe it, "this asshole talking about abusing sacred trust and corrupting and shit." The colonel was careful not to show any emotion during the lecture, but when Van Metre sentenced him to ten years—the maximum, just what Dutton wanted—John's knees nearly buckled under him. He felt, for a minute, as if he was going to faint. Still, he kept his cool and didn't break down until he left the courtroom.

Ten years in the Iowa State Reformatory for Men at Anamosa.

Van Metre had even said he didn't like sending first offenders to prison but that the sentence would "ensure that for some period of time you cannot seek out teenage boys to solicit them for immoral behavior of any kind." The kind of shit, John realized later, Van Metre had to say on account of all the publicity in the case. John would have been back in Illinois, on probation, except for the fact that Van Metre didn't have the guts to stand up to the media.

Ten years.

Dutton later rose from first assistant county attorney to county attorney. By exploiting John, who was still the dumb and stupid kid the Old Man always said he was.

On the same day he was sentenced, in the same building, Marlynn filed for divorce. So Freddy had his way on that one.

He would never see his son again, never see his daughter, all because they took the word of Voorhees over his, because Voorhees "outsmarted" him. "An asshole is someone who is trusting and gullible," John said later. "I was made an asshole and a scapegoat in Iowa, and when I look back I see myself more as a victim than a perpetrator."

A victim.

CHAPTER
8

EARLY MORNING IN THE yard at the Men's Reformatory at Anamosa, prisoners lounging about, doing lazy time, and here comes John Wayne Gacy, inmate number 26525, moving fast, a man with things to accomplish. Everyone else is in prison denims, but John is wearing his freshly pressed white shirt—a sign of status and privilege—and smoking one of his contraband Hav-a-Tampas. Cigars unavailable in the prison commissary could be gotten from the guards or other prison personnel. A cigar meant clout. John in a cloud of smoke, carrying his black briefcase, on his way to some important meeting.

The other inmates wondered when he ever slept. He was out of his cell after lockup almost every night on special passes. John told them a guy doesn't slow down just because he's incarcerated. Gacy: he'd been framed by political enemies in Waterloo and jailed on the chicken-shit charge of showing dirty movies to teenage girls, seventeen-year-old girls a few months shy of eighteen. Jail a guy on a charge like that—give him ten years—it stinks of a frame-up.

On August 28, 1969, the Iowa Supreme Court had dismissed Gacy's appeal. He was in for the duration, probably at least five years, given Iowa's "good time" system.

Everyone knew that the man with the white shirt carrying the briefcase and smoking the cigar had been married to the daughter of Harlan Sanders, the founder of the Kentucky Fried Chicken empire—a soft deal—but then John had been framed and his old lady couldn't stand up under the political pressure.

In Marlynn's divorce petition, she said that she had conducted herself as a dutiful and loving wife during the marriage but that Gacy's "cruel and inhuman treatment" had endangered her life and health. On September 18, 1969, a decree of absolute divorce was issued. Marlynn was awarded the car, the house, and most of the furniture. John was allowed to keep his movie projector—big joke on the part of Judge Heath right there—and his good-citizenship plaques, his Key Man award, that shit. Marlynn got custody of the children.

John let it be known that his political enemies were screwing him right into the wall, taking everything he owned, everything he had worked to achieve. They had even turned his own wife against him and taken his children from him. You had to feel sorry for the guy.

Inmate Gacy had once been a marine, but, in the intervening years, his health had gone bad on him. For the first time since his teenage years, John passed out, for no apparent reason. It was during orientation at Anamosa: all the new guys, the fish, standing in line, and Gacy flopped right over onto the hard cement floor, out cold. On his second day in prison.

After the standard two weeks in the fish tank, they put him out into the main population, and John made friends with the nonviolent offenders, first-timers like himself. He let them know about his heart condition, about how any little excitement could kill him, and his new buddies kept him out of any conflicts, just the way guys such as Richard Dalke had protected him when he was a teenager.

One of John Gacy's closest friends at Anamosa was a man named Ray Cornell, a twenty-one-year-old serving time for forgery and breaking and entering. Cornell, who was released from Anamosa in July 1970, was never arrested again and went on to become the respected prison ombudsman at the reformatory. Years later, Cornell recalled Gacy's rise to a position of power in the prison. "When I first came in," Cornell said, "I think he was simply working in the kitchen. . . ."

John's heart bothered him a lot the first few months. Maybe it was the aggravation. Anamosa—officially known as a "reformatory"—is a medium-security institution, and though the inmates were all convicted felons, most of them were young, younger than John Gacy, who was then in his late twenties. Early on, John had some problems with the young guys in the kitchen, inmates who didn't have his experience working with food. These guys could be dead wrong about something and they'd still argue. John would yell back, but then, suddenly, his heart would act up on him. Everybody'd have to stop yelling and get the gasping inmate to the infirmary right away. And then, when the supervising food-service coordinator investigated the argument, he'd find that John Gacy had been right all along.

"Very quickly," Ray Cornell recalls, "within a matter of months, he became number-one cook, or lead cook on the afternoon shift."

Cornell worked in the library, which he soon discovered was not a prime job in the prison hierarchy: you can't trade prose and poetry for aftermovie tickets or protection. Guys just come in and check out books: you give them what they want, and that's it. Cornell thought Gacy "enjoyed considerable power because of his control over one of the necessities of an institution, which is food."

Working in the kitchen, John was able to see that certain prisoners and members of the staff got special dishes: steaks sautéed in mushrooms, extra desserts, good stuff the assholes never saw. In return, Cornell noticed that Gacy got "cigars, not available in the prison commissary, that were brought in to him by employees. He got extra movement, pop tickets, and movie tickets that were often given in exchange for special things such as steak sandwiches and that sort of thing by officers on the evening shift."

In his freshly pressed white shirt, Gacy would come into the library where he'd sit and read *The Wall Street Journal* and *Barron's*. "The quality of the clothing that was available to him," Cornell remembers, "was superior to what the rest of us wore." The white shirts, Cornell said, "were a token of privilege in the institution." Gacy said he needed them to keep the kitchen sanitary. Cornell said he "got them from an officer."

Wherever he went inside the walls at Anamosa, John carried a black briefcase. He was a busy man. Anamosa was one of the first prison institutions in America with an all-inmate Jaycee chapter. John Gacy, Cornell recalls, "was the best Jaycee I ever saw." Initially, when Gacy joined, there may have been 50 Jaycees out of 650 inmates. In less than two years, there were over 230 Jaycees at Anamosa, the bulk of them directly recruited by John Wayne Gacy.

John was also active in the prison Jaycees' efforts to improve conditions at Anamosa. He and others worked through the legislature to get the rate pay for prisoners raised from twenty-five cents a day to fifty cents per day.

It was just as Ma always said: Hard work leads to success. John was elected chaplain of the Anamosa Jaycees. He won the Spoke Award, the Spark Plug Award, and Jaycee Sound Citizen Award. John Gacy, Cornell says, "is the hardest worker I have ever seen."

Take the miniature-golf course:

When an elderly couple in Anchany, Iowa, decided to give up on the miniature-golf business, they donated the structures to Anamosa. John Gacy made arrangements with the warden to have all the little windmills and open-mouthed dragons brought 120 miles to the prison; John worked on getting the cement foundation poured and personally supervised the actual assembly of the course. It was John who contacted a local department store and talked them into donating several rolls of indoor-outdoor carpeting so that prisoners could rehabilitate themselves playing miniature golf on a proper surface.

The Jaycees helped with the work, but Gacy personally put 370 hours into the project.

In the summer of 1969, the *Des Moines Sunday Register* ran an article about the golf course. In the picture that ran with the story there are four men posing in the middle of the course, with the stone walls of Anamosa rising behind them. John Gacy stands out in this photo. He is the only inmate not in prison blues: Gacy is wearing a pressed white shirt. He looks as if he might be a supervisor or a guard and not a convict at all.

Gacy's heart kept acting up on him at Anamosa. Cornell personally saw one of the attacks the Jaycee chaplain suffered there. John, Cornell, and a man named Larry were coming out of the movie that showed on Saturday afternoons at the reformatory.

Something was brewing, Cornell thought, between his two friends John and Larry. "We went down from the prison auditorium to the area where the golf course was," Cornell recalled, "and John had gone down ahead of us . . . and was already on the golf course. When Larry got to the golf course, all of a sudden, just as he stepped across the sidewalk onto the grass, he took his shirt at the collar and ripped it off and the buttons went flying everywhere and he was moving across the golf course to where John was."

Larry was a normally "gregarious individual," very "outgoing," but now he was in a fit of rage, running toward John Gacy, bare-chested, out of control, and Gacy had a heart attack. At least Cornell thought it might be a heart attack because John's "face went ashen and then gray. He began to shake and stumble. Obviously something was wrong. But, of course, he was the target of an attack by an individual—or at least an impending attack—by an individual somewhat larger than he. He stumbled and appeared to be on the verge of going down."

Gacy was gasping for air, clutching at his chest, hardly able to stand. Larry might have wanted to hit Gacy, punch him out, but he obviously didn't want to kill him. "At that time," Cornell said, "the entire incident ended in terms of any physical confrontation. And we walked to the prison hospital with Mr. Gacy."

John couldn't fight because of his bad heart, and he used his kitchen power base to secure the services of various bodyguards. One of his biggest fears was rape, homosexual rape, a sad and brutal fact of prison life. Ray Cornell remembers that Gacy expressed contempt for prison "punks," that he "hated" and "loathed" homosexuals. The idea of being forced to commit unnatural acts: everyone could see it scared the shit out of John Wayne Gacy.

The Old Man cried when they sent John away. It was the only emotion anyone had ever seen him display. John Stanley Gacy never cried, even at family funerals: the Old Man sitting in his chair, sobbing.

John never saw that. The family lived through it but John was in jail, building miniature-golf courses. "When I was sentenced," John said, "my dad, I don't think he was even surprised.

It was like he always expected it, like he knew it was going to happen. Right around in there, when I was sentenced, he said something about how I had to work twice as hard now to wipe out the blot on my good name. Except it was his fucking name he was talking about. Just like, I was the one who put the blot on his name."

John worked to clear his name for the Old Man's sake. "In Anamosa," John recalls, "I did the impossible. I finished high school in seven months: twelve credits in seven months. I earned four college credits, psychology. I was head of the inmate student council, I was the legal counsel for the Jaycees, I got two bills passed in the state legislature, I ran the whole kitchen. I was the most decorated inmate. A model prisoner.

"And my goal was to learn more about John Gacy the individual. Why I got involved with the kid. I couldn't figure it out. I mean, I had a wife, I had two children, I had wealth. So why get involved with Voorhees? If I wanted a whore, I knew where to go. They even had some boys there, that's what I heard.

"I did everything I could to figure it out. I took individual analysis and transactional analysis and group therapy, and about the only thing I could come up with was just what the doctors had already said, that it was curiosity on my part."

In later years, when fear and depression grabbed him by the throat, when anger, like steel bands, tightened around his chest and squeezed his heart, when thoughts of suicide, like pus or poison, flooded his brain, in those bad, down times, John was willing to believe that his "innocent curiosity" had finally killed the Old Man.

John was having a portrait done of his father, by an inmate at Anamosa with some painting talent. The guy was a killer—not murder one: something about a bar fight—and he lived in North House while John was in South House, but everyone came through the chow line together. John just approached the guy one day and asked him to do a portrait of the Old Man.

"I do 'em from photos," the guy said. "You got to get me a photo."

John wanted the painting done for the Old Man's birthday. He wrote Ma, and she sent a picture. The painter didn't seem to think the fifteen dollars John offered was enough to bust his ass on the work. "I had to keep on him, and keep on him about it," John recalls.

Fucking artist: it took him over three months to complete the painting, and John Stanley never saw it. On Christmas Day 1969, the Old Man died. He'd been sick and they wouldn't let John out to be by his side and that was a pain he'd never forget. It felt like God was running his heart through a wringer. After the Old Man passed on, they didn't tell him for a day or two, like the assholes didn't want to spoil his holiday in prison. "Merry Christmas, John, your old man just croaked." And then . . . then they wouldn't even let him out to attend the funeral.

He spent that day, the day they laid the Old Man to rest for the last time, with correctional counselor Lionel Murray, who recalled that John was "emotional about it. He requested to see me. He cried in my office."

John called Ma, who remembered that John was in the office of "a consultant or something. He was out there with him all day. He was all broken up. They would not allow him to come for the funeral, and that made it worse for him."

Years later, John found he couldn't talk about that day, really talk about it, without breaking down. "Yeah," John said, and there were tears in his eyes, "my dad was right about a lot of things. I let him down when he died." John made no effort to wipe away the tears, and he spoke in a choked whisper. "I let him down. And I've paid for it. My whole life . . ."

The words in John's mouth were injured things with no life of their own. He couldn't go on, couldn't talk about the Old Man's death anymore. He winced, as if something had suddenly ruptured deep inside. "The shame," John said, but he was unable to complete the thought. Impossible to say it: the Old Man died of shame.

In fact, the tumor Ma said was inside John Stanley's brain had held out to the last. It had never burst. The Old Man had died of cirrhosis of the liver, and all John had to remember him by was a portrait painted by a killer.

Christ, Ma could piss him off. He loved her, but she just got these dumb, wrong ideas and wouldn't let go of them. Just like Ma always thought that she got John out of jail. "I asked the governor, I wrote a letter to ask him to come home because I was alone. And I got a call that the parole officer wanted to see where he was going to live. This was on a Wednesday. And Friday the doorbell rang and John was there."

The way it happened, John said, "I was a model prisoner and I earned my release."

In May 1969, five months after being sentenced, John applied for early parole consideration based on his outstanding work with the Jaycees, his adjustment to prison life, and—as he explained to his counselor, Lionel Murray—his confusion over the crime he was supposed to have committed. Murray recalled that Gacy protested "being incarcerated. He felt that politics and power had a lot to do with the fact that he was there."

The parole board replied with a standard one-year kick, which meant they'd consider parole for Gacy again on the May 1970 docket.

In March 1970, Gacy made another request for early parole, and—since Gacy said he planned to live with his mother in Illinois upon release—a supplemental progress report was written for the out-of-state parole board. Gacy's request was considered on the May docket, and he was paroled in June 1970. Any prisoner whose record was clean might have expected parole on the same charges after five years. But John Gacy was a worker, and he served a mere sixteen months of his ten-year sentence.

As his parole date neared, John was transferred to the Riverview Release Center in Newton, Iowa. On the day of his release, Gacy was picked up by his friend Charles Hill, who still believed the colonel had been framed. Gacy had written frequently to Hill and continued to insist upon his complete innocence. He said it made it all that much harder for him, doing time with a clear conscience.

Hill and his wife took Gacy to dinner. The colonel said prison had been "awful rough" on him. He talked about his father's death and choked up a little, right there at the dinner table. The prison administrators hadn't even let him go to the funeral; they wouldn't even let him see his father one last time.

The conversation continued deep into the night, and somewhere toward the end, Hill said, "John, now that it's over, keep your nose clean."

Gacy stared at Hill. "I'll never go back to jail," he said.

There'd never be another Voorhees.

CHAPTER
9

MA HAD MOVED OUT of the house on Marmora, to a condominium at 4343 North Kedvale, where she and John Stanley had planned to live in retirement. The Old Man, so careful with money, had completely paid for the condo before he died.

John got a job as a cook at Bruno's Restaurant and Lounge on Wells Street, near Chicago's Loop. He was just out of the reformatory and "dating broads, having normal sex." Two of the busboys at Bruno's were real screamers, and one of the other cooks didn't like them because they were gay. But John defended them. He said, "Look, it's their life, what they do in private, they don't bother you."

So one of the gay guys said, "I like the way you think."

And John had to lay it on the line with this fruit picker, right there in the kitchen, in front of everyone. "Don't assume nothing with me," John said. "I respect you as an individual but that doesn't mean I get into any of that shit myself. Put your hands on me just once"—John was mad and everyone in the kitchen could see it—"and I'll split you wide open with a meat cleaver."

Still, the gay guys liked him. He remembers them well enough to imitate their voices in high-pitched fruity little

women's tones: "Oh, John, you're so organized. We get more
done when you're in the kitchen." John could make people in the
kitchen laugh doing that, talking like the queers who worked
there.

Bruno's customers would have laughed at what went on in
the kitchen, because it was pretty *macho* out in the bar. They got a
lot of business from the Black Hawks, Chicago's professional
hockey team, and off-duty cops from the nearby Hubbard Street
station.

There was one cop, back in the fall of 1971, who'd come in
for a drink after his shift. James Hanley wore civilian clothes, so
you could assume he was a detective. At least John thought he
was a detective, and this guy Hanley came in with a lot of other
officers who sat at the bar.

The night bartender introduced John to Hanley (all the
cops used their last names—"Hey, Hanley, your round"), and
sometimes John'd say hello, have a short conversation. Small talk.
Hanley thought that when John came out of the kitchen, he sort
of hung around the bar area, listening in on all the cop conversation. There are a lot of people like that: cop groupies.

It wasn't like they were friends, or even drinking buddies,
John and James Hanley. They just passed a few words every now
and again during the year and a half that John cooked at Bruno's,
and then John Gacy never saw James Hanley again. In fact,
John's memories of Hanley, in subsequent years, were factually
flawed. John always believed, for instance, that Hanley was a
homicide detective, but the man worked with the hit-and-run
unit.

He always thought James Hanley's first name was Jack. A
homicide detective named Jack Hanley, hard and muscular in a
way John had never been, a tough cop but fair. John may have
even invented certain attitudes for "Jack" Hanley. "He hated
queers," John said. "And he talked about his theories on homosexuals." It would be unfair to attribute these attitudes to the James
Hanley of the hit-and-run unit. John was talking about Jack
Hanley the homicide detective, Gacy's imaginary version of a
good cop.

In later years, cruising the homosexual haunts of Chicago,
John would identify himself as a homicide cop named Jack Hanley. Up in 3 North, in Cermak, Doc Freedman would ask John

about the use of the name. "All I remember about him," John said, "was that he was a homicide cop, which relates to death, and he was bent on removing all homosexuals and hustlers from the street."

On February 12, 1971, less than eight months after the day he was paroled, John was arrested and charged with assault of a teenage boy, who said that Gacy had picked him up at the Greyhound bus terminal. The boy admitted that he was homosexual, but he said Gacy had tried to "force" him into the act.

What happened, Gacy said, was that he had picked up the kid, who was hitchhiking, and that in the course of their conversation, the kid had made a sexual proposition. Gacy said he got so mad that he threw the kid out of the car.

Up in 3 North, in Cermak, John told the docs what made him so mad was that the fucking kid picked him out as someone who'd "get into it. And I didn't want to do that shit. The cop asked me, 'Couldn't you tell the kid was gay?' Well, no. Because at that time I was trusting and naïve. I didn't know one fruit picker from another."

"Jack" would have taken the kid on, though. John thought the reason he didn't was "simply because there was no Jack then. Jack didn't take over until 1975."

It was John Gacy who was arrested in 1971. He told people that the charge was "assault on a sexual deviate." He wanted to make that clear. Some people, they could hear the charge and think it was "assault, sexual deviate."

The case was dismissed when the boy didn't show up in court to testify. This proved, John contended, that the whole thing had been bullshit from the start. Assault on a sexual deviate: who'd ever even heard of such a charge, anyway?

Somehow the arrest was never registered with the Iowa Board of Parole. Gacy was released from parole on October 18, 1971. First-time offenders in Iowa routinely earn back their rights as citizens, and on November 22, 1971—less than forty-five days before Gacy's first victim was to die—the governor of Iowa granted Gacy full restoration of citizenship.

The cooking job was a real dead-ender, and John wanted to start his own business. One thing he knew how to do was paint, and he thought he could talk his way into some jobs in his off-duty hours. He and Ma came up with a name for the business: PDM Contractors, painting, decorating, and maintenance. Or you could call it Polish Daily Maintenance. Or Pretty Damn Messy Contractors.

John had to be in at 10:00 P.M., but he had so much faith in his vision of PDM that the parole officer allowed him to work nights. This is how he slipped into another bisexual episode. It wasn't his fault that it happened; he was working at the time.

It was a year after he'd been paroled, and one of the chefs, Roger,* wanted his apartment painted. John thought Roger was "kind of effeminate," but he would be painting the apartment while Roger was working his second job, teaching dance. There was no danger of the two of them "getting into it."

So John was working in the apartment when Roger's roommate, this Latin guy called Manny,* comes home.

The guy says, "Who're you?"

John told him and the guy says, "I'm Roger's roommate. I'm gay." It was weird to have a guy just come right out and admit something like that, but John said, "Hey, that's your thing." Because John had always had liberal ideas about sex.

A few nights later, this guy Manny shows John a picture of himself all dressed up like a broad and asks John, "Can I blow you?"

The way John looked at it, there was no love thing there, no affection. It was just like masturbation. Then, when they got talking, Manny told him a whole shitpile of things he never knew. Manny told him how you could go down to the Greyhound bus depot and pick up boys. He told John that the corner of Clark and Broadway was a big gay area where you could pick up hustlers and pay them to have sex anytime you wanted it.

It "floored the shit out" of him, that's what John told the docs up there in 3 North. Imagine: hustlers at the bus station.

Except that he had been arrested four months earlier for "assault on a sexual deviate" he'd picked up at the bus station.

About a month after meeting Manny, around late July 1971, at Clark and Broadway John approached a young man named Mickel Ried. Ried was new to the city, from Ohio. They

*Name changed.

talked a bit: mostly about construction and John's business and how much money a guy could make that way. Ried said he needed a job. The two of them ended up at the condo on Kedvale, where they talked some more and, according to Ried, had sex. John paid for it.

They met a few more times and talked more about forming a partnership in PDM. The work was going along pretty well now, and John thought he might need more help.

"He had a nice growing business there," Marion Gacy recalled. "He started from the condominium. He had boards and everything, painting in my storeroom. And they wouldn't allow that, so that's why we bought the home, so he would have his business."

The Old Man thought he'd been smart paying off the condo, but John had a hell of a time selling a place with no assumable mortgage. John Stanley outsmarted himself, with money, in death.

John and Ma finally found a place at 8213 West Summerdale, in Norwood Park township. It was a solidly constructed tract home built in the 1950s. There was a garage for John's tools, and a low crawl space under the house that could be used for storage if the Gacys could find some way to keep it from flooding. John, as co-owner, made monthly payments to his mother who, along with Karen and JoAnne, owned the rest of the house.

Ma and John moved out to the house on Summerdale on August 15, 1971. Mickel Ried helped them move, and because he was new to Chicago, John offered him a room. There was another guy living there, some guy from Bruno's named Roger, Manny's ex-roommate, whom Ma thought was "gay." John's Aunt Florence also moved in a little later, for three months. Everyone paid rent.

Mickel Ried stayed for a couple of months, and during that time he had sex with John Gacy "once in a while." Together they did several jobs: painting, house maintenance, little things. Sometimes they argued, mostly about money. Ried remembered a lot of quarrels about money.

Money was tight in the early days of PDM, and Gacy was able to save on landscaping by stealing shrubs from a local nursery. Once, after a money-related argument, Gacy took Ried to a desolate area, where he said they would break into a house. Ried got out of the car, and when he turned, he saw Gacy coming at him with a tire iron. Gacy stopped, the tire iron dangling from his right hand. It was, according to Ried, a "desolate" area, no one around, and he asked Gacy why he had the tire iron.

"In case there's trouble," Gacy said.

Ried was confused. It was dark. There was no one there. What kind of trouble could there be? Gacy went back to the car. Suddenly he didn't want to break into the house anymore.

Not long after that, Ried and Gacy went out to the garage to unload some equipment. "It was dark," Ried recalled, "and we got out of the car and the lights went out in the garage and John told me to get some fuses under the workbench. So, as I was doing that on my hands and knees, I got hit on the head. With a hammer.

"I stayed down a couple of seconds and I stood up and I saw that John was looking like he was going to hit me again. I put my hand up to stop his hand from coming back down, and at the same time I asked him what he was doing or why he wanted to hit me."

Gacy, Ried said, had a "strange look in his eyes," and they stood like that for a moment, the boy holding the man's arm, until Gacy's expression softened and he put the hammer down.

Just as he had done in Iowa after stabbing Edward Lynch, Gacy became very apologetic. Ried said, "He patched up my head. He said he was sorry he did it." They went into the house and talked for an hour, or at least Gacy talked, apologizing profusely while Ried listened.

The boy couldn't think how he might have provoked the attack. He and Gacy fought frequently over money, that was true, and sometimes the arguments turned into wrestling matches, a kind of horseplay with some serious intent behind it. Ried was living in the house, he was eating with the Gacys, and there was some infrequent sex, but they were supposed to be partners, and Ried said, "I never got that many payments."

That's what the fights were about, every single one of them. Ried thought there might have been one of those arguments just before John Gacy hit him with the hammer. Some argument about money, with just a little bit of sex wrapped up in the core of John's anger.

The next day, Mickel Ried moved out of the Gacy house.

*   *   *

Carol Lofgren had just gone through a divorce, and the later months of 1971 were not good ones for her. She had two daughters—Tammy, who was one, and April, who was three. It was tough making ends meet, frightening being out on her own, and she visited the Gacys often. She had gone to school with Karen and "became very good friends with the family. I felt like one of the family. I was at the house quite a bit when I was fifteen, sixteen years old."

John Gacy "felt like a brother" to her, but they did have one date when Carol was sixteen, and the two of them went to a drive-in.

Later, after her divorce, when Carol would visit at the condo and then the house on Summerdale, she found John to be "a very warm, understanding person, very easy to talk to, knew a lot of things. It was very easy to just listen to him. I always felt he knew what he was talking about. And I met a lot of interesting people through John." John knew hockey players and could get free tickets. He knew a dozen cops: he never introduced Carol to any of them, but he talked a lot about the police officers he knew, how they worked, cases he had heard about.

He was good with the girls, especially Tammy, the baby. Carol remembered that they called John "Daddy," even before she and Gacy were married. He had a soft, gentle way with the kids.

Later, Carol would say, "He swept me off my feet. I don't think I loved him, but I was still mixed up about my first marriage, and he treated me well."

For a while, there was a lot of mutual comfort in the relationship: Carol just coming off a bad divorce, John just out of jail. But when it seemed as if they were getting serious about each other, John told her about what had happened in Iowa.

"He told me," Carol said, "he did spend time in Iowa for pornography dealing with younger boys. He didn't go into too much detail about it. He said he served sixteen months and got out on good behavior."

Because it looked like they might marry, John felt a moral obligation to tell Carol one more thing about himself. "He told me he was a bisexual. At first I didn't understand what a bisexual was. So he explained it to me and I just kind of looked at him. I said, 'How do you know you're a bisexual? How can you just say, "This is what I am"?'

"He said, 'Because I am.' "

Carol "took it as a joke. I really didn't believe it."

Bisexual. Wasn't that something you studied in sophomore biology, like with earthworms?

John was intelligent, industrious, charming. Carol thought he was "just talking" about being bisexual. He certainly didn't act like a homosexual. In fact, he seemed to despise flagrant gays.

John Gacy, Carol saw, was manly, tough in his business, but not so *macho* he couldn't cry. The first time Carol saw him lose control was on Christmas Day 1971. John just let himself go, and he cried on Carol's shoulder, telling her that he couldn't stand the idea that he had let his dad down "because he did not make the funeral when his dad died. He was in Iowa at the time and they wouldn't let him come to the funeral." John said "it bothered him that he wasn't able to attend and see his father for the last time."

Carol recalled that every year she knew him, John would go out to Maryhill Cemetery, in Niles, and visit his father's grave during the Christmas holidays. Every year he'd come home upset. The first year, Christmas 1971, was the worst one. John just couldn't stop crying. He was totally out of control.

Just over a week later, John Gacy killed the first of his thirty-three victims.

CHAPTER
10

PATHOLOGISTS CLOSELY EXAMINED WHAT remained of each of
the thirty-three victims attributed to John Wayne Gacy. All of the
bodies, according to Dr. Robert J. Stein, Cook County's chief
medical examiner and one of the country's foremost forensic pathologists, could be described as "markedly decomposed, putre-
fied, skeletalized human remains." Ten of the bodies were in such
a state of decomposition that no certain cause of death could be
determined. Six of the bodies were recovered with ropes dangling
from the spinal column in the region of the neck. Others, more
recent and less skeletalized, were found with wads of cloth stuffed
far back into the throat. All this is consistent with Gacy's pretrial
statements, explanations, and "rationalizations."

He said the boys "killed themselves" with the rope. At
other times, in the early statements, Gacy said "Jack" must have
strangled them with the rope. He said he could only guess at this
because that is the way "John" found them in the morning. He
found them where they lay, found them dead, with ropes wrapped
tightly around their necks. He could only "rationalize" as to the
cause of death. He said that if he did, in fact, commit the
murders, then he might have stuffed rags down their throats to
prevent the leakage of certain fluids when he moved them. Gacy
didn't know this for sure, but it was a good rationalization.

The conclusions reached by Dr. Stein's team were consistent with John Gacy's statements. All the victims could well have died of strangulation or suffocation. There is only a single inconsistent instance: One victim was certainly stabbed to death.

The body was never identified, but since it was the ninth one recovered from the boneyard under John Wayne Gacy's house, the victim was named for the order in which his body was exhumed. Dr. Stein personally examined body number nine. He was dealing, for the most part, with bones.

Dr. Stein, along with a radiologist and an anthropologist, found that the fifth rib "had an incised area on the upper portion compatible with a stab wound. Also the left lateral or side aspect of the sternum had two areas which were also compatible with an incised or stab wound." Within a "reasonable degree of medical and scientific certainty," Dr. Stein concluded that the individual referred to as body number nine died from "stab wound, multiple, of the chest."

The boy known as body number nine died in an entirely different, but no less horrifying, manner than the other thirty-two known victims. This was a fact of special and intense interest to many of the psychiatrists and psychologists who studied John Wayne Gacy. Why did this boy die differently? Was there a special significance in this one stabbing? The doctors studied Gacy just as the pathologists studied the remains he had left behind. Body number nine became known as "the Greyhound bus boy." He was the first one whom John Wayne Gacy killed.

Everyone wanted to hear about the first murder. The psychiatrists, the psychologists, they were all interested in the first time, as if some special knowledge to be gleaned there would explain everything. The puzzle merchants were so goddamn interested in the first one it was almost funny. You could see them working it over, this first murder, trying to get down to the marrow of it, like a dog with a bone.

They were after the "why" of it, and the sense of their questions was this: If we can understand the first one, then it will explain all the others, every one; if we can only dig to the root of this one, then we should be able to see a pattern, see the entire dark flower whole. They seemed to think that all the rest of the murders grew from this first one and that once they grasped it, grasped the full meaning of it, the dark flower would unfold as flowers do in time-lapse photography. The first was the pattern, the genesis of the murders to follow.

This was absurd. John didn't know why they wanted to concentrate on the first one and on the last one. Both of them didn't fit the pattern. They were anomalies. He told them so. The first one was self-defense. Anybody who knew the facts would have to agree. Anyone, confronted in his bedroom by a man with a knife, would have done the same thing. Why couldn't they see that the first one didn't fit?

John told the story over and over. He told it the same way every time: clear and detailed right up to the episode with the knife. Then the story got hazy around the edges. It rippled and broke until the final ghastly scenes were wispy and without substance.

He always told them that he wasn't particularly depressed, though it happened just after New Year's Day 1972, and the doctors reminded John that the Christmas holidays had been a bad, unsteady time for him ever since that Christmas Day in 1969, when his father died without a son by his side to comfort him.

Sometimes, on Christmas Day, John would go out to the cemetery on the North Side of Chicago to stand by his father's grave. He said that those were times he had to talk to his father, but John's words burned inside his throat, and the graveside monologue became emotional, cathartic. His ex-wife Carol saw him sobbing helplessly by his father's grave on one of these holiday visits.

But no, John wasn't particularly depressed during the Christmas holidays of 1971. Out of prison, he was strong now, building a new life, working to became a new man, working to become successful. He had some things he needed to prove to the memory of his father. He wasn't depressed at all.

No matter that his Aunt Pearl, his father's sister, had died on New Year's Eve just as 1971 became 1972. The psychiatrists and psychologists could go ahead and assume that he was down. It always amused John that the doctors knew what he was thinking or feeling at any given time. He'd tell them one thing, and they'd go right ahead and figure the exact opposite.

So it was Christmas 1971, then his aunt died on New

Year's Day, and the doctors insisted on seeing some sinister emotional pattern. John told his story often enough; and no matter what his father thought, John wasn't dumb and stupid. He watched the doctors as intently as they watched him. And he knew what these doctors thought: They figured that the Christmas holidays preyed on his mind, that they reminded him of his culpability in his father's death. John could see it quite plainly: The doctors thought that all that Christmas music, all the cheer and laughter, all the parties and toasts to peace on earth conjured up images of death in his mind, visions of shame and retribution, of dark secrets and inevitable punishments.

On New Year's Eve, as his aunt was dying, John was working a private party at Bruno's. Carol's mother took the kids so that Carol could join John at Bruno's at about eight. John remembered that he paid for the cab. He always remembered little details like that. You could check them out, these little details, and see that John was telling the truth. He had nothing to hide.

John kept working, and he joined in the party when he could. It broke up at about 3:00 A.M., and John drove back to the house in Norwood Park where he and Carol fell exhausted into bed. They slept approximately four hours, rising at about eight in the morning. John had to drive Carol to Kennicott, where her mother was staying with the kids.

"I won't be able to see you for a few days," John told Carol when he dropped her off. He had just gotten word that his Aunt Pearl had died.

John drove back to his Summerdale house and slept until about 3:00 P.M. Then he got up and drove to his Uncle Harold's, where his mother had spent New Year's. From there they drove to Aunt Ethel's—a holiday with the family.

John told the doctors that there wasn't much talk of death that night: Aunt Pearl was on his father's side, Aunt Ethel was his mother's sister. It was just another holiday party, the end of a hectic week, and they drank and talked and played cards. Aunt Ethel mixed a stiff Scotch and water. John hadn't intended to get drunk, but he had worked hard the night before and he was tired and the drinks snuck up on him. It was Aunt Ethel's fault, really. She was one of those hosts who grabs your glass and fills it right back up again when you're only half done. Still, it was always a good time at Aunt Ethel's house. Everyone was talking a mile a minute—John and his mother and Aunt Ethel, all of them motormouths—and you had to watch the drinks. In a way, everything that happened that night and the next morning could be traced to those drinks. Nothing would have happened except that John got drunk. He sure wouldn't blame Aunt Ethel for what happened to the Greyhound bus boy. It was just the way she kept pouring all those drinks. . . .

The party began to break up at about 12:30 A.M. John's mother wouldn't get in the car with him. They argued briefly, but Ma just wouldn't drive with anyone who had been drinking. That was one of her rules; she told John that you never could say anything to a drinker. He'd just go and get belligerent and start to holler and that made driving with him doubly dangerous. Ma decided to stay with Aunt Ethel.

That was just another one of those details you could check out. John had no special plans that night. He never thought, This is the night I'll go out and kill the first one. He wanted to take his mother home. He argued about it in front of Aunt Ethel. If his mother had just driven home with him that night, the Greyhound bus boy might never have died. And maybe, if there hadn't been a first one, then there might never have been a second, or a third, or a thirty-third. John would never want anyone to think—God forbid—that his mother was to blame for a half-dozen years of killing. It was just one of those things you had to think about, another proof that there was never any premeditation. You could check it out.

John stepped out into the new year and walked to his car. The air was cold, bracing, and the Scotch had done its work on him. He wasn't tired. He wasn't thinking about the death of his aunt. He felt inexplicably charged up and thought he'd go out "looking around."

John started driving, and the car turned toward the downtown area. Maybe he'd just go down to the Civic Center and look at the ice sculptures. Of course, he knew that the Greyhound bus depot was very close to the Civic Center; and he knew from Manny that you could go down there to pick up "chicken hawks." John never quite got that terminology straight: it was the older men, cruising like sharks in the big cars, who were called chicken hawks. They picked up young men and boys at the bus station. The boys were chicken.

These definitions are not exclusive to the gay community. Cops use them. Straight people used to refer to a defunct burger joint near Clark and Broadway as "chicken delight." The place was a hangout for young hustlers; and blatant deals were struck with older men, there under the glare of fluorescent lights and amid the smell of frying burgers.

But John never quite got the terms right. He had seen his share of gay pornographic movies, kept gay pornographic magazines in his house; he had picked up hundreds of men and boys—by his own admission—over the years, and yet, even with an IQ tested in the upper 10 percent of the population, he called the boys he picked up "chicken hawks."

What could the doctors do with that one? You could suppose that he was naïve, that he hated the dark, night-stalking part of his life so much that he refused to think seriously about it or apply the proper definitions to himself. You could assume that he had heard the terms and thoughtlessly applied them to his own case. It was, after all, John Gacy who was the innocent, the chicken. The young hustlers were bent on outsmarting him, on cheating him out of his money, on blackmailing him. They were the chicken hawks.

At one or two o'clock on a cold January morning, after a long, lonely holiday weekend, what excuse did young men have for hanging around the bus station so late on such a frigid night? They weren't fooling anyone. Everyone knew that you could pick up the young ones there, the unsophisticated boys away from home for the first time. There were also some slightly older guys, hustlers who "got into it for money."

John knew a little bit about how the sculptures were made. It was "really an art." You have to hit the ice just right with the chisel, or the whole cake will break or shatter. It was something a professional chef could do and something John wanted to learn, so he went down to the Civic Center, near the station, to study the technique of ice sculpture at 1:30 A.M.

"I went down to look at the ice sculptures," John said. "But then, after I seen it, I got back in my car." There were people walking around, and across from the Civic Center he could see the Greyhound bus depot. "So I drove around the block and pulled up in front of there. That's when I seen the kid."

Picking up the kid was a fluke. This first one was an accident.

Up to this point, you could verify every detail of John's narrative. Carol's story would be substantially the same as John's. Records would show the exact time of Aunt Pearl's death. Ma would remember that she stayed with Aunt Ethel because John had been drinking. A quick call downtown would confirm it all: The ice sculpture exhibit was still standing outside the Civic Center in the early-morning hours of January 2, 1972. Everything John said was the truth. It all checks out.

The problem of verification comes after John picked up the Greyhound bus boy, because from that point on there are no witnesses and John must be taken at his word. The only other person who might have testified as to what happened that night is dead. John talked about the events leading up to the murder in dozens of interviews and, like the events leading up to the pickup, the story was always essentially the same. John had told the truth up to this point, had gone out of his way to supply a wealth of nonessential details, and he seemed to feel that if that part of the story checked out and was consistent, then the rest of the story should be believable as well. And the way he told it, the chronology of that first murder was at the very least consistent, even if it couldn't be verified. Why should he lie about something that only lived in his memory like a gauzy dream of death? He had nothing to hide, and he wanted to know. He really wanted to know.

John was frank about his thoughts at the time. He admitted things he never would have talked about had he not been arrested. Working with the psychiatrists, he was discovering things as he went along, just as they were.

John pulled up, rolled down the window, and as nearly as he could remember, said something like, "Hi. Whatta ya doing?"

The Greyhound bus boy, as John remembered him, was just about right: he wasn't tall, but he was well built, and young, maybe eighteen or nineteen, with "light or blond hair." He was wearing a plaid shirt and a pair of Levi's. There was a big buckle on his belt. John remembered the big buckle. The buckle stuck in his mind.

The kid said, "I ain't doing nothing. I got twelve hours to kill." He told John he had just come in from somewhere like West Virginia and was going somewhere else—or maybe he was going to West Virginia—and his bus wasn't due until noon or a little later. John couldn't remember where the hell the kid was going: he was just passing through, a naïve kid with no family or relatives in Chicago.

"You wanna drive around?" John asked him. "You wanna see the sights?"

They drove north, up toward the Old Town/New Town area, and John acted as tour director and teacher. "This here is the gay part of town," John told the kid. He mentioned that there were hustlers around, guys who got into it for money. John remembered that they talked about sex and he asked, "You ever get into it with a guy?" He couldn't remember what the kid said, whether he had or he hadn't, but they talked about it and both of them sort of concluded that there was probably nothing wrong with it. John thought he remembered that the kid might have been curious about it, but had never had the opportunity. Something like that.

Anyway, the kid was getting hungry, and they ended up at the house on Summerdale, and John fixed him something to eat. A sandwich with some lunch meat. John had to cut the meat from a big slab. He worked in a restaurant and knew that you saved money buying in bulk. So he cut the meat for the sandwich with a big butcher knife.

John left the knife in the kitchen and brought the sandwich out to his living room, where the kid was sitting right next to the bar. John mixed a couple of drinks. He might have had a beer, but the kid drank some 190-proof clear grain alcohol. John warned him about it, but the kid was bent on proving he was a man or something and threw down a couple of hefty slugs.

Sometimes John remembered to tell about the grain alcohol, sometimes he forgot, but what came next usually was the same. The conversation veered around to sex again, and the two of them "got into oral sex, both ways." Sometimes John said there was a discussion about who would go first. After it was over, John felt tired and said he wanted to go to sleep. He told the kid he could sleep in the house. He would drive him to the station in time for his bus at noon.

John lay down in his own bed and instantly fell asleep. Then—"it hadda be around four in the morning"—something startled him. Maybe it was a noise. Maybe he just felt a presence in the room, but John woke up. He looked to the doorway and saw the kid standing there, backlit from a light in the other room. It was almost like a dream, except the kid had a butcher knife in his hand—the same knife John had used to cut the meat—and he was walking slowly toward the bed.

John tells the story without any real feeling: he might be describing something he once saw on television. The emotion he says he felt was confusion. "I didn't know what the hell to do." He found himself leaping from the bed, charging the kid, grabbing for the knife. It could have been a dream.

They wrestled, and John thought, What? Why? The knife grazed John's arm, cut him. He still has the scar. They might have talked, shouted at each another, John doesn't remember. But if he said anything, it would have been, "What are you doing, for Chrissake? Why are you doing this?" And the blood was flowing from the wound on John's arm and they wrestled, fighting for possession of the knife.

It was, in fact, like something you might see on television, because they both lost their footing, and John didn't really stab the kid. "He just fell on the floor and I think he fell on the knife. He stuck himself with the knife because I had hold of his hand and I had turned the knife inward, toward him, toward his stomach or his chest, and he fell on it and I fell on top of him."

The chronology of events is not entirely clear in John's mind. He doesn't recall all the details, and those he does are not perfectly clear. There is a heavy, somnolent aura to his narrative: the sense of a man describing a confusing but particularly vivid dream. For instance, it seemed to John that after they fell, the kid just lay there, but then he remembered that he might have gotten the knife while they were wrestling; he might have stabbed the kid "four or five times." He might have stabbed him in the chest because—John seemed to dredge these details up from a great depth—he remembered the kid had no shirt. He was wearing the Levi's and had his socks on, but he was naked from the waist up, and John thought he might have stabbed him in the chest. The kid never moved after he fell.

None of this is very clear in John's mind. He remembers he got up from the kid, with the knife in his hand. He went into the bathroom and washed the blood off the knife, then washed the blood off his own body. In the bedroom he could hear this sound—a "gurgulation"—that seemed to go on and on and wouldn't stop. John walked through the house. He put the knife back in the kitchen where it belonged. He walked back to the bathroom, skirting the bedroom, then walked back to the kitchen, all the time listening to that never-ending gurgulation. When it finally stopped, he went back into the bedroom. The kid lay still as stone, silent as death. John assumed he was dead and tried to think what to do.

The kid had attacked him, so he could call the police. But no, he couldn't do that. The police would discover that he had a sex record in Iowa. Right away they'd say John attacked the kid. They'd framed him there in Iowa, so who would listen to him in Chicago? No, he couldn't call the police. The cops and the courts would just twist everything all around, the way they did in Iowa. No one would ever believe him. He had defended his life in his own home and he was going to have to keep it a secret.

These feelings and thoughts were hard for John to recall: he had successfully put them out of his mind for years. He knew he made no plans that day. It just didn't seem entirely real. Except for the blood and the body. The first thing John did was clean up the blood. When he had finished with that, he dragged the kid to the bedroom closet, opened up the trapdoor to the crawl space, and "just pushed him over into it." John couldn't bring himself to go down there, so he put the board back into place. It was easier to think then.

Ma would be home later that day. John walked around, checking for bloodstains he might have missed. Then it was time to pick up his mother at Aunt Ethel's and go to the wake for Aunt Pearl. John was running from corpse to corpse in the aftermath of the Christmas holidays, but if he saw some dark or sinister significance there, he never mentioned it.

At the wake, John's sister Joanne saw the cut on his arm. "What happened to you?" she asked. They were standing in the funeral home, and John lied. If you do a lot of good things in your life and only do a few bad things, you have to lie. It's best not to think too intently about it. It's best not to think of it at all: just let the explanations flow naturally. John hated lies and liars.

"I did it cutting carpet in the kitchen this morning," he said. "I slipped with the knife." Joanne, who had studied to be a nurse, was concerned. It was a deep cut, one that needed stitches, a cut that could lead to a serious infection. She advised John to have a doctor look after the arm right away.

There was a lesson to be learned there in the funeral home, one that John may have absorbed quite unconsciously. No one can see murder on your face: there is no brand that sets you apart from the crowd, no outward sign that the dark flower is growing in your soul. People will see you as they've always seen you if you can only bury fear and confusion and remorse along with the evidence. There is no reason a justified killing should have any effect on the life of a just man. You can see the truth of that in people's eyes as they speak to you, especially if you are hurt or ill. Sickness can be a measure of how much people care for you. It's good to feel that sort of sympathy at certain times. At certain times you really need someone to care for you.

John appreciated his sister's sympathy, and he took her advice. He left the funeral home and drove to the emergency room of St. Elizabeth's Hospital. After the doctor sewed up his arm, John went back to the funeral home, picked up Ma, and returned to their house, where the corpse of the Greyhound bus boy lay unburied in the crawl space.

Ma didn't often leave the house, and John knew that there would soon be an odor. It was the kind of problem a good, fast-working contractor could solve in a few hours. John took the board off the trapdoor in the closet, lowered himself into the crawl space, and, crouched over nearly double, with only two and a half feet of headroom, he dug a shallow grave and buried the remains of the young man the psychiatrists would eventually call the Greyhound bus boy.

That's why John started burying them in the crawl space: because of Ma. "It was just a nicely kept secret," John explained later. "Nobody knew about it."

In July, seven months after the first kill, John and Carol were married. They made love in the room where the Greyhound bus boy had died, just above the shallow grave where he was buried.

"If something works," John Gacy often said about his construction business, "you don't change it."

CHAPTER
11

MA AND JOHN, ALWAYS BICKERING about the little things. Just like while John and Carol were talking about getting married, Ma thought she was the matchmaker for her son. "Carol," Marion Gacy recalled, "lived with two children. I had John bring her home to Summerdale because they were on welfare and she was by herself and couldn't pay the rent. And I said she might as well move in with us."

This was just after the Christmas holidays in 1971. A few months later, when Carol and John announced their engagement, Ma said she would move out because "no two families should live together." She rented an apartment for herself in May. John and Carol were married on July 1, 1972.

Nine days before the wedding, John Gacy was arrested on charges of aggravated battery and reckless conduct. Police said that Gacy had picked up a young man on the near North Side, Chicago's nightclub district. The bridegroom-to-be had flashed a badge identifying him as a deputy sheriff; he had ordered the boy into his car and forced him to perform oral sex. Gacy then drove the young man some twenty miles north, apparently resting up for a repeat performance, but when they stopped, the boy jumped out of the car. Gacy chased him in his big Olds, trying to run him down.

119

Mysteriously, the charges were stricken and the case never came to trial. In later years, after John Wayne Gacy was charged with thirty-three murders, some reporters felt the case was dropped because of Gacy's Chicago-style clout, but it is doubtful he had much political sway in the summer of 1972.

Gacy's version of what happened is that a deal for sex had been struck and that he took the kid to a restaurant in Northbrook, where John held a temporary job as night manager. It was late, the place was closed, but Gacy had a set of keys. He didn't want to take the kid back to his house, back to Carol and Tammy and April. "What happened," John said, "this kid wanted me to take my pants off. I figured, shit, and let him run off with my pants and my wallet? Try to chase the son-of-a-bitch bare-ass? So I wouldn't, and he ran out the fire door. The sneaky asshole got his money up front. Fifteen dollars. Fucker outsmarted me. So I took after him in the car."

In this version of the story, Gacy is charged, but the kid makes the mistake of tracking him down through the restaurant. He calls Gacy at home and threatens to expose him unless John gives him a certain amount of money. John sets up a meeting, then tells the cops he's being blackmailed. When he hands the kid his money in some restaurant on the North Side, the cops come in, guns drawn, and arrest the kid. This is why the charges were dropped.

Whatever the truth is here, it's clear that by June 1972, John Gacy was cruising the nighttime streets of Chicago, looking for sex. It was a world of "greedy little bastards," of "jackrollers" who'd offer to perform sex for a price, then take the money and run. It was a city of dark streets populated by "all these little shitheads with trick minds." You had to be careful out there. You had to think in the Old Man's terms: fuck 'em before they fuck you; outsmart 'em with money, for sex. It was a game of wits: all money and sex and challenge, out on the street after midnight.

John and Carol were married in St. Paul's Lutheran Church. Gacy would have preferred a Catholic ceremony, but he was divorced, and St. Paul's was only a few blocks from the house on Summerdale.

John was a good lover and the only problem that really bothered Carol Gacy the summer of 1972 was the odor, a foul odor in the house that kept "getting stronger and stronger" as the weather got warmer.

There were some mice upstairs, and Carol set out traps frequently, but the odor seemed to be coming from below, from the crawl space. She wondered if maybe a lot of mice had died down there. Like when the crawl space flooded. It was the smell of something dead drifting up from the crawl space.

And then in the utility room Carol noticed "there were a lot of little black—I don't know if they were little gnats, but they almost looked like flies at times." Little flies, gnats, maggots hatching off the dead mice in the crawl space. Carol wanted to call an exterminator, but her husband told her not to bother. John said he'd take care of the smell, get rid of the dead mice in the crawl space.

John would drop through the trapdoor with a fifty-pound bag of lime over his shoulder, spread it across the puddled darkness, and still the smell got worse. John said it was a broken sewer pipe. It was almost unbearable.

Carol said, "The smell is getting bad and I'm here all day, while you're out. I think there must be a lot of dead mice down there."

It was as if John wasn't listening, as if his mind was on something else besides dead mice in the crawl space, because he said, "I'll go down there and set a few traps." It wasn't like her husband at all, saying something that made him sound stupid.

"John," Carol said, "if the mice are dead, how are they going to get in the traps?"

"Oh . . . yeah . . ."

"You really have to go down there and get them out."

And then, after Carol came back from a trip out of town, John told her that he had poured a slab of concrete down in the crawl space and he hoped it would take care of the odor. There were no more flies rising up out of the darkness below the house then, but as long as Carol lived in the house on Summerdale, she could detect a faint, sweet, sewerlike odor: a bad, dead smell.

Carol loved watching John with the girls. The first year of their marriage he worked eight- and nine-hour days, giving him plenty of time to play with Tammy and April. "He was a very good father to my girls," Carol said. "Never beat them, whipped them. He very seldom hollered. I was the one that was hollering, not him."

In that first year, Carol found John Gacy to be "very gentle, very warm" as a lover. He was "the aggressor," he was "passionate," but the "gentleness" is what Carol remembers most from those happy times.

By the second year of their marriage, John was working longer and longer hours. In mid-1973, he quit Bruno's and tried to make a go of PDM full time. Carol began to feel neglected. "It got to be he was working from early morning. He'd come home, have a fast break, something to eat, and just do paperwork or phone calling and go right back to work again. If it wasn't paperwork, it was puttering around the house, in the yard." John converted one room into a recreation area like the one he'd had in Iowa: there was room for a pool table and a fully stocked bar. He did a lot of work out in the garage, building stuff out there, and it was his private spot. Carol and the kids had no business in the garage.

With nothing but the profits from his own business with which to support his family, John Gacy would often work until two or three in the morning. "I think," Carol said, "John could go on about an hour of sleep, maybe none. There were times I thought he was going to take a shower and go to bed, and he'd come back out of the bathroom dressed and say he had to go on a few bids, check a building, or talk to someone. It always had to do with work, and he'd leave maybe somewhere around anywhere from twelve-thirty, or maybe it was one or after one. And he'd be gone all night."

Sex, so good at first, was getting to be a problem. "After a while," Carol recalled, "we didn't have too much sex at all anymore." Either John was out somewhere, or he fell into bed, exhausted, just "too tired."

It was during that time, when John was displaying less and less interest in sex, that a neighbor asked Mrs. Gacy if there were "any little ones on the way."

"You have to sleep with someone first," Carol said, and she did not smile, because, in the space of a year, she had begun to learn some disturbing things about the gentle man who "swept me off my feet."

Once, cleaning out under the sink, Carol found some magazines that contained "quite a few pictures of nude men." There was one that had "a kind of a bloody picture" of a man, or maybe it was a boy. Carol couldn't be sure. She didn't want to look at the magazines.

Then there were the silk bikini panties "John had but never wore." Carol found a pair in the bed once, under the covers, crusted with her husband's semen. There were other times: a soiled pair under the dresser; a pair under the bed. With her sex life sinking into near-nonexistence, Carol confronted Gacy with the evidence of his masturbation. John was angry: the silk panties weren't even his, they had been given to him as a gift, and he didn't like being accused of shit in his own house. It was an argument, brutal as only a sexual disagreement between a man and wife can be, and when Carol called Gacy "a jag-off," he grabbed her arm and half threw her across the room. It was the only time he was ever violent with her, and she learned that "jag-off" was a word she could never use in her husband's presence.

It pissed him off because jagging off had nothing to do with his lack of desire. John said he was just tired, mentally and physically. It was true to an extent. Carol could see "he had one goal in life and that was to make something out of his business, and he was doing a good job of it. His PDM Contractors was just a small thing, and he worked it, making it a corporation, and doing bigger things, working on drugstores and buildings. It wasn't just wallpapering and painting anymore."

As Gacy's business grew and his sex drive dwindled, he often slept on the couch, not even joining his wife in bed. Carol began to ask about John's odd middle-of-the-night business appointments. "Nobody does business at those hours," Carol said.

That only went to show what Carol knew. John insisted he had to "talk to somebody about a job," or "make a bid." It was more convenient to do these things at three in the morning because there was no traffic and he could get around faster, check more jobsites.

"Look," John said, "with the money I got coming in, this is the only way. I got to keep going. It's me and me alone." John could hear himself "sounding just like my dad," using money as a club.

Gacy's business would keep him out until sometime between four and six most mornings. Sometimes he wouldn't even sleep, just change clothes and go right to work. Carol never slept that well when John was out: she felt restless, unprotected, and one night, when she heard the car come in and out of the driveway several times, she got up and turned on the TV: Carol sitting in front of a feeble glow in the darkness of the front room. John was outside somewhere, probably puttering in the garage.

Suddenly the door opened, and when John saw his wife sitting in front of the TV he seemed startled, even frightened.

"What are you doing up?" John asked. He seemed "scared" to Carol.

"I couldn't sleep. I kept hearing the car going in and out and I decided to get up."

Gacy acted confused. He said he just stepped in to get something, then turned and walked out of the house without getting anything at all. "He went right back out to the garage," Carol said, "and as he went out there, I looked through the curtains and I saw a young boy, blond hair, get in the car and he hurried up and drove off."

From the window, Carol could see a light in the garage, not something a man could work under, just a small red light, barely visible from the house.

Carol wasn't allowed in the garage. "He really didn't like me in there," Carol said, "and I never had any reason to go." This night, however, after John and the blond boy drove off, Carol went out to investigate the garage where John did so much of his night work.

"In addition to a red light on the wall," Carol said, "there was a mirror and a blanket on the floor."

Carol never confronted John with what she found in the garage. It was like the jag-off argument: John always said, "Don't plant seeds." It was one of his favorite expressions: Don't plant seeds, and John told Carol it meant, "If I didn't know for sure what I was saying and I couldn't prove anything, then don't bring it up."

Only later did Carol learn John was having sex with some of the teenage boys he hired to work for PDM. When a former employee named Jackson* beat him up one day, John explained that it was a dispute over money. Jackson had come to the house and parked in the driveway, by the back door. John was standing there, not doing anything, and the kid jumped out of the car and hit him. Gacy fell back against the car and curled down, protect-

*Name changed.

ing himself without fighting back. Jackson hit him again, and Gacy fell to the ground. Carol's mother, who was living there at the time, ran out and stopped the boy from more violence.

This Jackson, John explained, was angry because his check had been withheld. "The kid was painting some steps," John said later, "and he did a piss-poor job on them: paint running, thick and thin spots. So I told him to paint the steps over before he went home. Well, he went home and never did the steps. Now, I had to do that job, because I wasn't going to get paid if the customer wasn't happy. Then he wants his check. For the work I did. So that's what the fight was about."

A few years later, Carol heard a different version of the story. In 1973, John went to Florida to look at some land he had bought and invited Jackson along for the ride. "Jackson claims that John raped him the first day there and he slept on the beach because he said he didn't want to stay with John anymore," Carol said. "And that was his reason for jumping him."

Carol didn't like to blame John for his lack of desire, to make accusations about where he was getting it—no more jag-off arguments—she only knew that her marriage had fallen apart on her. Less than three years after they were married, on Mother's Day 1975, John and Carol managed to get in bed together to celebrate the special time, the holiday.

"Happy Mother's Day," John said.

Carol said "Thank you" and something she doesn't remember, because the next thing John Gacy said jolted her.

"This, " John said, "is the last time we'll have sex."

Carol thought it was a joke, it had to be a joke, but then she looked into her husband's eyes and saw that he was as serious as death.

"How," Carol asked, "how can you say—"

"Because I did."

"But . . . you've got to be kidding."

"No," John Gacy said, "this is the last time."

Sex, with a woman, involved love and tenderness. The foreplay and the afterplay were just as important as the act itself. With a woman, John needed to feel the emotions flowing between them. He knew, from reading the Kinsey Report, that "women don't get off every time," and his goal was to satisfy Carol first.

That way he'd satisfy himself. It was good like that, beautiful, just the way Ma said it should be. It took time and tenderness, and it felt like a sacrament.

Ma was right on one other thing: No two families should live together, because when Carol's mother got divorced, she came to live with John and Carol, in the house on Summerdale. Her presence, John said, "ruined my marriage."

John had started working his long hours, and when the sex dropped off to something less than once a month, Carol asked him why he never seemed interested. "Shit," John said, "I work twelve to twenty hours a day. I don't have no sex drive. I'm exhausted."

But when some woman called about a bid on her kitchen, Carol's mother would "plant seeds" about how maybe John was banging her. He had to be getting it somewhere. "Every time I came home from work," John recalled, "I had to explain where I'd been and what I was doing. Defending myself in my own house. And I wasn't doing anything but working my ass off for Carol and the kids and her goddamn mother."

John tried to explain it to Carol: no matter what her mother said there was no way he could work sixteen, eighteen, twenty hours a day and still be out fucking every other broad who called the house on business. John told his wife, "Carol, I swear as God is my witness that I am not having relations with any females, okay?"

"Then," John remembered Carol saying, "you're having them with boys."

Carol couldn't seem to get it out of her head that John had been honest with her and told her before they were married that he was bisexual. "Well, goddamn," John said, "she knew I wasn't gay, because I told her that. I told her I didn't like homosexuals, that I thought they were weak, sick individuals."

But John had "young guys" working for him, teenage boys, and Carol started asking about them. Was John doing anything with his employees? Why did he always hire boys, fourteen-, fifteen-, sixteen-year-olds? And who were the boys he brought over to the garage late at night?

Jesus Christ, John had the house-mortgage payment to make, he had to float a second mortgage, pay his mother a hundred dollars on the house every month, had to come up with another couple hundred just to keep a roof over his head. No, he wasn't fucking around with the employees, or having sex with strange boys at four in the morning. He told Carol that he was working.

The crush of constant accusations weighed on John's bad heart, and in late 1973 he had a stroke because "I was working like a son-of-a-bitch and no one believed me and I couldn't take the pressure." You could trace it straight to Carol's mother. He was in the hospital two weeks and was forced to spend two more weeks at home in bed. Then he had to go out and make up for that lost time: work that much harder, be out more nights, and Carol's mother kept "planting seeds," making accusations. John had to get a court order, actually have a sheriff's deputy come to move his mother-in-law out sometime in 1974. It wasn't a pleasant thing to do, but John had to think of his health, his bad heart. The woman could kill him.

It was too late, anyway. John really loved Carol in spite of their problems, but she went around asking questions like some dumb cunt detective. "Once," John said, "I think Carol saw me smoke some marijuana with one of the employees out by the garage. I never saw what they got out of it, but it was after work, and that was the way they liked to relax and we were talking. So Carol says, 'If you're not having sex, you're dealing drugs in the garage.' Because she thought I was going out at night to deal drugs then."

The way John recalls it, Carol threatened to burn down the garage. John said, "Go ahead. Fine. Real smart. Burn down the fucking garage, you'll fucking go to jail."

John would work sixteen straight hours, checking out bids and jobs, running all over Chicago in his first PDM truck: the one he painted a big number "4" on so people would think he had at least four of those babies out on the street. He'd come in, take a shower, fall into the sack with Carol, and try to "get into it with her." But sex with a female takes time and tenderness and love and emotion. John tended to fall asleep, he was that tired.

Carol, her mind poisoned by her mother's suspicions, would say, "You don't want to do it with me." So John just gave up, thought, "Fuck it." If she was going to accuse him, he might as well go out and do something to be accused about.

So then, sure, he got it on with a few of the employees. A couple of them. One kid was only fourteen, a part-time worker making three dollars an hour. He was "real naïve," and John told him about the Kinsey Report: how it's "part of your manlihood" to have sex with a male before you have it with a female. It was such a crock of shit, the Kinsey Report thing, and John could rattle it off like it was a chapter out of the Bible. Just like Voorhees in Iowa, the kid was worried about "putting something dirty" in his mouth.

John told him how it wasn't any dirtier than any other part of the body; he suggested the kid try sucking on his thumb, like an experiment. John could hardly keep a straight face watching these dumb shits sitting there with their thumbs in their mouths. The Kinsey crock worked best with the young ones, the fourteen-year-olds. You had to come up with something better than that to outsmart them when they got to be sixteen, seventeen.

So, okay, some of the accusations were true, but John still had respect for the marriage vows he'd taken. He wasn't really cheating on his wife because he was having sex with boys and not with women. It was like a kind of masturbation, sex with some dumb and stupid kid, some hustler. There was no love, no tenderness, no necessity to satisfy: it was an animal kind of sex. The love part he saved for Carol. A boy on the street, ten minutes, ten bucks, it was done.

That's what John told the docs up on 3 North: The seeds planted in Carol's mind by her mother sent John Gacy out after midnight, looking for sex. That was in late 1974, early 1975, the time when Jack Hanley began to surface. Jack wasn't some alternate personality, John said, none of that science-fiction shit. Jack Hanley was just a name he used, because everyone on the streets used false names. It was part of the game they all played, trying to outsmart one another. John outsmarted the young hustlers with Jack Hanley.

In May 1975, when Gacy made his Mother's Day announcement, both Carol and John knew it was only a matter of time before the inevitable divorce. John was out most nights. It was like a compulsion for him, an uncontrollable urge to become Jack Hanley and haunt the night streets of Chicago.

It was also in May that Tony Antonucci met John Gacy while the contractor was remodeling the Antonuccis' house. Tony was fifteen, and John offered him a summer job at three dollars an hour. He often did that, hired boys he'd just met. In late May,

John had young Tony doing tiling, plumbing, electrical work, and general clean-up. Shortly after he started with Gacy, sometime in June, Tony helped John clean up the Democratic headquarters on Montrose Avenue. They were working alone and it was about eight at night when Gacy began making advances. "He asked about giving me a blow job," Antonucci said, "and I said, 'No.' "

Gacy suggested they sit on the couch. He produced a bottle of whiskey and encouraged Antonucci to have a drink with him. Then, Antonucci said, "he started asking me about homosexual activity. Offered money." Gacy was talking fifty or a hundred dollars.

Antonucci said he wasn't interested.

Gacy applied some heavy pressure. "What if it meant your job?"

And Antonucci said he said, " 'No.' I just continued with 'No' replies."

They went back to work then, and Gacy made the incident seem as if it had been a kind of exam. Antonucci thought his boss had made the proposition "to see how I would handle pressure." He knew Gacy had a wife and two kids; he had heard him make derogatory comments "about fags." Tony thought his boss was testing him.

But then Gacy started grabbing at the boy's crotch and buttocks until Antonucci finally "picked up a chair, like I would swing it." Gacy "sort of laughingly asked me why didn't I just say, 'Stop'?" It was horseplay, John said: just a joke.

First a test, then a joke.

Later, after work, Gacy took Antonucci out for a hamburger and explained that the incident had, in fact, been a "test of morals." Gacy was the kind of boss who needed to know if his employees would "break under pressure."

About a month later, in July 1975, Antonucci was sitting in his parents' home. His mother and father were on vacation. Tony had stepped on a nail at work the day before, and Gacy knew he was home alone, injured, so when John knocked on the door that night, Antonucci thought his boss was just stopping by to see if he was all right.

It was about midnight, and John said he had just been to a party. He had a bottle of wine with him. The boy and his boss drank some of the wine and, after about half an hour, Gacy said he had seen some stag films at the party. The films and projector were in his car. Did Tony want to see them? Gacy "asked me persistently," Tony recalled, "and I said, 'Okay.' "

They were heterosexual films, men and women, and after they were over, Gacy grabbed for the boy and started "wrestling around." It was just "regular collegiate-style wrestling," Tony recalled, all armlocks and headlocks, more horseplay, and not at all a serious fight. The boy was careful not to humiliate his boss, but after a minute or so, he felt Gacy trying to slip "a handcuff on my left wrist." Tony swung his other arm around but Gacy got hold of it and managed to get both of Antonucci's wrists cuffed, behind his back. They had been in a standing position, but now Gacy knocked the boy to the floor.

Tony Antonucci lay face up, his hands cuffed behind his back, and Gacy "started to unbutton my shirt and unbuckle my pants and pulled my pants down halfway to my knees." Nothing was said. Gacy went into the kitchen. Tony never knew why Gacy left or what he was looking for in there. The boy could feel that the right cuff was very loose on his wrist. He managed to work it off, but he lay, waiting, watching the entrance to the kitchen, hands behind his back, as if still cuffed. When Gacy stepped back into the room, Antonucci hit him with a football tackle at the knees. The boy weighed 150 pounds; Gacy weighed 230, but Antonucci wrestled on the high-school team, and this time he was fighting seriously.

The boy "took the handcuff that I removed from my right wrist" and slipped it onto Gacy's wrist. "I found the key" —Antonucci couldn't recall if he got it out of Gacy's hand or his pocket—"and unlocked the handcuff on my other wrist." Antonucci put the other cuff on Gacy so that he had him lying there, face down, both hands locked behind his back. The boy held his boss down for a minute, maybe two, then got up and let Gacy lie there, face down on the rug, for five minutes or so.

There was some conversation then: no cursing, no threats, everything very rational, and Tony recalled, "It was agreed he would leave. I just let him up. He didn't do anything then. Just left."

After Gacy was gone, Antonucci thought that one of the strangest things about the incident was the first thing his boss had said as he lay on the living-room floor with his hands locked behind his back.

"Not only are you the only one that got out of the cuffs, you got them on me," Gacy said. Like the guy went around putting handcuffs on people all the time: Antonucci couldn't make any sense out of the statement, "It really didn't have any meaning," it was "strange."

About a week later, another of Gacy's employees, John Butkovitch, failed to get out of the cuffs and was never seen alive again.

CHAPTER
12

TOO MANY ECHOES OF Iowa: a managerial position, young boys working for him, wrestling matches, boys with hands chained behind the back, a variation of Kinsey crock working well, boys whose jobs might or might not depend on sex. But now a new element: the Jack Hanley character, John's nighttime persona, was taking on a life of his own, a life wholly separate from that of John Gacy.

Maybe if the marriage had gone better, if Carol's mother had gotten out of there just half a year earlier; maybe if the work wasn't so demanding that "normal sex" could be a pleasure rather than a duty; maybe if Carol had been more aggressive in bed; maybe if he hadn't taken on so many jobs for PDM; maybe if he hadn't joined the Moose, or started performing as a clown for hospitalized children; maybe if he hadn't gotten so deeply involved in Democratic politics at the local level; maybe if he hadn't agreed to work like a bastard directing the Polish Day parade; maybe if he had learned how to sleep like any normal man . . .

Carol thought John looked "tired," "worn out," even "very . . . older-looking."

All this in the summer of 1975, a time when his business needed him more than ever; a year when he began drinking more steadily, more heavily, probably because the divorce was looming up, surely only months away now.

The way John saw it and explained it, in that summer when the Other Guy finally surfaced, circumstances had conspired to destroy him, to defeat him with anxiety and fatigue. Always on the go, never thinking about himself, never sleeping, working himself into the ground.

Then a period of blackout, and John Butkovitch was dead.

John Butkovitch was sixteen and working in a hardware store when Gacy offered him a job in construction. It was good work and good pay for a boy who had not finished high school.

Butkovitch, John said, "learned fast," a tireless kid. Carol thought "he was a very nice boy. He was over, spent several times with us, had dinner with us." Sometimes the boy would come over to pick up his paycheck and spend an hour or two, just playing with Tammy and April before he left.

When Ma moved to Arkansas to be with Karen and her family after they moved down there, John Butkovitch helped her move.

John Butkovitch and John Gacy: Carol called them Big John and Little John. They'd argue sometimes. Big John always argued with the teenage boys he hired to work for him.

Once Carol said, "Boy, if I ever worked for you and you did that to me, I'd turn around and say, 'The heck with you, John.' Because he was on them all the time, hollering. I said, 'Is it necessary to holler?'"

"You have to," John said. "I have to keep them in line. I have to make sure that they know I'm the boss. Otherwise they take me for granted."

Sometimes the arguments would degenerate into wrestling matches. Not serious fights, but a kind of wrestling where John just rolled around on the floor with one of his employees.

John argued with Butkovitch about money, or more properly, about the hours Little John claimed. Carol said, "Big John always felt that the boys would end up putting too many hours on the card anyway, so it was a little argument over the hours that Little John did spend on the job that Big John didn't think he did." Big John said he didn't owe Little John that money.

Little John worked almost a year for Gacy. During that

time, as their marriage degenerated, Carol did a lot of traveling with the girls. She'd go to nearby Shaumberg to visit Karen's family before they moved, or to Indiana to visit her relatives there. In July and August 1975, she went to Arkansas to help Karen care for Ma after she broke her hip.

When she came back from that trip, Big John told her that Little John had quit, run away, something. She never saw Little John again.

The Other Guy surfaced for an hour, maybe less, in the early-morning hours of July 31, 1975.

Little John Butkovitch was home early in the evening, complaining that Gacy hadn't given him a check for his last two weeks' work. His father, Marco, a Yugoslavian immigrant, had taken the money he earned as a janitor and invested in several apartment buildings. John, his son, was living rent-free in an apartment building the elder Butkovitch owned. Knowing a little about how the system worked in the new country, the father suggested that if Gacy did not pay up, young Butkovitch should threaten to inform the authorities that his boss was not deducting taxes from employee earnings, as required by law.

John Butkovitch and two friends left for Gacy's house that night.

The way Gacy remembered it, Carol was off on one of her visits when Butkovitch arrived with three friends at the house. John said, "They threatened to kick my ass unless I gave him his check." Gacy talked fast: "John," he said, "I'm not going to hold back your check because you earned the money, but let me just go get the file on you." Gacy offered the boys a drink while he sorted through the records in his office. When he came back into the living room, things had calmed down, and no one was going to get his ass kicked until the evidence was presented.

"Okay, look," John said. "Butkovitch has a hundred seventy dollars coming from work. But look here, it's all invoiced out." The records showed that Little John had spent six hundred dollars redecorating the apartment his dad gave him and had charged materials to the Gacy account to get a contractor's discount. Not only that, but he'd also been paying Gacy back out of his paycheck and still owed three hundred dollars.

"Look," Gacy argued to Butkovitch and his friends, "if John didn't owe me the money, why would he pay me back? Now, he has a fight with his dad, his dad's going to take away the apartment, and John wants to leave town. Why should I get stuck with a three-hundred-dollar debt?"

Butkovitch said, "The carpeting is worth three hundred dollars. Get the money from my dad."

"John, you signed for the carpeting. We got it for you. Your dad isn't going to pay me."

A compromise was reached. Maybe Little John could tear up the carpeting and take it back to the store for credit on the Gacy account. Then Big John would give Little John his check.

"Butkovitch and his buddies agreed to this," Big John said, "and we smoked some grass, drank some beer. I drank Scotch, and I must have got bombed."

Big John never said anything about a threat to expose the little tax dodge he was running. "We just all came to a reasonable conclusion, smoked and drank, and they all left together."

So Big John was alone in the house, stoned on the marijuana, drunk on the Scotch, and, because he was exhausted as usual, he fell asleep, right there in the big leather chair.

It had been happening more and more lately. John would drift off into a dreamless sleep, a sleep as dark and empty as death. But then he'd wake inside his car, "cruising" the streets as a cop named Jack Hanley.

"I wasn't out looking for Butkovitch," John recalled. The farthest stop south on his cruising run was always Bughouse Square, a one-block park on the near North Side where male hustlers congregated. From there, Jack Hanley would drift up Wells, past the gay area in New Town, then turn back down Diversey, toward the lake, to cruise Clark and Broadway. Nothing doing that night.

Jack Hanley might have given it up then and driven right back to Norwood Park, but there was one last area to cruise, and it was just a bit north, on the way home. There were always hustlers, poor kids with parents just up from Appalachia somewhere, hanging out in the doorways around Montrose and Lawrence. Maybe Jack Hanley would get lucky. He liked 'em poor, just in it for the money.

So Jack was checking out the dark streets, and there, at Sheridan and Lawrence, he saw John Butkovitch getting out of his car, waving. Jack stopped, and the John Gacy personality took over.

"I wanna talk to ya," Butkovitch said, and Gacy, drunk as he was, could see that the boy had also been drinking quite heavily.

"Jump in the car," Gacy said. "Hurry up, there's someone behind me."

They started driving toward the Norwood Park. Butkovitch wanted to go get the carpeting out of the apartment right then, but Gacy said, "I'm not breaking into your dad's building, you asshole."

Butkovitch was so drunk he could hardly talk. "If I was gonna kick your ass, I wouldna needed them other guys," he said, then switched subjects and said he wanted another drink. He looked in his pocket and couldn't find his wallet. John said he didn't have any money with him. They could go up to the house on Summerdale, have a drink there.

John Gacy later told the docs in 3 North that he remembers every bit of the conversation, even though it was one of the nights he woke up to find himself "cruising." He remembers driving up the Kennedy Expressway to Norwood Park, remembers parking, going into the house, and recalls offering Butkovitch a joint. It's all very clear. He liked to keep them in the refrigerator, already rolled, for the boys. Butkovitch had another drink and it dropped him over the edge, into a new rage.

"You shithead," the boy shouted, "gimme my check! I could pound the crap out of you right now!"

Gacy was soothing. "You know I got a heart condition. No way you couldn't kick my ass. Just the excitement alone, that could put me in attack. Probably kill me. What would you want to kill me for, John? For a carpet? You want to kill me for a carpet?"

John told the docs that the boy was drunk, ready to fight one moment and apologizing the next. "I figured I had to . . . subdue him some way," John said and, in later years, he'd act out the way it happened, how he got the handcuffs on Little John.

The cuffs—the same ones John had used on Antonucci a week earlier—were on the bar. John kept them on the bar or on the dresser in his bedroom and he said, very brightly, like there was an interesting story here: "Holy shit, you should have seen it; just before I picked you up, this cop threw a guy up against a car and put the cuffs on him. Man, you should have seen it."

Butkovitch was sulky, sullen. "Big deal."

"No," John said, picking the cuffs up from the bar, "you should have seen it." He was standing now, the cuffs dangling in his right hand. "Lemme show you what this cop did."

"Why ya gotta show me?"

"Cuz then you'll see. Here." John Gacy put a cuff on the boy's right wrist. "Okay, now put your other hand behind your back. C'mon, I'm just going to show you something . . . just for a second."

When the second cuff was on and both the boy's hands were fastened behind his back, John didn't have to make soothing noises anymore, he didn't have to talk about his bad heart.

"Now," he said, "you ain't gonna kick anyone's ass, you ain't gonna wreck anyone's house."

John, mimicking the boy's voice, said: "Motherfucker, I'll kill you when I get these off."

John, very cocky, said: "You ain't gonna get them off."

"I'll kill you."

"You just relax," John said. "I don't take the cuffs off until you sober up. Could take all night."

Butkovitch pulled at the cuffs, a futile effort that over-balanced him, and he stumbled. John "helped him to the floor because he was stumbling and he could hit his head on a coffee table, hurt himself." Once he got Butkovitch on his back, John thought he might "have sat on the kid's chest for a while."

"When I get these cuffs off," Butkovitch threatened, "you're a dead man."

But John Gacy was still John Gacy, because he remembers very well what he said. "Anyone gets killed, it's you, John. Just sober up, okay?"

Gacy told the docs that he himself drank a few more shots of Scotch—"I had been bombed earlier and I got rebombed" —then lay down next to Little John. He was going to lay with him all night, that's what John told the docs, he was going to lay there keeping the angry, drunken boy company until he came to his senses. "It must have been about three in the morning," John said, and that final act of compassion, laying down with the drunken boy, was the last thing John Gacy remembered that night.

John woke up in his own bed. He had one of those vague hangovers where you don't quite recall what happened or exactly where you are, and he had to look around to orient himself. He was in his own bed, alone.

It was still early and he had a sense that he'd been up late. After going to the bathroom, he wandered into the kitchen, looking for something to eat. A normal morning. There was a light still burning in the living room, and John thought, Son-of-a-bitch, who left that on? John fell asleep in his chair so often that waking up and finding a light on wasn't unusual. Had he been in the living room last night?

He thought: Butkovitch. Little John is still here. John Gacy thought: Might as well wake him up, fix breakfast for him. That's what John told the docs. He told them he was going to fix breakfast for a dead man. John Gacy still thought Butkovitch was alive.

He padded, barefoot, into the living room to get the light, and, as he came through the doorway, he could see some feet, legs to knees, on the floor; and then . . . then . . . there he was: Butkovitch, lying on his back, hands cuffed behind his back, just the way John Gacy had left him.

Except there was a rope around his neck, and the front of his pants was wet where he'd lost control of his bladder. Little John's "eyes were closed but his face was red, that kind of blue-red, and his mouth was wide open."

"I knew he was dead," John said later, "because the rope was so tight around his neck." John knelt by the boy, and the first thing he did was take the rope off. He tried to make himself believe "he's only unconscious." John put his head on the boy's chest, listening for a heartbeat. There was nothing, no sound of life, but he couldn't pull his head away, and he listened for several minutes. John massaged the boy's neck where the rope had been, and he thought about applying mouth-to-mouth resuscitation before he realized he wasn't thinking clearly. Little John was dead.

He turned him over and took the cuffs off, noticing then that the body was rigid but not completely stiff. John knew, from his experience working at the Palm Mortuary, that Butkovitch hadn't been dead very long. Rigor mortis hadn't fully set in.

John looked around in the early-morning stillness of the house. At least there was no blood to clean up this time.

How do you explain it?

John never put the rope around the boy's neck, never pulled it tight, never watched him die. But there was no one else there that night, so he had to be the one. But why didn't he have any recall? Why couldn't he remember a thing?

And why were there no feelings? Here was a boy who had helped build his business, who ate dinner with his family, who played with his daughters, and now he was dead and John couldn't picture him alive anymore. The death of John Butkovitch, however it had happened, was now something that was over, and no one had to talk about it again. That's how Big John felt about the body.

There was, of course, work to be done. John went into the garage and got a rubber tarp. He brought the tarp into the house, rolled the body into it, and took it out to his private workplace in the garage. "I had to drag it," John explained. "I couldn't hoist him up onto my shoulder because of my heart."

He did not understand why he had no feeling about the body. It was like a dog that had died: a pet that had passed on and there was nothing you could do for it anymore. You felt bad for it, but it happens. John left the body in the garage, wrapped in the rubber tarp for a day or so, just as if a pet had died. He would bury it when he had the time.

You'd think a man would be frightened—bury the damn thing right away—but John just left the body there, and then Carol came home that Sunday or Monday. Now he had a body in the garage and no way to get it in the house, into the crawl space. Carol was always in the kitchen, near the window that looked out at the big double doors of the garage.

When John thought about it later, he realized if he had actually committed the murder then—and he emphasized this to the docs—it couldn't have been sex-related. "Why," John argued, "would you put your thing in someone's mouth if he wants to kill you? Guy could bite it off." John told the docs he found Butkovitch fully clothed, so whoever killed the boy hadn't violated him. John was adamant: there was no sex with Butkovitch. If you were looking for motivation, John theorized, you had to rule out sex. The killings weren't any sex thing.

John had no time to think about motivation immediately after the fact, however. John Butkovitch's body had to be disposed of, and it was a problem in logistics. John looked at his garage: it was in a low-lying area, and the houses across the street were built up higher, so water ran downhill into the garage as well as into the crawl space in the house. John had put up cement walls around his garage, which meant that it held up to a foot of water in the spring, but John had planned for the flooding. When he poured the cement, he'd blocked off one area, leaving just a small square of dirt, where he intended to dig a drain so he wouldn't have to go wading through his garage to get his tools.

Short of taking out the cement, a two-day job with a sledgehammer, the only place John had to dig was this hole, which was really too small, only three feet by a foot and a half. The first thing he would have to do would be to dig it deeper.

Carol could see him dumping a couple of wheelbarrowsful of dirt in the backyard and could never figure what they were for. John was always "puttering," and it wouldn't pay to ask him what he was doing this time. A woman could take only so many lectures about how hard her husband works.

John said, "I took his clothes off, there in the garage, so there would be no identification. I thought I should bury him there. So I dug the hole and put him there, but I had to dig under the foundation because a three-foot hole is not big enough for someone who's five-five or five-six. Whatever. And it was hard to get the hole big enough. So I had to bend him over, and by this time he was stiff as a board. I just barely got him in the hole and I had to jump up and down on him to bend him over and get him deep enough in there."

Then Big John poured cement over the hole, smoothed it over, and he didn't have to think about Little John anymore.

Marco Butkovitch found his son's 1968 Dodge—"very special" to Little John—parked near the corner of Sheridan and Lawrence. Little John always put the car in the garage, and finding it out on the street with the keys still in the ignition meant something was very seriously wrong. Marco phoned the police and mentioned that the night before, his son had intended to confront his boss, a man named John Gacy, about a check. Marco didn't touch the car for fear of damaging whatever evidence it might contain.

The police came out right away and found several items in the car: the keys, a checkbook, a jacket, and John Butkovitch's wallet with forty dollars in it.

Gacy remembers that the police came out to talk with him about Butkovitch and that he told them exactly what happened: The boy had come out with some friends and they had argued about money for a while, until everything was settled. Butkovitch left with his friends. You could check with the friends on that one.

John Gacy spent hours thinking about Butkovitch, putting together the pieces of his life, the things he didn't understand. It wasn't until he was up in 3 North, at Cermak, that he remembered picking Butkovitch up the night the boy died. He probably wouldn't have told the police that anyway, but at least he remembered it. Things were coming back to him slowly, like images floating out of a fog.

The police told the Butkovitch family that their son probably was a runaway. At any rate, according to Illinois law, John Butkovitch, at seventeen, was no longer considered a juvenile but a minor entitled to leave home if he wished.

The family argued that even if John had left legally, the circumstances were ominous. Who leaves home without their car, their checkbook, their wallet? No, John Butkovitch was not a runaway, and the family feared for his life. Marco called Gacy, who said he was willing to help in any way; he was sorry Little John, a good worker, had run away.

The Butkovitch family phoned the police every week, urging them to go out to Norwood Park to talk with Gacy one more time. After two years and over a hundred conversations, the police refused to take any more calls from the Butkovitch family.

After John Gacy was arrested and charged with thirty-three counts of homicide, the police were severely criticized, and they were quick to point out that about 20,000 missing-person reports are filed in Chicago every year. Three quarters of the missing are minors, and a little less than half of these are juveniles: almost 7,000 boys and girls under the age of seventeen missing in

Chicago alone. Most of the missing juveniles and minors turn out to be runaways.

Nationally, nearly 180,000 persons under eighteen are reported missing to the FBI.

In 1984, the Justice Department proposed setting up a Violent Criminal Apprehension program as part of the department's Juvenile Justice office. Of the 20,000 homicides a year in the United States, over 5,500 go unsolved. The program proposed by the Justice Department would review these unsolved cases, looking for patterns that would identify serial murderers who most often prey on juveniles and minors.

Research on the phenomenon suggests there could be as many as thirty-five serial killers operating in America in the spring of 1984. "And that's a conservative estimate," said Robert Heck of the Juvenile Justice office.

James Stewart, head of the National Institute of Justice, said, "This is like trying to identify and cure a new disease. We've had it for a long time, but it's been overlooked for years and years."

The way John Gacy was beginning to figure it, up in room 318 in 3 North, a serial killer was born in the summer of 1975. It didn't matter what you called him—Jack, or Jack Hanley, even Stanley—he was the Other Guy, the one John didn't know, and he lived inside, skulking, hiding, waiting for his chance. And then he killed.

John told the docs he could really only recall five of the deaths, five burials actually. The first was self-defense, and it was John all the time, all through that. Then came Butkovitch, and the morning he found the boy's body in his living room, dead, for no reason. John had no recall, no idea how the boy died. For John Gacy, the world wavered and went completely dark when the Other Guy took over; he told the docs he had no memory of the thing inside him that killed.

It was like that with the other three he could remember: Greg Godzik, John Szyc, and finally Rob Piest. John could recall certain small details and then the boys were dead, hands cuffed behind their backs, the ropes tight around their necks.

CHAPTER
13

To Carol, the argument leading up to the divorce was "a little thing": she was just trying to balance the checkbook, save John some work. "I thought I was fixing it," she said, "and I did mess it up."

There was a fight then, one of the times John threw something. He'd throw a telephone or a glass, even a chair. Never at her—but he'd break things when he got mad, and this time he broke his marriage and it was irreparable.

When John looked back on the final fight he could see, in a way, that he really wasn't the sweetest guy to be around all the time, not the way he acted with Carol. He treated her like she was dumb and stupid: dense, naïve. He could see how he was acting just like the Old Man, denying "acceptance" to his wife. No one, man or woman, can live without acceptance.

John's attitude didn't have anything to do with the body buried in the basement, the body buried in the garage. Carol couldn't know about them. No one knew about them. They were just nice little secrets, their lives were over, and no one had to think about them anymore.

No, the arguments with Carol were common, garden-variety domestic disputes. Just like, Carol went through the credit cards like army ants through an orchard, and John had to take them away from her. He put a lock on the phone so Carol couldn't make outgoing calls. He even put a lock on his office door.

Then she was so dumb and stupid she didn't know how to buy anything. In shopping, John tried to explain to Carol, it's best to be on the offensive from the start. The thing about life is that the most anyone can do when you make a fuss is to say "No."

John told Carol how you can outsmart salespeople, make them give you discounts that don't even exist. Like when he wanted the bike for Tammy's birthday: no reason to pay full price for it, not if you're smart. Kids' bikes are just like cars. They put the base model on sale, and the extras cost like a son-of-a-bitch. John told Carol how to handle department-store clerks, using Tammy's new bicycle as an example.

"I just walked over to the bike that was loaded and told the salesgirl, 'This is the one on sale.' "

John went through the whole process so Carol could see how it was done.

"What did it say in the ad? It said the bike on sale has all this optional equipment, didn't it?"

"I don't think so, sir."

"Get the manager over here. The one on sale, it's got the horn and basket, the saddlebags, it's got the special handlebars."

The girl said, "No, the saddlebags . . . I know the ones with saddlebags aren't on sale."

John said, "Well, you're wrong. Get the manager over here."

"I don't think I am wrong, sir." John imitated the sound of the dumb girl's voice. "Besides, we don't even have any of the sale items in stock. We're sold out."

"Get the manager," John said with calm authority. "Because when you advertise something and you sell out, then the sale applies to the more expensive model."

"I don't think that's our policy," the girl said.

"Then you better either get the manager over here or give me your name."

When the manager arrived, John told Carol how he let him have it, good. "What's going on here? You guys advertised bikes for sale, I come in here to buy one for my daughter's birthday, this girl tells me you're not going to have that model in here for two weeks. My daughter's birthday is tomorrow, not in two weeks. What am I supposed to do, give her a sales slip? Tell her she'll get a present in two weeks? I do a lot of business in this store, and you're telling me I can't have this bike instead of one you don't even have in stock?"

The manager—John described him as some clerky guy in a shit-brown sport coat—said, "No, I'm not saying that."

"Well, isn't it a practice that when you don't have a sale item, the next one up goes on sale?"

"On some items."

"In this case, it should be the same. If you haven't got the power to do it, get someone over here who does."

The guy straightened his tie and said, "I have charge of this whole department."

"Then get me the one in charge of the whole store."

By this time he'd been arguing with these two assholes for twenty minutes, and they finally just caved in: he got the loaded bike for the sale price.

And that, John told his wife, is how you shop. Call it boldness, call it arrogance, John said it was just being "smart." But Carol—goddamn it!—wouldn't listen. She'd go around treating salespeople like they were doing her a favor selling her shit at full price. Paying full price for anything: it just infuriated John. It was dumb and stupid.

That sort of thing was bad enough, but the everyday problems really got on John's nerves. Just like the goddamn groceries she brought home: Carol was forever wasting money at the supermarket, buying center-cut pork chops when he told her—he *told* her—she could buy a whole pork loin and John would cut it down for her. That way the chops cost about half of what they did at the store. He had all the proper knives to cut down large chunks of meat, but Carol couldn't understand the simplest rules of shopping and thrift.

With his restaurant experience, John knew how to shop for a family of four and save money, but Carol wouldn't listen. She wouldn't do it his way: the right way. Pretty soon, on top of everything else, John had to do the grocery shopping, too, because Carol said every time she brought something home, he bitched about it. Carol would care for the kids, clean the house, do the cooking, but she wouldn't shop.

Carol begged John to quit PDM, go back to working forty hours a week. They wouldn't have to pretend that the business was going great guns and he wouldn't be so tired, so crabby when he came home, and John said, "Do you think that's going to make it for us? You go out and spend two hundred and fifty dollars for Christmas presents for Tammy and April, it's stupid. What you do, you buy them a favorite toy, then you get them clothes, shoes, shit they need. You got to be practical. Two hundred and fifty dollars, we aren't making that kind of money for Christmas presents."

She didn't even know how to shop for Christmas. Looking back, John could see that he was acting more and more like the Old Man. Locking shit up; hollering about shoes for the kids.

"What the fuck are these shoes you bought for April?"

"They're pretty. She likes them."

"They aren't practical. She's changing shoe sizes every few months." John reminded Carol that he had once worked for the Nunn-Bush shoe company; if there was one thing he knew as well as food, it was shoes.

"Sure," John recalled Carol saying, "you know everything, don't you?"

And there was a moment there, just a moment, when the comment seized his heart. He did "sound just like my dad": a fucking know-it-all.

But no, he was right. The shoes were a stupid buy. Of course he was right.

The way John saw it, looking back, it got so that Carol didn't want to do anything around the house because—it must have seemed to her—there was nothing she could do right. Nothing.

Even before August 1975 and the disappearance of Little John, Carol was making noises about a divorce. She said John wasn't giving her any money, nothing of her own, and the seeds her mother had planted made her angry and suspicious, ready for a separation. Before Butkovitch, John fought the idea. After he buried the body in the garage, it seemed as if he just didn't care anymore.

John could hardly figure out why he was such a bastard with his wife—he loved her. It was different than with Marlynn;

Carol was dainty, she needed protection, she needed his love, and it seemed—John could see it quite clearly—that he was destroying everything they had together. Almost like he was doing it on purpose.

The loving part of John came up with a solution: They'd be a team, work together on PDM, which, by 1975, was finally established and bringing in money. Carol could learn to drive: she could go deal with the bureaucrats for permits, pick up the materials he'd ordered at the hardware store and lumber yard. That way John could have more free time; maybe it would help their sex life.

"And what if I get the wrong stuff?" Carol asked, and her question was another accusation. "You can yell at your employees until you're blue in the face, but I won't have you yelling at me." Carol refused to learn how to drive. She didn't need someone telling her how "dense" she was all the time.

Later, John couldn't understand why he'd been so nit-picky, why he felt the need to make the person he loved feel so "dumb and stupid."

Just like the final fight with the checking account. It was in October. "That fucking account," John said, "what a goddamn mess she made of it. That's how she was going to help with the business: She was going to take over the checking account, and this was in 1975. But she thought if you wrote a check and didn't cash it, you forgot about it. The woman had never in her life heard the word 'void.'

"I told her, 'Carol, you don't throw away voided checks, for Chrissake. How is anyone going to make sense of this?'"

He went after her then, sitting at his desk, the checkbook spread out in front of him, yelling things like, "Okay, now where is check twelve-thirty?" And he'd have to fill out little sheets of paper so they looked like checks and put them in there. "Where's twelve-thirty-eight? Twelve-forty-two?" He was mad, yelling, because anyone knows things have to be in order, and a check-book has to balance.

Carol started crying then. "I didn't want to do this in the first place," she said, choking, emotional, and she could hardly get the next words out. "I can't do anything right."

John wouldn't let up on her though, not even then, because he was right, and getting a proper balance on the checking account is important. "Don't give me that crying shit!" John screamed. "Don't lay that crap on me. You don't want to learn. You're so dumb and stupid, you don't want to learn. Because you don't listen."

"I listen," Carol said. "I know you'd rather hang around with your employees than with me and the girls. I know some things."

"You know jackshit! You have no idea how hard I work for you, how hard I work for the girls. Because I want them to have the things they deserve, and you won't help me. You won't work with me. If I had some fucking help around here, I'd have time for you. You're so goddamn dumb, you don't even understand."

"It would be just the same," Carol said, "whatever I did."

"All you ever do is bitch!" John hollered. "Bitch from the time I walk in the door. If I was out banging every other broad in town, you'd have a reason to bitch. If I was gambling away our money, or fucking drinking it up, or buying drugs with it, you'd have reason to bitch. But I'm working! I'm working my ass off seven days a week, twenty fucking hours a day. Where does the money go? All the money goes to you. What do I ever spend on myself? Jesus Christ, Carol, what the fuck do you want from me?"

And Carol said: "I want a divorce."

Why?

Was he just tired of the fights, the bitching? Was he too exhausted to fight? Sitting up in his room in 3 North, putting the pieces of the puzzle together, John tried to understand his divorce, what brought it about.

He didn't want it, but he'd said, "Fine, go ahead, get a divorce." He even sent her to his own lawyer.

But he loved Carol, and she lived with him from October, when she asked for the divorce, until February, and then he used his trucks and employees to help her move. Does that sound like they hated one another? He continued to date her, seeing her often, hoping in some small way that they could find a way to get back together.

He missed her so much when she finally left with the girls. And later, up in room 318, a couple more pieces of the puzzle slipped together. It was John who wanted Carol and the girls:

John Gacy. It was John Gacy who felt love and compassion. But it was the Other Guy, the one who had surfaced with Butkovitch, who wanted Carol out. The Other Guy had used John Stanley's personality to drive Carol out of the house. John could imagine a voice in his head—after Butkovitch—a voice that wasn't a voice at all but a subtle tipping of his personality, and it wanted him to think, "The bitch is fucking up a good thing: get rid of her. I want the house to myself."

Later, John still wasn't willing to admit two people could live in one body; but how else could you explain Butkovitch? How could you explain agreeing to a divorce you didn't want? If the Other Guy was there, you could know him only through the things he did, things that John Gacy would never do. The Other Guy was like the Old Man's tumor, that small black heart, beating against his dad's brain. The only evidence of the poison inside was John Stanley's sudden and unexplained rage.

The Other Guy: you'd have to break down the elements, anything John could recall about him, because no one knew him, not even John Gacy. One thing, though: There was a lot of John Stanley in him, the Other Guy.

That was the kind of insight John thought was important. He told the docs about it, this breakthrough, and he hoped they could use it in their theories when he went to trial. And then, eventually, when the trial was over, they could use these theories to help John Gacy. With therapy and shit.

It was after Butkovitch that all these—John didn't want to call them "personalities"—all these "characters," aspects of John Gacy, began to emerge fully. They weren't like the Other Guy, someone hidden inside who might or might not exist. They were real aspects of the real John Gacy, and they might differ from one another, but they were John all the time.

John Gacy the politician really came to the fore that year. When he moved into the house on Summerdale, he discovered that one of his neighbors was a Democratic precinct captain, and John volunteered to be his assistant. That's how John Gacy met Robert Martwick, a Norwood Park attorney who was the Democratic township committeeman.

"I figured," John explained later, "that I could never run

for office because of Iowa. They'd dig that up. What I wanted to be was the adviser, like the power behind the throne."

Getting ahead in Democratic politics in Chicago wasn't much different than earning a Key Man award for the Jaycees. You volunteered for everything, did a great job, then volunteered for whatever else wasn't done. Gacy, for instance, made sure he and his young employees kept the Democratic headquarters on Montrose clean. Tony Antonucci had been helping John rise through the ranks of Chicago's Democratic Party the night John Gacy gave him a little "test of morals" at the headquarters.

John never charged money to run an errand for the party, to fix a door, to set up chairs for a meeting, to donate one of his trucks to cart crap from one office to another, to erect and man barricades for Democratic events. He painted and decorated the headquarters free and helped make sure the annual dance ran smoothly. He made himself invaluable to the Democratic Party on the far North Side of Chicago. "I was a do-gooder," John recalls. "Anything anyone wanted done, just call asshole John."

In 1975, after Butkovitch, John was finally appointed to his first political position: secretary-treasurer of the Norwood Park Township Street Lighting District. There is not much honor in the position, just a lot of work. John took care of the books for the lighting district, paid its bills, did all the secretarial duties, responded to complaints, and got streetlights installed where they were needed. As soon as John took over the job, he found that no one had ever thought to number the streetlights. If a light went out, people would call and try to describe where it was: "the uh, second or third one from the corner of . . ." Totally disorganized. John put a numbered box on each light and kept a map in his office. People could call in and say, "Number twenty-one is out." And John would know exactly where it was. With just a single sentence. He was the best officer the township lighting district had ever had. The job paid twenty-five dollars a month.

A year or two later, the party rewarded John Gacy for all that selfless work, and he was appointed Democratic precinct captain for the Twenty-first Precinct, Norwood Park Township. During elections, John was a dynamo, going door to door, getting out the vote. He asked people what the committeeman could do for them; or, if it was some small thing, what John himself could do. He was tireless knocking on neighbors' doors. Everyone in

Norwood Park knew John Gacy had important political connections. He came around a couple times a year to remind them of the fact.

It was also in 1975 that Gacy was named director of Chicago's annual Polish Constitution Day parade, a function of the Polish National Alliance. He was recommended for the job by Jack Reilly, the special-events director for Chicago under Democratic Mayor Richard Daley. Gacy was named for the job because of the orderly, almost military manner in which he'd directed the Christmas Day parade in Springfield in 1964 and because of his service to the party in directing the Democratic Day parades a decade before, during the State Fair in Springfield.

It was a headache directing that parade, but once John let them know he was the boss, things ran like clockwork. "Imagine trying to get ten thousand Polacks marching in unison." God in heaven, it was something. Every organization bitching about its place in the parade. "We need to be in front of this one; we want this one behind us."

John fixed their ass. Every float, every band, every set of marchers was given a number. That's how they marched, by the number, and no one but John Gacy knew which group would march where. Of course, he wasn't above providing a little help and information about parade positions to those who might enjoy doing something for him in return: some political favor, a little business thrown his way, shit like that.

And then there were the politicians. They descended on the parade like flies on a turd. Anyone in office, or looking to run for office in Chicago, is a fool to ignore the Polish Day parade. Politicians who wanted a favored position—anyone who wanted to look especially good to the Polish community—had to talk to John Gacy. He knew them all. Important assholes, and John had their phone numbers. He could call them up, they'd know who he was.

So, in 1975, Gacy was developing clout, becoming a politician himself. Which—John tried to fit this piece into the puzzle—was just the opposite of the Old Man. John said it hurt his head thinking about it every day in Cermak. You'd get an idea of the whole picture: "I am the opposite of the Old Man." So being a politician made sense when you knew the Old Man hated them. But what about that tilt, the Other Guy tilt, the thing inside his head that sounded just like the Old Man and actually wanted the divorce? The Other Guy, whose silent voice said, "Get rid of the bitch. I want the house to myself."

The year 1975 was also when John Gacy became Pogo the clown, a do-gooder who dressed like a moron so everyone could see at a glance that he was a man who gave of himself for the benefit of others.

Too old now for the Jaycees, John had joined Moose Lodge number 368, in River Grove. They had the Jolly Joker Clown Club, and there were only five or six clowns in it, who performed for kids at Easter, Christmas, and Halloween. There'd be as many as six hundred kids at these Moose-sponsored parties, and right away John could see they needed another Jolly Joker.

John had a costume made for himself and devised his own makeup. He performed with the other Jolly Jokers at the holiday parties, and visited hospitals, sometimes as often as twice a month. He loved to cheer up sick children—paralyzed kids, kids with spinal injuries, the mentally and physically handicapped, children who weren't taken to circuses and who would never otherwise see a clown in the flesh. Besides that, he clowned in "fifteen, oh, maybe twenty parades" a summer. All at no fee.

Jack Shields, a Chicago account executive who clowned with John, said Gacy was a good clown. "He prepared for the engagement and planned his entertainment. He used a series of two-hand puppets." The puppets were professionally made, very realistic, and the little skunk was the one that made the kids laugh. John could get the shiest children to talk to the squeaky-voiced little skunk. Shields recalled that Gacy "also had a rubber chicken he used. He had a dog leash and a harness he would use. He had a tubing that would run down through the leash to the collar, a bulb in his hand would contain water, and he would caution the children that his invisible dog was just a puppy, and they best be cautious. Like all puppies, sometimes it would wet their shoes, and about the time the child would believe that there was no invisible puppy, he would squeeze the bulb and wet the child's shoes and say, 'Now you excited my little puppy.'" The child would look down in wonder at his wet shoes, and hundreds of delighted children would scream out their laughter so loudly it almost hurt your ears.

John said he never went to clown school. "It just came naturally to me. In a way, I guess you could say I love to perform."

John understood that "Pogo was a tranquilizer for me. When I was Pogo, I was in another world." A clown does nothing but live for others, like a priest or a cop, except that a clown doesn't save lives or souls, he simply makes others laugh. Sometimes that's enough for a man; sometimes making others laugh is a way of saving his own life or his own soul. "Maybe," John said, "Pogo was a way of running away from myself. I enjoyed making people happy. I loved the laughing faces, especially the children. Why else would I do it, if I didn't have the time for myself?"

He wouldn't lie about it, either: John loved the attention, he "craved being in the limelight." Just like, one time he was clowning for the lodge and he was running late with all his engagements, as usual. It was time for the Wednesday night bowling league. He and Carol bowled in that league. So John raced over there all dressed up as Pogo.

Bowling was John's one sport: he hooked 'em hard into the strike zone from the right-hand side, hitting consistent 170s, 180s, but it was absurd watching a clown standing there studying the pins, then firing the ball down the alley like a pro. "They loved it," John recalled, "and they asked me to come out and clown for Christmas. And one woman wanted me to do something special for her daughter's birthday, so I went out there with my assistant clown, Patches—it was Michael Rossi, he was an employee then— and later on I got the cutest letter from this little girl." That's what clowning was all about: being in the limelight and making others happy.

Sure, there were times when he got paid for clowning, like for the grand opening of some ice-cream store in a shopping mall, shit like that, but it wasn't the same. Usually Patches—Michael Rossi—came along. Openings could be fun, but they were commercial ventures, you got paid for them, and they didn't make you feel warm inside, like coming out of church after confession.

There were times, too, when John Gacy as Pogo was a help to John Gacy the politician. He clowned at the Democratic organization picnic; he clowned at a fund raising fair for the retirement center across from Resurrection Hospital. A precinct captain had gone to John, the politician, and Gacy ended up helping organize the event. He donated lumber, the use of his trucks, and he built the refreshment stand. He and Rossi clowned as Pogo and Patches.

There were different clowns for different occasions. They were all Pogo, of course, but Pogo in a parade was not the same as Pogo at a birthday party. "Going to a parade," John recalled, "you have to get into the mood, real festive, before you even put on the makeup. And you have to be one festive son-of-a-bitch all afternoon. Sometimes I had to work, didn't even get any sleep, but when there was a parade, I had to be happy as shit all afternoon, running along the parade route for about four hours."

If John did it right, got himself into parade Pogo, he could go all afternoon, running beside the bands and horses, hopping in and out of the crowd—never mind his bad heart—and it was like "regressing into childhood." It was "like becoming someone else," a "whole different person," and he could do things he'd never do without the clown face on: He could run into the crowd, find himself a "strange broad and honk her boobs." Nobody ever said shit. "Oh, well, it's okay, he's a clown, you know."

The parade Pogo was not the same clown who visited the hospitals. "When you sit there, looking in the mirror and putting on your makeup," John recalled, "you had to get yourself up for it; you had to remember where you were going and why you were going. Just like a Democratic picnic is different than a birthday party where you want to concentrate on the birthday boy or girl. With retarded kids, you have to move like a son-of-a-bitch to keep their attention. Even if you worked all day, you have to keep jumping, always active. And you have to make them understand that a clown's life is all happiness, and there is no sorrow for a clown. You got to be compassionate and goofy at the same time. You want to make them feel the way you act: happy all the time."

There was a "whole other" Pogo who went to the hospitals to see physically ill children or kids who were the victims of accidents. What you have to deal with there is loneliness. "Just like I was in the hospital; I know what it is to be alone and sick. I been sickly all my life; I been alone all my life. I know what it feels like. So instead of an active, moving, goofy clown, like Pogo is for the mentally retarded, you want to be a more quiet Pogo. Still a compassion clown, but you want them to trust you and talk to you. They been lying there for days or weeks, they been lying there maybe a month, and they haven't had anyone to talk with.

So you get them talking, five-year-olds, and sometimes they don't make any fucking sense at all—see, it's all coming out, how they feel—and you stand there and smile and listen and laugh. Because I knew what a lonely life was, and I was spreading cheer, and it really, honestly made me feel good inside, talking to these kind of kids, going to the hospital. That was when it was best being Pogo."

Once, on one of his visits to a hospital—Resurrection or Northwestern, he couldn't remember—John rode up on the elevator with the other clowns: five bulky men in silly clothes and outsize shoes. The door opened on the children's ward and they came tumbling out. John leapt into one child's room and, he remembers, the boy was alone except for his mother sitting pensively in a chair by the boy's side. Pogo went into his antics, blowing up balloon toys, twirling his cane, having the hand puppets argue with one another: trying to cheer the boy up, make him laugh. The mother, John could see through Pogo's painted eyes, was staring at him with a strange, almost pained expression. The boy was in traction: a comic-strip hospital patient with a cast on his arm, plaster casts on both legs, and a bandage around his head.

Pogo capered about, gave the boy a few balloons, and then started talking to him in Pogo's goofy clown voice, trying to get the kid to open up, to pour out his loneliness.

"What's your name, young fella? And what happened to you? Why, you look like an accident on its way somewhere to happen. Looks like you need a balloon dog there, young fellow. . . ." And as Pogo capered and made the balloon animals—as the young boy smiled and began to laugh—John noticed that the mother's eyes had misted over and that tears were rolling freely down her cheeks. Suddenly she stood and walked rapidly out of the room.

The boy was focused on Pogo; he didn't even notice his mother leave. John pushed Pogo through another few minutes, then he left the boy, promising that he would stop back and see him again soon.

The boy's mother was standing in the hall, drying her eyes with a handkerchief, and John had to do a hard thing. He had to stop being Pogo and be someone else. He had to be John Gacy, a serious, compassionate man who just happened to be dressed like a complete lunatic.

"I hope," he said, "that I, uh, didn't offend you in some way in there. I was only trying to—"

And the woman smiled up at him, the mascara still streaked on her face. "Oh, no," she said, "don't think that. It's just that he's been in here six weeks since it happened and . . . oh, my God, this is the first time I've seen him smile." And the indescribable feeling shot through John like electricity: the full, welcome feeling you get after confession, the warm, peaceful feeling that fills your chest when you step out of church after Mass.

CHAPTER 14

JOHN TOLD THE DOCS up in 3 North that becoming Pogo was the best part of 1975. Even then, "sometimes it was bad for me to be Pogo." Sick kids, sure, they were easy, you had compassion, and Pogo was a compassion clown.

With healthy kids, performing as Pogo could be something else: like at a grand opening or a picnic, where the clowns were nothing more than ambulatory candy dispensers for a lot of screaming, greedy children. Or at the Moose Christmas and Easter parties, where Santa or the Easter Bunny were the main attractions and the clowns just kept order, like cops. Clown cops, watching to see that all the kids got their fair share. Pogo could watch selfish kids try to get more than what was coming to them and feel himself becoming a hatred clown.

So, John told the docs, if you really broke Pogo down, there were two of them: the compassion clown and the hatred clown. John wondered what that meant: a split in Pogo, one of the characters he was becoming in 1975, the year the Other Guy surfaced and Little John died.

Clowning was a calming influence on John Gacy, but it was harder to get up, mentally, when Pogo had to be a candy machine or a cop clown. John would sit, applying the makeup, carefully smearing on the white greasepaint. Pogo was a whiteface clown. That was John's decision from the start, because a whiteface clown is a happy clown. He didn't want to be a sad, pathetic asshole of a clown. The only place John Gacy liked sad clowns was in clown paintings. Then sadness seemed to give the goofy faces dimension.

In 1975, after Butkovitch, John started getting rid of the bullfight figurines he had collected, and began collecting clown paintings. He liked sad-faced clowns on the wall. Clowns staring out into the world with a secret sorrow in their eyes.

They made him feel sentimental, the poor, smiling sons-of-bitches with big, sad eyes shining out of happy, painted faces: a perfect example of how a guy can be right in the midst of a big social storm and still be lonely as a bastard.

John himself, as Pogo, was always a happy clown. Around the white face he drew a dark semicircle: a kind of upside-down horseshoe he left open at his white double chin. The eyebrows arched up in a ridiculous triangle on each side of his face. Then he drew a wide, dark mouth on his white face. John had designed his own makeup and had plenty of clown faces to work from, all those paintings hanging in his front room, but he liked Pogo's mouth to be slightly different from those of other clowns. It was bigger, like a huge moustache extending from chin to nose, and it curved up sharply, the smile tapering off to a knife point toward the outside corner of his eyes. A sharp-pointed, happy, clown's smiling mouth.

All the other clowns he had seen—all the professional clowns—used curved mouths. The pros said a sharp mouth can frighten children. John would look at Pogo's face in the mirror and sometimes, sure, it could look a little scary. Sometimes Pogo didn't mind scaring the kids just a little. That's when he had to be a hatred clown.

At those picnics or Moose parties when it was bad for him to be Pogo, he'd have a pocketful of candy, giving shit away to healthy kids who didn't really need it, and he could see "they were just greedy little bastards." Pockets full of candy and they'd say, "Please, could I have some? I didn't get any." Little shits with their pockets full of gumballs, lying to Pogo as if they thought he was dumb and stupid.

John would jump, caper about, frolic away from the little

fuckers, and they'd be after him, pestering him, pulling at his clothes, lying to him.

When it was like that, John told the docs, then it was bad to be Pogo; it was bad to be a clown who saw lying and greed. He'd be laughing because he was supposed to be laughing, but he could feel his heart swell with a kind of "hatred" so that the next kid who pulled at his sleeve, the next one who stood there with his pockets bulging and said, "Please, I didn't get any candy," that was the one John taught. He taught the kid with pain. Punishment was teaching.

"Oh, ho, ho, you didn't get any," Pogo would say, leaning down to the child and smiling his odd, sharp-pointed smile. He'd pinch the kid on the cheek, like clowns will do, only he pinched hard, so that it hurt and he could see the pain in the child's eyes. Smiling, and whispering so that no one else but the child could hear, Pogo would rasp, "Get your ass away from me, you little motherfucker. . . ."

And then he'd be up, capering around, a perfect fool, putting people and distance and laughter between himself and a suddenly sobbing child: Pogo smiling his dark, pointed smile.

Even while he was married, John felt a sense of loneliness, of being different, and the summer yard parties helped. Beginning in 1974 was the "Hawaiian Luau," where John cooked and wore a Hawaiian shirt. The second yard party was the "Western Barbeque," where one rough buckaroo roasted half a steer on a spit in the barbeque pit out in the backyard: John dressed up like Marshal Dillon. That was in 1975, the year of Butkovitch and Pogo and the divorce. John had just been appointed director of the Polish Day parade, and Mayor Daley had been invited to the party. John told everyone the mayor'd be out to the house on Summerdale for a little western hospitality.

Unfortunately, the mayor's busy schedule prevented him from attending, though John pointed out that "a lot of aldermen" were there.

John was the perfect host, never drinking too much, keeping an eye on the guests, and dancing with the women who had sat out too many Hawaiian love songs or western ballads. His house was open to anyone, and when some people mentioned the vague, musty odor, John told them about the periodic flooding in his crawl space and the darn broken sewer pipe down there.

By 1976, the summer-theme party had become too big for John to handle by himself—as many as four hundred people attended—and Jim Vanvorous, a heating contractor John worked with, agreed to cohost the "Spirit of '76" party. Gacy wore a colonial outfit with a white wig and a three-cornered hat, as George Washington. Even though they were divorced, Carol came as the hostess of the party. John had invited his mother-in-law, and it was the first time he had talked to her in a year. He enjoyed his party as much as anyone.

John and Vanvorous split the costs of mixers, a few kegs of beer, and a small band. Everyone was encouraged to bring his or her own booze, and, for the most part, all the neighbors were invited. There were important politicians there, and it was understood that John was a heavy in Democratic political circles. Some of John's wealthy clients attended. And John himself talked with these men, with other contractors, about plans to buy a bar and turn it into a disco, to put together grandiose projects in partnerships with contractors and clients. Permits and shit would be a snap with his connections; raising money would be a piece of cake because of the respect he had from certain well-to-do clients.

Some of the neighbors thought John was "boastful" about the money he made. Others just felt left out. Lillian Grexa, John's neighbor to the immediate west, said, "When you start quoting thousands and thousands of dollars and figures that an average person doesn't fathom, how can you make much comment on it?"

In 1977, the theme was "Southern Jubilee," with John a genuine Kentucky colonel frying up the chicken. In 1978, over four hundred people attended the "Italian Festival," and John dressed up like a peasant to piss off his "wop friends."

Lillian Grexa remembers John at the door after these parties, or others, and he would be carrying a big platter of turkey or beef. "Looks like I overordered again," he'd say, offering the plate to his friend. "Go ahead," he said, "you got kids, you can use it." Anything anyone wanted done in the neighborhood, John would do it. He was "boastful" about money and political connections, but he was "generous to a fault."

"No neighbor ever did things like that before," Lillian Grexa said, "and none has since."

*   *   *

As 1975 slid into 1976, when the divorce he didn't want would become final, John began drinking more and more heavily. Sometimes he needed pills to help him sleep, pills to calm him down, pills to get him going in the morning.

John would fall asleep in the big chair, then wake up staring at the test pattern on TV. Worse, sometimes he'd wake up driving down to New Town, to Clark and Broadway, to Bughouse Square and the male hustlers. John Gacy woke up "cruising," after midnight, when the dark flower blooms. In his mind, he knew, he was becoming Jack Hanley.

Jack had a theory—well, it was John's theory, but Jack used it on his nocturnal cruises—that most homosexuals have "light hair," sandy brown, blond in color. "Go into the gay area of any city," John once explained, "and you seldom see people with dark hair, moustaches, heavy builds, real *macho* look." "Queers" have a look about them: the fake innocence, the slight, muscular build. Light hair. A certain kind of ass, small and tight. Some of them, you could look at their hair and build and tell—and these kids, they wouldn't even know themselves. Not until they got off the bus and Jack offered them a ride. Then they'd find out about themselves.

Sometimes Jack skipped the Greyhound bus station altogether, because "the park" is where he ended up when he awoke to find himself cruising. Washington Park is a one-block-square area just north of the Loop and a couple of blocks south and east of the strip of nightclubs on Rush Street. In the 1950s, the park was a haven for soapbox orators, men or women who loudly declaimed wondrous theories. In those days, people began calling Washington Park Bughouse Square.

In the 1960s, the neighborhood began to deteriorate. Hotels that once strove toward a sort of genteel elegance became seedy, some of them little more than flophouses for transients. Within sight of the park, one of the larger bars began catering to the rougher homosexual crowd.

And Bughouse Square became a hangout for young male hustlers. On sunny afternoons, elderly people eat their lunch on the park benches, but after midnight, the park belongs to young men trading on their youth and looks. Their customers are older men, generally from nearby suburbs, who drive down Chestnut

Street, staring at the young men standing under the streetlights or sitting on the hoods of cars.

A car pulls to the curb; a young men steps over to the open passenger window, but not before thrusting his pelvis forward—"throwing the basket"—so a heavy bulge at the crotch is clearly visible. A pair of socks stuffed down the front of the pants makes for a more impressive basket and helps bring a better price.

The exchange of service for money at Bughouse Square is often characterized by a sort of mutual contempt. Many of the boys do not consider themselves homosexuals: they'll sell what they have to the pathetic old jerks who need to buy it, but the hustler's attitude is one of swaggering superiority.

Negotiations are marked by mutual distrust. The men in the big cars often consider the boys whores, to be taken advantage of, to be cheated. There is always an argument about money: how much, for what, whether it is to be given up front. "Jack rollers" will perform if they have to, but they'll run if they can get the money first.

It can be a rough place, Bughouse Square after midnight. Men have been beaten and robbed by groups of boys. Some of the young hustlers have been badly injured by the men who picked them up. A few boys, after a month or a year, have simply disappeared, perhaps gone to another city. There are always rumors of death.

Jack thought of the boys of Bughouse Square as "scum, weak, stupid, degraded." But something about the park drew him to it, "like a compulsion."

If nothing was happening at the park, Jack would cut over, making a slow run through New Town, a neighborhood of young singles with some elegant cafes and restaurants and a sprinkling of gay bars. Prostitutes, male and female, work the bars and streets of New Town, and Jack knew that if a young man caught his eye, it was a signal.

John said, "I'd just pull over, ask them what they were doing. Sometimes they'd say they were homosexuals, talk about how long they'd been out of the closet and shit, and then I found that I didn't really like to go with them."

From there, it was only a few blocks east to the corner of Clark and Broadway, where there are a number of gay bars and a few hustlers hanging around: young men standing on the corners, looking to pick up twenty or fifty dollars for a quick trick after midnight. Boys anxious to earn a few bucks from older men cruising the dark in their big cars.

"I didn't want to be down there, cruising," John said. "But then, I always said, 'As long as I'm here, I might as well get my rocks off.' Because I didn't have the time to be doing that, and if I was there, I could get it over with, and the next night I wouldn't wake up and find myself out cruising again. Because anyone who knows me knows the one thing I always say, I always say, 'I haven't got the time.' So if I was already cruising—even though I didn't consciously set out to—I would look for someone who'd do it quick: you know, 'Blow me and get the fuck out of my sight, you piece of shit.' " It was "a quick animal thing" John wanted, and he used Jack to get it.

Still, it made him mad, the Jack part, if there were no suitable boys out on any given night. Jack was angry because of the compulsion, because of the time he was stealing from John.

Uptown, at the northeast corner of Chicago proper, was on the way home from the park. John could have taken the expressway, but if Jack was still mad and looking for action, they'd cruise Uptown.

Years ago, uptown had been a good, solid area of fine apartment buildings. The neighborhood usually is described as "lying in the shadows of the skyscrapers," and every few years there is a newspaper story about how depressed the area has become, a story about some young mother whose baby sleeps in a hammock to avoid rat attacks.

The streets narrow as they move in from the lake, and they are littered with broken glass and blowing paper. The solid old three- and four-story buildings have fallen into disrepair, and tattered signs advertising "apartments for rent" are taped to dirty windows. There are boarded-up storefronts—the remnants of some failed restaurants or hardware stores—and an occasional burned-out building, a dark shell, looks out on the world with broken, windowless eyes. Clothes hang drying on lines strung across iron fire escapes.

The neighborhood has its share of pimps and pushers working the tough streets under the el tracks; prostitutes work streets full of pawnshops, used-furniture stores, and storefront barrooms. The blinking orange signs read, "Checks Cashed," or "Submarines," or "Jesus Saves."

It is a strange neighborhood, a mix of American Indians, newly arrived immigrants from the Orient, a few blacks, and hundreds of thousands of people from the mountains of the South. It has been estimated that over four hundred thousand people from Appalachia have moved to Chicago in the past forty years. The majority of these people settled in Uptown.

During the day, people sit on the stoops, chatting. Sometimes a couple of dozen neighbors—people of all colors—can be seen moving some family's possessions down the street to a new apartment. Teenage boys along the curbs restore old cars. In the summer, they work naked to the waist, young men with Appalachia in their genes: blond-haired boys, some of them short, slight, but muscular.

These Uptown kids: so many of them were the very kind of boy John could spot as a homosexual on sight. John Gacy, in his silver Oldsmobile station wagon with the contractor's sign in the window, would cruise uptown during the day, recruiting the short, blond-haired boys for PDM.

But after midnight, when the part of himself John called Jack liked to cruise, the streets of Uptown belong to the gangs, to the pimps, to young male hustlers who seem to outnumber female prostitutes. You see these male hustlers in faded jeans and T-shirts, on the corners, in the dark doorways, waiting. They watch for the big cars, new ones not ordinarily seen in uptown, expensive cars with no dents and with suburban parking stickers in the windows.

Business is done in the car, under the el tracks; it is done by the vacant lots, or parked at the curb under a streetlight that has been broken for months; business can also be done a few blocks away, in the park by the lake.

Jack could do it that way, but he liked to take them home, to the Summerdale house. It wasn't a very long drive, ten minutes or so, and Jack liked it best at home.

John told the docs that Jack wasn't some alternate personality. Forget what he told the cops after he was arrested. He didn't remember any of that shit, anyway. Jack was nothing more than another version of John, like Pogo, and he was useful because he could be tough with potential jack rollers and shit. Just the way Pogo could be a compassion clown for sick kids, Jack could be a cop on the lookout for thieves, liars, jack rollers, homosexuals.

He thinks the first time the name occurred to him, he was driving around Bughouse Square with one of these hustlers in his car, when he saw a squad car pull slowly by, the cops glancing at him. It came to him then, all at once, that if they arrested him, he could use the name Jack Hanley to get out of trouble. Jack, the cop buddy he used to drink with down at Bruno's. The squad car pulled by, and John thought, But that's who I'll be, Jack Hanley. Because John Kennedy was called Jack, and John could be Jack, too. A street name, so that you wouldn't have some little shithead running around telling the mayor, "Pogo the clown's queer!" Jack Hanley—he would be a kind of fatherly cop. John had always been fascinated by police and police work. Being a cop came as naturally to him as being a clown.

Everyone on the street used false names, anyway, all the greedy little hustlers. They'd say, "Hi, I'm Billy." Get them home, say something like, "Want a drink, Bobby?" and the kid'd say, "Sure." You could trap 'em that easy, they were so dumb and stupid. Most of the people Jack had sex with—and by 1976 he was going down to the park twice a week, a hundred times a year—were dumb and stupid. The scum of the earth. That's how you could tell the sex was all bisexual: there was no love, no "fondering." Just blow me and get the fuck away from me, you filthy scum. That was Jack's attitude.

Sometimes he even picked up women, and it was the same deal: Blow me and get lost. Or go blind, die. Just like the one he picked up in Old Town, some Eastern European broad, hardly spoke English, and she blew him as he drove up Lincoln. The broad needed to get off at Irving Park, but John didn't get off until Lawrence. He told her he didn't have time to drive her back but that it was only a short walk away.

Like a couple of miles. Talk about dumb and stupid.

Jack was another character, like Pogo, and John knew him just about as well. He knew Jack mostly went for boys and didn't like them dirty-looking; he hated hippy assholes with long, straggly hair. He wanted them young, clean-cut, but virile-looking. They should have blond or brown hair, with tight butts and short, muscular builds. He especially liked them young so he could "have the fatherly image over them." Young, and "small enough so you wouldn't have no trouble with them" if it came to that.

Jack hated queens, though, shitheads dressed up like women, talking like girls. Sick motherfuckers. A man should know he's a man: a boy has to know what he's got between his legs. The ideal pickup shouldn't be an actual homosexual: Jack liked a kid struggling to make the price of a meal and not really sure he "should get into it." A first-timer.

Sometimes they'd lie to you, and you'd get real homosexuals. Guys who weren't bisexuals at all. But John could get into Jack as well as he could get into Pogo, and with these lying assholes he was a law-enforcement officer. He had to track down the homosexuals, like a cop. He didn't even have to tell them he was a cop. It was just a way of acting that did it, a kind of natural performance that made it easy to outsmart them.

John knew what Jack was doing. He'd bring them back to the house, get what he wanted, say he was going to give the kid his money when he dropped him off again at the park. But if the little bastard was a real queer, or if he raised the price on him— and they always did: so naïve and stupid they thought they could outsmart a streetwise homicide cop—if they raised the price, Jack could handle greed as well as Pogo. "Oh," Jack would say, driving the kid to whereever he wanted to go, "wait, there's a vending machine, I need a paper. Get me one, will you? Here's a quarter." And he'd pull up a few feet in front of the machine so that when the kid got out, Jack could speed away without the little asshole grabbing onto the door handle. No fight, no argument: Jack just outsmarted them, left them standing miles from anywhere with a quarter in their hand.

Once he got into it with a kid for hours, some hitchhiker he'd picked up during the day, and Jack offered to wash the kid's dirty clothes while they were doing it. Later, driving to that night's bowling league, John gave the kid a few bucks and told him to go in a burger joint and get them both something to eat. As soon as the dumb little shit was out of the car, Jack hit the gas and was gone. He threw the kid's clothes in the first trash dumpster he passed.

Just like with Pogo, there was a split in Jack, too. Sometimes he'd pick up a good kid, real naïve, and he couldn't bring himself to have sex with the boy. Jack'd be a good cop then, tell the kid about the jack rollers down at the park; tell him he could get himself killed down there, about how he was degrading himself, selling his body for money.

So there was a split in Jack: He could be a good cop, or a cop bent on outsmarting the hustlers. None of the people Jack met, or had sex with, died. John knew that. But—and here was the central piece to the puzzle—what if there was another Jack? What if the Other Guy split off Jack? John didn't know that Jack. He never met the killer.

He tried to fit it together, up there in 3 North. All these characters came to the fore in 1975, after Butkovitch. Pogo could split off into a compassion clown or a hatred clown. Jack could be a compassionate cop or a smart cop, a real bad-ass cop. John could love Carol and still act enough like the Old Man to force her into a divorce.

John thought about it, and he asked the docs, What if Jack split a third time, a time that John didn't know about? Because in 1975 and 1976, when all the other characters were rising up out of John, the Jack Hanley part kept getting stronger and stronger. And 1976 was when the majority of the killings began. What if a part of Jack—say, Smart Jack, Bad Jack—split off into the Other Guy, the one who destroyed John Gacy's marriage, the one whose silent voice said, "I want this house to myself"?

CHAPTER
15

JOHN DIDN'T REMEMBER THE boys of '76. There was an image—something seen through a shimmering, nearly opaque vapor—of a boy who had died near Christmas: Greg Godzik, an employee. The others: John couldn't even recall disposing of their bodies. Most of them.

The first known victim that year was Darrell Sampson, last seen alive on April 6.

Five weeks later, on May 14, Randall Reffett disappeared. On the same day, a fourteen-year-old boy named Samuel Stapleton left his sister's place to walk home. Home was one block away, and it was 11:00 P.M. Sam Stapleton and Randall Reffett, who disappeared on the same day, were found buried together in a common grave under the house at 8213 Summerdale. It looked as if they had been killed on the same night.

The body of William Carroll, who disappeared only twenty-seven days later, on June 10, 1976, was the twenty-second body exhumed from the crawl space under the house on Summerdale.

Less than two months later, Rick Johnston, eighteen, never came home from a concert at the Aragon Ballroom in the uptown area. His was the twenty-third body exhumed.

Then it was December, and John Gacy recalled some of

the events leading up to the death of Gregory Godzik. John had a recollection of Godzik and had some knowledge of the death of John Szyc, who disappeared a month later, on January 20, 1977. Gacy could almost bring back the moment of the rope with the two of them, but he saw it only vaguely, in the way a man recalls the sharp, cutting edges of a bad nightmare, one of those dreams where you wake sweating in terror but can't truly recall the horror you've seen in your sleeping mind. It was almost as if he'd been a witness to part of a pair of murders someone else committed. He could envision the boys alive in his house, and then there was a blank time several hours long.

And in the morning, he found them dead. That's the way John explained it to the docs.

The psychologists gave him another IQ test: prison docs were big on IQ tests, as if the answers would prove you were dumb and stupid and that's why you ended up in jail. Except that John wasn't dumb and stupid and he got better on the tests; he got a lot better as he went along.

Even up in 3 North, with all the pressure, the trial nearing, his life at stake, he kicked ass on the same IQ test he had taken in Iowa. On the Wechsler adult intelligence—a test that is given individually and considered by psychologists to be among the best, if not the best method of measuring intelligence—John Gacy scored a 119 in verbal abilities and 129 in the performance aspects. Dr. Thomas Eliseo, the clinical psychologist who administered the test, said the scores indicated that Gacy is "of superior intelligence and about the top ten percent of the population, very bright."

John used his intelligence to evaluate the docs, just as they evaluated him. Cavanaugh, the prosecution's guy: every criminal he ever analyzed, John figured, turned out to be a sociopath. Happy personality disorder, and jail for you, asshole. Cavanaugh didn't give a shit about John Gacy or helping anyone. He just wanted to advance his career, always trying to outsmart John with questions. Just like John remembered Cavanaugh asking him, "If you don't remember these deaths, do you think you have amnesia?"

Fucking amnesia! Actors have amnesia on silly-ass soap operas; people don't have amnesia. At least John didn't think he did. He thought Cavanaugh was just giving him some easy psy-

chological bullshit excuse to cling to—amnesia—and then when
the case got to court, Cavanaugh would show how you couldn't
have amnesia thirty-three times, selectively, or some shit. The
guy was about as subtle as a poke in the eye with a sharp stick.
John wasn't about to help Cavanaugh; this was one doc John
would outsmart when he could. It would be easy enough.

Morrison, for the defense, she was big on his youth; stealing, liking the feel of silk panties and shit, but one day she called
him at Cermak and told him she couldn't help him unless he quit
lying. Morrison thought she could shake him up somehow: your
favorite defense doc quits on you. She was looking to "outsmart"
him. What was he supposed to do, make up a bunch of shit about
things he knew nothing about? Tell her some fairy tale about how
all those assholes who died and ended up in his crawl space?

Either Morrison would come around, or he'd "outsmart"
her, then "fuck over her." You can't shit a shitter. If the docs
wanted to advance their careers studying the guy who was accused of killing more people than anyone else in American history, (if they wanted information for their papers and scholarly
reports) they would do it his way. Who did Morrison think she
was? Life is a two-way street. You scratch my back, I'll scratch
yours.

Rappaport, for the defense, was smart, able to draw correlations between things that made John think. This doc didn't come
right out with his theories, but John could tell, by the tone and
push of his questions, where Rappaport's mind was going. Just
like if John really did hate the Old Man, which was still hard for
him to admit, then maybe there was a kind of thing where he,
John, became John Stanley, dominant over the hustlers, who were
dumb and stupid. Then as the Old Man, he had to teach the
hustlers, who were really him as a young man. Follow that one
through—John took and expanded on Rappaport's questions—to
realize that the Old Man thought teaching was punishment.

So what's the ultimate punishment?

And then where would you hide your secrets? If you were
the Old Man? John felt puzzle parts slipping together with
Rappaport. The Other Guy and the Old Man. Twist those pieces
around. See how they fit together.

Rappaport worked differently from Freedman, who was
the most distinguished of the defense docs. John thought of Freed-

man as "that fucking old man," but it was an affectionate nickname, because John liked him and thought he was tough. Freedman just took everything and picked it apart. "John," Freedman once asked, "do you realize that the phrase you use, 'dumb and stupid,' is redundant?" The doc was right, of course, and John had to sit around thinking how dumb and stupid he sounded saying dumb and stupid all the time. The fucking old man knew a lot and he was closer to the disease, whatever it was, than anyone else. One day Freedman and John were sitting alone in the doc's office, and this little fucking old man said, "Is Jack Hanley in? I'd like to speak to him."

Just like that, at 11:00 A.M. John had to explain that Jack Hanley was a name he used when cruising. The Other Guy might not be named Jack Hanley, if that guy existed, and John, after nearly twelve months in jail, thinking about it, putting the pieces together, was coming to the conclusion that yes, crazy as it sounded, there might be someone else living in his body. It was pretty nutty, but if the Other Guy existed, John didn't know him, much less know his fucking name. Besides, whoever it was hiding inside—you could call him Bad Jack—if he came out, he came out at night, after midnight, when John was drunk or stoned on pills. Maybe you had to make John mad for Jack to come out. You don't just ask to meet him, like you would some celebrity at a party. "Oh, my goodness, isn't that the Other Guy, the one who is supposed to have killed thirty-three people? Could you introduce me to him? I'd like to have a little chat."

Jack didn't come out like that. There were probably special circumstances that caused him to surface, that triggered him. Maybe it was a combination of alcohol and drugs, of fatigue and anger. Maybe the trigger was something the victim did or said, some wrong move that released the killer.

The doc just filed that one away. No expression. He didn't share his theories, and John was never sure what Freedman was thinking. John had to guess about Freedman's theories, but now the tough old fart was asking to meet Jack, and John thought the doc was closer to the truth than the others. Real close. John'd work on it, try to bring the murders in out of the fog.

He warned the docs that he wasn't talking about what he knew, what he really remembered. It was all what John called "rationalization"; it was all "supposition." Just like Butkovitch:

there was a stretch of five, maybe seven hours he couldn't recall. Then Gacy woke up and found Little John Butkovitch dead, the rope tight around his neck.

But, John thought, maybe if he talked about how it "must have" happened, he'd just flow into the Other Guy's thought patterns. With Rappaport and Freedman he'd be a real motormouth, rationalizing and supposing without even thinking about it. Because that's how he remembered one detail he'd forgotten about the Greyhound bus boy. He'd forgotten about the sound of the boy's breath bubbling up through the holes in his chest—"the gurgulation that went on and on"—and he'd gotten that just by going over the story. Telling it over and over again.

Years later, John said that was his technique with the docs who really wanted to help. He tried to motormouth his way into something he'd forgotten, like the gurgulation. If it worked once, maybe it'd work again, maybe he could motormouth his way into the Other Guy's personality.

Just like, if he found a body in the morning—and he couldn't even recall burying some of them—but if he found a body and it was handcuffed and it had a rope around its neck, he'd try to visualize slipping the cuffs on, try to see the rope going around smooth young neck.

Start with the handcuffs. Okay, John Gacy, sometimes when he wanted sex, he handcuffed guys. You could say he raped them, but that was bullshit.

The thing about rape, John explained, is that, in some way, it has to be consensual. Even if the guy does it because of force, it's consent. If the kid has an orgasm, that's proof of consent. When John got some dumb kid cuffed, on his knees, terrified, he had to be sure the kid wouldn't bite it off if John stuck it in his mouth. No one ever tried, so that was consent: the proof was right there between his legs. No one ever bit it off. When they were done—the hustlers and the naïve first-timers—it was fun to belittle them, show them up as the lying little queers they were.

"If you never done it before, how come you know what to do? Huh? How come you're so good at it, you never did it before? Answer that."

Show them they were fruit pickers in their own minds and that they had consented to it.

Later on, right in the same conversation, John would revert to the fatherly image he had over younger kids, offer them a drink, use his Jaycee chaplain voice to explain about morality: "Nothing is wrong unless you make it wrong in your own mind."

Before he got to that point, though, John Gacy had to get the cuffs on them. You couldn't wrestle around with these little assholes, try to sneak the cuffs on, using force. Antonucci proved that in the summer of 1975.

What you wanted to do, you wanted to "plant seeds" in their minds about sex, see how they responded. If the seeds seemed to be growing, the handcuffs came next. Some kids were straight. Antonucci, you could plant seeds all night long, the kid wouldn't go for nothing. But John had learned from Tony Antonucci. There was a better way to get the handcuffs on them. You could trick them.

Just like Michael Rossi, the employee who sometimes clowned with Pogo as Patches the clown: John said Michael was the first one he remembers using the "handcuff trick" on.

There is a problem here: John told this story to the docs and to the cops. He told it to a reporter years later, how sixteen-year-old Michael Rossi was the first to fall for the handcuff trick. During the police investigation of the crimes committed by Gacy, Rossi admitted to investigators that he had a continuing sexual relationship with John Gacy and that the sex was a condition of his employment. When Lieutenant Kozenczak of the Des Plaines Police Department put Rossi on a lie-detector test and asked about the disappearance of one particular boy, investigators felt Rossi was "basically truthful," but the official report read that because of "erratic and inconsistent responses" they were "unable to render a definite opinion." The question here was not sex; it was murder. Could Rossi, after working for Gacy for two years, have some guilty knowledge? Did he know anything of the murders? The state's attorney's office declined to prosecute Michael Rossi. What the boy knew or might have guessed—whether he knew anything at all—was not as important as what John Gacy had done.

Later, testifying under oath, Rossi denied ever having sex of any kind with John Gacy. Under oath, Rossi claimed that Gacy never got the cuffs on him.

Maybe John's story is a fantasy about the perfect employee. A young kid, he wants work, you plant some seeds, slap the cuffs on him, rape him until he shows consent, and then the kid comes back and works for you. That way you can have him any time you want.

Rossi said he met Gacy on May 22, 1976, when he was working with Max Gussis, a plumbing contractor who was helping remodel the kitchen in the Summerdale house. John was putting in a new dishwasher, and Rossi went down to the crawl space to install the waterline. A week earlier, fourteen-year-old Samuel Stapleton and fifteen-year-old Randall Reffett were killed, probably on the same night, and buried in a common grave under the house. It was dark in the crawl space except for the work light Rossi was using, so he didn't notice anything unusual down there. Just sort of a damp, musty odor.

Rossi was doing morning work for Max the plumber at twenty-five dollars a day, but Gacy offered the boy a job at three dollars an hour and promised him a full forty-hour week. According to Rossi, the job interview was held at Gacy's house around lunchtime. Max the plumber was there.

Rossi, who was about 5 feet 7 and weighed 160 pounds, had sandy brown hair. According to Rossi, John planted a few seeds at the first interview, asking the boy how "liberal" he was in regard to sex. Rossi didn't say where Max was while John was planting seeds, and Max later testified that it was two years later when Rossi told him, "John is queer."

Max Gussis said, "Mike, you're crazy. I never seen anything wrong with this man." So Max, who was sitting in on the lunchtime interview, according to Rossi's testimony, apparently missed the reference to "liberal" attitudes toward sex and all that the conversation implied.

Rossi testified that he told Gacy, "I don't want to hear about that stuff," and John dropped the subject. Rossi said he never went back to Gacy's house that night. He said that in the time he knew John, he sometimes saw handcuffs in the house. Gacy, Rossi swore under oath, never put him in handcuffs.

John's story is at odds with Rossi's testimony. He said Max brought two boys to help him with the plumbing work and told John he was going to have to let them both go. John asked which was the better worker and Max said, "Rossi."

John told Rossi he might have a job for him but that he didn't have time to talk just then. As John recalled the conversation, he said, "Tell you what: I'll be done around ten tonight, I'll pick you up by your house."

Rossi said, "I live on the forty-seven-hundred block of Drake."

John said, "Fine. Ten tonight, be standing out on the corner by your house, I'll pick you up. We'll talk about the job."

Rossi was on the corner at ten sharp, and the two drove back to the empty house and discussed the job. Maybe John dropped a Valium. "I told him," John said, "that I was liberal-minded about sex." They were smoking marijuana, according to John, and drinking heavily.

"What would you do if some guy approached you for sex?" John asked.

Rossi, in John's version of the story, said, "I don't know. It never happened." The boy was behind the bar, where the handcuffs were, and he was "fiddling" with them. John said, "Hey, I'll show you a trick. You can put these things on and take them off without the key."

Rossi didn't believe it.

"You can. It's a kind of magic trick."

"Yeah?" Rossi put the cuffs on, snapped them on tight, like John told him, so the trick would work right. "All right, they're on tight," Rossi said. "How do I get 'em off?"

And then John told Rossi the secret of the handcuff trick. "You don't get 'em off. The trick is, you need the key."

Rossi didn't seem scared or upset. "I thought you could slip your hand out or something."

John said, "No way, asshole. And now . . . I'm going to rape you."

Years later, in this version of the story, John described in detail what he did with Rossi, how he stripped the boy, sat on his chest, forced him to perform oral sex, and how he, John, "got into it orally" with the handcuffed boy. There were orgasms and there was no biting, so actually the whole thing was consensual sex.

Afterwards John took the cuffs off and they had a few more drinks and talked, John said, about how it wasn't as bad as people made it seem. Nothing wrong with it: it was bad only if you made it wrong in your own mind. Business, John explained to Rossi, was a process of mutual benefit. You scratch my back,

I'll scratch yours. There were ways a young man could get ahead, make a lot of money, earn promotions at PDM.

It was getting late now, around 2:00 or 3:00 A.M., and John drove Rossi home, telling him they had to be at work early the next morning.

"Eight that morning," John said, "there he was at work." When he caught Rossi alone sometime around eleven, he asked him how he felt about the handcuff trick. Rossi said that when he got home to his mother's, where he was living, he thought about finding a gun, coming back, and killing John.

"So why didn't you?"

John, in this version of the story, recalls that Rossi said, "I need the job. I want to get ahead."

With the docs, John motormouthed through his "suppositions" about the murders.

Randall Reffett and Sam Stapleton disappeared on the same day. Since they were buried in a common grave, is it possible they were killed together, on or about the same time? It stands to reason that if one boy was being killed before the horrified eyes of the other, the second boy would surely flee. Unless he was somehow restrained. Unless the Other Guy knew the handcuff trick before John Gacy.

The conscious John Gacy thought he discovered the trick while raping Michael Rossi sometime during the early-morning hours of May 23. Reffett and Stapleton disappeared on May 14, nine days earlier. Was it possible that the idea—the handcuff trick—rose in John's subconscious mind and surfaced consciously?

The trick worked; that was the only thing John knew clearly.

John Gacy didn't remember William Carroll, who was last seen on June 10. John Gacy didn't remember anything about Rick Johnston, who vanished less than two months later.

John wondered whether there was something about getting the cuffs on these kids, the fact that it was "a trick," that brought out the Other Guy? John thought, "You'd have to be pretty dumb and stupid to let a stranger put you in a pair of handcuffs."

The conscious John Gacy discovered, in the summer of 1976, that the handcuff trick wasn't foolproof. Not yet. He hadn't quite perfected it. At least one more boy managed to fight his way out of the cuffs.

On the night of July 26, 1976, David Cram, eighteen years old, was hitchhiking down Elston Avenue when a chunky man in a silver Oldsmobile station wagon pulled up and stopped. There was a PDM Contractors sign in the window, and Cram, who had been working at a tire-repair shop, asked how a guy got into construction and what it paid. The man, who introduced himself as John Gacy, said he could top Cram's salary. The boy would start out at $3.66 an hour, with the 66 cents going for deductions. If Cram was interested, Gacy said, he should call that evening.

Cram made his call, and Gacy had an employee pick him up. They drove to Gacy's house, where some other employees, all teenage boys, were waiting. They had an urgent job that night, painting Oppie's hot-dog stand. The other boys drove the truck to the jobsite. Gacy and Cram were alone in the Oldsmobile.

David Cram felt that Gacy "built himself up" in the conversation. The contractor said he had a degree in sociology but that his other collegiate degree, in psychology, was "good to have" in his trade because you could "manipulate people a lot easier." A man with a degree in psychology, Gacy said, could talk to you and "plant the seed in your head and let it grow like a forest."

Gacy was talking about planting seeds and "describing his company and how an individual could progress," and then "he just kind of faded into a conversation that he was bisexual." An employee of PDM Contractors, Gacy said, "could progress in the company on their own standings, or morals." Cram understood it to be a "you scratch my back and I'll scratch yours" situation. A guy who scratched John Gacy's back could make a lot more than three dollars an hour.

That was the end of the conversation on bisexuality. It was either then or soon thereafter that Gacy told Cram he was knocking down about "half a million a year and he projected a million for the next year." A lot of money there for someone who didn't mind a little back scratching. Cram was young and "I wasn't too familiar with construction companies at the time." The "image he painted for me," Cram said, "was like, bulldozers and cranes, you know, tall skyscrapers and that's what I thought we'd be doing." They were, however, on their way to paint a hot-dog stand.

Gacy said he had a fully stocked bar and that he didn't

mind if employees came in for a few drinks after work. He said that he had just given a Bicentennial party at his house and mentioned the names of prominent people—politicians, lawyers, judges, "very impressive officials"—who had attended.

They arrived at the hot-dog stand and began painting. John told Cram that if he had any questions, just ask. If he made a mistake, it was his own fault for not asking. Gacy was a perfectionist about the work, but he pitched in and did as much physical work as any of the boys.

Cram worked steadily for Gacy for the next few weeks, and one day, cleaning out the garage beside the house on Summerdale, he found "a couple of wallets with identification in them," and the physical description on the driver's license of one fit Cram pretty well. He never could remember the actual name on the license, but he asked Gacy if he could have it. Cram was underage, too young to buy liquor legally, and he thought he could use the license for that purpose. According to Cram, Gacy "just chuckled it off and said that I didn't want those, those were from some deceased person or something like that, something that had to do with some kind of syndicate." What he did, Gacy said, besides contracting, he worked for the Syndicate. He set people up for hits. He didn't do it himself, kill the poor sons-of-bitches, but he set them up.

Once, after Cram had been slightly late for work, Gacy gave him a watch he said had belonged to "one of the deceased persons" the Syndicate had hit on John's say-so.

After knowing Gacy for some time, many people simply dismissed his more outrageous statements as an odd sort of bragging, self-administered fodder for his big-man complex. Syndicate killings: what impressive connections; I certainly better be careful around you, John Gacy. The man tended to exaggerate.

It's likely Cram didn't take all this assassination talk very seriously either, because on August 20, or 21—a couple of weeks after Rick Johnston disappeared—Gacy told his new employee that because of his recent divorce "he had plenty of space in his house. Three bedrooms." Cram could have one of the bedrooms for twenty-five dollars a week. John made it sound as if the boy would have the whole house pretty much to himself. For only a hundred dollars a month.

Cram moved in on August 21, 1976. The next day was his

nineteenth birthday, and he spent most of the night with a couple of his friends, driving around in a truck and drinking. Cram got back to the house well after midnight, and he was fairly drunk. Maybe a little stoned. Cram couldn't recall if he'd been smoking any dope.

It sure must have seemed like it, though, because when he came in the door, John Gacy was standing there "and he had a clown suit on." All 230 pounds of Pogo, smiling his dark, sharp-pointed smile.

There was no goofy-clown voice that night. John told Cram he was "preparing for the next day. He said he had some kind of benefit, charity to do with some kids, with the clowning, and he thought it would be rather cute if, you know, seeing as how it was my birthday, that he leave the uniform on. . . ."

They moved off to the barroom, a kind of sunken living room in the back of the house, where John's big lounge chair was in front of the TV. Cram was pretty bombed already, but John, still dressed as a clown and acting all jolly, poured them both a couple of hefty shots of pure grain alcohol, the fiery 190-proof stuff. Cram didn't recall if they smoked any marijuana—it wouldn't have been unusual for Gacy at that time of night—but Cram remembers that John took some kind of tranquilizer. A Valium, maybe. John had started taking a lot of Valium. They both had a few more drinks.

Pogo, all made up to entertain kids, was pouring down the drinks, popping pills, probably taking the occasional hit off a joint. Something—the alcohol or the pills, maybe just the costume—turned Pogo into a genuine Jolly Joker then, and he began to perform. Cram said the man in the clown costume "was showing me some of his puppets and so on and so on. Then he came up with a handcuff trick, how you can escape from handcuffs. He demonstrated them, and he shook them off. I was so plowed, I didn't, you know, really pay attention to it."

Pogo asked if David would like to try the trick.

John Gacy told Cram, "Maybe someday you'll need it."

He held his hands out in front of him for Pogo to handcuff him and show him the trick. He felt cold metal tight around his wrists; he saw a big clown face with a dark, sharp smile, inches from his face.

Cram couldn't get out of the cuffs. "The trick was," he said later, "you needed the key." The boy held his hands up to the man in the clown suit, said he was locked in solid, and asked Gacy to "get them off." But the clown "grabbed me by the chain between the cuffs and swung me around the room a couple of times."

Cram was screaming, "Get these off me!"

But Pogo swung him around another time, and John Gacy's voice came rasping out of the dark mouth on Pogo's face: "I'm going to rape you."

Gacy let go of the chain between the cuffs then and Cram stumbled back against the TV stand, but he did not fall down.

Huge Pogo, merry as only a clown can be, lumbered toward Cram. The boy was cuffed, and the clown was going to rape him. Pogo moved slowly, very sure of himself now.

But Cram had spent a year in the Army and knew something about hand-to-hand combat. He kicked high and hard, catching Pogo in the head, smearing the greasepaint there. The clown fell heavily and lay still for several moments. Cram had plenty of time to get the keys and unlock the cuffs.

By the time Pogo could stand, Cram, who had "sobered up" quite a bit, was standing there, both hands free. The boy and the clown stared at each other for a moment. Nothing was said. Except for the paint smudge where he'd been kicked, Pogo looked like one of the sad-faced clowns hanging on the wall in the front room.

Cram said he "went and locked myself in my room."

More "motormouth suppositions" on Gacy's part.

John Gacy, in 1976, knew nothing of the Other Guy. But what if they learned from each other somewhere below the level of consciousness? What if there was a sort of telepathy going on between them? What if the Other Guy knew about John Gacy? What if he was smarter than John and learned from his mistakes?

John "rationalized it out" for the docs:

The conscious John Gacy could use Pogo for a number of things. So then, in the summer of 1976, John Gacy had learned that you could use Pogo to trick people into putting on a pair of handcuffs. This was the conscious John Gacy, who was "totally nonviolent" and interested only in "consensual sex."

But what if the Other Guy was watching, learning all the

time? Just like with Cram—it was a disaster. A smarter John Gacy would have tricked Cram into putting the cuffs on behind his back. Try to kick with your hands behind you; you'd fall flat on your ass. A smarter Gacy wouldn't announce he was going to rape somebody. You want to keep tricking them, outsmarting them.

If the Other Guy was in there—and John was beginning to think he was—then it's possible that he learned from the incident with Cram. The only thing: The Other Guy was "bent on violence." Using Pogo, Bad Jack could trick them into being handcuffed, but with their hands behind their backs.

And that made sense, because that's the way John found some of the victims in the morning: with their hands cuffed behind their backs.

And if the Other Guy tricked them into the cuffs—hypothesis again—he probably tricked them with the rope.

Because John knew something about the other victims: He found them all strangled, ropes wrapped tightly around their necks, fastened with a tourniquet knot John Gacy learned in the Boy Scouts. So the Other Guy was using things John Gacy knew, like the knot.

The Other Guy—Bad Jack—was perfecting the rope trick in the black hours John lost before he found the bodies in the morning. It must have been Bad Jack who killed Godzik in December 1976.

CHAPTER
16

ABOUT A MONTH AFTER he'd moved into the Gacy house, David Cram was sleeping in his room, wearing an old pair of jeans for protection. Gacy occasionally visited him in the night, erection in hand, and the fastened pants slowed him down, gave Cram a chance to protest. This night, as they lay in their separate rooms, Cram woke to a strange sound. Gacy was calling out to him from his own bedroom in a high-pitched singsong voice:

"Dave, you know what I want."

Cram chose not to reply. Later he told police that Gacy came into his bedroom and said, "Dave, you really don't know who I am. Maybe it would be good if you gave me what I want."

Gacy stepped forward, then jumped on the bed and put his forearm to Cram's throat. He was growling, like an animal, deep in his throat. Cram recalled, "I knocked him off me. He came back in and grabbed a hold of my pants and I moved one way and he was moving the other way, and they ripped . . . we fought a lot more, and finally he laid there." Cram told investigators that he managed to straddle Gacy and was about to hit him, but then it seemed as if the older man passed out. Cram pulled his punch, and Gacy regained consciousness. Then, as Cram recalls, Gacy "got up, walked to the doorway, turned around, smiled a little bit, and said, 'You ain't no fun. . . .' "

Cram moved out after that incident. He quit PDM and tried to make a go of his own contracting business.

John now had an empty house again, and Mike Rossi moved in not long after Cram moved out. Rossi paid the same rent as Cram, which was the exact amount John was sending Ma each month to pay off the house.

The way John saw it—having Cram and Rossi stay, paying rent—was part of his "do-gooder" personality. If you looked at it, his house was always open. First there was Roger, from Bruno's, the one Ma thought was "gay"; there was Mickel Ried, the boy who had some sex with John and who caught a hammer blow on the head when he argued about money; there was Cram, hand-cuffed by Pogo; and now Rossi.

John compared himself to one of those animal-lovers who always take in strays. John said he "felt sorry for them, and I liked to help them out."

Rossi was a hard worker who earned his raises, and soon John had him supervising jobs. Rossi became John's right-hand man at PDM. Rossi was ambitious and learned fast. John saw a lot of himself, his own youth, in the boy. He knew he "browbeat" Rossi, just the way his dad had hollered at him, but together they got the work done, on time and on budget. Rossi, who testified that he never had sex with John Gacy, stayed the better part of a year in the house at 8213 Summerdale.

John insists he did, in fact, have sex with Rossi, "whenever I wanted it." It was, as John remembered, the usual bisexual stuff, "no kissing, no fondering," none of that ugly shit. John liked to "dominate" Rossi, order him around—"Get on it, Rossi, right now!" When Rossi wanted something—he didn't have a car and he was forever asking to borrow the truck to take his girlfriend on a date or some shit—John let him know how he could earn the truck for the night. "Get on it, Rossi!"

He taught the boy that one hand washes the other, John said, and sometimes Rossi would do something when he didn't want anything at all from John. In this version of the relationship, John would ask, "Okay, whatta ya want now?" after it was over, and Rossi would just smile. The little fucker was saving them up, like in a bank. He was smart.

Then, according to John, sometimes Rossi would "tease me

with it, get me all hot" and then put in his request before capitulating to John's dominance.

Carol, who was seeing John occasionally, noticed "that Rossi manipulated John and John manipulated Rossi. They were both doing it to one another." The two of them, Carol thought, were "very close," and John told her "that Michael felt like a son to him."

Greg Godzik was seventeen, about five feet seven, slight, and muscular. He went to Taft High and was on a school work program doing afternoon labor at the Republic Lumber Company for $2.35 an hour. Gacy, who shopped at Republic, offered Greg a job at almost twice the salary. The boy lasted just under three weeks on that job, then disappeared.

Greg had been dating a girl named Judy Patterson—he was popular with the girls at Taft—but she was special. As Judy recalls, her old boyfriend and Greg "got into a little jealousy thing," sometime around December 1. Greg went to work looking a little worse for the fight: a few bruises and a cut over his right eye.

On Saturday, December 11, 1976, at about 7:00 P.M., Greg was preparing for a date with Judy. His sister, Eugenia, noticed "he was just very, very concerned on how he looked. He had on new pants, new shoes, and a new shirt. He was very excited about going out."

Judy recalls the date lasted until about midnight; then they picked up Judy's mother, who was visiting friends, and Greg drove them both home. Judy's mother went into the house, and Greg and Judy sat in the car for another half hour. It was the last time Judy ever saw Greg.

When the docs remarked on John's lack of remorse, he told them that he was just trying to figure it out, understand why it happened. He was too confused about everything to feel remorse, and he could talk about the deaths dispassionately, over a prison lunch, as you would talk about a movie you saw a few years ago: images seen as if on an imperfect screen, something that didn't actually happen to you.

Just like Godzik. The kid worked for him for two weeks. John knew Greg was having trouble with a girl and that some older guy laid his head open over her. But John really didn't see Godzik more than five or six hours, all told. The boy was working under Rossi, who was supervising that crew.

John recalled that one day he stopped to see how the Rossi crew was doing, and he heard the boys talking about marijuana. He thought that, the way Godzik was talking, he might have a connection to get some, and John liked to have it on hand. He was beginning to enjoy it himself, but hell, he was thirty-four years old; there was no place he could buy it.

So he got Godzik aside and asked if he could buy any dope. Godzik, according to Gacy's story, said maybe he could get some Saturday.

Sure enough, Saturday night—apparently after his date with Judy—Godzik called John about the dope. There was some confusion about Greg's car: his friends had dropped him off. Could John come pick him up?

So asshole John got in his car long after midnight, picked up Greg, brought him home, and the kid didn't have any dope. They smoked some marijuana that John had and drank quite a bit. John "must have got pretty bombed," because that's the last he remembers of that night.

John "supposed" that maybe he started getting mad at Greg. A conversation such as, "First you tell me you have the dope, then you say you don't." You could theorize that they argued that way, over dope and money. Maybe something inside John came out then, thinking Greg was trying to "outsmart" him.

All theory, though. What John clearly remembers is waking up the next morning and finding Greg with his hands cuffed behind him, a rope around his neck, dead. Godzik, John recalled, was sitting in a chair in the living room, and all he had on was his underwear. He had been dead for some time, and rigor mortis had set in.

John had started sort of a hole for a drain tile in the crawl space, so he dumped Greg Godzik down there and dropped him into the hole, burying the boy's body on its side in a stiff sitting position. Then he smoothed the dirt over and didn't have to think about Greg Godzik again. Not until 3 North.

John told the docs that there didn't seem to be any sex involved with Godzik, as far as he could theorize. Just like the first one—the Greyhound bus boy—was self-defense; the second—

Little John Butkovitch—was about a carpet; and Godzik was about dope.

Whoever was doing the killing, John speculated, wasn't killing them for some sex thing. Spend months looking for a "motive," and John just couldn't come up with a thing. Self-defense. A carpet. Dope. The motive thing was a real head scratcher.

Mrs. Eugenia Godzik awoke early on Sunday morning and went in to wake her son, Greg, only to find that his bed had not been slept in. She called his friends. No one knew where he was. At about ten-thirty that morning, Mrs. Godzik called the police.

Greg's maroon 1966 Pontiac was found parked in a northern suburb. It was his first car, a prized possession, it didn't seem likely that he would simply abandon it if he was going to run away. He had no reason to run away: he and Judy were close; he would graduate in June; he got along with his parents; and he had a good, high-paying job.

About the middle of the following week, Mrs. Godzik called Greg's employer. John Gacy said he had a message from Greg on his phone machine. The boy had called on Tuesday or Wednesday after the Saturday he disappeared and said he'd be at work by noon the next day. He never showed. Gacy told Mrs. Godzik he couldn't play the tape for her because he'd already erased it.

Mrs. Godzik called the police and suggested they talk to John Gacy.

At this time, Marco Butkovitch was still calling the police, begging them to interview John Gacy about the disappearance of his son a year and a half earlier.

Butkovitch was calling the police's Area 6.

The Godzik family was calling the police's Area 5.

There seemed to be no communication between the two departments.

After John Gacy was arrested and charged with murder, Harold Thomas, commander of the Chicago Youth Division, explained to the *Chicago Tribune* how a serial killer could slip through holes in the system: "You must realize that you don't treat every missing-person case [as] a possible homicide."

The Godzik family—like the families of other victims—conducted a private search for their son. They contacted the Salvation Army and other groups dealing with runaways and street people. After six months of fruitless searching on their own, they hired one of Chicago's most famous and expensive private investigators, who also came up empty-handed.

Judy Patterson, thinking Gacy might be able to help her find her boyfriend, visited his house a few weeks after Greg disappeared, sometime between Christmas and New Year's of 1976–77.

Judy said that Gacy "seemed like I was bothering him and he didn't have time for me." She was in and out of the house in five minutes, but in that time Gacy said that Greg had planned to run away and that he had mentioned these plans to his boss. Judy recalls that Gacy said he wanted the name and address of the guy Greg fought with in early December. "I'm in the Syndicate," Gacy said, "and we'll look into this our own way."

Years later, John recalled quite clearly how a seed sort of dropped right out of his subconscious mind. He was up in 3 North, working on a kind of written variation of the motormouth approach to finding the Other Guy: some deal where he had the names of the victims in front of him, the five he remembered, and he was supposed to describe them in adjectives, without really thinking.

When he got to John Szyc—who disappeared on January 20, 1977, about five weeks after Greg Godzik—John was motormouthing along with the pencil, not thinking, and he found himself writing pretty much the same stuff as he did for all the others: dumb, stupid, greedy, naïve . . . and right in the middle of all those adjectives, a name: "Rossi."

John remembers, right away, he stopped and started erasing what he'd written. The doc, John couldn't remember which one it was, noticed and asked him what he was doing. John explained that he was supposed to write adjectives and here he'd written a name: "Rossi." The doc said, "Just leave it."

John wished the doc would let him erase the name. Coming out under Szyc like that, it was almost like an accusation. God forbid that he should accuse someone else of "the crimes," even subconsciously.

The whole thing with Szyc was pretty foggy, anyway. John remembered that it was raining and that he was cruising when he saw this kid walking along and struck up a conversation. This guy Szyc—John remembered the name because later he had to spell it and it was all consonants—said he was about to leave town and wanted to sell his car.

"Oh, yeah," John said. "You got the title?"

Kid walked back to the car, got the title. John said, "Let's go back to my place, talk about it."

They got back to Summerdale, and here John's memory began to fade in and out. Was Rossi there? Did he tell Szyc, "This guy might buy your car"? Or did Rossi come in later? It's possible that Rossi wasn't there at all. John said he honestly couldn't recall.

John knows there was some drinking, some discussion about the car, some talk about drugs, and then there was a long blank period and John woke up at seven-thirty or so to another of those mornings.

There were three people in the house, and one of them was dead. In his mind's eye, John could see that morning as clearly as if it had just dawned. Szyc was lying on the floor in the other bedroom, the rope tight around his neck.

Rossi was sleeping on the couch in the front room. He was still wearing his jacket. John didn't know what Rossi knew about the dead boy, didn't recall what had happened at all. Still, he figured that if Rossi didn't know, he wasn't going to tell him. As quietly as possible, John dragged Szyc's body to the crawl space and dumped it down there. No time to bury the kid just then.

John recalls that Rossi said he'd just gotten in and didn't mention anything about meeting some guy who wanted to sell a car, but the title Szyc brought with him was still on the bar, and John said it was for some vehicle. It was Rossi, according to John, who said, over breakfast, "Well, let's go get the car."

They drove down to Clark Street and found the car, a white 1971 Plymouth Satellite. Rossi drove it back to the house, and by the time they got back to Norwood Park, he was sure he wanted the car.

John recalls that there was an issue of fairness involved. "Michael," he said, "you can have the car, but what do I get out of it? Because that car's worth at least six hundred dollars."

So they argued about the price for a while, and Rossi didn't have it in cash, but John sold it to him, anyway. He let him have it for three hundred dollars, about half of what it was worth, and Rossi paid John in weekly installments deducted from his check.

Just like the Old Man had done when John bought his first car, Gacy put his name on the title along with Rossi's. When Michael paid the entire three hundred dollars, he could have clear title. It was the sort of thing a father does with a son.

The police later discovered that John Szyc's name on the title looked nothing like John Szyc's signature.

Michael Rossi testified, under oath, that he had never met John Szyc. In court, Rossi said that Gacy told him John Szyc was selling his car "because he was going to California."

After John was charged with the murders, after the hints about Rossi's possible guilty knowledge had been dropped, investigators were forced to consider the etiquette of murder. The police and the state's attorney's office didn't believe in the existence of the Other Guy.

Perhaps they worked it out like this:

If Gacy had killed Szyc in Rossi's presence, Rossi could blackmail John for the car in return for keeping the murder secret. Instead, Rossi paid for the car.

If Rossi killed Szyc, how is it that John considered himself the owner of the car?

Rossi's story sounded more credible, and he was never charged in connection with the murders, nor was he charged with any crime in connection with the car.

Gacy seemed to think that whatever it was that happened entitled him to the car. He even kept the things he found in the trunk of the Plymouth: Szyc's clock radio and his TV. The only reason John kept the TV, he said, was that he wanted to give it to Carol for the girls.

It pissed John off: in the nearly two years between the time Szyc died and the day he was arrested, he never got around to taking the TV over to Carol's place. The police found it in his bedroom, and they were going to use it to try to tie John to the death of Szyc.

After his arrest, John told the police the reason he moved Rossi out was that it looked odd, a teenage boy and a man living together. He didn't want the neighbors to think he was strange that way. Rossi found an apartment in April 1977. A woman John had been dating off and on since January, Doreen,* moved in with him toward the end of that month.

Doreen met John at some family function. Like Carol, she was a friend of Karen's. John and Doreen got engaged in the spring of 1977. Neighbors said John seemed happy about his engagement and his relationship with Doreen, but the couple "didn't see eye to eye" from the start.

John had a "sexual relationship" with Doreen, but there were problems. They'd start necking, begin to get undressed, and John was almost ready, almost hard. But she had had a colostomy, a serious operation in which an artificial anus is constructed, and when she took off her clothes, John would feel himself "get soft again."

John thought his problem with Doreen was the result of her colostomy. He couldn't get an erection with her, and it was because he was afraid he might hurt her.

John even went to his doctor and asked about it. The doctor listened to the problem and agreed: John probably had difficulties getting an erection with Doreen because of the operation. That was what John thought from the first, but it was good to have a solid medical opinion backing him up. The colostomy set up a "mental block" that prevented John from having erections with his fiancée.

There were other problems with Doreen, problems not unlike the ones he'd had with Carol. John told people he liked women with backbone, who didn't put up with any shit, who talked back, but Doreen really went overboard that way. She read "women's lib" books, and her mind was all full of those kinds of attitudes.

John's business was picking up then, and he was always working on three or four projects at the same time. He had crews out all over the city and was running himself into the ground trying to keep up. That was the PDM work, but in March, John was hired as a construction supervisor for PE Systems, a firm that

*Name changed.

specialized in remodeling drugstores nationwide. He had to do a lot of traveling for PE Systems, and it was exhausting keeping both businesses running smoothly. "I did almost eighty buildings in 1977," John recalled. He even rehired Cram but still never had any free time. Then clowning and politics stole more of his hours, and when Doreen moved in, he was getting ready to direct that year's Polish Day parade.

The women's-lib stuff got all twisted in Doreen's mind, the way John saw it. She wanted to go out to eat every night, she didn't like to cook, she didn't like to clean up the house. She wanted a housekeeper. She'd ask questions like, "John, why is it that I can't do anything right for you?"

Just like Carol, she wouldn't help with the business, but she'd spend the money. Once, during an argument, John remembers telling Doreen that she wanted all the gravy and none of the responsibility.

Doreen said, "I don't want to be your assistant contractor. You expect too much." John finally had to have it out with her. "Doreen," he said, "this just isn't working out." He told her it would be best if they broke off their engagement. John said he was leaving on a business trip for PE Systems and he'd be gone for a week or so. That'd give her plenty of time to move out.

John said, "Doreen, I want you gone when I come back."

In June of that year, when he came back to the empty house, John knew he was "going through a bad low point." Business was booming, but John felt "confused." He began thinking about Carol, wondering if they could get back together. Carol, he thought then, was the only person who could somehow "save" him.

John told the docs he didn't know who Carol was going to save him from: the house was empty. Ma would come for her summer visit, get on his nerves, and restrict his freedom for a month, but then the house would be empty.

Sometime in August 1977, after Ma had gone and the house was empty again, Michael Rossi recalls that Gacy told him "to go down into the crawl space and dig a trench line for some drain tile." The trench was to be a couple of feet deep and a foot wide. Gacy gave very specific instructions about where to dig and, according to Rossi, "he would actually mark it out with sticks." If someone deviated from the line, according to Rossi, Gacy "would get very upset."

Rossi dug only one trench down there, but he supervised more digging done by other employees, and Gacy ordered that the job be done right. He'd stick his head in the crawl space and holler when someone took a shortcut and dug off-line.

After John's arrest, after he was charged with murder, he told police that he had his employees dig trenches so he would "have graves available."

But that was after the trauma of arrest, after not sleeping for a week, after the shock of being charged with monstrous crimes, and Jack was out then, saying strange things to the police: weird, incriminating, contradictory things that John swore he couldn't remember.

As for the trenches, John, to the best of his recollection, told employees such as Rossi where to dig in very unspecific terms. Sometimes they dug the pits too deep, like they were graves or something, and then, sure, he yelled about the work. You don't need to dig drain trenches that deep.

John certainly didn't want to implicate anyone else in the murders, but what if someone, or some group of his employees, had been killing? Lots of people had keys to the house, and John was traveling all over the country for PE Systems, so what if some kids had a party in the house while he was gone and someone OD'd on drugs? They could bury them in asshole John's place.

That's why John was still mad about the way the state charged him. How could they connect all those bodies to him? Okay, they were in his house, but he didn't remember putting them there. What if someone else did some of them?

The proper charge, John figured, would be "concealing evidence of a homicide." Because, okay, he did remember burying some of them. Say he was charged with every one, even the ones he didn't remember, or the four the state said were "mine," that the cops found floating in the river. John read in some lawbook that concealing evidence of a homicide is a 10-year term. If he served consecutively, that would be 330 years.

Of course, he could always serve it concurrently. That would be 10 years. Just like Iowa.

John figured that if he could just see it whole, understand

it, bring back an image of someone else doing even one murder, it would muddy the state's case. They'd have to amend the charge.

And something in the back of his mind, something floating in the fog, always connected Rossi with Szyc. That's what John told the docs.

If Rossi said John was specific about where to dig in the crawl space, he was lying. John remembered that he really didn't give a shit where Rossi dug.

If the cops were saying he told them he wanted to "have graves available," they were lying. He didn't recall saying that. It was "a self-serving statement" on the part of the cops, a statement designed as part of a frame-up. They had a lot of bodies and needed a "scapegoat."

Because it didn't make sense: if it was during working hours when Rossi dug down there, then he was talking to John Gacy. Not Jack. Jack came out only at night, and then only when John was drunk or stoned on pills. John didn't think Jack, Bad Jack, if he existed, could get a sober John Gacy to provide graves for him. Not in the summer and fall of 1977.

Nothing fit together, but the cops and the prosecution wanted to make it look like a rational John Gacy planned to kill, and they wouldn't admit that the proper charge was concealing. It wasn't fair and it wasn't legal, but the state had John and they needed to convict him of the murders. Because of the publicity. Gacy told the docs he felt like a "victim" in the whole deal.

Aside from John Szyc, the boys who died in 1977 were a mystery to John.

He could recall nothing of Jon Prestige, a twenty-year-old just in from Kalamazoo, Michigan. On March 15, Jon told a friend he was going to take a look at this Bughouse Square place he'd heard about. The boy's body was the first one exhumed from the crawl space under the house.

John told the docs he didn't recall Matthew Bowman, nineteen, who disappeared on July 5, after Doreen moved out.

The victim labeled "body twenty-five" was Robert Gilroy, eighteen, who probably died the day he disappeared, September 15. Gilroy was a horseman and, because he didn't own a car, was hitchhiking to a place called the Blue Ribbon Stables when he disappeared. That would have been after Ma finished her annual summer visit and the employees dug the trenches.

Only ten days later, a nineteen-year-old ex-marine named John Mowery disappeared. Gacy said he honestly couldn't recall how Mowery's body ended up in his crawl space.

Russell Nelson graduated on the principal's honor roll in the small town of Cloquet, Minnesota. He attended the University of Minnesota and, at twenty-one, was planning to get married. Nelson and his fiancée had already picked out the names of their children, but on October 17—less than a month after John Mowery disappeared—Nelson, who was in Chicago visiting friends, did not come back from a disco near Clark and Broadway. His body was found in the wet mud under the house.

The victim labeled "body eleven" was identified as Robert Winch, a sixteen-year-old runaway also from Kalamazoo, who disappeared on November 11.

Exactly one week later, on November 18, Tommy Baling was watching *Bonnie and Clyde* on TV at a North Side bar. He was twenty years old, about five feet eight, and weighed 135 pounds. Tommy left the bar, intending to go home to his wife and infant son. He had been married in a double-ring ceremony, and his wife identified the ring the medical examiner found on "body twelve."

A few weeks later, on December 9, David Talsma—a nineteen-year-old just out of marine basic training and living at home until he got his active-duty assignment—told his mother he was going to a rock concert in Hammond. He left the house at about seven that evening and ended up in John Gacy's crawl space.

John didn't remember any of those boys. Two of them were U.S. marines. How could a guy with his health problems kill a couple of marines? Up in 3 North, the docs gave him photos of the victims to study, but they were a gallery of strangers to John, and he told the docs that he honestly couldn't be sure that any of those boys were "mine." The only one he recalled was Szyc, and he probably remembered him because of the TV set, the clock radio, the car, and the funny way he spelled his name.

Mrs. Rosemary Szyc didn't think her son, John, had run away. The boy had an apartment of his own, a car, a girlfriend. He had left all his clothes in his apartment, and his income-tax papers were spread out on the table, as if he had been working on them. Mrs. Szyc called the police and reported her son missing. The boy's car couldn't be found, and his TV and clock radio were missing from the apartment. Mrs. Szyc supplied the police with those serial numbers. She and her husband paid a month's rent on the apartment and tried not to touch anything in case the police might want to search it for clues.

During the next two years, Mrs. Szyc or her mother frequently called Area 5 police, who told them there was nothing new—they were unable to find a trace of John Szyc.

Sometime in the late summer or fall of 1977, police picked up a young man in a white 1971 Plymouth Satellite. A service-station attendant had accused him of filling up his tank and driving off without paying. The man was Michael Rossi, and he said his boss, a contractor named John Gacy, could explain the problem about the plates on the car.

Gacy talked to Area 5 police, paid for the tankful of gas, and said that a kid named John Szyc had sold him the car in February. It wasn't much of a car, but the kid needed money to leave town.

Not long after that, John Szyc's parents received a letter:
"Dear Mr. and Mrs. Szyc,
"I was unable to locate your son, but I did learn that he sold his auto in Feb of '77 and told the buyer that he needed money to leave town."

The letter was signed by an Area 5 police investigator.

CHAPTER

17

UP IN 3 NORTH in Cermak Hospital, John tried to recall the moment of the rope. He told the docs it was almost like making it up, like inventing a near-murder, but he could pull one isolated incident out of the fog. Some kid, his face so twisted in fear you could almost laugh. Big eyes straining like balloons blown past the bursting point. And John Gacy, moving in slow motion now, fighting his way in, out of the glittering mist. Taking over. Seeing it whole and clear: a boy about to die. And thinking, Jesus Christ, what am I doing?

There was a rope around the boy's neck—a length of ordinary clothesline—and it was fastened on the side, just above the shoulder in the simple tourniquet knot John had learned in the Boy Scouts. Easy to tie, that knot. You just place one end over the other and pull tight: a crossover knot, the first thing you do when tying your shoes. The knot was tight against the boy's neck. John found a broken hammer handle up against the first twist of rope, and it was secured there by a second crossover knot.

One knot, a hammer handle, the second knot. That's all there was to the rope trick. You could turn the handle and control the flow of blood to the brain.

John quickly undid the knot and told the docs he let the boy go. He couldn't even remember if the kid had been hand-cuffed—though thinking about it, John figured he must have been.

And if he tricked the boys into putting the handcuffs on behind their backs, John could "suppose" that he tricked them with the rope. Same deal: "Just one more trick, I won't hurt you." First the handcuff trick, then the rope trick. John figured he must have instilled confidence in them at this point, the way he could with his customers. Just like the time he was asked to build that roller rink, paid fifty cents to get into a skate palace and took notes on construction techniques because he knew nothing at all about building roller rinks. Still, he got the building done in forty-five days. You had to be a good con man in his business, and maybe that part of John Gacy came out with the rope trick. John asked the docs: "What if it was all a game with me? What if it was a game and I let it get out of control?"

It was hard to think about. Everything had "double mean-ings." Perhaps another side of his personality—the do-gooder, nonviolent one—came out as the rope tightened around the boys' necks. Dying, that way, was quick. It wasn't messy, like the first one—the stabbing—with all that blood to clean up, and the boys wouldn't have suffered long. There were no everlasting "gur-gulations." Maybe he gave them the rope trick, this gentle gift, out of compassion. Death came unbidden, just the way John had prayed for it when he was their age. It was a kind of suicide that left no sin on your soul, a dying that came out of the night, like a gift from God.

John could recall dozens of boys he'd had sex with, boys who were still alive, and they'd seemed so lost to him, so afraid of life. He knew what they felt, because he'd suffered in the same way at their age: the shameful desires, the loneliness, the sense of being "different." And hadn't John prayed for a death that came from outside himself? So maybe he was doing them a favor. Maybe he killed them "out of compassion."

All hypotheses.

Compassion and the need to outsmart teenage boys: maybe they were all wrapped up in a bundle with two other aspects of John's personality—John Gacy the alcoholic drinker, and John Gacy the drug taker.

He had to draw it out, define his terms to the docs. An alcoholic, as John saw it, is a person who gets drunk all the time and can't help it. An alcoholic drinker is one who drinks too much on occasion and who may "consequently black out" and not remember what it was he said or did.

So, okay, what if he went into a sort of blackout, then picked up someone at the park, strictly out of "compassion," out of a desire to help? "I could have been trying to be nice to someone." So the alcoholic drinker picks up someone basically as a happy drunk, a drunk who exhibits his mother's virtues: trust, compassion. But the alcoholic drinker would have his mother's major fault: He would be naïve. So—this was John's supposition—when the drinker realized that he was with some hustler who was "really bent on greed," it broke something loose inside him. "My father's side," John said, "could have come out then with my dad's distrust, and his violence, with the idea that everyone is out to fuck over you and you got to fuck them before they fuck you. See, that attitude came out more in my dad when he was drinking." And maybe it came out in John that way. Maybe there was more of the Old Man in him than he was willing to admit.

If you really wanted to examine "the crimes" independent of the sexual component, John thought you had to look at all the drugs as well, you had to analyze yet another aspect to his personality: John Gacy, the drug taker. If drinking to black out didn't develop mistrust in and of itself, maybe all the other drugs he took in tandem worked like one deadly chemical cocktail to bring out "the Other Guy," the killer. John used Lasix, a diuretic, because "I hold water." He popped one pill two or three times a week. He took a prescribed pill, some little brown thing, for his thyroid, and a little yellow pill to curb his appetite. He was smoking marijuana after work with his employees, and with some of the hustlers he picked up.

In 1976, when his divorce from Carol became final, John began hitting the Scotch heavier than ever. He also started taking Valium: at first only one ten-milligram pill a day.

The next year, John said he began dropping twenty-five or seventy-five milligrams of preludins every twenty-four hours. He needed them to counteract the Valium, to speed up, to complement his natural drive. But it was like a seesaw: with all the preludins, he needed more Valium to calm himself down, and in

December 1978, just before he was arrested, John figured he was consuming at least four Valium a day.

The pills were easy enough to get. While remodeling drugstores all over Chicago and as far away as Detroit and Oregon, he would talk to some of the pharmacists about his health problems—his strokes and heart attacks and leukemia—and sometimes they'd give him pills right off the shelf. There was never any need to steal drugs from a jobsite. He could get anything he asked for. Some of the pharmacists talked about how they laid broads in the back room in exchange for drugs. You could get anything you wanted from these guys, and you didn't have to steal. Police and prosecutors tried to say that all the drugs they found in the house on Summerdale were stolen, but John insisted that they were actually given to him by pharmacists in exchange for construction favors.

However he got them, by 1978 John would wake up from two hours of sleep, walk to the bathroom and pop two Valium, a Lasix, the thyroid pill, a seventy-five-milligram preludin, and rush out to put in a sixteen-hour day. Back home he might drop two more Valium, smoke some marijuana with one of the employees, drink half a bottle of Scotch, take a sleeping pill, and fall asleep in his big reclining chair.

And the strange thing: An hour later, two hours, he'd wake up and find himself driving around the park and "not know what the fuck I was doing there." Maybe drugs and alcohol set loose the Other Guy tilt to his personality, the thing inside him that ruined his marriage to Carol, that wanted the house to itself. There was, John told the docs, a lot of the Old Man in the Other Guy tilt. Now, take the Other Guy tilt during a blackout and apply it to some greedy little hustler. You would get an angry, punishing father, an irrational alcoholic father who had to strike out, who thought he had to fuck the world before it fucked him. The corpse would be found in the morning with the dawning of sobriety, and it would be hidden in a father's hiding place, in the basement, to be covered over and forgotten, like a father's helpless drunken ravings.

If drink and drugs set loose the killer, it would explain one thing that John said puzzled him. Looking back on his life, trying to recall the crimes, was almost like waking up with a bad hangover and knowing that you must have done a lot more last night than you remember.

With Butkovitch, John could see only broken fragments of the time he lost in a darkening mist. It was so goddamn crazy, he told the docs, because an image came up, a flashback maybe, but it wasn't at all as if he was seeing it out of his own eyes. During these flashbacks, he seemed to be standing off to one side, like a ghost or something that couldn't talk, couldn't even be seen. One of the figures he saw was a boy, some kid who looked like Butkovitch, but he couldn't really be sure because there was a hazy fog in the room, a glittering mist that flickered like a failing light in a storm. What gave him the creeps was the other figure. "It was me," John told the docs. "Or similar enough in build to be me." When the rope came out, the fog would purple down into blackness, and John never saw the image of himself committing the crime.

He'd been having these flashbacks even before he was arrested, John told the docs, but the witness in him wouldn't go to the cops and confess. How could you turn in an image of yourself seen through a darkening haze? "You'd look dumb and stupid." They'd think you were nuts. So you keep your mouth shut about it. Out of fear.

Same thing with the images John saw in flashback. Same fear. That's why he buried the bodies in his own crawl space, where no one would ever find them. Out of fear.

John told the docs that looking into the fog like that, searching for a motive, was like working on a jigsaw puzzle. The problem was, he had only a few of the parts. There was a smooth, white piece you could label "compassion," and a dark, jagged one you could think of as "outsmarting the other guy." Then you had John Gacy the alcoholic drinker, and John Gacy the drug taker.

There were other pieces, and John began isolating them for the docs. He sat in his room in 3 North, ripping his personality into little shreds he called characters. The first one was "John Gacy the workaholic," the top dog of them all. Other characters included the person who was naïve, the religious person, and the lonely man; there was the guy with the sex drive, the sick person, the politician, and the criminal who was always stealing. You had Pogo, who split into the compassion clown and the hatred clown.

Many of the characters John developed contradicted one another: On one side you had Gacy the miser, the tightwad. On the other there was Gacy the do-gooder, the selfless, community-minded man.

It took weeks to break John Gacy down, but eventually there he was, scattered all over the yellow legal pad, his whole life spread out like a puzzle ready for assembly. And he came to see soon enough that there was a split in the single person he knew as John Gacy: all these contradictory characters were battling with one another, right there on a lined sheet of paper.

You could divide these ill-fitting pieces on two sides—call them right-hand and left-hand. On the right was his mother's side, and the pieces that belonged there were the religious person; the do-gooder; the softhearted person; Pogo the Clown; and the trusting, naïve person. Put sex drive on Ma's side, too, but make it the good, wholesome kind of sex that involves love between a man and a woman.

The left was John Stanley's side. Most everything over there was a contradiction of the Old Man, and John told the docs that in what he was doing in his life, he must have been trying to "destroy the father image." You only had to look at the left-side character pieces to see that. The Old Man hated politicians, so John became a politician. Dad didn't like being an alcoholic, so John became an alcoholic drinker. John Stanley despised drug takers and criminals, so his son took drugs and became a criminal.

There were some good aspects on the left, though. John could be a tightwad, just like the Old man, but in its best light, you could think of that as being thrifty. The distrustful John Gacy could be a con man, sure, but "by the same token, most people are bent on fucking over you," and it's dumb and stupid to imagine that they aren't. Thinking the worst about anyone—it was only being "smart."

When John thought he had the pieces pretty well divided between the right- and the left-hand sides, he took the Bible a visiting priest had given him and sketched in all the characters on the flyleaf. The drawing looked like a big tree with branches on either side. The top dog, the workaholic, was the trunk, and he nourished everyone on both sides of the tree.

John told the docs that the workaholic "derived from never being accepted, never being good enough." And when John thought about it, he realized "I was a slave to myself, constantly striving for acceptance." Little John Gacy yearning for one kind word from the Old Man.

Talking with the docs, John was able to add a few more characters. Pogo was on the right, with Ma, but that was Pogo as a compassion clown. When he was a hatred clown, Pogo belonged over on the left, with John Stanley. And then, sitting there talking with one of the docs, John had another revelation. There was a split in the sex-drive piece! Because, okay, you had sex between a man and a woman, and that was like a sacrament, done with love. But over on the left side, sex could be had coldly and without emotion. On John Stanley's side, sex could even be a hatred drive.

John Gacy on the right-hand side: He wanted to have loving sex with a woman, but goddamn it, the workaholic didn't have the time. Still, there was a physical need, a drive, and the fastest way for "the motor-driven John Gacy to get his rocks off" was to pay for it. Relieve himself and get back to work. But even with a whore John said he felt emotion slipping in there. That and the infuriating thought that he had to waste his time actually trying to satisfy her. He kept slipping over to Ma's side with a woman.

The part of him that simply needed sex and no more, wanted it cold, hard, and fast: sex "reduced to an animal status." The workaholic, with no time to waste, "came down to the point where he could just relieve himself with a male." Some kid on the street, you don't have to satisfy him. There's no "fondering": you don't make love. And you never go back to the same one twice: too much danger of emotional attachment, which is the very thing you're trying to avoid.

That was how John rationalized it, sex on John Stanley's side. He could even put a name on the sex-drive character over there. The guy who went cruising for animal sex with males was named Jack Hanley.

Police reports on his arrest said that John Gacy had drawn a map of the crawl space, dropped his head, as if asleep, and then looked up and said, "Did Jack . . . I see Jack drew a diagram of the crawl space." Well, that was bullshit. John couldn't recall ever drawing such a map. The cops probably drafted it themselves in "a self-serving" effort to make him a "scapegoat." Also, to the best of John's recollection and with God as his witness, he never said anything about someone named Jack. Jack Hanley was just a name he used when he was out cruising for animal sex.

The docs, however, took that seed, Jack Hanley, and let it grow. Freedman was even asking to meet him, like Hanley was actually the Other Guy Gacy found himself fighting during the divorce with Carol. Like the Other Guy was his own person, "a whole other personality" lurking inside, raging against the person he knew as John Gacy. The way John saw it, the docs actually planted the Jack seed in his mind. They brought it up. Now they were going to have to convince him they were right, that Jack was the Other Guy John saw in his flashbacks.

At first John wouldn't accept any of this crazy crap. He told the docs he didn't want to apply that Jekyll and Hyde shit to himself. He didn't even want to think about it because "that's running away from reality." John was committed to honesty in analyzing himself, and he hoped the docs could see that. He told them he wasn't going "to blame somebody else" for something he did. The problem was that none of the docs had been able to convince him he had committed "the crimes," which forced him to examine seriously their split-personality theory. What if there really was someone else inside who killed people and left John to shoulder an unearned guilt?

So, okay, since the docs made the suggestion, he'd consider the possibility that he had "a dual personality." The personality tree, with all the characters branching out on right and left, was a first step in helping the docs pry the Other Guy to the surface.

Even so, it sure was hard to conceive of two people living in the same body. The whole concept was a real brain buster. John told the docs that he had never caught himself actually going from one person to another. Then again, there were long periods of time—hours upon hours—when he couldn't recall anything at all. Every time that happened, the return of consciousness brought him another boy to bury. And then, in flashbacks, John could see the image of himself with some boy he knew was dead, a boy already buried in the crawl space. But the kid was alive in the misty vision, and the two of them, man and boy, were laughing, drinking, arguing. John could see the rope dangling from his hand, see the hammer handle, and then the mist became an opaque fog, thick and black.

*   *   *

Looking for the Other Guy:

Examine the tree, right-hand side, left-hand side. If death was a gift, it was given out of compassion, but the killer clearly couldn't split from John Gacy the do-gooder. The Other Guy didn't belong on Ma's side at all. John concentrated his search on the Old Man's side of the tree.

And it kept coming back to the sex-drive guy, Jack Hanley. Through the haze, John said he could see elements of the drug taker and the alcoholic drinker, the con man, the tightwad, and the criminal. But these characters, in and of themselves, weren't "strong enough or smart enough" to split off into the Other Guy.

Which left Jack Hanley standing alone over there on the Old Man's side. But Hanley was nothing more than a convenient name John Gacy used to hide his identity when he went cruising for animal sex. Like everything else in John's life, though, the name had a double meaning.

John Gacy told the docs he knew all about Jack Hanley. When John got drunk or stoned, Jack came out and went down to the park because John Gacy, sober, didn't have the courage. Jack was just a braver, more aggressive version of John. So how could he split off into someone John didn't know? How could he become the Other Guy?

It was like following a path that kept doubling back on itself, a trail that eventually disappeared somewhere in the fog. That's how John saw it. And then he had another revelation: It seemed as if he had actually been, well—it sounded crazy—fighting with Jack Hanley from the time he invented the name. It was almost as if Jack was a real guy, sort of a semipersonality on the left who had set himself in opposition to everything that was good on the right-hand side. John followed that trail all the way down into the mist, and he used a car he'd bought in 1977 to get there.

"I bought my first black car after the divorce from Carol," John said. A new Oldsmobile Delta 88 that John had stripped of any extraneous attachments except for a red spotlight on the driver's side, a white light on the passenger's side, and the pair of CB antennae on the trunk. The vanity license plate read "PDM 42" for John Gacy's business and his year of birth. The cops were saying that he had tricked the black Olds out to look like an unmarked police car. They said he posed as a cop to pick up boys, intimidate them, kill them.

Not true. First of all, the car looked official, almost presidential, and he could use it for parades and shit. John told Cram that Norwood Park picked up part of the cost because the Olds could be used as "the township car." There were more "double meanings" here: John told the docs, "When I bought the black car, I was fighting the Jack Hanley side." He had been battling the Other Guy about Carol, and after the divorce he was fighting Jack, trying to outsmart him with an Oldsmobile that looked like something a police detective might drive. A cop car.

"I figured," John said, "that no hustler is going to come up to a car that looks like an unmarked police car. That way, if I woke up and found myself cruising the park, I wouldn't be able to pick anyone up. I thought, 'I'll fix the son-of-a-bitch.' "

Look at it in that light: Any doc could see that John Gacy never had that much control over the Jack Hanley part, anyway. Why would you be constantly fighting with yourself?

The black car didn't work as well as John had hoped, however. "Some of the hustlers were awful damn bold," John said. "How do you figure it: prostitutes coming up to a black car like that?"

The workaholic John Gacy, who needed his time, came up with another way to "make it hard for Jack to go down to the park." Gacy stopped carrying cash. There were double meanings here, of course. The boys who worked for him were forever whining about money, asking for advances on their salaries. John didn't like to lie, he said, and he didn't like to pay for work that hadn't been done. The solution was simple: Don't carry money. If John Gacy needed gas—if he wanted to pay for a dinner out—he had his credit cards. You made big purchases by check.

"But see," John said, "on the same token, I was fucking over the Jack Hanley side. Because prostitution is a cash business. Some of them want to see the money up front. You can't show them a credit card or a check."

This is where a second aspect of Jack Hanley came out. "This guy, Jack number two, he figured a way around it," John said. Without a dime in his pocket, the second Jack Hanley could talk a hustler into the big black car with only a promise. But this Jack Hanley, the second aspect of Jack, even outsmarted John

Gacy because he used the car as a prop to get sex free. "See, this guy," John said, "he'd have the kids thinking he was a cop." John had bought the car to fuck over Jack, but Jack was so smart, the car actually made it easier for him to outsmart hustlers. "Jack didn't even have to tell them he was a cop," John said. "He just planted seeds."

Jack was so smart he could even deny being an officer in such a way that the seed erupted like a jungle in a boy's mind. It was a good way to "dominate" hustlers, to "have the master control" over them.

The second Jack Hanley was a tough, streetwise homicide cop who could track down homosexuals, then "cunningly trap them." He was "a genius at what he did," but he "wasn't such a bad guy": certainly not a killer. Jack just "outsmarted them" and discarded them.

There was a *third* Jack that John knew about, another character that split off the second Jack. He was still a cop, the third Jack Hanley, but he wasn't "bent on outsmarting" the boys who hustled their bodies down at the park. He was a good cop, the third Jack. Just like John Gacy on the right-hand side, he admired police officers. It was a tough job with a lot of character roles to play. You had to be a violent person sometimes, and you had to be smart. A good cop, the best sort of officer, has "humanity"; he has compassion for the people he deals with every day, even the scum. A cop can be like an understanding father figure to young boys. He can help them straighten themselves out.

The third Jack was like that. He was a compassion cop.

John could recall bringing boys out to the house on Summerdale and not having sex at all. Sometimes he'd just talk to the kid. If the boy told a genuine hard-luck story, the third Jack might even give him a few bucks out of compassion. But sometimes John Gacy lost the third Jack Hanley in that fog. Sometimes, John told the docs, the boys who came home with the compassion cop died.

In the darkness of the fog, during the time lost to John Gacy, the Other Guy split from the third Jack. John told the docs he was sure of it. But who was he, the fourth Jack? John was blundering around in the flickering darkness of the fog, looking for the killer, and he was armed only with "suppositions" and "rationalizations."

They gave him pictures of the victims, and John spread them out on his bunk up in 3 North. He recognized Butkovitch, Godzik, Szyc, and the last one killed, the one who got him caught, Piest. The rest of them were ciphers.

The only way to think coherently about the boys in the pictures, John thought, was to catalogue their similarities and build a composite picture of the typical victim. One thing, most of the dead boys were of a single physical type. The typical victim was slender, muscular, short. Seventeen of them had been between 5 feet 2 and 5 feet 9, and all had weighed less than 150 pounds. The composite victim was young—twenty of them were under twenty, and the youngest was fourteen; the rest were under twenty-two. The overwhelming majority of them, nineteen of the victims, had light-colored hair: sandy blond, red or light brown. Six had brown hair.

Picture some kid who was young and muscular-looking, with light-colored hair and blue eyes. Why did the composite victim remind John of someone? Who the hell. . . ? It came to him one day, John said, in a flash of insight: Donald Voorhees looked like that! Voorhees, the boy who had outsmarted him in Iowa, who blackmailed him, whose testimony before a grand jury sent him to prison on a ten-year rap for sodomy.

Voorhees had been young, fifteen at the time, and he was short, muscular, with brownish-blond hair and blue eyes. A clean-cut kid—no beard or moustache, none of that dirty hippie shit—Voorhees had this cunning air of innocence about him.

The dumb-looking, dewy-eyed ones, John knew, were the most dangerous. They could use it, the naïve act, to outsmart you. Greedy little bastards with "deviate minds." Healthy boys who wore tight-fitting clothes on a small, tightly muscled frame. Trick minds hiding behind innocent baby faces.

John examined the pictures of the victims, working rapidly through the large stack, shuffling them like a deck of cards. Butkovitch looked a lot like Voorhees. The Stapleton kid, the fourteen-year-old, John couldn't remember him, but he had that dangerous, baby-faced Voorhees look: an innocent, naïve-looking boy with blond hair falling across his forehead. The rest of them didn't look exactly like Voorhees, but every one of the little assholes had something of Voorhees in his face. The eyes, the hair, a smile, the sense of being lost or lonely or troubled—every one of them had that look.

All the victims, John told the docs, were Voorhees.

The composite victim was a key piece of the puzzle, and it fit neatly into its spot on the personality tree John had drawn on the flyleaf of his Bible; it slid right in there next to the breakdown of the various Jack Hanleys. The edges of the composite-victim piece matched those of the piece John was calling the fourth Jack Hanley. Bad Jack. The Other Guy.

The compassion cop picked them up because they were young and innocent. He wanted to help them. But then the "Other Guy switched on."

John's rationalization:

"Remember what happened in Iowa?" Bad Jack says. "Remember how you wanted to help the kid out and he blackmailed you? Remember how he outsmarted you and fucked over you? Remember Voorhees?"

John said he could hear the Other Guy screaming, "This is the son-of-a-bitch who destroyed you in Iowa. Get the motherfucker, now."

That scenario made sense to John, and he began to "theorize" about "a trigger" that caused Bad Jack to split from the third Jack. Maybe the victim said something that Voorhees had said and that caused "the switchover." It could have been something as simple as money. Maybe the kid tried to take advantage of the compassionate cop, tried to outsmart him for money. Then the fourth Jack took over and outsmarted the kid with death.

Another theory: Maybe Bad Jack was still a cop, but not a cop who was "bent on getting his rocks off," like the second Jack. He may have been a cop who hated homosexuality because he knew what it had done to him in Iowa. What if the sex act itself switched on a cop who was "bound and determined to exterminate homosexuals," a cop who wanted to punish boys for prostituting themselves, for tempting him, a cop who killed to reassert his own "manlihood"?

John told the docs he was bringing more and more pieces of the Other Guy in, out of the fog. Even in the fourth Jack, John was beginning to sense some deep well of compassion. This guy could actually have given his victims the gentle gift of death because they were lost, because they wanted to die just the way

John Gacy wanted to die when he was their age. This was crazy in a way, because that meant he was killing himself, committing a kind of suicide, except that a stranger, some boy he'd picked up on the street, had become young John Gacy.

John couldn't get the new pieces organized. How could the victim be Voorhees and John Gacy at the same time? The Other Guy, what the hell, he could be as complicated as John Gacy himself. Maybe he had a dozen or more characters in his break-down, too; maybe he split off into different aspects. Just like there was an aspect of Bad Jack that John began calling "Stanley." No reason. There was just some hazy quality to the Other Guy that John thought of as "Stanley."

When someone pointed out that Stanley was his father's middle name, John said he almost slapped his forehead like a dumb Polack in one of those jokes. Of course: the Old Man! He'd been telling the docs all along that he suspected that there was a lot of John Stanley in the Other Guy.

But if the victim became young John Gacy, and if the killer was the Old Man, then maybe Bad Jack had a father's interest in teaching hustlers right from wrong. Just like John Stanley thought punishment was teaching. And John Gacy, when he took a word-association test the docs gave him, "correlated punishment with teaching." Follow it through: death was the ultimate punishment, the final lesson. You kill someone, now you've taught him: he won't do that again.

This new guy: John told the docs that he didn't think Stanley was another personality. He was only a character part of Bad Jack, just the way Pogo was a character in John Gacy.

Stanley, Hanley—they were the same guy. They were both Bad Jack.

The puzzle was coming together, but John still couldn't see the whole picture. These character aspects of the Other Guy wouldn't fit together in an organized pattern. Did he kill for different reasons? Did he give one boy the ultimate lesson and another the gentle gift? Were boys murdered because they said something that reminded Jack of Voorhees? What if all the character aspects came together in one compulsive bundle at the moment of the rope?

It was almost done, the thirty-seven-year puzzle of John Gacy's life. There were only two things left to do to complete the picture. John had to work with the docs to "find the trigger that makes the Other Guy split off of Jack number three."

If one of the docs could find that switching mechanism, isolate it, he would be able to talk to Bad Jack. Then you could do a breakdown of Jack Hanley, just like the breakdown of John Gacy. The docs could analyze that, the killer's personality, and use it to help John, with therapy. They could take the breakdown to his trial and explain murder to the jury with science. Docs sitting up there in the witness stand saying something like, "After an exhaustive search and with the help and complete cooperation of John Gacy himself, we find the defendant to be suffering from a type of mental illness that involves a dual personality, and we emphatically recommend that he be found innocent by reason of insanity."

Before that could happen, though, the docs would have to find the trigger and pull it. The trial was bearing down on him now, and John knew the prosecution would surely ask for the death penalty. He began a frantic search for the trigger.

Releasing Bad Jack so the docs could talk to him: it was worth John Gacy's life.

CHAPTER
18

ON JANUARY 6, 1978, Chicago police investigator Ted Janus, who worked the homicide and sex detail in Area 6, the North Side of the city, pulled near the house at 8213 Summerdale, spotted the Oldsmobile in the driveway, and noted the license number: PDM 42. Janus went down two houses and parked by the curb, motor running and lights off as he called for a backup unit. Suddenly a portly man came out of the house, got into the big black Olds, and began backing out. Janus put his own car in gear and blocked the driveway. He got out, told the man in the Olds to put his hands on the dash, and placed him under arrest for kidnapping and deviate sexual assault.

The man, John Gacy, listened to Janus read him his rights, then said he knew nothing about a kidnapping and invited the investigator into the house for a drink. Instead, Janus took Gacy to Area 6 police headquarters, where they went into an interview room. Gacy was again advised of his rights and agreed to talk. No, Gacy said, he didn't need a lawyer.

What happened last week, early on the morning of December 31, John Gacy explained, is that Robert Donnelly, this nineteen-year-old kid making the complaint, was walking along Montrose Avenue a little after midnight. Gacy pulled over, offered the boy a lift, and as they were driving, a sexual bargain was struck: They would perform a kind of slavery-sex thing, and Donnelly agreed to a certain price for his services. It was all "consensual."

The "slavery sex" took place inside the house on Summerdale. Gacy said they bound one another with handcuffs and chains and committed various sexual acts using chains and dildos. The slavery continued through the night, about seven hours, and at eight that morning, Robert Donnelly took a shower and Gacy drove him to work. That must have been when the kid got the license number off the Oldsmobile.

Gacy planted an important seed. "I didn't pay the kid," he told the investigator.

Janus had interviewed Donnelly previously, on the day after the incident, when the boy's wrists were still bruised from the handcuffs. The investigator had written up a "basic summarization" of Robert Donnelly's statement.

Donnelly himself recalls that he told Janus and other law-enforcement officials the whole story: how Gacy had impersonated a police officer and pulled a gun to get him in the car, how he was immediately handcuffed. There was no talk of money: Donnelly was neither a hustler nor a homosexual. At the house, Gacy threw a drink in the boy's face, then poured another down his throat. Donnelly said he was raped in various painful ways, that Gacy tied something—he couldn't see what it was—around his neck and choked him. The boy said that Gacy pointed the gun at him and told him there was one live shell in the chamber. Gacy pulled the trigger more than a dozen times until there was a loud report, obviously the sound of a blank. Donnelly said that Gacy, using only his hands this time, choked him until he passed out. When he came to, he was still cuffed, and there was some sort of gag in his mouth. He remembers telling the officers that his head was thrust into a bathtubful of water until he passed out. Donnelly said the man held his head underwater, nearly drowning him like that, four times. The man, John Gacy, kept him on the brink of death all night long. Donnelly, in fact, was in so much pain he had begged the man to kill him.

A lot of this wasn't in the "basic summarization."

After listening to Gacy's version of events, Janus called in assistant state's attorney Jerry Latherow, who talked with both Robert Donnelly and John Gacy in separate interviews. Janus asked that charges of kidnapping and deviate sexual assault be brought against John Gacy, but Latherow refused.

One witness said the "slavery sex" was a matter of mutual consent.

One said he was viciously sodomized, terrorized, nearly killed.

The state's attorney noted that Gacy had, in both versions of the story, first offered the boy a drink. He had driven him to work in the morning. Gacy was too "nice."

Donnelly, by contrast, appeared to be mentally unstable. Actually, he had recently completed therapy designed to relieve stress after his father died. Donnelly, the eldest of eight children, had to take care of the family by himself. He entered therapy because his doctor "noticed I was having a stress buildup." He was still in shaky condition when he met John Gacy.

Worse, Donnelly spoke slowly, with a kind of stutter.

Gacy, on the other hand, was intensely fluent, the owner of a prosperous business, and a respected—indeed, an influential—member of the community in which he lived. The man had political connections.

Latherow found evidence of Gacy's sodomy conviction. Still, it would be impossible, the assistant state's attorney thought, to get a felony conviction on the latest incident. In his summary report, Latherow found "too many difficult matters to believe in Donnelly's story." Gacy was a "better" witness. "Even though Gacy had a sex-offense conviction several years ago," Latherow concluded, "he was much more credible than Donnelly."

If Bad Jack—or whatever you wanted to call the Other Guy—felt like torturing some boy nearly to death, then releasing him, he couldn't have chosen anyone more suitable than Robert Donnelly.

Call it Bad Jack's little trick on Asshole John: Release the bad witnesses; let the space cadets complain to the cops. John Gacy would have to outsmart the police to save himself. Just a little message from Bad Jack to John: "Don't fuck with me, asshole."

The way John was beginning to see it, 1978, the year he was finally arrested, was a time of conflict: John against the Other Guy, each out to outsmart the other, each one looking to take over.

*   *   *

The Other Guy knew John. Asshole John, the goody-goody, could plant seeds, pull "a reverse" when he needed it.

Just like a few years before, driving back from Schaumburg a little drunk with his mother, John was doing a hard seventy miles an hour when a cop pulled up behind and started beeping. A state trooper in an unmarked car: John would have seen him five miles back if he hadn't had a few J&Bs. The only thing to do was bluff it out.

Bad Jack probably remembered that reverse as well as John, who could recall the conversation with the cop nearly word for word. "I waved him on," John explained. "Moved over a lane so he could pass. Guy stays right on my ass. I step on it, go on up to seventy-five to get out of his way. The guy puts on the revolving light, and he's beeping like crazy. So I start waving over my head like, 'Go on by, ya son-of-a-bitch.' We must have gone fifteen miles like that: he's got the red light going on his dash, and the siren's screaming. I turns to Ma, I says, 'I think he wants us to stop.' "

Just before the place where 90 runs into the Kennedy, John pulled over. The cop walked over to the car, steaming. John looked up and said, "Damn, I got to get my mother here to the hospital."

The cop said, "Yeah?"

"Yeah. She's got a heart condition. I'm taking her to Resurrection, right down on Talcott. I don't get her there on time, anything happens to Ma, it's your fault. You want to stand around, you better give me your name."

John laughed, remembering the whole thing. "Shit, I reversed the whole thing on him. I says, 'I want your name and your badge number, because if anything happens to my mother, I want to know who to sue.' "

The cop walked over to Ma's side of the car and asked her if she was all right. John's Ma is fair, and she can find excuses for bad behavior, like the tumor that pressed on her husband's brain when he was drinking, but Ma is straight-out honest and doesn't lie. Fortunately, John had been driving with the window open, and Ma was half frozen, so she said, "I'm just so cold, I feel numb."

John explained how the feeling came over him then. His

mother was sick, and he needed to get her to the hospital. The poor woman was numb, for Chrissake, and this cop wanted to stand around and bullshit. John exploded.

"That's it, damn it!" he shouted, righteously angry. "I'm taking my mother to the hospital RIGHT NOW!"

The cop walked around the car, grabbed John's arm, and said, "You better watch your mouth, buddy."

John said, "Now you're putting your hands on me? Do you know who the fuck I am?" In Chicago—more than any other city in America—that question can give a cop pause. He looked at John, then looked at the new Oldsmobile with custom plates.

"Just lead me to the hospital," John said, backing off, giving the cop an out, using psychology.

"I can't do that without authorization."

"Well, just let me get my mother to the hospital. Can't you see how sick she is?" John recalled how he felt the tears beginning to burn in his eyes then. His Ma: her heart. How he loved her.

"Yeah, okay," the cop said, "just drive a little slower on the way. You're almost there."

John turned off, on his way to Resurrection, in a hurry to get medical attention for his mother, and when he was sure the cop had gone, he pushed the big Olds up to eighty and started laughing. Almost gave Ma a real heart attack. "I feel numb," she says. Shit.

Reversed the whole damn thing on that cop.

Just like in Cermak, John reversed a priest there. John asked to see the first one, but he sure felt like an asshole because he had to ask, "Father, can you confess to something if you don't even know you did it?" John recalled that the priest told him the Church didn't "require a confession if you have no knowledge of the sin."

"God knows what's going on," the priest said, and John didn't make a confession.

That priest didn't give John any pressure, but the next one they sent him, when he got sick in April 1979, John had to show him his place. "By the time he left," John remembered, "he was asking me to forgive him. I told him he was overstepping his bounds as a priest."

"I says, 'Do you believe in God?'"

"He says, 'Of course.'"

"I says, 'Why do you think I need God just because I'm down and out right now? Don't you think about God when you don't need him for nothing? That's the trouble with the world. People only think about religion when they need it. You should thank God for the good days and he'll be there in the bad ones.' "

John said that "I switched the conversation around on him. And he actually did, he asked me to forgive him. Because he wasn't sure he was being Christian."

John told this pushy priest that God is around all the time; anyone can feel him. "I had this priest second-guessing himself," John said years later. "He thought I needed him just because I was in that situation, and I told him, 'Bullshit, I got God around me all the time.' "

John told the priest that his religion was something he lived every day, not something he turned to in hard times only. If that was why the priest had come, John said, "Then I don't need you." John "proved that I had stronger faith than him. And he left feeling like an asshole, I think."

To "work a reverse" with the psychiatrists was a little tougher, though.

John recalled one of his sessions with Doc Freedman, "when we were trying to get the Other Guy out, and I jumped his ass because we weren't spending enough time. I said, 'You have to get me going, and that takes time. Especially because the Other Guy don't come out unless I'm taking Valiums or drinking. He don't come out in the day. He don't come out until after midnight.' I says, 'You'd have to get me drunk, get me mad to have the Other Guy come out and then he could tell you about all those assholes in the crawl space.' " If the rules said they couldn't look for Bad Jack with Scotch and Valium, John thought, then they had to put in hour after hour: they'd look for the Other Guy using time.

John said, "Doc, I come all the way over here to your office in chains, and you been late twice. What is this shit? You got no reason to be late. We can't get the Other Guy out because we don't spend enough time and then you're late."

John recalled that he looked around at Freedman's office and saw that it "was totally disorganized." The whole place needed to be remodeled for efficiency, and John explained to the doc how work is done. "First of all," he said, "in any job, you are not late.

Because you're getting paid. If I was doing this office, I would not be late." John felt his mind going so fast that he skidded right by his point, and he was off, motormouthing about work. "And if you came in and told me to do the shelves before the floors, I'd tell you to get the hell out. Of your own office. Because when I do my work, we do it my way. That's just how I am. Then later, if you don't like what I did, or you want it done some other way, then we can talk about it. But don't try to tell me how to do my job when I'm doing it."

John remembered that Dr. Freedman just looked at him and very softly said, "John, taking that all into consideration, you should remember that I'm the psychiatrist and you're the patient. That's why we're going to have to do it my way."

Years later, the memory of that confrontation still made John laugh. "He reversed me, that fucking old man."

Although some of the jigsaw puzzles John did at Cermak took over a hundred hours, it took longer to fit the pieces of his life together. He had been in 3 North for almost a year before he could see that in 1978, his last year as a free man, he was actually at war with himself. John Gacy and the Other Guy, fighting for dominance.

After breaking up with Doreen, John Gacy had begun seeing Carol again, hoping they might be able to get back together. There was a thought in the back of his mind that he could give up PDM, liquidate his assets. The whole family could move somewhere, some small town where there wasn't a park, a place to cruise, and they'd open a fried-chicken place, Brown's or a Kentucky Fried. It would be a family operation, with the girls, Tammy and April, helping out. The young employees—employees John would have nothing to do with sexually—could take over in the night shift so that the family could be together, at peace, in the evening. In the night. No more Pogo. No more politics. No more parades. He'd pour cement in the crawl space, sell the house, start a new life. Maybe they'd go down South, someplace like Arkansas, where things were slower and he could be closer to Ma and Karen. John Gacy wanted a close family life down there, in the South, with no place to cruise.

John said that was his plan in the spring of 1978. Get away

from the park, from Uptown. Get back with Carol. Live at peace with himself.

The Other Guy didn't like that. It was like the Other Guy said, "Why fuck up a good thing?" And he gave John another little warning in the spring of 1978.

On the night of March 21, 1978, Jeff Rignall, twenty-six, left his girlfriend's apartment in New Town. Rignall—who later testified that though he had sexual relationships with women, he preferred men—was the sort of proud, unashamed gay man John Gacy called "a faggot."

Rignall had just had an argument with his girlfriend about their relationship, and he stepped out to have a drink and think it over. As Rignall started walking, a big black Oldsmobile with spotlights and antennae pulled into a driveway, blocking his path. It was a cold night, but the window was rolled down and the driver said, "Hey, where did you get such a good tan?"

"I just got back from Florida," Rignall said.

"Where you going?"

Rignall said he was going to a local bar frequented by gays, and the man in the car said, "Hop in, I'll give you a ride." The driver was holding a joint, about to light up. Rignall figured the man would offer him a toke on the way to the bar and he stepped around the car—noticing a customized license plate: three letters and two numbers—in order to get in on the passenger side.

The driver seemed friendly enough, and Rignall figured him for one of those poor suburban guys with a wife and kids, some guy who couldn't admit his homosexual tendencies and cruised New Town in the dark, looking for sex. It was sad the way some of these guys hid in the closet. They came into the gay bars, and they were almost pathetic in their efforts to fit in.

The driver was talking about his property in Florida, just a normal conversation, and he passed the joint to Rignall, who hit on it and passed it back.

They were driving toward the bar, and when Rignall turned to accept a second hit off the joint, he was hit in the face with a wet cloth or dishrag. "It had a cold feeling to it," Rignall said, "and I immediately started having like a buzzing-bee sensation in my head, and I went unconscious."

Chloroform, a heavy, toxic fluid with an etherlike odor,

can be used as a general anesthetic. It is also a good solvent that contractors use in cleaning buildings to be remodeled.

When Rignall came to, he found himself strapped to his seat and saw "amber lights going out the car window above, like they were a spaceship flying by, one right after the other." The lights of an expressway. The driver put the rag over Rignall's mouth and nose again, and he passed out. Once, when he regained consciousness, Rignall noticed an exit sign: "Cumberland." Chloroformed again, he felt his head bump against the window as the car turned left off the expressway onto Cumberland.

When Rignall awoke, he felt that the man was "carrying me. My head was against some kind of screen door. . . ." Rignall felt the rag again, and when he woke, he was on a couch. There was a bar in the room, and a picture of a clown above the bar. Little Christmas-tree-type lights were blinking around the picture. The driver was fixing a drink, and Rignall asked, "Why did you do that to me?"

The driver "came back with a very stern, deep tone in his voice and said, 'There is a gun under the bar and I'd just as soon kill you as look at you.' "

The man—Rignall could see now that he was very fat, pear-shaped—walked toward the couch and lit up another joint. He seemed entirely relaxed and even offered Rignall a hit. The second time he passed the joint, the man fell on top of Rignall and put the dishrag to his face.

The driver was slapping him in the face, bringing him to consciousness once more. Rignall had been stripped, and he was restrained in a kind of pillory device: it seemed to be a flat wooden board with three holes in it. His head was locked into the hole in the center of the board, his arms were extended and locked into the holes at either end. The device seemed to be affixed to the ceiling with chains. Rignall felt that his feet were locked into another device.

The driver was standing in front of Rignall and was nude, and masturbating, talking all the time, "making it clear" to Rignall "that he had total control of me and he was going to do what he wanted with me, when he wanted, and how he wanted, and he had the power over me." Rignall noticed the man's stomach protruded almost over the genitals—folds of fat there—and veins and stretch marks covered his belly.

On the floor between them, Rignall saw "several long leather whips curled around wood and leather handles." Some of the metal instruments looked like fireplace tools, and they were scattered among several plastic and rubber dildos.

The driver forced Rignall to perform oral sex and ordered him to say, "I love it, I love it."

Rignall felt the rag over his face again. When he woke, his face was burning from the chloroform. The driver "picked up one of the instruments, told me what he was going to do with it, and started injecting it until I showed physical pain. . . ." Rignall tried not to moan or scream; somehow he felt that might excite the man.

"You love it," the man said. "I want to hear you say you love it." It was a voice full of contempt. Another, larger instrument was shoved roughly into him.

"Say you love it."

The rag went back over Rignall's face.

When he came to again, Rignall felt the driver's "head on my shoulder. He was behind me and inserted something anally. I believe it was himself. And there was someone on his knees in front of me."

All Rignall could see of the accomplice was that he had brown hair and that it was parted in the middle. When the one in front realized that Rignall was conscious, "I was put out again."

Rignall woke in the snow at the base of a statue of Alexander Hamilton in a park near where he'd been picked up. His pants weren't zipped up, and he "was in total pain. My face was burning, and I was really unaware of what had happened to me at that time."

Rignall managed to get back to his girlfriend's apartment. His face was badly scarred, and he was bleeding. He reported the rape to the police, then spent a week in Grant Hospital, where he was treated for facial burns, rectal bleeding, and pain. Later Rignall discovered that the chloroform had severely damaged his liver.

The police told Rignall they could do nothing with the information he gave them. There were thousands of black cars with spotlights and customized license plates in Chicago. Rignall, however, "wanted revenge." He and two friends rented a car and spent a month parked by the Cumberland exit off the Kennedy

Expressway. They were waiting for the Oldsmobile sedan John bought to fuck over the Other Guy.

Jeff Rignall is, perhaps, an easy man to underestimate. A reporter who interviewed him after Gacy was arrested said, "He comes on sort of dingy, a little spacey." Just the kind of guy Bad Jack turned loose to teach goody-goody John a lesson.

John Gacy had absolutely no recall of the incident, and it seemed awfully farfetched to him. Sure, the police had found a bottle that might have contained chloroform in his house; John used it as a commercial solvent. But you wouldn't use it to kidnap someone. What if a cop stopped you? How would you explain a guy passed out in the seat, the smell in the car? The Jack John knew, either of the first two Jacks, would never use a gun, never carry drugs in the car.

And then what about this "rack gadget"? John never had anything like that in the house. And the blinking lights around the clown picture: cheap shit you'd see in some wop bar or something. John wouldn't have blinking lights around a picture. Jesus.

And who was "the guy with brown hair parted down the middle" supposed to be in front of Rignall while "I was poking him in the ass"? Rossi had brown hair and parted it that way: so did a lot of guys. Sometimes John, calling himself Jack, got into three-way sex—all by consent—with a pickup and an employee.

But John had no recall at all of Rignall. John didn't like anal sex. John didn't have a rack. John would no more use chloroform than he'd use a gun.

What John figured is that this Rignall was a friend of some hustler John might have neglected to pay. The two of them—this disgruntled hustler and Rignall—could have gotten together and cooked up the rack-and-fireplace-poker story to sue John Gacy. Rignall might have been a guest at one of the summer yard parties; John never knew everyone there. That's how Rignall could describe some of the house.

That was John's main theory on Rignall: It never happened.

But what if it did? Say Rignall's story was even partially true. John "theorized" that the Other Guy, from what he'd been able to "suppose" about him, would "be smart enough" to let Rignall go because there was a witness present. Some employee, maybe, or a second pickup, who might report a murder.

Or maybe Bad Jack planned it that way to outsmart John, since the Donnelly thing had been so easy. Two potential witnesses. A clear warning: "Stay away from Carol and the kids."

In late April 1978, Rignall and his friends finally spied the big Olds pull up off the Kennedy onto Cumberland and followed it to 8213 Summerdale. The license was PDM 42: three letters, two numbers. Rignall gave the license number and address to his attorney, then notified the police.

At the Area 6 station, where Gacy had been questioned on the Donnelly matter only three months before, Rignall was told that Gacy had a sex-offense conviction in Iowa and that the police would get a mug shot for him.

"At that time," Rignall said, "they asked me if I was gay. I was honest with them. I said, 'Yes.' From that point on I got no cooperation at all."

Rignall called the police daily, sometimes twice daily, about the mug shot. After two or three weeks, he was allowed to look through several books of mug shots. He identified John Gacy because "I will never forget his face."

After positive identification, Rignall met with an officer and an assistant state's attorney who clearly didn't believe his story. "When I started getting into the physical aspect of what the man had done to me," Rignall recalled, "they began to make me believe *I* was the crazy one, that he was quote unquote a model citizen."

Once again, an assistant state's attorney at the Area 6 police station refused to charge John Wayne Gacy with a felony. Rignall was told that he could issue a civil assault warrant if he liked, and on May 7, 1978, Rignall's attorney wrote Gacy informing him that Jeff had issued a warrant for his arrest.

The letter might just as well have been signed by the Other Guy. Not that John was aware of Bad Jack's existence in the spring of 1978. "The conscious John Gacy" knew only that "I was just constantly fighting with myself. I was thinking: Do what you want to do. But then I didn't know what I wanted to do. If I woke up cruising, I must have wanted to do that somewhere inside my mind. Even though I hated what I was doing, I must have wanted it, or I wouldn't have been doing it.

"But then Carol and I were becoming close again. It's so hard: everything has double meanings; I loved her and thought she could save me, but then I had to protect her, too."

John hadn't been to bed with Carol since the divorce, but one spring day in May—just about the time John Gacy got a letter from Jeff Rignall's attorney—they drove up to Wisconsin with the girls, a family again, enjoying the warm spring weather, the sense of a world reborn, everything new, the promise of summer. They got home at about nine that night, and Carol remembers that "John and I had both, I think we were looking very forward to the time again to be together, and we started, tried to start to make love. And John broke down and cried.

"He couldn't do anything and he said it didn't have anything to do with me, that he waited for this, for the day for me to be back in bed with him. And he said he was afraid he was going the other way.

"Well, when he said that I just figured that he was having sex more with men and couldn't do anything with a woman anymore."

Years later, John Gacy would look back at it as the worst moment of his life. He could still feel the pain of failure, of weakness, and he remembered the tears, like surrender. . . .

"Going the other way."

It wouldn't work with Carol because Bad Jack was beginning to take control, able now to bubble to the surface whenever he wanted. The Other Guy: he took what he wanted when he wanted it, and he destroyed what he hated. At that moment of failure with Carol, Bad Jack killed John Gacy's dream of a new life. The bastard destroyed everything: the little restaurant in the South, a quiet family life with Carol and the kids, a decent work schedule. No more drugs, no more cruising, nothing bad . . .

John cried, and it was as if something inside had ruptured and he was in physical pain. Carol didn't know what to do, "so I held him and he cried. We just didn't—he didn't talk anymore, and I just let him finish out his crying, and that was it. We ended up going to sleep."

CHAPTER
19

WHILE JEFF RIGNALL WAS going through mug shots, Gacy was making preparations for the most important parade he'd ever direct. He even had Secret Service help on this one. It was the Polish Constitution Day parade, and it consisted of fifty-four floats, twenty bands, and, as John recalls, "twenty thousand marching Polacks," though the actual number of marchers was closer to half that.

The parade was held on May 6. Rosalynn Carter, wife of the President of the United States, was a special guest of honor, on hand to improve her husband's relationship with the Chicago Democratic machine. As far as John was concerned, he told friends one night, she was just another of those political flies buzzing around the big turd. No—he wanted to take that back—the parade wasn't a turd. Or if it was, it was clockwork turd: two hours, exactly, of precisely positioned Polacks hitting their marks when John cracked the whip; Polacks like lions hopping through hoops. It was the best ethnic parade in Chicago, and John was proud of the job he did.

Because Mrs. Carter would officially review the parade along with about fifty others, John recalled that "the Secret Service came from Washington." There were, John doesn't remember, half a dozen, maybe more of them, gray guys in gray suits who wore sunglasses on gray days so you couldn't see their eyes. He sat with them around a big conference table, and together they hammered out the protocol for the parade.

And John told them—maybe he was bragging a little bit about this little speech, exaggerating—he said, "Goddamn it, there's a wrong way, there's a right way, and there's my way. I been running parades for fifteen years, I been running this parade for three years, and this is gonna be done my way."

It was a matter of attitude and experience, and John let Mrs. Carter's Secret Service contingent know who was running the show. He thinks they respected him for that, for telling 'em they could can the big-deal White House shit right there because John Gacy was the man in charge. "Look," John said he told the Secret Service, "this is how it's going to be done. . . ."

John was wearing his special "S" pin, a sign that he'd already been cleared by the exhaustive Secret Service check-out procedure. The Secret Service was expected to examine the credentials of the fifty or so people who'd officially review the parade with Mrs. Carter, and of the dozens who'd meet her later at a reception in her honor at Daley Center. Gacy's name, Social Security number, and birth date were all on a list given the Secret Service.

As is standard procedure, this list, including Gacy's name, was checked for subversives, criminals, and potentially embarrassing crazies known to local Secret Service and FBI agents. The name "John Wayne Gacy," apparently, was run through the National Crime Index. Years before, upon his parole, Iowa had provided Chicago police with Gacy's record as a felon and convicted sex offender.

Somehow John Gacy slipped through the interstices of the system, and the Secret Service decided he was a fit man to meet Rosalynn Carter.

The "S" pins, indicating clearance up to and including personal contact with the President's wife, were sent to the Polish National Alliance and distributed before the planning session in which John told the guys in the gray suits how it was gonna be.

Later, probably bragging a little bit, John described how the guys in sunglasses tried to take the whip right out of his hand on the day of the parade. "Mrs. Carter," one of the assholes told

John, "is ready." The guy had a little electronic gadget in his ear and said, "The motorcade is on the way. Let's be ready when she gets here."

The way John explained it later, he really lit into this Washington jag-off. "Hey," John said, "look at the fucking program here. What time does it say the parade starts? Does it start at eleven-fifty? Huh? Does it start at eleven fifty-five? The motherfucking parade starts at noon sharp, so you get on your little gadget there and tell Big Rosie that this bastard starts at noon. She can sit in the car, she can ride around the block, I give a shit, but she gets here at noon sharp . . . and then the fucking parade starts."

John said he got a lot of compliments about how he ran that parade. Cops coming up to him and telling him it was more military than the marines, which, as John probably pointed out, had been his branch of the service.

Later that night, at the private reception for the President's wife, John Gacy shook the First Lady's hand. A picture was taken. Both Gacy and Mrs. Carter are staring at the camera and not at one another. Mrs. Carter wore a white blouse, scarf, and cardigan sweater. John Gacy wore a dark suit and tie, with his security clearance button worn rather low on his left lapel, over his bad heart.

Mrs. Carter signed the photo:

To John Gacy
Best Wishes
Rosalynn Carter

A little later that month, toward the end of May, John and Carol had what amounted to their last date. The two of them were having a drink in a North Side bar called the Good Luck Lounge. Carol recalls that "John asked me what type of fellows did I think that he would have anything to do with. He said, 'You know, look who is in here, look around who is in here and pick them out.' "

Carol understood that John's question was a sexual one: Which of the young men in the bar would he want to "have sex with"? Carol had overheard one of John's phone conversations in which he mentioned these preferences, "so I picked out a few

fellows, most of them had light-brown hair, medium-brown hair."
John agreed; it was a good guess on Carol's part. He told her he
liked boys with "light hair, had buttocks kind of firm, small, they
were small build. Not real big built, not big boys."

Almost a year later, after John had been arrested and the
bodies exhumed from under the house where she had once lived,
Carol realized Little John, John Butkovitch, "had that kind of
build." His body, recovered under the cement in the garage, had
been grotesquely twisted to fit the tiny grave where a storm drain
should have been.

"Maybe," John said later, "I should have asked Carol for
help. But I didn't think she was strong enough, and I tried to
protect her from it."

That's why he buried Little John in the garage, to protect
Carol. That and the fact that there was a small drainage hole
there, already half dug.

In the spring of 1978, seven months before John was
finally arrested for the murders, there was a groundbreaking
ceremony for the retirement center where he had built the refreshment stand and donated his trucks and clowned with Rossi to
raise money. Now John Gacy the politician took care of the gate
and controlled traffic. Michael Bilandic, then mayor of Chicago,
was there for the ceremony, and John asked a friend to take a
picture of the two of them shaking hands.

That was the photo the police found in John's office.

Rignall couldn't get the police to serve his civil warrant on
John Gacy. He "was calling the police department on a daily basis
and becoming totally frustrated because they were totally neglect-
ing it." One officer told him Gacy's house was "too far of a drive."
Rignall, who weighed 150 pounds when John Gacy picked him
up, now was down to 110 pounds.

After two months of excuses from the police, Rignall drove
out to the house on Summerdale. Ma, back in Norwood Park on
her annual summer visit, opened the door. It was July 15, the
morning before a party, and Ma's hair was done, dyed brown, Jeff
thought, and her lipstick was neat and freshly applied.

Ma said that John wasn't home, that he had taken the van
to get the dog clipped.

"Are you coming to the party tonight?" Ma asked. She was very pleasant.

"Are you kidding me?" Jeff said.

The woman, still pleasant, still smiling, invited Jeff inside. John would be back shortly. "I'm John's mother," Ma said, and Rignall could hear pride in her voice.

"I don't know if your son told you," Rignall said, "but there's a warrant out for his arrest."

Ma let the screen door slam and said that John's business dealings weren't her concern. Jeff could come back later, talk to him then. And suddenly Jeff wanted John Gacy's mother to know about her son, really know him. He wanted to tell her about the chloroform and the rack. "Do you know," he began, "your son was convicted of a sex crime in Iowa?"

In a book Rignall subsequently wrote about his experience with John Gacy, Rignall said that "the woman's face turned a bright crimson and [I] could see it harden. Her voice came out harsh and cold."

" 'That was years ago,' she said firmly. 'We don't talk about that anymore. Anyway, it was a bum rap.' Then she slammed the door in [my] face."

Rignall went back to his car and a little later saw the van pull in. He called the police and gave the warrant number. Eventually, entirely at the insistence of Jeff Rignall, the police did come. They couldn't find Gacy, but a young gentleman with brown hair parted in the middle came up to Rignall and "asked me if I would please not say anything about the rape to John's mother."

Rignall wasn't going to give up.

John, however, figured he wouldn't need a lawyer to reverse the little bastard in court. He filed a countercomplaint that charged that Rignall had "without legal justification made physical contact of an insulting nature with John W. Gacy, by shoving him with his hands and shoving a bottle of Rush in his face."

Rush is a brand name for isobutyl nitrate, a liquid whose fumes, when sniffed, are thought to intensify sexual pleasure. Rush, sold in head and porno shops, is perhaps more popular with the gay than with the straight population.

"See," John said, "I figured if I charged him, the complaints would cancel one another out and the case would be thrown out of court."

Rignall's lawyer had a copy of the complaint filed against John Gacy by the boy who had been taken to Northbrook, the one who said that Gacy, impersonating a police officer, had picked him up in June 1972 and tried to run him down in the car.

Gacy had countercomplained that the kid was trying to blackmail him because of a sexual encounter.

Back in 1972, the complaints did indeed cancel one another out, and the case was dropped.

Rignall's lawyer thought pretty much the same thing would happen with the criminal case against Gacy when it came to court on September 13, 1978.

On that date, Rignall and his lawyer met early at the courthouse and went to "felony review." The criminal charge against Gacy was still a misdemeanor—punishable by a one-hundred-dollar fine—and Rignall wanted to get it bumped up to felony assault, which would make the civil case in preparation stronger.

The state's attorney who reviewed the facts, like the police investigator, seemed "hostile." Rignall later testified that the "state's attorney stood up, took the file, and said, 'What the hell. This is only a butt fuck. People get shot in this city and they're not charged with a felony.' "

When the case was called, Gacy was not present, and the same young man who had asked Rignall not to talk about rape with Ma—the one with brown hair parted down the middle—appeared for the defendant and said that Gacy was in New York on business. It was a stroke of luck for Rignall. Had John been present—taken the thing more seriously—it is likely both complaints would have been dropped.

In his absence, Rignall's lawyer got Gacy's countercharge dropped, and a warrant was reissued.

Meanwhile, Gacy got his own lawyer to reply to the Rignall civil case against him, and the matter was settled out of court. Gacy paid Rignall three thousand dollars. Rignall's lawyer thought that was the best they could do, though Jeff's medical bills ran to twenty-five thousand dollars.

*   *   *

A month after an assistant state's attorney decided that John Gacy was "too nice," and a "more credible" witness than Robert Donnelly—the boy who claimed that Gacy had choked him into unconsciousness and nearly drowned him in the bathtub four times—a muscular nineteen-year-old named William Kindred disappeared from Chicago's North Side. Kindred was 5 feet 8, weighed 155 pounds, and had ash-brown hair. A tough, streetwise boy, Kindred lived in the New Town area, where he was known as "Shotgun." Only three months before, Billy Kindred had gotten engaged and planned to marry Mary Jo Paulus as soon as he landed a good job. There were no rings exchanged, but Mary Jo had given Billy a religious medal on a chain. On the night of February 16, Billy left Mary Jo's apartment. She noticed that he was wearing the chain around his neck. Back at his own apartment, Kindred told his roommate that he was going out to a bar.

When Billy Kindred didn't call the next day, Mary Jo was worried. For the next few weeks, she drove around the New Town area, asked after her boyfriend, and posted information-wanted posters throughout the neighborhood. Finally, along with Billy's mother, she went to the police and reported him missing.

A half year after the arrest of John Gacy, in the summer of 1979, sheriff's police officers asked Mary Jo if she could identify some articles of clothing and a piece of jewelry. She said the belt buckle looked like the one Billy had on the last time she had seen him; the chain was a Catholic medallion, the gift she had given to her fiancé. Billy "Shotgun" Kindred was the eighteenth identified victim.

There were ten other bodies recovered from the crawl space under the house, and one other found buried beneath the barbeque pit in the backyard. Police and coroner's officials were unable to identify these bodies before John Gacy went to trial. As one prosecutor said, "All we know is that they were boys. All we know is that they ended up in Gacy's graveyard." The victims remained unknown perhaps "because they were from out of state, maybe because they were drifters, maybe because their dental or medical records were never sent in because their parents just didn't want to know that they ended up at Eighty-two Thirteen Summerdale."

Burial and periodic flooding in the crawl space had slowed putrefaction of the bodies, but applications of lime and muriatic acid had macerated them, so there was no way even to estimate a time of death for the unknown victims. John Gacy couldn't help; he said he remembered nothing of the unidentified boys. "I don't even know if they're mine."

What he did remember, what he told police shortly after his arrest, was that the crawl space was filling up, and digging new graves, bent over in that confined space, was hard on his health. Imagine pitching over with a heart attack and dying right there in a grave dug for someone else.

The last four victims definitely attributed to John Gacy were not buried at all. They were found floating in the Des Plaines River. All of them had been thrown from the bridge on Interstate 55, an hour and a half drive south of his house. Gacy had crammed the corpses into the trunk of his black Oldsmobile and tossed them into the dark waters of the Des Plaines River in the dead of night.

Police called the last four bodies "floaters," and the first of them was identified as Tim O'Rourke. One night in mid-June of 1978, O'Rourke told his roommate that he was going out for cigarettes. His body was found about two weeks later, floating face down in the Des Plaines River, six miles downstream from the bridge on I-55. O'Rourke, who stood 5 feet 9 and weighed 150 pounds, was a tough, dark-haired boy who idolized the late martial-arts movie star Bruce Lee. O'Rourke had a crude tattoo on his left biceps that read: "Tim Lee."

Dr. Munesh Ahluwalia performed an autopsy at the Blackburn Funeral Home in Joliet, Illinois. Ahluwalia said the body was "that of a young white male," but the changes, "the gross changes attributable to putrefaction, characterized by peeling of the skin," led some police officials to conclude, from the name "Lee," that the dead boy might have been Chinese, and they scoured Chicago's Chinatown, asking about a missing person.

Several months after the arrest of John Gacy, Donita Ganzon, a presurgical transsexual, read a newspaper story about the unidentified body. Ganzon, who had lived with O'Rourke for three months, recalled the "Tim Lee" tattoo. She also remembered that O'Rourke had talked about a contractor on the Northwest Side who might have a job for him. When Ganzon asked if this contractor was gay, O'Rourke just smiled. The contractor's name was Gacy.

Dr. Ahluwalia, examining O'Rourke's body on June 30, 1978, concluded that it had been in the water for "approximately seven to fourteen days or longer." Tim O'Rourke was murdered a few weeks after John Gacy posed for a photo with Rosalynn Carter; he was killed a week after John Gacy was photographed shaking hands with the mayor of Chicago and less than three weeks after John failed for the last time with Carol, failed and fell sobbing into her arms, sure then that he was "going the other way."

John Gacy's fifth annual yard party, the Italian Festival, was held in July, and it was the largest gathering yet, with more wealthy clients and influential politicians in attendance than ever before. It was a bitch to organize—just to find the time—considering all the work John was doing for PDM and PE Systems. He was constantly on the road for PE, remodeling drugstores across America. He estimated that he covered nearly sixty thousand miles in 1978. In the first week of February, he was in Woodburn, Oregon, and arrived back in Chicago on the seventh, nine days before William Kindred disappeared.

In early April, before the Polish Day parade, he worked in Brainerd, Minnesota, and Pompton Lakes, New Jersey. John did two stores in Michigan, one just outside Detroit, where he took a side trip to Windsor, Ontario. Then, in late summer, after the death of Tim O'Rourke and after the Italian Festival, he did a four-day job in Knoxville, Tennessee.

Back in Chicago, in September, John struck up a business relationship with a fellow contractor named Richard Rapheal, who had just organized his own company, Rafco Incorporated. Rapheal was remodeling and building retail stores, and he asked John to subcontract his drugstore bids. Gacy did the carpentry, the fixture installation, and acted as superintendent on a number of drugstore jobs being done at the same time.

There had been no known deaths—no boys killed at John Gacy's hand—for almost five months.

John theorized about this fact, this marked contrast to the holocaust of the previous year. Perhaps the do-gooder in him, the Asshole, knew—somewhere below the level of consciousness—that the Other Guy had been set loose in late May, when John Gacy failed with Carol, when his dream of a clean new life died. Could it be that he was working himself into the ground, outsmarting Bad Jack with fatigue? John knew only that he didn't do much cruising in those months. What with his work for PE Systems, PDM, and Rafco, with his political duties to fulfill, the yard party, and his clowning to think about, John was "too tired" to set the black Olds spinning down to the park. Let the docs chew on that one. No boys died for five months; John just "didn't have the time."

And then, at the beginning of November, John learned that Carol was getting married. Her decision was irrevocable, and the killing began anew.

On November 3, Frank Landingin, a nineteen-year-old who was known to hustle drugs and to pimp, was released from jail, having made bond on a battery charge. Landingin had been arrested several times, mostly for assault and auto theft, and this charge had involved an assault on his girlfriend. At about two in the morning of November 4, Landingin met his father, Francisco, in a North Side bar. Frank told his father he was going to look for his girlfriend, apparently to make up. Frank Landingin was last seen walking west on Foster Avenue, just off Broadway, at about three in the morning.

Eight days later, the body of a young white male was found floating in the Des Plaines River, downstream from the bridge on I-55. The victim had been gagged with his own underwear before or just slightly after sex, and something, perhaps the gag itself, or, more horribly, some unbearable external stimuli, had caused the victim to retch and drown in his own vomit.

After exhumation of the bodies under Gacy's house, police saw a familiar grisly pattern: The underwear gag was a Gacy trademark. Twelve of the victims had died not of strangulation but of asphyxiation related to clothlike gags shoved deep into the throat. The body found floating in the Des Plaines River on November 12 was the thirteenth victim to die choking on his own underwear. He was identified as Frank Landingin.

Less then three weeks after Landingin disappeared, a short, brown-haired, twenty-one-year-old man from the suburb of Elmwood Park had Thanksgiving dinner with his family. James Mazzara was living with friends on Clark Street, three blocks from Bughouse Square, and when he returned to the city, he found that he'd been evicted. James Mazzara, who called himself MoJo, was last seen alive walking alone in the direction of Bughouse Square, carrying a suitcase.

A month later, the body of James "MoJo" Mazzara was found floating in the Des Plaines River, only a mile downstream from the I-55 bridge.

Financially, 1978 was the best year yet for John. He expected to report about two hundred thousand dollars in gross receipts. He owned three new vehicles: a Chevy van, a pickup truck, and a new black Olds. PDM, PE Systems, and Rafco were all off and running, moving ahead on their own momentum and John's own considerable drive. He looked forward to doubling his gross in 1979: close to a half-million-dollar year.

Politically, John had solidified his position in North Side Democratic circles. No need to brag, to exaggerate: John Gacy had clout.

The Rignall and Donnelly matters had been settled with a minimum of fuss. A quarter-million-dollar-a-year businessman, a precinct captain, with clout, could reverse a fruitpicker or space cadet in any cop house in the city. Barring a bad mistake, something dumb and stupid, John Gacy was bulletproof.

There were the bodies to consider, of course, and just after the Christmas holidays, in January 1979, John planned to pour about thirty yards of concrete in the crawl space. Cement one foot thick, covering everything, "but not," John told the docs, "because I thought there was anything buried there." The concrete floor would eliminate his seepage problems, and get rid of the musty odor, the bad, dead smell that rose out of the crawl space when it flooded; the faint, sickly sweet odor that filled the house on hot summer days. The concrete would strengthen the foundation so John could build a second story onto the house. Make the whole place into a recreational palace. John thought he might install a whirlpool and a sauna on the second floor. Just lie back in the Jacuzzi after a hard business day. And down below, under a foot of concrete, there'd be a nice little secret.

That way, with the concrete down there, he could start a new life. The past would be over and done. No one would have to think about it again.

*   *   *

On December 11, 1978, John Wayne Gacy killed his last victim, a fifteen-year-old high-school sophomore named Rob Piest.

The boy died between nine and ten o'clock at night, and witnesses who talked with Gacy slightly before the murder said he was neither drunk nor on drugs. Gacy even took two business calls while the boy was dying, and the men who talked to him said he seemed calm and rational.

John couldn't understand why the Other Guy came out with Piest: it sure didn't look like the same guy who had to get drunk and stoned to kill; the one who killed in the early-morning hours, who covered everything as he went along.

The murder of Rob Piest: it was dumb and stupid. Atypical. Not like Bad Jack at all. To get caught.

CHAPTER
20

ROB PIEST, A FIFTEEN-YEAR-OLD sophomore at Maine West High School, loved woods and rivers, all the wild places of the Midwest. He was two merit badges shy of becoming an Eagle Scout, and he planned to earn scouting's highest award with a community service project that involved cleaning up a portion of the Des Plaines River. He was a good student—on the honor roll as a freshman—a passionate outdoor photographer, and a member of Maine West's gymnastic team. Rob was a developing athlete, a boy of medium height with a gymnast's trim, muscular build and supple grace. A good-looking young fellow with shaggy brown hair, Rob tended to date girls a year or two older than himself.

Rob's mother, Elizabeth, regularly picked her son up at school after gymnastics practice and drove him to his part-time job at the Nisson Pharmacy in Des Plaines. The drugstore was only eight blocks from home, but Rob's schedule was so tight that his mother usually brought a dinner for him to eat in the car on the way to work.

The boy worked almost every night, often filling in for other employees when they called in sick. In only four months at Nisson, he'd managed to save nine hundred dollars, which he planned to use as a down payment on a Jeep. With a four-wheel-drive vehicle, Rob could get out into the wilderness more often, take more photographic safaris. It was going to be tough, though; he was making only $2.85 an hour at Nisson, not nearly enough to cover payments on the kind of vehicle he wanted. Worse, he'd just been turned down for a raise. Rob would be sixteen, old enough to drive, in three months. There wasn't much time.

On December 11, 1978, Elizabeth Piest picked Rob up at about 5:00 P.M., a little early, and they had time for a quick dinner at home. It was his mother's forty-sixth birthday and the family would wait on the cake and ice cream until Rob finished work at nine that night. He arrived at the Nisson Pharmacy a little before 6:00 P.M.

John Gacy was really running. It was another "drugstore day," and he was checking out jobs all over the city, pushing his new four-door Olds 98 hard. The first black car hadn't stopped Jack, and John never could explain why he hadn't given up the stratagem, why he traded that car in for a second black Oldsmobile, a Royale, equipped, like the first one, with red and white spotlights and a CB antenna.

By three in the afternoon of December 11, John had already put in an eight-hour day. He knocked off for an hour to visit at Northwest Hospital his Uncle Harold, who had been so helpful to the family when John Stanley was sick. He was John's favorite uncle, a goodhearted guy who "took the brunt" of John Stanley's rages.

At Northwest, John learned that Harold had slipped into a coma and wasn't expected to live through the night. It was two weeks until Christmas, the beginning of another hollow holiday season. The Old Man had died the day Christ was born: died of shame, John knew, without a son by his side to comfort him. Because of Voorhees. Now Uncle Harold was passing on and there was nothing John could do, nothing anyone could do about the dark season, about Christmas.

John left the hospital at 4:00 P.M. He felt "a little depressed." Goddamn bells ringing all over the city, carols on the car radio: sounds of death and shame. Christmas.

An hour later, at five o'clock, Richard Rapheal talked with John Gacy on the phone. A Rafco business meeting was scheduled for seven that evening. Rapheal wanted to introduce Gacy to another superintendent and discuss a job that was supposed to start the next day.

Gacy said he'd be there, at Rapheal's house in Glenview, at seven sharp. Rapheal said he'd order John a pizza.

Phil Torf, the co-owner of Nisson Drugs, Rob Piest's employer, had called John Gacy that day and asked him to stop over and "give me an assessment of how my store was put together." About a year before, Gacy had enlarged the store and "given it a general face-lift." Torf wanted to do some "minor rearrangement." Gacy wasn't much of a craftsman in Torf's opinion, but he knew the pharmacy business—knew, for instance, which items to stock on the top shelves and how to funnel people through the impulse-buy aisles to the pharmacy counter in the back. Torf thought the contractor was ambitious and a bit of a braggart, but he got the work done fast.

Half an hour after his conversation with Rapheal, Gacy walked into Nisson Drugs. It was about 5:30 P.M. He made some measurements, then talked with Torf for over an hour. Gacy wanted sixteen hundred dollars for the job, but the pharmacist said he thought he could do the work himself. Maybe Gacy could just give him a little advice. The two men were standing by the pharmacy counter in the back of the store.

Rob Piest came in at about six, walking to the back of the store, near the pharmacy, where he sat down and began putting price tags on merchandise to be stocked.

"Looks like you got a new crew," Gacy said. "A lot of new faces." He was looking directly at Rob Piest, who was near enough to hear the conversation.

Torf said he hired "a lot of high-school kids," but they usually went on to college or full-time jobs.

"I've been hiring a lot of high-school boys to work for me," Gacy said. He glanced over at Torf's new stockboy.

Rob Piest didn't say anything.

Linda Mertes, who worked at Nisson Drugs, remembered Gacy from the work he'd done there in 1977. She talked briefly with the contractor when he came in, did some work, then joined

Gacy and Torf by the pharmacy in the back of the store. She stood just in front of Rob Piest.

Linda asked Gacy about Mike Rossi. "He's doing much better now," Gacy said. "I started him at two or three dollars an hour. Now anyone who works for me starts at seven dollars an hour."

"Hey, Rob," Linda said, "you want a job?" It was a joke, and neither Gacy nor Piest said anything. It would have been bad form with Phil Torf standing right there.

"I never talked to the Piest kid," John said. "I went in, measured the store. I was there for a couple of hours. And we were just bullshitting about old times." There were some seeds dropped, though. "We started talking about money," John said. "Okay, I know the kids were listening, but I never offered any one of them a job. The Piest kid, I never mentioned anything about a job. But I knew he was pissed off about what they paid him there." John didn't say how he knew that.

After the seeds were dropped and Torf rejected his bid, Gacy left Nisson Drugs, at about seven. Torf noticed that John had left his appointment book on the desk behind the pharmacy counter.

Where the hell was Gacy? He'd never missed a business meeting before. It was after seven, the pizza was cold, and Rapheal had two other guys, just sitting there waiting for Gacy. There was no way even to get ahold of the contractor: every time he called the house, Rapheal got the phone answering machine.

"It was snowing," John said, "so I went back to my house to change vehicles because I had to do some plowing. I cleared my phone machine and Phil Torf had called, said I left my appointment book there."

Phil Torf told police that he never phoned Gacy about the book. He was adamant on that point.

John didn't recall any messages from Rapheal.

"Nisson Drugs is on the way to Glenview," John explained. "I figured I could pick up my book, then drive out to Glenview for my meeting." This is the only reason he went back to the drugstore.

*   *   *

Sixteen-year-old Kim Byers was working Nisson's check-out counter near the front door. It was a cold night and every time a customer opened the door, Kim caught a blast of frigid air. Rob Piest's parka was draped over the counter, where he'd left it after taking out the garbage. It was a blue Pacific Trails parka, and Kim put it on against the cold.

At about seven-thirty, when business was slow, Kim took some photographic negatives out of her purse. They were photos of her taken at a homecoming dance. Kim wanted reprints and enlargements to give to her sister for Christmas. She tore off the top receipt—number 36119—and absentmindedly put it in the pocket of Rob's parka. She filled out the photo logbook with the date and put the envelope in the "to be developed" bag.

John Gacy parked his black Chevy pickup in front of the liquor store near Nisson Drugs. The plow on the front was pointing out, toward Touhy Avenue. It was a little after eight. When he walked into the store Phil Torf said, "Forgot something, huh?"

John said, "Yeah."

Even though he was over an hour late to his meeting in Glenview, John began walking up and down the aisles, measuring shelving, examining the construction. "I thought I might work a deal with Torf," John explained. "He could do the work, I'd supervise. He'd save some, I'd still make some."

John figured he might be able to help Torf bring the job in cheaper if they used some of the leftover shelving from the last job. That's what John said he was looking for in the back of the store at about eight-thirty. There was a door open and John could see the new kid, the one who was pissed off about his pay, kneeling in the snow and folding boxes. They were alone back there, and John asked the kid about the shelving. The boy didn't know anything, and John swore with God as his witness that was the only time he talked to the kid. Just asked him about some shelving.

About ten minutes later, sometime around eight-forty, John Gacy left Nisson Drugs. He was almost two hours late for the Rafco meeting, but he sat out in the parking lot, by the liquor store, for at least ten minutes. John couldn't recall "what the hell I was doing. I must have been writing down figures, which is a standard thing to do after you leave a client."

While John Gacy was sitting in his truck, "writing down figures," Elizabeth Piest arrived at Nisson Drugs to pick up her son. It was eight-fifty. Rob was on the register at the front counter and had ten more minutes to work. Elizabeth Piest began browsing to pass the time.

Just before nine, Rob asked Kim Byers if she could take the register for the rest of the night. He said he wanted to go "talk to that contractor guy about a job."

Rob was now wearing his blue parka. Kim had entirely forgotten that her photo receipt was in the pocket.

A moment or two later, Rob found his mother walking down one of the aisles and said he would be a few more minutes. "Some contractor wants to talk to me about a summer job," he said.

"No problem," Mrs. Piest said, "I'll browse around the store and I'll wait for you."

Elizabeth Piest noticed that Rob was wearing his parka.

The cops and prosecutors wanted to make it look like John talked to the kid in private, offered him a job, then waited for him outside in his truck. The truth was, John said, that he was writing down figures. Why would you sit there waiting for a kid you talked to once about some goddamn shelving?

John snapped his notebook closed and was about to pull out onto Touhy when Piest came running out and banged on the hood of the truck. Or maybe it was the window. John wanted to be totally accurate, not make anything up. He knows he rolled down the window. The kid asked if there was a summer job available. Some shit like that.

Ten seconds later, John would have been gone. But the kid came out to talk to him on his own initiative. Was that John Gacy's fault?

"I ain't got time to talk about it," John said.

Still, the kid seemed ambitious and he looked so eager about the job you could almost feel sorry for him. "Well, hell," John said, "get in the truck. I gotta pick up something at my house. Then I got a meeting in Glenview. I'll drop you off on my way."

It must have been John Gacy who picked up Piest, because John remembers the conversation pretty clearly. He told Piest that he couldn't hire a fifteen-year-old, and the kid started getting "pushy." Greedy. He kept after John, talking about what a good worker he was and shit. John finally said, "You need money that bad, you ought to hustle your body, make money that way."

The Piest kid just let that one whiz right on by him. Didn't even respond to it. He kept "pushing" about a job. But John had planted the seed, and the kid hadn't actually said no, so maybe he was receptive. He could be one of the sneaky ones who had to be convinced with money. Or with tricks.

"John Gacy was with the Piest kid twenty minutes," John told the docs. Then—and this was "supposition"—the Other Guy came out and "fucked over the kid." But why did he come out so early, at nine-thirty in the evening, and when John was almost dead sober? It sure was hard to figure. Maybe it was "because Carol had remarried," John said. "I think I felt torn apart by that, like I had nothing to live for anymore. And when we got to the house, I cleared the phone machine and learned that my uncle had died. I was upset about that."

Even so, the Other Guy wouldn't have come out unless Piest gave some indication that the seed was growing inside his mind, and John could see "he was into it." That would bring out one of the three Jacks: either the guy who "just wanted to get his rocks off," or the one "who tracked them down and tricked them," or the one "who felt sorry for them." There had to be a trigger somewhere: money, sex, something.

The kid didn't say anything about how it was his mother's birthday. That would have been a whole different trigger. It was "speculation," of course, but "because of my respect for mothers and motherhood," John figured, "I probably would have given him a present for her and taken him home."

But the kid just wanted to talk about a job, and John figured Piest pulled the trigger on Jack during the conversation they had about money in the house. John recalls that they both had a drink. The kid drank 7-Up—wouldn't touch liquor—and he sat at the bar. John had a Scotch.

He asked the kid if there was anything he wouldn't do for the right price and Rob Piest said he didn't mind hard work, that he'd do just about anything for money.

That sounded like a hint, and John planted a few more sex seeds, but Piest was "totally unreceptive." The kid just sloughed off the sex talk and kept pushing about a job even after John told him PDM didn't have any openings right then.

"You want to earn money, there's good money in hustling," John reminded the kid. Piest ignored that one, too. "He never responded to anything that involved sex."

Piest asked about the clown pictures on the wall, as if he were trying to change the subject and get friendly all at the same time. The handcuffs were on the bar, near where the kid was sitting, and "he picked them up and started fiddling around with them."

"What are these for?" Piest asked.

That was the question, John figured, that probably triggered the second Jack, Smart Jack, the guy who outsmarted boys for animal sex. Because, okay, you've just been talking about hustling, about making money that way, and now the kid wants to know about the handcuffs. One of the sly ones, pretending he doesn't have a clue. A kid, you could tell by his build, by the color of his hair, what was going on in his mind. Acting naïve so he could earn more money. A trick mind behind the baby face. The Voorhees look about him.

That must have been the way it happened, John figured, because the next thing he knew, Smart Jack was showing Rob Piest a trick with the cuffs, telling him to put them on behind his back.

"Why," John asked the docs, "if you had just been talking about sex, would you let a stranger talk you into putting on a pair of handcuffs? If you weren't into it?" The docs and the cops and the newspapers could say that Piest was some kind of superstraight-arrow kid until "they're blue in the face," but John wouldn't believe it. Not after the kid put the cuffs on himself.

"I'm going to rape you," John heard Jack tell the kid, "and you can't do nothing about it." It wouldn't really be rape, though, because there was no force involved and the kid put the cuffs on himself, which showed consent.

John would have gone with it that way—one of those consensual rapes engineered by Smart Jack—but there was a mist now, swirling in wispy shards around the images moving through his memory. He does recall unzipping the kid's pants. "And I seen he wasn't into it at all. He was scared at this point. He had tears in his eyes, and you can't get no erection like that. Well, I had the meeting in Glenview and I had to go to the hospital about my uncle, so I thought, might as well take this kid back. We had just been horsing around with the cuffs, and if the kid told anybody, it would have been my word against his."

John led the handcuffed boy into the bedroom, but he really didn't know why they went in there, and the mist had thickened into a fog that was beginning to obscure his recollection. "Why would I take him into the bedroom if I was going to let him go?" John wondered. "The only reason: I think the key for the cuffs must have been in there because I always kept it in the top drawer of the chest by the bed." John—he figured the boy's tears switched on the character John knew as the third Jack, the guy who felt sorry for them, the compassion cop—went into the bedroom with the full intention of taking the cuffs off Rob Piest. That's what he told the docs.

The bedroom was dark, but light from the barroom streamed through the open doorway. In the darkening fog, Piest looked like one of those black cardboard silhouettes. Not even a human being. It was too dark to see if the cardboard boy still had tears in his eyes. The last thing John recalled before the fog filled the room with darkness, he was reaching around inside the drawer, looking for the key.

Then there was, John said, a sense of some time lost to the darkness—only a few minutes—and he must have snapped right out of it because the next thing he recalled, the phone was ringing insistently.

John Gacy was three hours late for the seven-o'clock meeting. Rapheal called Gacy so many times he doesn't actually recall who placed the final call, but he does remember a phone conversation with John Gacy at about ten that evening.

"I asked him where he was," Rapheal later testified. "I was perturbed because I had two other people sitting there. He elaborated on a number of excuses. He said he had a flat tire, then he had something about an uncle dying, and then he said he was tired and he was sleeping. . . ."

Rapheal later testified that John Gacy was entirely coherent and that he spoke in a normal tone of voice. The two men agreed to meet the next morning, at the house on Summerdale.

"When I came back into the bedroom after answering the phone call," John said, "I found Piest lying on the floor with the rope around his neck." The boy's body was wedged between the bed and the wall, where he'd fallen, and John said he had "a hell of a time getting it out of there." He put the body up on the bed, careful to "roll it over on the back because he'd already urinated his pants."

The boy was dead, and there was a moment, John said, just a moment, when he felt a shaft of pure anger that seemed to come from outside his rational mind. He was disgusted with the kid. Because Rob Piest didn't have to die.

It was the same knot: crossover, hammer handle, crossover. John figured what happened, he must have been looking for the key in the drawer, ready to let the boy go, when his searching hand fell on the rope and hammer handle. That must have been what switched on the Other Guy and brought the fog down on him, John said.

Looking at the rope around the boy's neck, he could see that it had been twisted only twice. The hammer handle was turned a bit so that it rested behind the boy's head. All Piest had to do, he could have ducked his head and lowered his shoulder. The hammer handle would have spun loose. It looked like Bad Jack had only just started with Rob Piest—two minutes lost in the fog—when the phone rang. It was like he escaped.

The docs kept pushing about the Piest kid, and John tried to help, but he couldn't really explain it himself. Some doc'd have to get Bad Jack out, talk to him, before John himself really knew what the hell had happened in the bedroom. Otherwise, talking about how the Piest kid died was just a matter of "rationalization."

As the trial date finally approached and the pressure to find Bad Jack mounted, John motormouthed through his speculations on what must have happened, in an effort to bring back the moment of the rope. Sometimes, during a long session with one of the docs, he'd say something—a sentence or two—and the words that came out of his mouth would have no meaning.

"I don't know why the fuck I should feel sorry for them. It's just a weakness, feeling sorry. They don't deserve to live, so you don't let them live. You fix 'em. You fix 'em good. What the hell's to explain? You can outsmart somebody and fix him good. Make him trust you. They trust you, you can trick 'em into doing anything. Anything you want. All you do is, you put the rope around their neck. Tell 'em it's just a trick, there's nothing wrong with it."

John would hear himself saying something like that, and it wouldn't make any sense. He told the docs he didn't understand what the fuck was going on. "I was just talking, but I don't know what I said. It sounds crazy, talk like that." Words with no meanings. Except that with John, the words would seem to have meaning when he said them; then they'd drift off into the mist.

When he first came to Cermak, John almost laughed in their faces when the docs asked him if he thought he had a dual personality. He told them they were full of shit. But then, when he broke his personality down and discovered the four Jacks, he began to sense a familiar hostility kicking at the weak parts of John Gacy's mind. Jack in there. Fighting with John again. So the docs had been right all along. And maybe Jack was beginning to surface because the trial was coming up hard on him now, and John was nervous and frightened about it. Jack came out when John was "weak." So it was John's fear, his weakness, that allowed Jack to surface in short, garbled bursts.

He never stayed out for more than a few sentences, though. Nobody could really interview Jack. It was like he was experimenting with the docs, playing a game of hide-and-seek in there. Bad Jack, acting like some neighbor's three-year-old boy visiting with his parents. First thing, the little kid ducks behind the sofa. He peeks out, you wave at him, and, bang, he ducks out of sight, giggling. About ten seconds later, there he is, peeking at you again: a little bolder this time. You know he really wants to come out and play, but the kid's shy and you have to coax him.

That's what Bad Jack was doing: He was peeking out every once in a while, experimenting with the docs. Bad Jack was looking for a doc who wanted him to come out and play. That's the way John figured it. Why else would he hear himself say:

"They're scared and they can't get no erection. You just tell them that when the rope goes tight, they'll get hard. Nothing wrong with it, unless you make it wrong in your own mind. No struggle. They put the ropes on themselves. They get excited; they kill themselves."

John heard himself saying those words, and he had to think about them for days. Maybe Jack didn't commit "the crimes" at all, and that's why John could never bring back the moment of the rope. Why didn't the docs jump on that? What Jack said sure sounded like a clue. Why didn't they look into the idea that Piest, or any of the little bastards, actually killed themselves? By accident. Jagging off with the rope.

Every year, an estimated five hundred to one thousand Americans die from autoerotic strangulation. The victims range in age from nine to seventy-seven, and include both men and women, though the majority are teenage boys. The body usually is found behind a locked door, a noose around its neck. There is evidence of masturbation.

The use of near-asphyxiation to heighten solitary sexual pleasure is a dangerous gamble. Dr. Robert Litman, a Los Angeles psychiatrist who has studied the phenomenon, told *The New York Times* that "there is an extremely sensitive area of the carotid artery. Just turn the wrong way and you become unconscious. You may do it right forty times, but on the forty-first, you may make a wrong move and die."

The folk myth about the hanged man's erection, forensic pathologists say, is based on fact. The carotid arteries, located on either side of the neck, carry oxygen-rich blood from the heart to the brain. When these arteries are blocked, as in strangulation or hanging, the abrupt loss of oxygen to the brain can often cause erection and even orgasm in a dying man. There is no sexual pleasure in such a death: the victim is either unconscious or dead at the point of orgasm.

In Chicago, the Cook County coroner sees about thirty cases of masturbatory strangulation a year. It seemed unlikely that thirty-three boys had come over to 8213 Summerdale to have their autoerotic accident.

John wished Jack had never opened John's mouth, never

mentioned the rope and erections. It was like Jack made some kind of bad slip that fucked them both up. Because now the docs thought there was something sexual in "the crimes." John could imagine that thought festering behind the doctors' eyes and non-committal expressions. They might think that he handcuffed them and used the rope to make them hard. Against their will. But you can't have an orgasm against your will. If you're not into it. And even if some kid went and got hard under the rope, who's he gonna tell? A young kid like that, he thought he wasn't into it. Now he's worried about his manlihood. He doesn't want anyone to know that he's actually a fruit picker in his own mind. Because if you have an orgasm, that means you're into it.

You can let that kid go.

And then maybe every once in a while, Jack took it too far and there was an accident and someone died. Even so, if there was no struggle, then it was consensual. They wanted to die. Orgasm was proof of that. They were fruit pickers in their own minds, and they wanted to die.

That's how someone could read it. It's how John figured some of the docs rationalized the crimes. So how come that theory didn't fit in at all with the four Jacks; or the gentle gift, given out of compassion; or the way Jack became the Old Man and punished the boys because they were young John Gacy and Voorhees combined?

If Bad Jack used the rope to get the little bastards hard, there was sex in there, right at the core of everything. That cheapened everything, the sex idea, and it just wasn't true. John had already shown the docs—by going over the victims he could remember—how none of them were sexual. Just like:

The Greyhound bus boy was self-defense.

Butkovitch was about a carpet.

Godzik was about dope.

Szyc was about a car.

And Rob Piest was . . . what?

John didn't know. Piest was a real puzzler, all right. One thing, though: The more he thought about the Piest kid, the more he began to like him. John told the docs he felt real affection for the dead boy. As the trial neared, John began referring to Piest as "Robby." He heard later that it pissed off some of the prosecutors because the kid's name was Rob and no one ever called him

Robby. Never mind the assholes: John would call the kid what he liked.

Because Robby did what all the cops in Chicago couldn't do: He stopped Jack.

A revelation here: It wasn't just Robby who stopped Jack. You had to give John Gacy a lot of the credit. Ma's side, the good side, had to be working in there, and that's why the Piest thing didn't fit in with the others. It was a totally different crime, committed, for the most part, by a totally different person.

First of all, John wasn't drunk or stoned, which meant he wasn't weak enough to let Jack out, anyway. Second, it all happened between nine and ten o'clock at night, well before the time Jack went cruising. Third—and this was the major difference right here—the crime itself was pretty dumb and stupid.

"Everybody saw me in the store," John explained. "The kid goes out, says he's going to talk to a contractor. Who else could it be?"

The Other Guy didn't operate like that. He went cruising under cover of night. He carefully picked the little bastard he wanted, and he covered his tracks. Bad Jack was a "criminal genius." With Piest, there was a trail that led right to the door of John's house. So it was just as John thought all along: He had picked up Robby.

The puzzle was coming together now, and John had to put it in context so the docs could understand. John Gacy had been fighting with Jack for years, but after Carol remarried, Jack was gaining the upper hand. And then, with Christmas coming and Uncle Harold dying, Jack was coming out whenever he wanted. There was only one way to stop him.

What happened, John brought Piest home, then stepped aside and let the part of himself he couldn't control kill the boy. There was a kind of tragic heroism here, as John saw it: he had purposely left a trail that led right to his door. He was going to sacrifice himself to stop Jack.

It may have been all unconscious in there, but John told the docs that it was almost like he sat back and waited for the coppers to bust him. Because killing Robby was so dumb and stupid, they couldn't help but find "the perpetrator."

John Gacy had finally outsmarted Jack, with stupidity.

CHAPTER
21

ELIZABETH PIEST SAT BY the candy counter in the Nisson Pharmacy, waiting for Rob to come back from his job interview. At nine-twenty, she asked Kim Byers to call if Rob came back, and went home to wait.

"Something's wrong," she told her husband, Harold. "I can't find Rob."

At nine forty-five, she called Nisson Drugs. Rob wasn't there. Ten minutes later she called again to ask Phil Torf who "this contractor" was.

Phil Torf said, "John Gacy."

Rob Piest was already dead.

John left the boy's body on his bed. He showered, changed clothes, and drove to Northwest Hospital. Uncle Harold "wasn't there," John recalled, "and his bed was already stripped down." It was eleven o'clock, during a shift change, but several nurses saw a man fitting Gacy's description on the floor.

John's aunt had already left, so he drove over to her house, even recalling the route he took: down Addison to Harlem, Harlem to Kullum. She was next door at a neighbor's, and John visited with her for two hours. "I had two or three beers," John said, "then left there about one-thirty."

250

Back at his house, John phoned his older sister and told her that Harold had died. He wondered if he should call Ma, but John's sister thought it would be best to wait until morning.

"I went into the bedroom," John said. "The kid was lying on the bed. Well, it didn't belong there. I pulled down the stair ladder to the attic. Went back to the bedroom, picked it up, put it over my shoulder, and carried it up the ladder to the attic. Closed the thing up, got undressed, and went to sleep."

John insisted that he didn't sleep with the body. Why would you want to sleep with some kid, he's already dead?

While John Gacy was inquiring about his uncle at Northwest Hospital, Elizabeth and Harold Piest were at the Des Plaines Police Department, filling out a missing-persons report on their son. The report contained a description of Rob and the clothes he was wearing, as well as the name of a man he had planned to ask about a summer job: John Gacy.

The police told Harold and Elizabeth to go home and wait. Des Plaines is a small suburban station, and the case would be handled by the juvenile division in the morning.

The Piest family couldn't wait until morning. They felt Rob was in trouble. He could be hurt, unconscious somewhere out in the frigid night; perhaps he was being held by the contractor. They could find no "John Gacy" listed in any of several local phone books and decided to search for the boy themselves. Rob's twenty-one-year-old sister, Kerry; his twenty-two-year-old brother, Ken; and Harold Piest took their cars and began driving slowly down the empty streets and back alleys of Des Plaines. They gave the family's two German shepherds, Caesar and Kelly, bits of Rob's clothing to smell and set them loose in likely spots. Maybe the dogs could find Rob if he was unconscious. Elizabeth Piest stayed home by the phone to coordinate the effort and check off areas already covered.

The family searched all night while John Gacy slept.

John woke early, and he met with Richard Rapheal about the drugstore jobs a little after seven that morning. Gacy, according to Rapheal, seemed like the same old John, coherent and normal in every respect.

Sometime that morning, John called his younger sister in

Arkansas and asked her to tell Ma that Uncle Harold died. He said he would call late that night about the funeral arrangements.

John put in his usual workday and arrived home about seven-thirty that night. He cleared the phone machine, made a few calls, and waited for Rossi, who was coming over later. John was going to take him out late and "look for Christmas trees."

"See," John explained, "the year before I had found some Christmas trees." He was hoping to find some good ones this year, after midnight.

At eight-thirty that morning, the Piests went back to the Des Plaines Police Department and spoke with officer Ronald Adams. The family was exhausted, frantic with worry. Adams was an experienced youth officer, and this didn't look at all like a typical runaway situation.

Adams called a phone number Phil Torf had supplied. John Gacy said, yeah, he'd been to the Nisson Pharmacy last night. He'd asked Torf about some fixtures and he hadn't said anything about any job to any kid. Adams thought the whole deal stunk. He asked for investigatory help.

A detective named James Pickell checked out the number Adams called and found it was listed not to John Gacy but to PDM, a corporation at 8213 Summerdale, Norwood Park. He drove by the house and took the license off a new Olds 98 in the driveway. Pickell ran a registration check on "PDM 42," then called Chicago police headquarters and asked for the rap sheet on John W. Gacy. He learned that Gacy had been convicted of sodomy in Iowa a decade earlier.

Gacy's record showed an arrest in June 1972. A man named Jackie Dee said that Gacy had picked him up on Chicago's North Side, tried to handcuff him, hit him from behind, and attempted to run him down in the car when he fled.

Six years later, in July 1978, Gacy had been arrested for assault on Jeff Rignall. Pickell reported to Lieutenant Joseph Kozenczak. It looked bad: This guy Gacy had a record of sodomy involving teenage boys, he seemed to be violent, and he was, in all probability, the last person to see a boy who was missing.

Ronald Adams told Kozenczak that the Piests were genuinely worried. He had checked out Rob's friends at school: no way the boy was a runaway. It was time to talk to Gacy face to face.

Lieutenant Kozenczak and three other officers drove over to the Summerdale house. They were standing at the front door when a van pulled into the Gacy driveway. A young man who identified himself as Michael Rossi said he and John had planned to get Christmas trees that night. The police told Rossi to wait outside.

At nine-thirty, John was in the family room, watching TV, when "Asshole Kozenczak" knocked on the door. "He came in with another officer," John said, "and there were two more outside."

The more John thought about Joseph Kozenczak, the more he realized what an absolute, gaping "asshole" the man was. "He played a hunch," John said years later, "and he got lucky. Big, smart cop. You know what he was wearing? Kozenczak? A brown suit. How can anybody wear a brown suit? Brown is the color of shit!"

John sat in his reclining chair, imperious, while Asshole kept pushing about the missing kid. And John told him the truth: same thing he told Adams on the phone earlier. He hadn't talked to anybody about any job.

Kozenczak took it all in calmly, almost smiling, and asked John if he could come down to the Des Plaines police station and fill out a witness form.

It was out of the question at that time: John was busy arranging his uncle's funeral. He had to call Ma in Arkansas. Kozenczak said, "Call her now."

So John had to talk to Ma about her brother's death while these two cops sat there, listening and waiting. It pissed him off enough to really bark at Asshole when he got off the phone.

"I haven't got the time to come down now," John almost shouted. Jesus Christ, his uncle had just died, and Ma was upset.

Asshole kept pushing it. "When can you come down?" he wanted to know.

"I don't know," John said. "Maybe in an hour." He was exasperated. "You guys are very rude. Don't you have any respect for the dead?"

Years later, John explained what was going through his

mind when he said that. "I was pissed because here I had a death in my family and Kozenczak didn't give a shit. All he was interested in, he wanted to know about some missing kid. See, things come and go in my head, and at that time, I had completely forgotten that Robby was up in the attic." The prosecutors wanted to make it look as if John had tried to manipulate the cops with death.

Anyway, the comment and John's promise to come to the station in an hour finally got Asshole out of the house. Rossi came in, and John told him the cops were asking about some missing kid. He didn't know anything about it. Rossi wanted to borrow some Christmas tree lights. They were in the attic and John said, "I'll get them." He acted as if he didn't want Rossi to go up there, and he handed the three boxes down from the darkness of the attic.

Gacy still had business to attend to: He had to go get some lighting district checks signed. Rossi met him afterward, back at the house, at about eleven o'clock. John recalls dropping a Valium, having a couple of beers, and smoking a joint. They decided against trying find any Christmas trees that night. Just after Rossi left, the drugs and drink went to work on John. There he was, sitting in the black recliner chair, grieving over his uncle, and the thought hit him, "Shit, the little bastard's still in the attic. Gotta dump it tonight." It was like some light that snapped on in his head, the way John explained it. "I thought, Boy, I really would have been up shit creek if Asshole searched the house."

Even though John was "exhausted" from working all day, he went up to the attic, "got Piest, wrapped it in a blanket: I carried it through the kitchen and out to the driveway." He put the body in the trunk of the Olds, dropped Rob Piest's clothes in a Salvation Army box somewhere, then drove south on I-294 to the bridge on the Des Plaines River.

On the CB, John heard a warning about an "unmarked Smoky" on the bridge, and he made several passes, back and forth, until he decided that someone had figured the black Olds for a police car. When the bridge was clear—no vehicles approaching from either side—John hoisted the body over the rail and let it drop into the river that Rob Piest had planned to clean for the merit badges that would make him an Eagle Scout.

*   *   *

It was a cold night after a warm day, and the ice-covered roads were hazardous. John was late for his talk with Asshole and was speeding north toward Des Plaines when the big Olds spun out on I-294. Dennis Johnson, working for the Illinois tollway system, spotted the disabled car at the twenty-nine-mile marker, about twelve miles north of the bridge over the Des Plaines River. It was two-thirty in the morning of December 13.

The car had spun about six feet off the road, broken through a thin crust of ice, and settled into the mud below. Johnson stopped and asked the man if he wanted a tow truck. The driver said he'd get the car out himself. He jacked up the back end of the Olds, put his spare tire under the right rear wheel, and tried to drive out. It was no good. The car was stuck, and the driver asked Johnson to call a tow truck.

On any such call, Johnson was required to note the license. This one was PDM 42.

The driver, Johnson said, was coherent, normal in every way. The guy just seemed to be in a big hurry. He said he was a police officer and that he had to get to Rockford. There was a murder up there.

The tow-truck driver, Robert Kirkpatrick, arrived twenty minutes later and winched the Oldsmobile out of the mud. The driver tried to get Kirkpatrick to charge the tow to "the Cook County Lighting District." There was a brief argument, and the guy finally paid for the tow in cash.

At 3:20 A.M., John Gacy walked into the Des Plaines police station and asked for Lieutenant Kozenczak. He was late, he said, because he'd had an automobile accident. The watch officer told Gacy that Kozenczak had waited for him and gone home at about one o'clock. He noted that Gacy seemed nervous and that his pants and shoes were muddy.

Later that morning, Gacy called Lieutenant Kozenczak and told him that he had been unable to keep last night's appointment because he'd gotten stuck in the snow.

"Where?" Kozenczak asked.

"The corner of Cumberland and Summerdale," Gacy said, a few blocks from his home.

"You still interested in talking to me?" Gacy asked.

"Yeah, I am."

"I'll be right in."

Gacy arrived at the Des Plaines police station just before noon, and while he sat in a conference room telling Detective Pickell that he never even talked with Rob Piest, Kozenczak was next door talking with Terry Sullivan, the supervising state's attorney for the northwestern side of Cook County. The Gacy thing looked like serious business—a kidnapping at the very least—and, if a bust came down, the lieutenant wanted to make sure it was clean.

Kozenczak gave Sullivan a brief rundown on the case: the sodomy conviction, the evidence of violent behavior. Worse, there wasn't much time. It looked like Gacy was holding Piest captive. The family was frantic—they wanted police to storm the house.

Sullivan; his chief investigator, Greg Bedoe; and Kozenczak began drawing up a search warrant on the basis of unlawful restraint.

Gacy, meanwhile, had made a written statement and was discussing his million-dollar-a-year business with James Pickell, who was trying to keep him in the station until a judge signed the warrant. Gacy dropped a few names, and Pickell acted as if he were impressed. A personal friend of the mayor, of Rosalynn Carter's—wow! Director of the Polish Day parade. No kidding? Norwood Park precinct captain. Geez.

Pickell was an appreciative audience, and Gacy talked for nearly four hours. The warrant was signed at three-ten. Informed that the police were about to search his house, Gacy grudgingly gave Kozenczak a set of keys. The search team pulled up in front of his house at about four o'clock. They would be looking for anything that would show that Rob Piest had been in the house: clothing, blood samples, hair. Anything else in plain sight was fair game.

In two and half hours, police and evidence technicians found:

In the master bedroom: a large quantity of varied pills that looked as if they had come directly from some pharmacy; a stash of marijuana, some pornographic films, a small Motorola television set, and, in a dresser drawer, a Maine West High School ring bearing the initials "JAS."

In the second bedroom: a pair of handcuffs, and a two-by-four with holes drilled on either end that looked like a restraining device.

In the hall in front of the bathroom: a bloodstain on the carpet.

Officers searching the attic rolled away the insulation and found several police-type badges hidden in company with a large dildo. Downstairs, evidence technicians found a starter pistol, a bag of blank shells, and an empty brown bottle that smelled of chloroform.

Gacy's books were varied: *It's a Good Life* by William Brownfield; *Dr. Atkins Diet Revolution;* a biography of Cardinal Cushing; *Neurosis and Human Growth* by Karen Horney; a biography of Abraham Lincoln; *Criminal Law and Its Practices; Principles of Salesmanship; Laws of Illinois; Birth Control and Catholics; How to Increase Your Self-Confidence; How to Work Under Pressure;* a Bible; and a Sunday missal.

Several of the books had been stolen from the library at the Anamosa men's reformatory.

There were other books, hidden in the attic: *The American Bi-centennial Gay Guide; The Rights of Gay People, 21 Abnormal Sex Cases; The Great White Swallow; Heads & Tails; Bike Boy; Pederasty: Sex Between Men and Boys; Tight Teenagers.*

In the kitchen trash basket, Lieutenant Kozenczak found a photo receipt from the Nisson Pharmacy: number 36119. Beside that was an eighteen-inch length of nylon rope.

Two officers used a flashlight to look down into the crawl space. There was a thin crust of lime evenly spread over the dirt below and no evidence of fresh digging. Rob Piest wasn't buried in the crawl space.

John Gacy was still at the Des Plaines Police Department. He had called his attorney, LeRoy Stevens, who advised him to sign the Miranda waiver since, John insisted, he had nothing to hide.

Kozenczak got back to the station at about eight o'clock and told Gacy that both his car and his pickup had been impounded. A young man named David Cram had driven the PDM truck into the drive while the police were searching the house, and he had given them the keys. Gacy exploded. "How am I going to get home? Why am I being treated this way?"

LeRoy Stevens cut the interrogation short, and Gacy left the station.

*   *   *

David Cram had been doing a painting job for Gacy at the Democratic headquarters, and he had simply been returning the PDM pickup when the officers confiscated it.

After Gacy left the station, he picked Cram up in his third vehicle, the PDM van. Over cheeseburgers at a restaurant, Gacy told Cram that the cops were looking for some kid who disappeared. John didn't even know what the hell they were talking about.

Gacy was nervous, Cram thought, actually afraid to go back to his own house. He almost begged Cram to come with him. Just inside the front door of the house, Gacy found a clot of mud that might have come from the crawl space. It seemed to frighten him badly. He told Cram to "turn off the lights in case anybody's watching." They moved through the house with flashlights, like burglars.

"You think anybody's still down there?" Gacy asked Cram.

"I doubt it very much," Cram said.

"Why don't you go down there and see."

Cram, who was wearing his good shoes, said he didn't see any sense in that.

Gacy opened the hatch over the crawl space and dropped down into the lime and mud himself. Cram could see him down there, turning in a circle and shining the flashlight into the darkness. Apparently satisfied that nothing was amiss, Gacy climbed back out and put the hatch cover back in place.

"I wonder what they were looking for down there?" he said.

Cram thought Gacy seemed "kind of shook up about it."

John Gacy left and drove to his sister's house, where he spent the night. It was as though he was afraid to sleep in his own house.

The next day, December 14, Kozenczak and Sullivan decided to put John Gacy under surveillance twenty-four hours a day.

Terry Sullivan's investigator, Greg Bedoe, went to the intersection of Cumberland and Summerdale, where Gacy said he'd gotten stuck the night he was supposed to talk with Kozenczak.

There were no ruts in the mud. Gacy was obviously lying. Hiding something.

Michael Rossi was brought in for questioning. He said he just worked for John Gacy. That was about it. The police asked Rossi to give them a call if he thought of anything that might help them in their investigation.

The next day, Friday, police called John Gacy's ex-wife. Carol said she could come in on Saturday. No, she told police, John wasn't violent. The only time she'd been afraid of him, seen his anger out of control, was the time she'd called him a jag-off. It was officer David Hachmeister who put that one in his special file, for use as a psychological ploy. Jag-off, John didn't like to be called a jag-off.

If the police wanted to interview any employees about John, Carol said, they might talk with an employee named John Butkovitch. He and her ex-husband had been very close, but they might have some trouble finding the boy. He'd disappeared three years ago. Probably a runaway.

Late that afternoon, Rossi called back with some information. If the cops were looking for missing persons, there was a kid named Greg Godzik, a PDM employee who'd disappeared around Christmas a couple of years ago.

Two missing employees?

Meanwhile, Greg Bedoe had tracked down the owner of the Maine West High School ring: the boy's name was John A. Szyc, and, like Butkovitch and Godzik, he was missing. John's mother, Rosemary Szyc, told police that her son disappeared on January 20, 1977. She mentioned that a small TV set was missing from his room. Later that year, she said, the police advised her that her son had sold his car, a white Plymouth Satellite.

An officer named Rafael Tovar recalled that Mike Rossi drove a white Plymouth Satellite.

Police obtained a copy of Rossi's title on the car. He owned it free and clear. The previous owners were Michael Rossi and "John Grey," who lived at 8213 Summerdale. "Grey" and Rossi had bought the car, so the title showed, from John A. Szyc, whose high-school ring was found in John Gacy's dresser.

It was four days after the disappearance of Rob Piest. Kozenczak and Sullivan now feared the boy had been murdered.

It was possible that three other missing boys—Butkovitch, Godzik, and Szyc—were also dead. The entire Des Plaines Police Department was working on the case, everyone putting in sixteen- to twenty-hour days.

Terry Sullivan wanted to be very careful with Gacy. A few months back, higher courts had reversed the convictions of serial killers Juan Corona and Elmer Wayne Henley. When Gacy was arrested, Sullivan wanted the charges to stick.

As Sullivan and Kozenczak built their case, the surveillance teams were told to make themselves obvious, to let him see them. Maybe the son-of-a-bitch would crack under constant pressure.

On the morning of Saturday, December 16, police interviewed Richard Rapheal, who said that Gacy had been acting irrationally since Wednesday, the day after his house was searched. Gacy, Rapheal said, was scared, almost incoherent.

David Cram, who was working the job with Rapheal, told police that Gacy was running around like "he was afraid of his own shadow."

If Gacy was nervous in the presence of his employees and business acquaintants, he was putting on a good front for the public. It was Saturday night, and John Gacy was out having a good time. At about midnight, he stopped into the Moose lodge.

Instead of waiting outside, as they had done in the past, Gacy's tail, two plainclothes Des Plaines police officers—Michael Albrecht and David Hachmeister—followed him into the club. The officers took a seat at a table and watched Gacy move through the room, glad-handing, smiling, laughing, drinking.

A waitress stopped by the officers' table and gave them two drinks they had not ordered. "Mr. Gacy," she said, "wants to take care of his bodyguards."

John talked with a number of people, then swept by the officers' table, moving toward the door. "I'm leaving," he said.

The caravan—Gacy in a rented car, Hachmeister and Albrecht in a pair of wheezing beaters they usually used for stakeouts on drug cases—drove to a nearby restaurant. Gacy invited the officers to sit with him at a table in the back of the restaurant. He wanted to talk.

"Why are you guys following me?" Gacy asked. "Exactly who are you?"

"Des Plaines police officers working on a missing-person case," Hachmeister replied.

Gacy thought that was "bullshit." Two teams of cops following him everywhere, every day. They had to be "feds," because, okay, sure, John would admit it, he worked in drug-stores. He "got into" a few drugs.

"Nothing that big," the officers said. They were just Des Plaines police officers trying to find a missing boy.

Well, shit, John said. He had already talked to the Des Plaines police. He gave them a signed statement and didn't know anything about the Piest kid. What he was going to do, John was making arrangements to take a lie-detector test, on his own, which would clear him in the matter and let the cops get on with more important work.

Kozenczak "was barking up the wrong tree," John said. Hell, he was a clown—"a registered clown"—and he entertained bedridden children in hospitals all over Chicago. Would a regis-tered clown, a man who publicly loved children, have anything to do with a missing boy? John had a special affection for sick children: he understood their fear and pain and loneliness, because he himself had "leukemia" and wasn't expected to live long.

Gacy, friendly as a convention of insurance salesmen, paid the bill.

Hachmeister and Albrecht followed Gacy to a Northwest Side bar, where John had his third or fourth drink since midnight. After an hour or so, Gacy led the officers to another bar, where he sat at a table with two women. When one of the officers followed Gacy to the rest room, John began talking about the women's bodies and what he'd like to do with them. At about four, the caravan set out for another neighborhood bar, the Unfor-gettable, where Gacy sat with three men and discussed, in a loud voice meant to be overheard, local politicians and high-ranking police officials who happened to be his personal friends.

At about five that morning, the officers followed Gacy into the Golden Bear Restaurant, where all three sat at the same table.

"C'mon," Gacy said, "you guys are feds working on a drug bust, right?"

Gacy, with six or seven drinks in him, started getting

tough. He was suing the city of Des Plaines, Kozenczak, Sullivan, and a few others: a big goddamn harassment suit that would ruin reputations and put the city in hock. His lawyers, Sam Amirante and LeRoy Stevens, were in the process of preparing it.

The suit would go through the courts like shit through a goose: John told the officers he was "one of the heavies" in North Side Democratic politics. His cousin was another heavy: Gacy mentioned the name of a notorious Chicago underworld figure. Gacy let the cops know he wasn't going to take this shit: he was going to come at them from both sides of the law. See how long Kozenczak could stand up to that kind of pressure.

And the surveillance teams should watch their asses, too. Gacy said he'd hired a real "bodyguard," a guy named Nick who "carries a three fifty-seven magnum and wouldn't think twice about wasting you."

John didn't seem to be striking much fear into Dave Hachmeister's heart, though. "You get back to your bodyguard, John," he said, "and advise him to look over his shoulder because there may be more guys on our surveillance team than he knows about."

John went off on another tack. "You guys sure you're not feds?"

"Just Des Plaines police officers on a missing-person case," Hachmeister explained for the second time that night.

Gacy suddenly wanted to be pals again—it was all on a first-name basis now: John and Dave and Mike having breakfast after drinking all night. About the kid, John said, he was just as concerned as Mike and Dave were. He himself hired young boys: they were good workers, energetic, and they'd do the work the way John wanted it done. They weren't set in their ways. Oh, sure, he had to browbeat them, but that was only so the work would get done on time. He paid them well, and it was intricate work, the drugstore stuff where you constructed the shelving so the impulse-buy items were at eye level, trick stuff like that. It was a good business, John said, and he'd fixed it so that all the money was in PDM. He himself wasn't worth much, but his companies were worth a small fortune.

Gacy talked for an hour, with no prompting, and went home at six in the morning. It had been a remarkable perform-ance. The guy babbled incessantly, and he was firing all his guns, all at once, in every direction. It looked as though John Gacy was beginning to come apart at the seams.

The next day, December 17, was a Sunday, but no one at the Des Plaines police station was taking the day off.

Rafael Tovar confirmed that Gacy's employee John Butkovitch had been missing since July 1975. A set of trained police dogs were given articles of Rob Piest's clothes for scent, then set loose in the police garage where Gacy's truck and car were arranged among fourteen other vehicles. Terry Sullivan, in *Killer Clown*, a book he cowrote about the Gacy investigation, said, "I got a chill down my spine" when one of the dogs got in Gacy's black Oldsmobile" and lay down on the seat. That was the "death reaction." Rob Piest—the officers almost felt as if they knew the boy—was dead.

Meanwhile, officers Bob Schultz and Ron Robinson, the day surveillance team, spent the afternoon drinking beer with John Gacy at a restaurant bar and then a bowling alley, where Gacy made a point of grabbing the women he bowled with and feeling them up. "Nice tits and ass," John confided to the officers, "and that one's an easy lay." Later, Gacy took Schultz and Robinson to dinner at a North Side restaurant.

"Would you answer a question honestly for me?" Gacy asked Schultz.

"Depends on the nature of the question."

"Why are you guys following me?"

Schultz said it had to do with a missing boy, but Gacy felt it "had to be bigger than that." His guess was that "the FBI put you onto me for narcotics."

Schultz denied that, but John was already off on another subject. Babbling. He'd actually hired his own detective to find the Piest kid and get this bullshit out of the way.

"What caliber guns do you guys carry?" Gacy asked suddenly. Did their guns carry as much stopping power as, say, a .357 magnum? Because John had hired a bodyguard who carried a .357. It would be nothing for a guy like that to blow away a couple of cops, anytime.

Not that John was a bad guy. He was pals with a mayor, a good friend of Rosalynn Carter's, and he clowned for sick children in hospitals. Clowning in parades was fun. You could run along the sidelines, walk up to some broad, feel her up, and she'd just slough it off. Okay, it was a little naughty, but a clown could get away with shit like that.

Gacy looked directly at Schultz. "A clown can get away with murder," he said.

At midnight, when Hachmeister and Albrecht took over, John took them back to a restaurant, where he talked about his marriage to Carol, and Hachmeister thought, just for a moment, that John Gacy might break down and cry.

The guy was definitely losing control.

CHAPTER
22

ON MONDAY, DECEMBER 18, one week after the murder of Rob Piest, Rosemary Szyc gave police her son's papers, which included a warranty for the small TV. Officer Tovar recalled that Gacy had a small Motorola TV in his bedroom.

Pickell and Adams had traced the Nisson Pharmacy photo stub that had been found in Gacy's garbage to Kim Byers, and they were attempting to contact her.

Gacy spent the day racing the rented car all over the North Side of Chicago. Had the police talked to Richard Rapheal? Gacy had to get up to Glenview, quick. Were they talking to Rossi? Cram? Gacy was now running a step or two behind the police, trying to find out who they'd talked to, what they knew. He drove like a man on fire, and the surveillance team ran more than one car into the ground chasing him around Chicago. They wouldn't cite Gacy for speeding, though, wouldn't harass him, give him ammunition for a possible suit. Rob Piest was dead, and they wanted him for murder.

That evening, at his house, Gacy, who had been trying to elude officers all day, suddenly wanted to be buddies again. Schultz and Robinson were invited inside for dinner. John said he'd been a chef for the Chicago Black Hawks. He had a lot of pals who were hockey players. Tough guys who got in fights and went out with lots of women.

The officers were given a tour of the house. John pointed out pictures of himself with the mayor, with Rosalynn Carter. He explained how the collected clown photos made him feel warm inside. Jesus Christ, why the hell were officers following him, anyway? He was a good guy, with political connections: the kind of man who hung out with hockey players.

Why did the cops want to harass a man with leukemia? They were killing him, killing him, destroying his business, his reputation, everything. Even his closest friends were beginning to wonder if maybe he didn't actually have something to do with the Piest boy. Guys asking him over drinks and shit about a kid he never met. Wondering if maybe he wasn't queer or something. Him, John Gacy.

On Tuesday, December 19, while Gacy was meeting with one of his lawyers, Kim Byers told police that she had left her photo receipt in Rob Piest's jacket the night he disappeared. Sullivan and Kozenczak knew that Rob was dead. Now they could place him in Gacy's house.

There had to be something they missed on the search of the house, something that would tie Gacy irrevocably to the death of Rob Piest, of John Butkovitch, of John Szyc, of Greg Godzik. They desperately needed to search the house again, but getting a judge to sign a second search warrant on a complaint of murder, even multiple murder, was extremely difficult in the absence of a body. Sullivan thought he could use Kim Byers' photo receipt as the basis for the warrant, but he wanted more than that. He needed a strong backup. The procedure had to be clean all through this one. Irreversible.

Once again, the day surveillance team of Schultz and Robinson were invited into Gacy's house. Schultz asked if he could use the bathroom. Robinson kept Gacy talking—no very difficult task—while Schultz went into the bedroom to get the serial number off the Motorola TV. Later, police would see if it matched John Szyc's warranty number. There was a faint, sickly sweet odor in the hallway.

After copying the number, Schultz went back to the bathroom and flushed the toilet. As he did, the central heating system forced warm air up out of the vent beside the toilet. The odor Scultz had noticed in the hallway was stronger now, here in the bathroom. Whatever it was that made the house smell had to be coming from the basement. There was probably a break in the ductwork down there, and the forced-air system was pumping that sick, damp basement smell all over the house. It was a nauseous odor, not seepage exactly, and Shultz thought it was familiar, something he'd smelled before, somewhere else: an odor that didn't belong in a guy's house. He couldn't put his finger on it.

On Wednesday, Gacy's lawyer Sam Amirante gave Terry Sullivan a copy of a $750,000 suit that had already been filed in Federal District Court and was set for hearing on Friday. The complaint named the city of Des Plaines, Kozenczak, and several other officers. Gacy, according to the suit, had been subjected to unreasonable search of his home, unreasonable seizure of his vehicles. The surveillance was ruining his business.

Sullivan thought Amirante was likely to win a temporary restraining order on Friday. The police would have to cease and desist. No more surveillance. If there was evidence inside the house that tied Gacy to the death of Piest or anyone else, it would surely be destroyed while Des Plaines and Sullivan were occupied defending the suit.

Sullivan had one more day to put together an ironclad search warrant. He needed a backup for the photo receipt that placed Piest in Gacy's house.

At noon, when Schultz and Robinson relieved Hachmeister and Albrecht, Gacy ran out of a store he was inspecting and began taking photos. Four officers, four disreputable-looking cars; the photos could be used in a harassment complaint.

Later that afternoon, Gacy shifted gears again and offered Schultz and Robinson—his friends Ron and Bob—the services of a hooker. It looked like a blackmail situation, but Gacy backed out of the deal, claiming that the woman he had in mind wanted too much money.

No doubt about it: Gacy was beginning to crack. Police interviews with Cram or Rossi seemed to piss him off even more than the surveillance. Every time the officers talked to one of his employees, Gacy exploded. He pushed his rental car to a hundred miles an hour, speeding through residential areas to get to them. To find out what they told the police. Kozenczak and Sullivan decided to tighten the screws.

Rossi and Cram were asked to report to the Des Plaines police station, one after the other. From the outside, it must have looked as if the cops had put something together. Like they were tying up a few loose ends. Like they had stumbled onto a nice little secret. By playing a hunch.

Kozenczak leveled with Rossi, trying to shake something out of him. John Szyc probably was dead, Kozenczak said, and you're driving his car. The lieutenant was going to put Rossi on the polygraph. Did he want to say anything first? Michael Rossi, according to Terry Sullivan in his book, broke down in tears. Rossi admitted to having sexual relations with Gacy and said that he thought Szyc's car had been stolen. That's what Gacy told him. On the polygraph, Rossi swore that he knew nothing about Rob Piest. Kozenczak told Sullivan he thought that Rossi was "basically truthful" but that the "test results were hard to interpret."

Sullivan and Bedoe talked with Cram. They told him about Szyc, the sodomy conviction, everything they had up to that point. David Cram was cooperative.

"You been in the crawl space, David?"

Cram said he'd been down there a couple of times, spreading lime and digging.

Digging?

Cram told them about the trenches he'd dug for the pipes that Gacy was going to lay to drain the crawl space to get rid of his seepage problem. Cram drew a diagram of where he'd dug. The trenches didn't go to the sump pump. No, Cram had never actually seen any pipes.

How big were they, these trenches?

About two feet by two feet. Really long.

Trenches that didn't go anywhere, that were too deep and too long for pipe that didn't exist, anyway.

They knew now. The son-of-a-bitch was burying them in the crawl space!

John was waiting outside Rossi's house when Rossi got home from the Des Plaines police station. Gacy was smiling, but Rossi didn't want to be alone with him and asked Schultz and

Robinson inside. As he had done with Russell Schroeder in Iowa, Gacy told Rossi he'd get him a lawyer. He wasn't to talk to the cops again, John said, not without a lawyer present.

The police left, and Gacy talked with Rossi for another half hour. John didn't remember what they talked about, though. His thoughts were spinning off into the mist. Rossi knew that Kozenczak was certain that John had killed both Rob Piest and John Szyc. Did Rossi tell him that? John didn't remember, he said.

Gacy stormed out of Rossi's house just before midnight. Gacy seemed almost crazy with rage and fear. The surveillance team followed him, hitting a hundred miles an hour on the way to Sam Amirante's office in Park Ridge.

"I went in there to talk about the suit," John said years later. "I had taken a lot of Valium because I was under so much stress. Sam had a bottle of Scotch in his office, and I remember I drank what was left. Maybe half, three quarters of the bottle."

After that, John's memory drifted into the fog, and it must have been Jack who talked to Sam that night. So John "rationalized."

Albrecht and Hachmeister came on at midnight, waiting for Gacy outside Amirante's office, in their cars. Two hours later, the lawyer invited them inside. The officers could sit in the hallway just outside a glass wall that looked into the office reception area. Would the officers like coffee, a drink? Amirante, in the midst of preparing a harassment suit, suddenly wanted cops inside the building. What had Gacy told him?

At 3:30 A.M. the officers, who were sitting behind a glass wall, saw Amirante and Gacy's other lawyer, LeRoy Stevens, lead John to a couch in the reception area. Gacy flopped down and fell into an exhausted sleep.

Amirante and Stevens talked with the officers. Whatever Gacy told the lawyers was privileged material, but instead of asking the police to call off surveillance, as they had done repeatedly in the past, Amirante and Stevens were practically begging Hachmeister to arrest their client.

Amirante suggested that the officers block Gacy's car with their own vehicles so he couldn't leave. Shoot out his tires. Both lawyers seemed stunned, afraid of their own client. Whatever

Gacy told them had shaken them badly. LeRoy Stevens was taking deep drags off an unlit cigarette.

Terry Sullivan had one day to produce a proper search warrant. It was Thursday, ten days after the death of Rob Piest, and the eighth full day of surveillance. Gacy's harassment suit was due for a hearing early the next day. A restraining order to halt surveillance was almost a certainty.

Officer Schultz came into the Des Plaines police station at daybreak and talked with Larry Finder and Lieutenant Kozenczak. That smell, that bad smell that had come belching up out of the heating duct in Gacy's house? Schultz had been thinking about it all night. He knew what it was. The realization had hit him just before he went to bed and had kept him up all night. It was the smell of death, of human remains. Schultz knew the odor. As a police officer, he had made over forty trips to the morgue. The odor was unmistakable—it just wasn't something you expected to come wafting up, sickly sweet, from someone's basement.

Sullivan, Bedoe, and Larry Finder began drafting a search warrant for Gacy's house. They would use Kim Byers' photo receipt to place Rob Piest in Gacy's house. The odor that Schultz described was the backup Sullivan needed to show probable cause.

They had less than twenty-four hours to draw up a warrant that a judge would sign. After that, Gacy's harassment hearing would be the end of it. If the warrant wasn't perfect, if a judge refused to sign it, Gacy could walk away from the investigation without a scratch.

That same morning, John woke up in Sam Amirante's office at about eight-thirty, hung over and unshaven. John's memories of his last day of freedom are hazy.

He recalls leaving Amirante's office and pulling into the Park Ridge Shell station, where he usually bought gas. Hachmeister began shouting in his face, cursing him for speeding through a school zone, putting kids in danger.

The officer dug the worst one he could think of out of his mental file on Gacy: he used the word the man's ex-wife said might move him to violence. "You . . . jag-off!" Hachmeister screamed.

The words seemed to hit like a double hammer blow to the

heart. Gacy apologized profusely. He seemed confused and looked terribly hurt.

John Lucas, the owner of the station, saw Gacy walk by Lance Jacobson, a young employee who was checking the car's oil. Gacy very obviously slipped something into the young man's pocket. Lucas asked what was going on. Jacobson reached into his pocket and pulled out a plastic bag containing three marijuana cigarettes. The police were fifteen feet away, watching the whole thing. It looked as if Gacy wanted the police to arrest him on a drug charge.

What the hell, did jag-off John think that his pal Dave was going to be satisfied with a minor drug bust, that he'd forget about Rob Piest and John Szyc, about John Butkovitch and Greg Godzik if he could bring John Gacy down for three joints? Hachmeister stayed behind at the gas station and picked up the joints anyway, for evidence.

"I didn't want to take it," Jacobson told Hachmeister. "He said, 'Take it. The end is coming. These guys are going to kill me.' "

Gacy was driving fast, recklessly, and he spun into a ditch, then screeched back onto the blacktop. He pulled up to his house, stayed for half an hour, then drove a few blocks to the home of his friend Ron Rhode.

Rhode was a forty-seven-year-old cement contractor, a married man with four children and a reputation as a tough, no-nonsense guy. He'd poured a few jobs for John Gacy and gotten friendly. The two pals had taken their wives to Las Vegas on a vacation once.

The John Gacy whom Ron Rhode knew didn't take drugs, hated homosexuals, and was good with Carol's kids. John always brought Rhode's wife a gift for Christmas.

At nine-fifty on the morning of December 21, Rhode's wife told him Gacy was at the door and wanted to see him. John was "ragged," unshaven, "shabby-looking," and he asked for a Scotch and water. Rhode had never seen John drink in the morning.

Gacy took a seat, and while he drank, Rhode said he could understand how a police tail could make a man nervous.

"Why don't you sit here and we'll talk about it," Rhode said.

Gacy couldn't be still. "I got to go, Ron," he said. "I've got to go to the cemetery." Gacy wanted to visit his father's grave. "I really came to say good-bye to my best friend for the last time," he said.

"What the hell are you talking about?" Rhode said.

"Them sons-of-bitches out there are going to get me."

"John," Rhode said, "there's no way a police officer can pull a gun and shoot you."

Gacy didn't seem to be listening. He walked up to Rhode, put his hands on his "best friend's" shoulders, and began crying. "Ron," he said, "I've been a bad boy." Gacy was crying "like a ten-year-old."

"Aw, c'mon, John," Rhode said. "You haven't been that bad."

John Gacy put his head on Rhode's shoulder. He was sobbing uncontrollably. "I killed thirty people," he said, "give or take a few."

Rhode later testified that he "didn't know what the hell to say. . . . I asked him who the people were. He said they were just bad people. They were blackmailers."

Rhode looked at Gacy and said, "Okay, John, you're full of shit."

"Remember," Rhode said later, "I'm knowing John approximately five to six years and I thought I knew this gentleman very well. And I mean, it would be like somebody's best friend coming up there and giving you a shot right between your eyes . . . you really don't know how to handle it."

Gacy grabbed his jacket, like he was leaving, and a rosary fell out, onto the floor. Rhode had never seen John in any church. "Hey, you son-of-a-bitch," he said, "when did you turn so religious?"

Gacy picked up his rosary, started for the door, and Rhode grabbed the back of his jacket. He pulled his friend back into the house and shook him.

"John," he said, "you just gave me a shock. I want to talk to you. For once in your life, tell me the truth. Do you know the Piest boy?"

Gacy swore he didn't. If Piest walked through the door, John said, "I wouldn't know him."

John was trying to say good-bye to his "best friend," and

Rhode was asking about the Piest kid. No one was concerned with him, with his health, with what the police were doing to him. Even his best friend wanted to know about Piest.

John pulled himself away from Rhode, who stood at the front door trying to get Gacy to come back to talk. The police could see tears in Gacy's eyes as he walked to the car. He had one hand in his pocket, on the rosary. He couldn't stay, couldn't talk with the living. He had to visit the Old Man one last time. Had to get to the cemetery.

Gacy drove back to the gas station, talked with Lucas a second time, and cashed a fifty-dollar check.

"I've just about had it," Gacy said. His eyes were red-rimmed from crying. "I don't think I can take it much longer." Lucas thought John Gacy looked exhausted: a "very nervous, very tired, very drained" person. "You've been good to me," Gacy said, "always gave me good service. I want to thank you." To the intense embarrassment of the station owner, Gacy embraced him. Lucas looked over Gacy's shoulder at the surveillance team. He rolled his eyes as if to say, "The guy's gone around the bend."

Suddenly Gacy broke the embrace, clutched at his chest, and began gasping, audibly. He bent over the counter, bowing in respect to some intense internal pain. When the attack was over—when everyone had finally seen what the police were doing to him—Gacy stumbled back to his car.

John prayed on the expressway at seventy-five miles an hour, with the surveillance cars dogging him, pulling alongside for a better look at his misery.

Albrecht, who was abreast of him in a chase car, saw Gacy mumbling over the beads of his rosary. The man was driving crazily, weaving in and out of traffic, drunk on Scotch and Valium, on prayer and fear.

Gacy pulled up to David Cram's house. Michael Rossi was standing out front. Gacy jumped out of the car and asked Rossi to come into the house with him. He needed to talk to his two employees, his two closest friends, in private. Rossi didn't want to go anywhere with Gacy, not without a couple of cops present.

"Please," John begged, and his voice was broken, pitiful. "This may be the last time you'll ever see me."

Rossi reluctantly followed Gacy into the house, where they met Cram. Rossi thought his boss "was very emotionally disturbed . . . very nervous." Gacy was "breaking into tears," Rossi later testified, and he "proceeded to tell myself and David about confessing to his lawyers the night before to over thirty killings."

As David Cram recalled the conversation, Gacy said that he had spent the entire evening in his lawyers' office and that he confessed to thirty Syndicate-related killings. Today he "wanted to go around, saying his last good-byes."

"This is the last time you will see me," he said again. Tears streaked his face, and a clear mucus ran from his nose. Rossi left the house: he didn't want to hear any more, didn't want to be involved.

"Syndicate-related killings," Gacy tried to tell Cram, but he was breaking down completely, hardly able to talk. "I swear," he said, "with God as my witness"—and he was crying freely, tears running down his cheeks, the words wet in his mouth—"I never had anything to do with this boy being missing."

Gacy clearly was in no condition to be behind the wheel, and Cram agreed to drive. John stopped to see James Vanvorous, the heating contractor who cosponsored the annual yard party—another good-bye—and then it was time to meet his lawyer LeRoy Stevens at a North Side restaurant. Cram parked while Gacy went into the restaurant. It was just noon, and the day surveillance team came on shift.

With Gacy inside the restaurant, Cram had a chance to talk privately with the cops. Schultz thought the young man looked dazed. Gacy, Cram said, was depressed. It was crazy bad. Gacy was eating Valium like popcorn and babbling about his father, about going to the cemetery. The guy had been up all night, Cram said, at his lawyers' office, where he'd confessed to killing "over thirty people."

He was going to talk with his lawyer LeRoy Stevens, then visit his father's grave. It seemed to Cram that this visit to the cemetery was the terminal trip, the last good-bye.

"I'm really afraid the guy might try to kill himself and kill me with him," Cram said. "When we leave here, don't lose us. Please."

Gacy came lurching out of the restaurant about fifteen

minutes later. He told Cram to drive him to Maryhill Cemetery, where John Stanley Gacy was buried. John gave Cram a ten-dollar bill. "He wanted me to go to McDonald's and pick him up a hamburger or something like that," Cram said, "and then I was to meet him back at his father's grave."

If Gacy was going to kill himself, it looked as if he'd make the attempt at the cemetery, over John Stanley Gacy's grave.

Gacy had cracked. That much was clear, and the entire surveillance team was on hand: Hachmeister and Albrecht, Schultz and Robinson along with supervising sergeant Wally Lang. Hachmeister had the marijuana that Gacy had given Lance Jacobson at the Shell station. Lang, after consulting with Kozenczak on the radio, made the decision. They weren't going to let Gacy off easy. They weren't going to sit by and watch him commit suicide—if that's what he had in mind. They'd take him down for "delivery of marijuana," a felony.

At the point where Elston crosses Milwaukee, they boxed the car—just cut Cram off, with one chase car slicing over from the left front, and one on the rear bumper. The entire surveillance team surrounded the car, and it was Hachmeister who jammed his pistol in Gacy's ear.

"We got you now, you jag-off," he said.

Terry Sullivan finished up what he knew was an airtight search warrant as John Gacy was being processed on the marijuana charge. At about the time Judge Marvin J. Peters signed the warrant, steel bands began tightening around John's chest. It was a heart attack, just like the one John suffered before the fight at Anamosa, like the stroke that put him in the hospital because of all the unfair accusations Carol's mother had flung at him.

Paramedics rushed Gacy to Holy Family Hospital. At the same time, a dozen law officers arrived at the house on Summerdale, where evidence technician Daniel Genty plugged in the sump pump and waited for a foot or more of water to drain out of the crawl space.

Doctors at Holy Family carefully examined Gacy and found that there was nothing to suggest that he was having a heart seizure. Nothing at all. If the guy said he was having a heart attack, he had to be "bullshitting." There was nothing physically wrong with John Wayne Gacy.

Daniel Genty, meanwhile, had dropped into the darkness and mud of the crawl space. It was there, in the southwestern corner of the house at 8213 Summerdale, on the first experimental excavation, that Genty's trenching tool hooked the skeletal remains of a human arm. There were bits of white flesh on the bones, which hung from the blade of the shovel by an elbow joint. Genty shouted up to Joseph Kozenczak: "Charge him! Murder!"

CHAPTER
23

THE COPS USED THE good guy/bad guy technique on John, who saw through it right away. The psychologists used their tests: crazy shit where you're supposed to tell them what color your stools are or whether people are always following you, as if they didn't know that the police had followed and harassed John Gacy twenty-four hours a day for eight days before they finally arrested him. The cops had their "confessions," the lawyers had their strategies, but it seemed to John as if everyone wanted to play psychiatrist, even his lawyers. As his trial approached, the pressure became more intense. Dr. Morrison called and told John to stop lying, that she couldn't help him, either medically or on the stand, unless he told the truth.

John could see through that one: she had called from his lawyers' office, so it must have been Sam who put her up to it. They simply didn't believe that he could remember only five of the victims and that even those memories were necessarily "rationalizations." To find out about the other murders, they were going to have to talk to Jack. No one seemed to have been able to meet or talk to Jack, and that worried John, because he knew Jack was there, seething, raging, a killer lurking just under the surface of consciousness, hiding in the synapses, alive and laughing in one of those lobes Freedman showed him on a chart of the brain.

As the trial date approached, John begged for more time. The psychiatrists, the lawyers, his entire defense team were all pushing him, insulting him, getting tough with him. The defense team needed to meet Jack to save John's life—and if Jack was there, he was lurking in John's mind like the mists of half-remembered dreams. John remembers that time well; he remembers how they demanded that he "take them cruising." It was just another game they played, the lawyers playing psychiatrist, the psychiatrists playing lawyer. They sat him on a chair and insisted that he pretend he was behind the wheel of his big black Olds.

"Just tell us how you picked them up."

"How should I know? I was just an observer."

"Do it right-hand, left-hand. You're on the left, Jack is on the right. Tell us what Jack is doing. You be the observer, you tell us how Jack killed."

"Jack doesn't come out like that."

"Let the son-of-a-bitch out!"

They wanted him to relive a killing—any killing—just so it wasn't a reprise of his standard story, not his "rationalizations" about the five victims he vaguely remembered. They wanted him to start from the moment when drugs or drink or weakness put him in the big black car and sent him spinning down to Bughouse Square.

"What the hell," John said at Menard Correctional Center in Chester, Illinois, "I took 'em cruising with me."

In the conference room at Menard, years later, John remembered how he took them cruising, how someone sat next to him, to his right, facing in the same direction, as if in the passenger seat of a car. Sitting in a chair at Cermak Hospital, he played their game. He drove an imaginary car down to an imaginary park and hoped he'd be able to pick up an imaginary kid. Maybe the kid would be a greedy little bastard, a hustler, and maybe that kid would meet Jack. He'd know what to do with a kid like that, Jack.

It was less than a month before the trial, and John needed more time. He was scared, and he could feel the pressure on his chest. He tried, he really tried: he played their half-ass game.

In his ankle irons, with handcuffs loosely connected to his waist chains, John hobbled around his chair, demonstrating how he took some members of his defense team cruising there at Cermak, before his trial. He is no mime, but his clowning experience has served him well, and his actions are entirely self-explanatory. John just opens the door, slides into the seat—which is really a chair in a prison conference room—puts the key into the ignition, looks out the back window, stomps on the accelerator, and goes roaring back out of the driveway.

Spin the wheel. Hit the brake hard—John's body rocks back in the chair as the inertia hits him—shift into drive, stomp the accelerator, and go tearing up Summerdale, right out to the expressway. It's the park, Bughouse Square this night.

"They got me to go cruising," John said, "and they tried to piss me off."

He imitates a voice, a high-pitched voice that is perhaps a woman's. He gives a silly, grating intonation to the voice.

"John, there's a stop sign."

"No, there isn't."

"Yes, there is."

"Who's driving, you or me?"

"You, but there's a stoplight. Stop!"

John plays both parts, himself and the antagonist sitting beside him there in Cermak.

"There's no goddamn stoplight. I know how to drive."

"There is a light," the high-pitched voice grates, "a stoplight and you just blew it, you asshole."

Some part of John Wayne Gacy loves to perform, and he is performing now, getting into the part of John Gacy at Cermak: John the victim, pushed too far, rebelling, angry. It is difficult to figure out who is sitting beside him because this is only a supporting role—no need to change position, turn his head, show us the configuration of his antagonist's face—it's just a silly, grating voice that is pushing him. Pushing John. Forcing him to react. It is odd watching John's angry face but hearing this earnest, high-pitched, indefatigable voice coming out of his mouth.

"Don't tell me you know how to drive," the odd voice insists. "You don't know how to drive. You can't drive. You just blew a light. Shit. You oughta let Jack drive. . . ."

"Jack don't . . ."

"Look! Over there. Look at that guy. Tight pants. What is he, maybe sixteen, seventeen? Let's pick him up."

"Not my type."

"Shit, just look at him. Young, nice ass, tight pants, blond hair . . ."

The whole game made John mad, really mad; you can see it in his face, in the tremble of his hands on the imaginary wheel of the imaginary big black car.

"Kid's cock isn't big enough," he says, a naughty boy, trying to shock.

And the pushy, grating, insistent voice comes back: mean, sexy, insinuating, knowing. "Maybe not for you, you faggot, but Jack would like him. Jack would . . ."

Now it's hard to tell if John is still performing, because his anger is intense, entirely real. "I'm not a faggot, you asshole."

The woman's voice is calm and soft but cuts like a blade, it is so knowing, so irritating and assured: "Yes, you are," it purrs. "You're a faggot. Jack told me. . . ."

John's eyes are glazed, but he keeps his hands on the wheel, keeps staring off into the middle distance, like a man driving at night. "I told you, goddamn it, I'm not a faggot. I'm a bisexual. Not a faggot . . ."

"Oh, yes, you are." A woman's mysterious taunting voice. "Sure you are. You're a fruit-picking faggot. Jack told me all about you. Just ask him."

John is not going to ask anyone anything. His face is red, curiously swollen, and the eyes are deep as sin and shame, dark and empty as an open grave. Looking into John's eyes now is like staring into a hole so deep that darkness swallows the light.

This is rage beyond performance, and John—or is it Jack? —rises from his seat, the imaginary car forgotten. His face is now devoid of expression, but there is a growling noise that seems to emanate from deep in his chest. It is guttural and continuous. Jack's fingers are hooked like talons. His elbows are bent stiffly, but his arms are stretched out before him. Jack takes a step forward, unsteady on his feet. Then his eyes roll out of focus and he steps back, falling onto the chair in a rattle of chains.

There, at Menard, John slumps in his chair, his head lolling to the side, his eyes closed. He could be asleep; he could be acting out his pretrial performance for the lawyers and psychiatrists at Cermak. He begins to snore, which is something people do when they are asleep and something people often do when they are pretending to be asleep.

Minutes pass. Eventually the snoring stops and John struggles up out of sleep, moving ponderously. He can't quite control the extremities of his body.

"What happened?" he asks, eyes swimming vacantly in his head. "What happened? Is everyone all right?"

John shakes his head and shoulders, throwing off sleep and confusion like a wet dog. "Was that Jack? I can't . . . I thought I heard someone yell, 'Sit down, Jack.' I . . . are you all right?" He appears to be talking to someone on his right, and there is no one there. Sitting in chains at Menard, he is still at Cermak.

John turns and stares into the middle distance for several seconds. When he opens his mouth, a woman's high-pitched voice, less confident-sounding now, says: "I'm all right."

"What happened?"

"I was talking to Jack."

"Yeah? What did he say?"

The woman's voice is coaxing now, a tone you might use to encourage a small child to let go, to take the first run of his life down a shiny new slide. "Why don't you ask him?"

"Cuz he don't talk to me."

"Try him."

"I can't. He don't come out like . . ."

The high-pitched voice begins to grate again: "I know your secret," it seems to say, "I despise your weakness"—and the tone is taunting, bleeding with contempt, falsely reasonable. "All I can say is that Jack confirmed my feeling that you're a faggot."

"Fuck you," John says angrily. "You're a liar."

"No, I'm not. He called you a faggot. He knows all about you: You're nothing but a faggot, a dumb, stupid faggot."

"Jack wouldn't, Jack doesn't . . ." John's face is red, swollen with a blood rush of anger, and he can't find the words he needs to say. "Liar!" he shouts.

And out of the same burning face, out of the same shouting mouth, the woman's calm, reasonable, taunting voice says: "You know I don't lie. And you know I don't want to talk to you. I want to talk to Jack."

"Jack!" John howls. He is silent for a moment, then he

speaks more calmly, imitating his own imitation of the woman's voice. "Jack doesn't want to come out." The sentence is both a taunt and a challenge.

"Sure he does, John," the womanly voice says, all appeasement now. "He likes to come out when you go cruising, doesn't he? Let's get back in the car again. Let's ask Jack to come along."

"Aren't you afraid?" John asks, challenging again. "Aren't you afraid that if Jack comes out he might kill you?"

"I want to talk to him. Just get in the car."

Once again John stands, opens an imaginary door, takes a seat, starts driving. "Where are we going?" the woman's voice asks.

"The park."

"Bughouse Square?"

"Yeah, the park."

"You going down Clark?"

"Yeah."

"What do you see?"

"I see . . . I see the streetlights coming up the hood of the car. They're like spotlights."

"Are you in the spotlight?"

"Not my face . . . my hands."

"How do they look?"

"Big. Strong. My hands on the wheel, they're in the spotlight. They look . . . powerful." John's voice is dreamy; he sounds like a man reliving a pleasant memory.

"There's a guy," the woman's says. Her voice is sticky with honey and sex. "He looks right, doesn't he? Nice tight ass, not too tall, slender build, blond hair. He big enough for you?"

"He looks," John says scornfully, "like a fruit."

"Ask Jack what he thinks of him."

"Fuck Jack," John says, exasperated.

"Kid looks about eighteen, nineteen. How old does he look to you?"

"Maybe eighteen," John says with a sigh, capitulating, playing the damn silly-ass game.

"How tall is he?"

"Five-seven, five-eight."

"What's he wearing?"

"White pants. Tight white pants," John says without hesitation, "brown leather jacket, white T-shirt . . . white tennis shoes."

"What color eyes has he got?"

"Who gives a shit?"

"Let's ask Jack what he thinks of him."

"Jack's not coming out. Jack's not coming out because I don't want to pick the kid up."

"You asshole!" The woman's voice is no longer breathless and sexy. "You dumb stupid asshole." The voice grates, like a rat clawing on glass. "I don't want you to pick him up. I want Jack to pick him up." And now hard, like a slap at full force: "Jack says you're a faggot."

John's head jerks back, as from a blow, and the woman speaks out of the mouth in his stricken face. "Jack says you're a faggot. I don't want to see a faggot pick this kid up. I want to see how a real man does it."

Now John speaks in his own voice, softly, slowly: "Son . . . of . . . a . . . bitch . . . son-of-a-bitch . . . son-of-a-bitch, son-of-a-bitch." The dead-level intensity of John's voice is unsettling: it is like that strange green calm that settles over the Midwest just before a tornado howls over the land. "Son-of-a-bitch," John says again, and his voice is deeper, more guttural, "son-of-a-bitch."

"John!" The woman's voice again. "John, keep your hands on the wheel!"

"Son-of-a-bitch." Louder, deeper, hoarser.

"Jack," the woman says suddenly. "Is that you, Jack?"

There is no reply, just a sepulchral mutter, a hollow, grinding rasp.

"What are you feeling?" the woman asks, and her voice is almost tender. "What are you feeling right now?"

Jack's voice is that of a man wakened from deep sleep; it is a rumbling full of rust and broken glass. "I am going to kill you. . . ."

"Hello, Jack," the woman says, sounding both shaky and certain.

John stares straight ahead with Jack's tunnel-deep, unseeing eyes. There is a low vibration, a growling in the back of his throat, the sound of a large dog about to attack.

"Jack," the woman's voice says quickly, "look at that guy,

why don't you. He doesn't look like a fag, does he? He looks like a hustler."

Jack's voice is very deep, very hoarse: "Yeah. Little son-of-a-bitch. I see what he's up to." Jack moves suddenly, swiftly, but his movements are curiously stiff, like a man miming a robot. He flings open the imaginary car door, swings his legs to the side, ducks under the imaginary door, and stands as at attention. He does not close the door. The man is in chains at Menard State Penitentiary, and he is demonstrating something that happened at Cermak Hospital before his trial. Perhaps he is not performing; perhaps, in his mind, he is standing on a dark Chicago street corner at 3:00 on a cold, windy morning. Perhaps he can see, in his mind's eye, a blond young man in tight white pants, a young man who is staring at him, waiting, a half smile pulling at his lips.

Jack's eyes are opaque, flat, dead as onyx. He walks to his left—toward a boy standing on the corner near Bughouse Square this cold Chicago morning—and just for a moment, his knees seem to be locked. He moves one jerky step at a time: elbows at his side, arms out before him, the fingers hooked like talons. One step, two, three—this is the way the monster moves; everybody knows how the monster walks; everyone's seen Boris Karloff as Frankenstein's monster—and suddenly, like a punctured balloon, the odd tension dissolves. His arms drop to his sides, and his eyes live inside his head.

"You," Jack says, "you kid, get your ass over here." The voice is deeper than John's speaking voice but not so hoarse nor so guttural as it was a moment before. "I'm a cop, and I want your ass right here." Jack waits a moment, then makes a flipping gesture, as if displaying a badge in a wallet. "I know what the hell you're doing out here. I'm a cop and you're hustling."

Jack's face is stern—a good, tough cop's face—and he doesn't change position, but the boy's voice whines out of his mouth. This tone is more realistic than that of the woman; it sounds very much like the cadences of a young man, a teenager. "Hey, man, I ain't doin' nothin'."

Now Jack's deep voice, a cop at work: "You're hustling."

"No, hey, I'm not. I'm just, you know, standing here. Waiting for a few buddies, you know." The voice shakes a bit.

The kid is young, a little naïve. He's trying to tough it out and not doing too well.

"When they coming, these buddies of yours?"

"I don't know," the boy's voice says, sounding trapped. "They should be here soon."

It is easy to picture the man in chains on a dark street on Chicago's near North Side. He and the boy are standing on the sidewalk, well away from a bright circle cast by the nearest streetlight. They are dressed much alike: both wear leather jackets, white T-shirts, light-colored slacks. The older man is paunchy, and his pants are loose-fitting; the younger man is slender, very taut, and he wears his pants tight. In the dark, they might be the same man, separated by the cruelty of fifteen or twenty years.

There is a sense of others in the gloom of the park behind them, a sense of men sitting in the cars parked along the curb. No traffic disturbs the night this late: only a few big cars—all of them with suburban parking stickers in the windows—drift occasionally down the dark and otherwise empty streets. Sometimes a shadow detaches itself from the gloom of the park and moves toward one of the cars. A window is rolled down. There is a hushed discussion.

"Look, asshole," the older man says, "I know you're lying. You ain't waiting for nobody. Fucking liar. I hate liars. Now I got to figure out, do I want to bust you and go through all that goddamn paperwork."

"Hey, man, please," the boy says, "don't bust me. Don't take me in."

There is a sudden sound of laughter in the shadows. A young man walks under the light in the center of the park, stumbling slightly.

The older man grabs the boy roughly by the upper arm and spins him toward the big black car. "Get over the hood of the car. Spread your arms and legs." The man frisks the boy. He stops, cups the groin, then moves on briskly. It is dark out of the streetlights, and the car is black with no chrome but for the two spotlights just under the windshield on the passenger's and driver's sides; no chrome but for the two conspicuous CB antennae that give the car an official look. It's a plainclothes cop's car. An older man frisking a boy spread out over the hood of a car like that is nothing new to Bughouse Square. If there are watchers in the dark, no one says anything.

"All right," the man says, "get your ass in the car."

"Hey, no, please, man . . ."

"Get in. Now!"

"Okay, okay, but can't we talk about this? Please don't bust me. Man, I just couldn't take—"

And the man shoves the boy into the big black car. He puts his hand on the boy's head, a protective gesture cops use when the TV cameras are on them.

At Menard, John—or is it Jack?—walks around his chair, as around the front of a car. He does not open the imaginary door. He never closed it when he lurched out, stiff-kneed and growling. There is no provision made for the other voice, for the antagonistic woman.

The man sits behind the wheel, driving. He makes four consecutive right-hand turns—one complete revolution of the single block that is Bughouse Square—until the boy's voice, pathetic and pleading, finally says, "Okay, you got me. What do you want? Don't take me in. Please."

The man is not so gruff now. He sounds thoughtful, almost friendly. "I'm supposed to take you in." This is a cop who sometimes does not like what he has to do. "It's my job to take you in."

Neither the man nor the boy says anything for another complete revolution of the park. "I'm supposed to bust you." The tone suggests that there is a difference between justice and the law; the tone suggests that sometimes a cop is torn between his duty and his humanity. "I'm not like a lot of these cops," the man says, as if speaking to himself. "I'm pretty liberal-minded." The man looks over at his passenger and he almost smiles. "Why don't we just take a ride and talk about it."

It is as if, on the second full revolution of the park, the car has worked up enough centrifugal force to break the gravity that held them, man and boy, to the park. The car swerves off to the north, toward Norwood Park and the house on Summerdale.

"You do drugs?" the man asks.

"Where are we going?"

"I asked you if you do drugs," the man says, sounding just slightly angry again.

"I . . . not really," the boy says uncertainly, but he must know that he can't fool this experienced cop, and he adds, "I do 'em a little. I mean, I've tried 'em once in a while. I'm sure not heavy into 'em."

"No?" the cop asks, friendly again, rewarding the little bit of honesty in the boy.

"No," the kid says, sounding very sincere. "Just a little, now and then."

"You live in Chicago?"

"No."

"Got relatives here? Any friends?"

"Not here."

"Where you from?"

"Out of state."

"Your parents know where you are?"

"My parents suck," the kid says, suddenly angry.

"They do, huh?"

"Yeah, damn straight."

"You ever just try to talk to them?" the man asks. "You ever consider their side? You get a little older, you find out they aren't so bad. Maybe just a little set in their ways. Hell, my own old man, he never understood me, and I was never close to him. Now he's dead and I wish I woulda been closer. I wish I wouldna done some of the things I did. You ever think about how you're going to feel when your parents are dead?" The man is a good cop, one who really cares about kids, one who would rather help them than bust them.

"I never thought about them being dead," the kid says, and then the full force of the thought hits him. "Shit," he says.

"They don't even know where you are, do they?" the cop asks.

"No," the boy says, suddenly thoughtful. The black Oldsmobile cuts left, hits an entrance ramp, and rises up onto the Kennedy Expressway, heading north toward Norwood Park.

"And here you are, down at the park, standing around. Don't you know you can get hurt down there? You can get jack-rolled, beaten up. You could get killed down there. As God is my witness, I hate to see kids hustling their bodies down there."

"I wasn't hustling."

The man turns to his right and pierces the kid with a flat black stare. He hates liars.

"I was just, uh"—the kid stumbles, knowing that this cop will bust him for a lie and reward him for the truth—"just, well, I heard you can make some money that way. I can't get a job, and I don't have any place to live. I needed something to eat."

"Look kid," the good cop says, "I see a hundred of 'em like you every week. What I do, if they're straight with me, I'm straight with them. There's bad people down at that park. Real bad people. I tell the good kids I got to pick up, I warn them about the jack rollers, and the queens, and all the sick ones. Just like you, first thing tomorrow, you ought to call your parents, at least let them know where you are. You ought to think about going back to them, maybe going back to school. See, you get so upset they don't understand you, and you don't make no effort to understand them. See what I mean? You make an effort to understand them, they're gonna try harder to see what it's like for you. One hand washes the other, see what I mean? It's a two-way street."

The kid hesitates, and when he finally says, "Yeah, I see what you mean," he sounds entirely sincere. The good cop glances toward his passenger and smiles: he feels warm and sees himself as a caring cop who does a lot of good things in his life. The big black car turns left, off the Kennedy Expressway, and follows the signs reading "O'Hare." The car is moving north and west, toward Norwood Park. The man drives for some time, smiling.

And then, suddenly, from out of nowhere, there is a new voice in the big car, a loud woman's voice, rat claws on glass. "Look, he's trying to open the door! The little shit is trying to get away!"

The older man, the cop, responds to the action but does not reply to the disembodied voice. He reaches over, grabs the kid by the collar of his leather jacket, and yanks him savagely back into the car. "Get back in here!" he shouts, and then his voice drops into a deeper register. "I'm trying to be nice to you." And deeper still, "You little fucker." Under his breath, in a low, vibrating growl, the angry cop says, "Dumb stupid little fuck. I ought to kill you right now." He is breathing heavily, as if in rage or passion.

"Dumb and stupid little fuck," the disembodied female voice whispers. There is, in the voice, a hint of sex, of shared secrets, of dark pleasures yet to be savored. "Little bastard," the voice says, panting, and its message is, "I want to watch, I want to see it all. Turn me on, make me hot, show me, oh, please, show me."

But the older man is a good cop, a cop who can understand why a kid might be frightened, and he says to the boy, "Look, just don't be scared, okay? There's nothing to be afraid of. We're only going to take a little ride. Have a little talk."

"What are you going to do to him?" the woman begs. "Tell me."

The man turns to the boy sitting at his side: "I'll decide what to do with you later," he says.

"You're not going to bust me?"

"Look, kid, I told you: I'm a good cop. I like kids. I ain't here to do you no shit. No shit you don't deserve, anyway. Let me ask you something. Are you homosexual?"

"No."

"You're not, huh?"

"No. I got . . . okay, I got it on with a guy once or twice, but only when I needed some fast bread." They drive for a moment in silence. The big car turns off the freeway onto Columbus.

"Where we going, man?" The boy sounds more confident now. He's heard about cops like this and has some idea of what will be expected of him.

The black Oldsmobile takes a left and drives down a quiet, empty street of modest homes and neatly kept lawns. The street sign reads, "W Summerdale."

"Let's just go over to my house," the good cop says. "We'll have a drink. Maybe we can work something out."

The kid knows now. "I . . . thank you. I'll, you know, do anything you want. Just don't bust me."

"Anything I want," the man asks, chuckling. He seems to think this is a funny thing to say.

"Sure," the kid says, all confidence and conspiracy now.

The big black Oldsmobile turns into a driveway, proceeding past a one-story brick house and stops in front of the garage.

At Menard—and probably at Cermak—the man opens an imaginary car door, steps away from the driver's seat/chair, rises to his feet, and, at Menard, stretches as grandly as his chains will allow.

It is a brisk morning, cool and bracing. A full moon, low in the sky, throws shadows on the lawn. The man's moon shadow is elongated, huge, satisfying to see, so much more powerful than life.

"C'mon, kid," the man says, "let's go inside."

Somewhere nearby, on an adjacent lawn, a large dog, hidden by a row of shrubs, begins barking insanely.

CHAPTER
24

AT MENARD CORRECTIONAL CENTER, the man in chains speaks like an impressed teenage boy: "Hey, man, is this your house?"

In a tone only slightly deeper than his ordinary speaking voice, the man responds to the boy's question: "Yeah, this is my place. I do all right." He sounds nonchalant, but if he is actually living through the scene in his mind, he certainly hears a dog barking from the neighbor's lawn.

The owners of the dog live on Berwyn, directly across from the empty lot where John Wayne Gacy's house stood. They remember Susie, their dog, barking—barking insanely, hysterically—one night in the summer of 1978. Out of a back window, they could see into Gacy's yard. A light from the Gacy garage fell across the lawn, and they could see a young boy stumbling between the house and the garage. The dog wouldn't stop barking, and the boy stumbled and fell to the ground, out of sight, behind the shrubs. The dog kept barking, and it scratched at the door; the neighbors stepped out onto their own lawn to investigate. They could hear labored breathing, and that was all. It didn't seem right, and they called the police, who came over but could find nothing amiss.

"I never thought anything of it," said the neighbor woman.

"Not until this happened. Now I suppose this was probably one that got away from him. And lots of times, I heard crying at night. Crying and screaming: one o'clock, two o'clock, three o'clock. At night. I'd wake up my boy and say, 'Where does that come from?' He says, 'I can't tell.' I say, 'This is terrible, terrible, all those screams. The sound is close by.' But we can't tell where it comes from and we think, Well, the neighbors, someone who is closer to it, they can tell where it comes from. They will call the police. At night you can't tell where it comes from, a screaming sound like that. But the dog was always barking and the screams would fade away, so maybe it was just my imagination. The next day and the day after, I'd listen to the news and they never said anything about screams, so I thought, It's my imagination. Another week would go by and the dog would start barking late at night, and I'd wake up and I'd hear it again: these terrible high-pitched screams."

Those night screams from the Gacy house strongly suggest—despite John's vehement statements to the contrary—that many of the murdered boys were tortured before they died. The most horrifying bit of evidence supporting that theory comes from the forensic pathologist, Dr. Edward Shalgos. Dr. Shalgos, who provides professional services to coroners outside Cook County, was asked to autopsy the body found floating in the Des Plaines River on November 12, 1978. The next day Dr. Shalgos began to work on the body. The victim, Frank Landingin, had been dead for some time before the body was thrown in the river. Dr. Shalgos also noted "something being very firmly packed into the mouth of the individual effectively plugging . . . his airway. . . ." This clothlike object was "pushed up against the backward opening of the nose and also pressing backwards and downwards on the tongue."

Dr. Shalgos "struggled a great deal to remove this object, which was wound and forced into the mouth very, very strongly. It took a great deal of effort to get this object out." When he was finally able to extricate the cloth, Dr. Shalgos discovered that it was "a pair of intact bikini pants, dark blue with a marginal rim of red, white and blue, quite narrow."

In trying to ascertain the cause of death, Dr. Shalgos examined the contents of the stomach and found "a very generous amount of rather well-digested food, including varied vegetables" and small fragments of meat. John Gacy—or a manifestation of Jack—often fed the boys he picked up; John liked to think of himself as "the perfect host."

Dr. Shalgos also examined the victim's seminal vesicles, which were very firmly contracted and had no content, indicating that "within a few hours of death, the individual had had sexual relations." Aside from those findings, the pathologist could find no traumatic abnormalities: the upper respiratory tract was intact and undamaged, indicating that "there was no strangulation. . . ."

What Dr. Shalgos found were food elements, similar to those found in the stomach, in the upper respiratory tract. He found well-digested food that completely filled the bronchial tubes. "The individual," Dr. Shalgos concluded, "died of asphyxia related to regurgitive occlusive aspiration of gastric content, all related to the mouth gag that had been placed." In effect, the boy drowned in his own vomit. It was impossible to say if the sickness, the vomiting, had been caused by the gag or by some unbearable external stimuli.

Thirteen of the thirty-three victims attributed to John Wayne Gacy were found with clothlike material stuffed into the back of the mouth and pushed deep into the throat. John insisted, in his early statements, that if he had placed anything in the victim's mouths, he "must have" done so after the death of the individual. John "rationalized" that because of his work with corpses in the Palm Mortuary—because of his firsthand knowledge of the various indignities of death—he "probably" gagged the victims to prevent "fluids leaking out." The gags were a sanitary precaution, placed after death to save the rugs. John gagged the corpses he found in his house because they were messy and he is a very neat man.

None of the victims, John said, had been hurt before their deaths, none of them were tortured as far as he could remember and as intently as he could rationalize. John was a gentle man, a "completely nonviolent" person. And yet the boy found floating in the Des Plaines River on November 11, 1978—one of the victims definitely attributed to John Wayne Gacy—had been alive when the gag was stuffed into his mouth.

John didn't remember killing any victims aside from the first, and for that reason, he said, he obviously couldn't remember gagging anyone while that person was alive. But if he did—and the evidence from Dr. Shalgos is incontrovertible—then he must have done it for a reason.

There is only one reason to gag someone—to silence that person. Jack may have been a murderer, but he apparently shared John's concern for the neighbors. Too much noise too late at night sets the dogs to barking; people who hear screams in the dark of the night end up calling the police.

So if the man in chains is truly living through the pickup—living through a murder scene—he certainly hears the dog barking outside when he says, "Yeah, this is my place." He's expansive but modest, not at all overbearing, like some well-to-do people. He's a nice man, an authority figure certainly, but almost more of a father than a cop. "I do all right," he says. "You want a drink?"

"Yeah," the boy says. "Whatcha got?"

"I got beer, I got Scotch. . . ."

"I'll try the Scotch," the kid says, and the man in chains goes through the motions of fixing a couple of drinks. He extends his hand, as if offering a drink.

"You hungry, kid?" he asks.

"Yeah, I'm starved."

"Want a sandwich?"

"Yeah."

"Okay. I got some ham, I got some cheese."

"Sounds okay."

"You want ham and cheese?"

"That's what I said, didn't I?"

"No." The man sounds annoyed. "You said it sounds okay, but maybe you want only ham, maybe you want only cheese. Maybe you want both, but you didn't say, did you?" There is a warning here: Just don't piss me off.

"I want both," the kid says. And then, because this cop blows hot and cold, because any little thing seems to set him off, the kid adds carefully, "I'm sorry. I should have said I wanted both right away."

"That's okay," the man says, smiling slightly. He likes it when they know their place. "You know," he says, "I'm a cop, but I got a construction business on the side."

"Yeah?"

"I got four trucks on the street. A lotta guys your age work for me. I pay good." The man is cutting thin slices from a large ham. "I'm always looking for good help," he says mildly, planting another seed. He smiles vaguely and glances affectionately over his shoulder. He really seems to like this kid.

"What kinda work is it?" the boy asks.

"All kinds of contracting."

"Whatta ya pay?"

"I pay good. We can talk about it later if you're interested."

"I'd be interested," the kid says. There seems to be a contract in the making. The job may or may not be offered later, after the boy does whatever it is the man wants. "I'd be interested," the kid says again, and there is, in the voice, the slight hint of a hustler who smells money. "I'd like to talk about it . . . later."

"Later," the man says, while slicing cheese for the boy's sandwich. The boy is wandering around the house, and he stops in the den, looks for a moment at the walls, and shouts to the man in the kitchen, "Where did you get all these pictures, man?" The boy is looking at a series of oil paintings. The paintings are all of clowns, and many of the clowns, under their makeup, seem to be terribly sad, melancholy. Some of them look to be at the point of tears. It is a blatant and obvious sort of imagery: the clown who presents a happy face to the world, who makes people laugh; the clown who is really lonely and sad inside, racked by some secret sorrow. It is an image that obviously appeals to the man, this idea of the clown of sorrow.

"I collect clowns," the man says. "See, I do a lot of clowning myself. I entertain at hospitals, for sick kids. I do parades, shopping-center openings. Stuff like that. You like clowns?"

"Sure," the kid says. Who doesn't like clowns? "When I was real young, I wanted to run away with the circus."

"No shit." The man is pleased to hear this. "You wanted to be a clown, huh?"

"Sure did."

"Well, that's funny, because right now I got so many jobs booked I need an assistant clown. See, I'm Pogo the clown, and my assistant is Patches. If you're interested, we'll talk about it—"

"Later," the kid adds, knowingly.

"Right," the man says in a gruff, somewhat deeper voice. He doesn't like smart-ass kids who go around completing sentences for him. Shit like that makes him angry. He is not really himself when he's angry.

"Right," the man says again, "and if you're real nice to me, maybe I'll show you my trophies." The man frowns: what an odd thing to say. "I keep 'em downstairs." His voice trembles a bit, as if to smother a sudden sob, or, more probably, an unbidden laugh. "I keep 'em in my crawl space."

"What did you get 'em for?"

The man stares into the distance, as if searching for something, a thought perhaps, the outline of an idea he can no longer recall. "Never mind," he says. Secret sorrows imply the glimmerings of dark knowledge.

There is something vaguely sexual here. The boy knows what the man wants, he just doesn't know what form it's all going to take. He can play along, maybe make some money—maybe even score a job—or he can get all prissy and take a chance that this cop will bust him. Maybe this guy has a sex thing about his trophies.

"I'd really like to see 'em," the kid insists, and there is, in his voice, the slight hint of a hustler's feigned fascination and passion.

"Maybe later, kid," the man says sharply, an obvious attempt to change the subject. The boy seems to sense something beyond his understanding, seems to think this man is somehow making fun of him. He doesn't like older people humoring him. "You almost done with that sandwich?" he asks coldly. "I'm starving, for Chrissake."

The man in chains continues cutting, but his movements are suddenly tight, furious. They are the gestures of a man pushed to the limits of his very considerable tolerance. "Dumb son-of-a-bitch," he mutters under his breath. The voice is somewhat rusty, a rasping whisper. "I bring you to my house, I offer you a job, I try to feed you, you . . . son . . . of . . . a . . . bitch. . . ." The tone falls quickly into a deeper register—this is the voice of a man falling, falling into darkness.

The knife stops cutting. The man looks about, angry and inexplicably confused.

"Jack," he says suddenly, and there is no one there.

"Jack," he says, as if calling for help.

"Jack," he says, and there is a catch in his throat, a whining note to the new deepness in his voice.

"Jack, the motherfucker's trying to take advantage of me," he says, pulling the trigger.

The man raises his arms as far as the chains will allow and stares down at the palms of his hands. "Oh, God, look at my hands." He holds them out away from his torso and stares as if he has never seen them before, as if they don't belong to his body at all. "Look at them. They're getting bigger, stronger. Look! Look!

"Oh, my God," the man says as if in terror. These are Jack's hands: not the Jack who splits from John, the one who "knows what he wants," who "cunningly traps 'em," who really "isn't such a bad guy." These are a killer's hands, Jack's murdering hands, the huge, powerful hands that gripped the plunging knife the very first time. The trigger has been pulled, and these are the killer's hands.

"God," he shrieks.

The man's eyes roll in their sockets. "My head," he mutters. "My head hurts." He doubles over, trying to put his head into his chained hands, but suddenly straightens up, quickly, stiffly. He stares down at his hands in horror. The fingers are spread far apart, and now they slowly curve into the palm until they look like talons. "Oh, God, Jesus, my head," he whimpers.

"Jack!" A man dying of thirst might call for water in the same tone.

"Jaaaaaaack!" It is a deep, guttural call, very much like the sound of sickness, of a man vomiting.

Suddenly the man stiffens, makes a quarter turn, and steps forward as if his knees are locked. His arms are bent at the elbows, his fingers hooked like talons. He takes one more step— the man moves like a movie monster: a powerful zombie, a Frankenstein's monster—and picks up the knife off the cutting board.

"I'll take over now," Jack says, a new Jack who spews out his weakness in a hoarse groan of delirious agony and anger. He slams his fist down as if plunging the knife deeply into the cutting board, then turns and lunges forward, muttering, growling, his knees stiff. His elbows are at his sides, and he holds his hands before him, the fingers hooked and lethal, powerful.

A boy's voice, frightened, quavering, bursts out of the twisted mouth in Jack's contorted face. "Hey, whatta ya doin'? Man? Hey, man—"

But Jack has the boy in his invulnerable hands, and he is shaking him. "Shut up," he growls, and there is, in his voice, the rumble of something not entirely human, a guttural growl: something dark and bestial heard from a distance in the jungle at night. "You fucking little bastard."

From the same mouth, from the same throat, there is a sudden, strange sound, almost a whimper. "Man . . . hey, please . . ."

"Dumb bastard," Jack grates. "Dumb stupid bastard, think we're all assholes, just so dumb and stupid." But he has stopped shaking the boy and is simply holding him in those huge hands. "Just like all the rest," Jack says, and his voice is less rasping, more human, "trying to take advantage . . ."

"I'm not," the boy says weakly. "You . . . you offered me a job, man." Jack takes his hands off the boy and stares at them for a moment, as if he has never seen them before.

"What did I do?" the boy whines. "Really, man, I want to work with you. I want to be your assistant clown, really."

"Okay," the man says. He turns his head to the right as if looking for someone who isn't there. His voice is less deep, less harsh. "Okay, yeah, sorry . . . I . . . I must have got you confused with someone else. . . . I . . . I'm sorry." Jack is a busy fellow, and if he sounds a bit distracted, it may be that he is in the process of making up his mind about some niggling matter of minor importance, some nasty bit of work that has to be cleaned up right away.

"We were just talking about, you know, how I could maybe be your assistant clown." There is blatant manipulation here: The boy would like to avoid the subject of the goddamn sandwich—which inexplicably seems to piss this cop off—and turn the conversation back to a safe subject, like clowns.

"Yeah, sure . . . that's what . . . I'm sorry." Jack might be entirely sincere but for the strange smile on his face.

"It's okay," the boy says, relaxing a bit. "I really like clowns," he adds with transparent cunning.

The man stares at his hands for a moment, then gives the boy a shrewd, appraising look. "You wanna be my assistant, huh?"

"I sure do, man, really, hey." The boy is an artless manipulator, just a dumb stupid kid.

"You know anything about clowning?" Jack sounds like a man whose mind is made up.

"Just what I seen in the circus."

"Well, shit," the man says, bantering now, "how do I know you're good enough?"

"I don't know." The boy's voice suggests he senses a new joke behind the man's easy tone. Perhaps they're finally getting down to it. "Why don't you give me a chance," the boy says, all sex and saucy impertinence, "just try me out once." He's got a finger on this cop; he knows how to deal with the sudden rages now.

The man in chains turns his back, walks a few steps, and appears to pick something up off a waist-high platform: off the top of the bar, or off the dresser in the bedroom. "You say you want to work for me, you gotta show me how good you are."

"You'll see," the boy says. It's a whore's promise.

"All right. I'm going to show you a trick. Show you how to do it." The man proffers something he is holding in his right hand. "Take these," he says, "and put them on."

"Handcuffs?" the boy asks uncertainly.

"They're trick cuffs. There's a hidden button. I'll show you how to get out of them."

"Is this in the clown act?"

"Yeah. It's not much of a trick. You do it for young kids. Put the cuffs on, put a white cloth over 'em, take the cuffs off, and slip 'em up your sleeve, then throw your hands up over your head. See, you made the cuffs disappear."

"Yeah, but"—the kid isn't too sure about putting on the cuffs—"how do I know I'll get out of these things?"

"Look, idiot," Jack says in his bantering tone, "it's just a trick."

"I know, but—"

"See, you either trust me, or you don't. Either you want to work for me, or you can forget it."

"I wanna work for you."

"All right, then put the fucking cuffs on like I told you," Jack says in a *macho*, mock-gruff, half-joking tone, "asshole."

And the boy, who has been subjected to the threat of arrest, to generosity and job offers, to sudden rage and equally sudden apology—the boy who is from out of state and has no friends or relatives in Chicago—snaps a cuff loosely onto his left wrist.

At Menard Correctional Center, John Wayne Gacy stares intently at nothing at all. "No, no, no," he says, still joking and almost at the point of laughter. "Asshole," he says with a laugh, as if to say, "You're a funny kid."

"That's no trick," the man says in mock exasperation. "Why are you all alike? Why are you all so dumb and stupid? Put the fucking"—the man is laughing continuously now, this is fun stuff—"cuffs on behind your back. That's it. Now keep 'em loose. We just put the cloth over 'em and then you come right out of 'em. It's a simple trick for kids, five- and six-year-olds."

The man in chains is nodding and chuckling. Perhaps he envisions the boy before him: a boy who responds with his own nod, his own bright grin. "Turn around," the man says. "Lemme see if you done it right."

Jack looks down at the boy's wrists. He puts his powerful hands over each cuff and stands there smiling for just a second. Then, with a grimace of effort, he squeezes the cuffs tightly closed with both his huge hands.

"Christ," the boy howls, "Jesus, that hurts."

"Shut up, asshole," the man rasps. His voice has suddenly dropped into a deeper register, and the humor that was there just a moment before has been transformed into a kind of triumphant glee. The man is as merry and malignant as a magpie.

"It really hurts." The boy sounds as if he is about to cry. "Where's the button? How do I get these off?"

"That's the trick," the man says. "There is no button." He might be explaining an exceedingly simple procedure to an idiot. "You need the key," he explains patiently. There is just the barest hint of suppressed laughter in his voice. His tone suggests that this is such a good trick the boy should surrender to laughter; he should be as amused as the man at this absurd predicament. How stupid, how dumb and stupid, to let a stranger slip the cuffs on you without a fight. This kid really needs a father to teach him.

But the boy is not amused at his own stupidity, and this is not such a hot joke to him. "C'mon, man, please," he says pathetically, "take 'em off. They hurt."

"I told you," the man says calmly, "to shut the fuck up."

And then, at Menard State Prison, the man in chains moves with a startling suddenness. He lifts his right arm as high as the waist chain will allow, then delivers a fast, hard, open-

handed slap to the empty air. He stares down at the floor, shaking
his head in mock sorrow, but there is laughter in his eyes. This is
one of those jokes where the punch lines keep on coming, one
after the other. It just goes on and on, this peculiar joke.

"Look, kid," the man says, "you want to get out of those
cuffs?"

"Yeah, please." Total capitulation.

"Then," the man says—he is the soul of reason now—
"gimme a blow job."

"I ain't into that," the man says in the boy's whining voice,
"I ain't good at that. . . ."

"You do it right, maybe I'll take the cuffs off."

At Menard, John Wayne Gacy fumbles with the catch of
his pants, then lets them drop around his ankles. On the outside
he wore sheer briefs, almost panties, in various colors. Now he is
wearing prison-issue shorts, and under them is the hint of an
erection. He glances down at himself.

This, he seems to be saying, is the proof. Here, between
my legs, is the truth. I am Jack; I am the one who lives in John's
mind. I am out now and I make no apologies, I have no regrets, I
feel no remorse. All those things goody-goody John consistently
denied—all the atrocities, the very worst of them—really happened. I am Jack, and Jack did it all. See my proud proof. Yes, I
played the cop; yes, I hurt the boys; yes, I forced them to perform
sex acts; and then, yes, I hurt them again and again and again.
The proof that this, finally, is the way it all happened, the hard
evidence of my sincerity is here. See, here!

But he does not pull the shorts down over his fleshy hips.
Some things must remain hidden. Perhaps the entire performance
is nothing more than an exciting fantasy; perhaps there is something else here that remains hidden. You will not see my cock,
and you will not see my soul.

The man in chains squats, as if straddling the fallen boy.
"You bite my dick and I'll cut your fucking balls off," he says,
and this makes him smile again: it is another hollow joke, hauled
up out of darkness like some eyeless and primitive thing found in
a fisherman's net. Breath burns harshly in his throat: another
evidence of Jack's vehement passion. He is on his widely spread
knees now, in a straddling posture, the pants bunched around the
chains on his ankles. He does not touch himself. His hands are

held out low in front of him as if he is holding the boy's head, and he grunts with passion or effort, breathing hard, hyperventilating, rushing toward certain culmination.

And then, out of the same mouth, the kneeling man makes another sound. It is a wet, slurping sound, strangely avid, intermingled with soft whimpers.

Jack gasps, then throws his head back and moans, as if in ecstasy, or pain. He grunts once—the wind driven from his body as if by a punch—then again and again and again. Breaking into this sound is another, one that doesn't belong at all to Jack's frenzy or passion. It is a sound of helpless gagging followed by a wet, choking cough. The man sighs—an affectionate accolade from the sated lover—then falls over onto his side and lies motionless for several long moments.

Finally, a boy's pleading voice: "Okay, okay, you said I could go now."

"I lied," Jack says mildly.

CHAPTER
25

"PLEASE, TAKE THE CUFFS off," the boy begs. "Please let me go."

"I'll tell you when it's time to go," Jack says calmly, then shouts, "you fucking asshole!"

The man in chains struggles up off the floor, pulls up his pants, fastens them, then walks to his chair, a thoroughly exhausted fellow. He sits perfectly still, his eyes closed, the manacled hands folded in his lap. Minutes pass and the man appears to be asleep, but then his shoulders begin to shake subtly. A series of wet, spluttering sobs bubble up out of the silence. It might be the sound of a boy softly crying, but the man's face is dry.

The eyes suddenly snap open and Jack looks out at the world inside his head. It is Jack who seldom blinks, who carries his eyelids high so that the whites show all around the iris. It is Jack whose eyes focus to some distant point beyond the walls. An actor playing Rasputin, or Charles Manson, would stare out at his audience in precisely the same manner. These are a madman's eyes; this is the theatrical maniac's glare.

But Jack walks normally now, though it is two steps to the spot where he lay a few minutes before. He bends, strikes at an empty spot a foot above the empty floor several times, then jumps back as if struck or kicked in return.

"Ow, goddamn it, motherfucker!" he shouts. "Shit. I'll show you. I'll teach you, you stupid son-of-a-bitch."

He lurches about, as if looking for something hidden low. He bends to the floor; his gestures are those of a man pulling something out from under a bed or a chair. His movements are confusing now, but he appears to be dealing intently with some simple mechanism.

"See this, kid?" His arm is held away from his waist as if offering some object for inspection. "Now, this has a lock on it," he says, a good father teaching his dumb and stupid son. "You'll never get out of this," he says, then bends to the floor, huffing in effort, as if engaged in a brief struggle.

"Now," the teacher says, "there's just a couple more tricks I want to show you. I'm going to taste you now, kid." He kneels and fiddles with something—a button? a zipper?—then makes a lifting, pulling gesture.

"Well, shit," he says in mock surprise, "I can't get your pants down over this board, now, can I? Whatta you think, kid? Think I should take it off you?" There is no reply. "But see, if I take the board off, you'll just kick again, won't you?"

The boy's weak voice, "I won't, I swear. . . ."

"You must think I'm dumb and stupid."

"Please take it off."

"Naw. We do it my way."

The man in chains reaches out for something near at hand. He mimes picking up a light object, then holds it out, as if letting the imaginary boy inspect it. Jack extends the first two fingers of his right hand and closes them until they meet his thumb. It is a slow, pinching motion, a strangely suggestive and threatening gesture.

"We'll use this," he says, opening and closing his thumb and first two fingers. His hand moves slowly, slowly, as if traveling down the boy's prone and helpless body. He grabs something in his left hand, jerks it in an upward direction, then moves the right hand close to the clutching left, still opening and closing his fingers slowly, suggestively.

And a boy's voice screams out, "Oh, my God, no, NO-NONONO—"

"Awwww," the man says in mock sympathy, "you didn't think I was going to snip it off, did you?" He opens his left hand

and moves the right lower. "We're just going to have to cut these pants right off, aren't we," he says with the professional patience of a nurse or a teacher, someone used to irrational outbursts. "We have to cut them off because you kick, now, don't you?" The man continues to move, as if back up the boy's legs, as if cutting and ripping away at the pants with a pair of scissors. "A last cut here," the man says, quite delighted with his work, "and then one here, and we'll just get rid of these." The man lifts, pulls, tosses something behind him. He stares down at the empty floor as if at some illicit treasure suddenly his.

"This your best underwear, kid?" the man asks.

"Yes," the boy says, pathetically eager to please, "they're my best pair."

The man's grin erupts into a broad, sarcastic smile; the boy's attitude makes him laugh. It is a contemptuous laugh, borne out of real pleasure. "Then we'll have to be real careful with them, won't we?" He begins a careful cutting gesture just above the empty floor. Then he shifts position, cuts again, tosses something out of reach to the rear—the scissors, probably—then lifts and pulls as if removing the boy's carefully slit underwear. Shifting again, the man neatly folds the thin cotton briefs. It is a curiously affectionate gesture, almost reverent, very much like a young father folding his new son's clean diapers.

"Now," he says, "we'll just see how you taste."

Jack kneels, as if at prayer, then bends from the waist and purses his lips like a thirsty man about to drink from a cool, clear pool. Suddenly he straightens up, then rocks back into a more comfortable sitting position on his heels. "Awwww," he says in theatrical disappointment, "c'mon, get it hard."

"I can't, mister, please. I'm scared." A boy's voice, weak and quavering.

"I said, 'Get it hard.' "

"I'm too scared, honest."

"Well," Jack says, tolerant of these little setbacks and ever ready with alternative plans, "I'm hard." The man in chains lurches to his feet, bends from the knees, gathers something into his arms and slowly, as if dealing with an unwieldy and inert weight, straightens his back and his knees. He might be a laborer lifting a sack of potatoes onto a flatbed truck.

The man shifts the weight to some waist-high object. Perhaps he sees the boy—naked from the waist down now—bent limply over the back of a chair. Jack's powerful hands are waist high and he extends them in a quick, brutal, spreading gesture, a ripping, tearing motion. He does not drop his pants. Moving forward, his right hand before him as if holding an erect penis, the man wiggles his hips slightly—a stripper's studied obscenity— then begins thrusting so viciously the chains rattle about his waist.

"Am I hurting you, kid?" the man asks, and he responds to himself with a boy's muffled scream.

"Awwwww," he says, ever the concerned lover, bucking his hips and grunting with effort now as the chains jangle at his waist. "Awwwww," he says again, but there is no more false pity in the expletive; it is more like a groan of relief. "Ahhhhhhhh." The man thrusts forward, his hands before him, as if gripping something with a great deal of force. His body jerks in three quick, spastic movements—"oh, oh, oh"—then he takes one slow, stumbling backward step, his eyes vacant and heavily lidded. "Ahhhhhh."

He glances almost tenderly toward the spot where his passion was spent, and then, quite suddenly, his eyes snap open into Jack's stare. Something terribly wrong there. The boy is doing something obscene and unforgivable: he is doing something so dirty, something so foul that despite postcoital satiety, Jack is infuriated.

"Don't you bleed on my carpet!" he shouts, and his voice rips through the prison conference room like a buzz saw tearing through a pine knot. "Don't you fucking bleed on my chair! You fucker!" he howls. "You little fucker!"

The man in chains begins to pull the boy across the floor. "C'mon," he says very gentle now, as if calling a skittish dog, as if the imaginary boy were not bound and helpless, unable to walk, "c'mon, let's go in here, get more comfortable." He lugs the inert weight across the floor, glancing down toward it every once in a while. "Stop that bleeding, goddamn it!" he shouts, angry again. "You're going to clean up this mess." And then calmly, with real affection: "This is my bedroom. You like it?"

There is no reply, and the man asks again, "You like it?"

"Yes," the boy says in a broken whisper, "I like it."

"Good," the man says pleasantly, "because we'll just get you up here"—Jack lifts the boy onto the bed and rolls him over—"where I can show you another good trick."

The man walks about the room and appears to select some object more pleasing than others in a dresser drawer or on a closet shelf. He turns back to the imaginary bed. "Man," he says, "I gotta tell you, you are tight." He holds the imaginary object out at waist level. "See this?" he says, jerking his right hand in a vicious, jabbing motion. "See it!"

The man shifts positions. "We're going to have to loosen you up," he says, more in sorrow than in anger. The boy has to learn. "You're so tight you hurt my dick, so we'll just use"—here the man in chains makes another jabbing motion, and the weight of his bulky body falls fully behind the piston thrust of his right hand—"this." There is a sharp groan: the sound of sudden, lacerating pain.

"This ought to loosen you up real good." Jack applies the lesson with maximum vigor, but he is not above appreciating the humor in this particular course. It's just that for each thrust and guffaw, he emits a sharp, staccato scream. The screams and laughter feed one upon the other.

"Aren't we having fun?" he asks, but there is no reply, only intermittent cries of pain.

The man bends to his work with total concentration. There is some obstruction here, and he shoves the imaginary object forward with sudden and intense force. Jack grunts—in effort, or perhaps it is the sound of the boy's pain—then, like a man making the last half turn on a screw set into a hard metal surface, twists the object—there is a long, piteous scream here—until it will go no further.

"Isn't this fun?" the man says, as if speaking to a very young child, or an idiot. "Aren't we having fun now?"

"Oh, God, please . . ."

The man releases the object and stands back to admire the results of his efforts. He is laughing softly to himself, but the hissing chuckles are interspersed with a certain wet snuffling, an injured child's helpless sobs.

Well, no one ever said learning was easy, and a teacher's job is never done. No time to rest now. The man walks a step or two and selects another imaginary object, perhaps from the top of the bedroom dresser. He kneels on the floor in a straddling position and throws both hands up and then down. "This trick," the teacher explains, "is called horsey. See, you're the horse, I'm the rider, and these"—the man rocks back on his knees, a rider pulling a frisky horse to halt—"are my reins."

There is the sudden sound of gagging, a startled, strangled gasp.

"Giddiyap, horse, c'mon."

"Oh, my God, you're hurting me, please, you're hurting me."

The man in chains kneels on the empty floor. He yanks his hands back occasionally, lets them fall loose in front of him, yanks them back, lets them fall loose. Now he leans forward and makes a cuffing motion with his right hand.

"Faster, giddiyap, horsey." Leaning back on his heels and yanking his hand toward him, he shouts, "Whooaaaa, horsey!" A swift, vicious pull on the reins. "I said, whoa, now."

"Tell me you love it," he says, as if to a lover who likes it a little rough.

"Tell me," he says, breathing heavily, his tone a mixture of contempt and excitement.

"Tell me you love it," he says, a triumphant child making a fallen adversary say "uncle," a rapist forcing his victim to admit to unfelt pleasure.

He loosens the reins. The boy gasps for air, coughs, but whatever words he tries to say are mangled in his throat.

Jack says, "Don't you pass out on me now, you little son-of-a-bitch, don't you dare pass out."

"Please," the boy manages finally, "pleeeeeese. . . ."

"Okay," the man says, "okay, we're done now. Just one more trick." He drops the reins, looks behind him, and staying on his knees, shifts position somewhat. "What's this?" he asks. Golly, his tone says, what a surprise to find something so large so deeply embedded in the horsey's rectum. "We'll just have to take this out and put it where it belongs."

The man snaps his fingers—he has just realized the obvious. "Let's dump you off the bed," he says, making the appropriate motions. Then he reaches down and mimes grabbing some object. "You shit and you'll eat it," he says, then yanks his clutched right hand upward with considerable force. He examines the imaginary object with some distaste and tosses it on the floor behind him.

Jack stares down at absolutely nothing in total disgust. "I

can't look at that," he says, kicking at the floor as if turning the boy over onto his stomach. "Ugh," he says. "So dirty." John may be a goody-goody and Jack may be a killer, but they both share a certain love of neatness and order.

The man sits in his chair. He has brought cigars and matches with him to the prison conference room, but he mimes peeling cellophane off an imaginary Antonio and Cleopatra. "Hey, kid, you want to hand me those matches on the dresser," Jack says, clearly the superior fellow but one who is not above an occasional witticism.

"I can't. . . . I can't move. . . . Oh, God, please . . ."

"Forget it, asshole." The man reaches over and grabs the imaginary matches, shaking his head in amused disappointment: kids today. He bends forward, hampered a bit by the manacles on his hands, and lights a nonexistent cigar, which he smokes importantly.

"One more trick," Jack says, moving back into his strad-dling position. He holds the cigar in his right hand, between the thumb and forefinger, then lowers it slowly toward the floor. "Does that hurt?" he asks, and he answers himself with a weak scream. He moves his hand lower. "You'd think it'd hurt more"—he holds the cigar motionless for a moment, just pausing for effect, then lowers it gently, experimentally—"here."

Another scream, one that goes on and on and gets progres-sively weaker and weaker.

He holds the cigar up and to his right, as if over the boy's face. It hovers there, ready to drop at any moment. "Tell me you love it," Jack says in a threatening whisper.

Pain has stolen the boy's breath, and it takes him two false starts before he can say, "I love it, please, I love . . . it."

Jack lifts the cigar to his mouth and takes a long, satisfying drag, but it is an imaginary cigar, after all, and he is still able to mimic the sounds of a boy's pained sobs.

"You love it, huh," Jack says, a father truly interested in a son's reaction to new experiences.

"God, no," the boy says, pleading. "Please, no. If you're going to kill me, kill me. Kill me or let me go, please. . . ."

Jack nods to himself as if noting, for the record, this new element in the boy's pleas. "Look, fucker," he explains cordially, "I'll kill you when I want to kill you." He bends to smoke. His manner with the imaginary cigar—even hampered by the very real chains—is full of grand swoops and flourishes.

"Hey," he says, "you stink, and you're still bleeding. Why don't we clean you up." Shifting position, Jack works intently for a short time, then says, "I got the board off. You can walk to the bathroom."

"I can't. . . . I don't think I can walk."

"Then," Jack explains, exasperated—why, why do they have to make everything so fucking difficult—"crawl." He puts the cigar in his mouth, rises to his feet, and strolls quite slowly, grandly, across the room, smoking in a contemplative manner and staring down toward his feet, as though at a boy crawling painfully before him.

"That's right. Right here, on the floor."

Jack kneels to turn on the taps in the tub. He glances down at the boy, puffs on his cigar, then disposes of it, perhaps in an ashtray, perhaps in the toilet. There's work to be done now: a thorough cleansing, a purification. He extends his left hand, then pulls it back, and turns sideways while he makes gentle, circular motions. "That doesn't hurt, does it?" he asks sympathetically, and he answers the question with a long, bubbling sob. "It's just a washrag," Jack says gently, "it doesn't hurt."

This sudden sympathy opens the floodgates and the boy cries helplessly, more a child now than a man.

"I'm sorry," Jack says sincerely. "I'm really sorry if I hurt you. Tell me if I'm rubbing too hard. Is this all right?" He waits, as if for an answer, but the boy will not speak. "Say something." There is no reply, and this annoys Jack. You do something nice for someone and they snub you. They just lie there with their eyes closed, hoping to pass out or die or some damn thing.

"Please," the boy says weakly but with the dignity of one who has made a difficult decision, "if you're going to kill me, kill me now. No more torture."

Jack nods, as if in assent, then drops to his knees. "We got to clean your face," he says reasonably. "First we got to clean you off." He turns off the taps in the tub, which must be full now because his gestures are those of a man grabbing someone by the hair and plunging a head into the water. He holds the boy's face underwater for several long moments and stares up to the ceiling.

In John Wayne Gacy's home, there was a single ceiling

light in the bathroom, and Jack must be staring up at that bulb because he mutters, reverently, almost inaudibly, "Light." The single word sounds like a prayer.

Then, as if remembering a trivial but annoying matter— damn, left the water boiling on the stove, something like that—he tears his eyes away from the glowing bulb and lifts the boy's head out of the water. Immediately, there is the sound of someone gasping for air, spluttering and coughing weakly.

"Oh, God," a boy's voice pleads breathlessly, "oh, God, help me."

Jack holds the boy's head—blond hair bunched in a huge right hand—and he stares up into the Light. "Yes, my son," Jack says, as if intoning some liturgical ritual, "God will help you." These are the soothing words of a priest, a father's blessing for the deeply troubled. "But first," the father says, "you must be puri- fied." And he plunges the boy's head back into the water and stares into the Light.

There is a limit to how long a person can hold his breath, so that there would be bubbles rising up around the boy's face by the time Jack lifts it from the water a third time. He allows the boy time to spit what water he can from his lungs, then holds the gasping, crimson face inches from his own.

"Yes, my child," Jack says, "God is here." He can't really help himself now: Jack just has to laugh in the boy's contorted face. "But first you must be purified," he says, thrusting the boy's head back into the water. And the ritual goes on. Jack lifts his own head, lifts his mad eyes to the wonder of the Light.

God is here: God the Father.

When the bubbles rising up around the boy's head become smaller and less frequent, when the boy's body stops those annoy- ing spasmodic upward jerks—the man in chains has been kneeling on the empty floor a long time—Jack drops his eyes from the Light. He pulls the boy from the water and dumps him on the floor by the tub.

"I'm tired of this game," he announces petulantly. "Get up."

Jack himself rises to his feet and stares down at the bare floor. "Can you get up?" he asks, but there is no answer. "Well, can you at least crawl?"

When there still is no reply—only the prolonged sounds of

helpless gasping—Jack smiles ruefully and shakes his head. He is a man unfairly put upon. Why must he do everything himself? He reaches down, grabs the boy by his blond hair one more time, and drags the limp weight of the body back into the bedroom.

"Well, shit," Jack says, staring down at the floor as if disappointed. Suddenly a new thought hits him. "I'm hungry," he announces. "You hungry, kid?" A sly intonation to the voice: it is the same joke as before, just put another way.

The man in chains shuffles across the floor of the prison conference room. He stands against the wall and mimes opening a door, a refrigerator door. Some good stuff inside. "You want your sandwich, kid?" Jack calls. But there is no answer, and he says, "I'll eat it, then."

When the ham and cheese is finally eaten, it's back to work for a bit. Just a few more things to clear up before bed. "Well, kid," Jack says, rising from his chair and walking to the bedroom where the boy lies, "I gotta get up early tomorrow. Time for you to get out."

Jack yawns expansively.

"I'll go," the boy says, still very weak, very obsequious. "I won't tell anybody. . . ."

"I know," Jack says. "I know you won't because there's one more trick. You'll love this. It's the rope trick." He turns and grabs two objects from some platform that stands just above waist level.

Jack kept the necessary implements on top of Asshole John's bedroom dresser: the trick requires a short length of nylon rope and a hammer handle. John must have wondered about Jack's tools sitting there on his dresser day after day. Did they have some relation to the strangled bodies he found in his home all those bad, hung-over mornings?

"This is the last trick," Jack says. He is a very sincere fellow, a little tired now, but this is a serious trick. "When we're done, I'll drive you back, okay?"

"Yes," the boy says, and there is fear and abject submission in that one word.

"Lemme help you up," Jack says, and he stoops, grabs the boy under the arm, and helps him struggle to his feet. "You going back to the Square?" Jack asks.

"I . . . no," the boy's voice is unsteady, and it is likely that he sways from side to side, a severely abused boy, almost a child, barely able to stand.

"Wait'll you see what this rope does for you," Jack says. There is a smirking and coarse sexuality in his tone, a nameless obscenity in his smile. "You'll love this," he says, his voice deep, not much more than a growl of excitement and anticipation.

And now Jack is making all the requisite motions: He is wrapping the rope around the boy's neck, he is tying the first knot—cross one end over the other and pull gently. It is the same knot Asshole John makes every morning when he ties his shoes, the simple crossover knot that begins a process that holds the tongue immobile.

"Noooooo?" A boy's questioning plea: horror without hope.

"Aw, c'mon," Jack says, breathing heavily now, "stand still. It's just a trick, for Chrissake. Feel how loose I've got it. It doesn't hurt at all." And then, lewdly, "Wait'll you see what this does for you."

Jack, his breath coming in ragged gasps, places the hammer handle over the first knot, then carefully ties a second knot, precisely the same as the first, over the splintered wood of the much-used handle.

"Oh, God, don't . . . don't hurt me any more."

"It's okay. This is the last trick."

Jack turns the hammer handle once, twice, three times. He lodges the end of the handle behind the boy's head and steps back to examine his work. The boy's hands are cuffed behind his back and the hammer holds the rope tightly, but not too tightly, around his throat.

It's a game, the boy would have to think, only a game. He would believe this because no one dies when he's eighteen; it's just one of those sex games, one of those strange, bad sex games. That's what it is, that's what it has to be: one of those games people play, a sex-and-danger game. A game of fear.

Maybe the boy already knows the game. You play it with a rope and slipknot: just loop the rope around the neck and pull during masturbation; time the ejaculation or orgasm to the point of passing out.

But if the boy knows of the game—if he's heard gossip about slipknots and ejaculations—there would be, in his mind, in his heart, a helpless explosion of hope. It's just sex, and I won't die. I can't die: I'm only eighteen, and this is only a game, a trick, "the last trick."

"Please," the boy says, whimpering, "please loosen it a little."

The man in chains takes a step forward. He grabs something—the hammer handle—and twists his hand as if turning on a faucet.

There is a choking gasp, a few strangled words: "Oh, God, please help me, God. . . ."

Jack turns the handle as if the motion costs him some effort. "God will help you," he says, and there is, in his voice, the rumbling solemnity of an organ as played at solemn services.

"God is here," the man says, but there is, in his voice, a religious or sexual mania so overwhelming that it is difficult for him to catch his breath, and he sinks slowly, slowly to his knees. He is moaning now, a sigh beyond love or life, and yet, out of the same mouth, at the same time, there is a strangled gurgling as well so that it is difficult to know if the sound is a rush of passion or the rattle of death. They merge now—the gurgling, strangled sighs, the ecstatic moans of extinction and release—so that one sound is indistinguishable from another and they both come from the same mouth.

Jack falls to his knees, his tongue loose inside a gaping mouth, the groan and gargle of his breath rattling in his throat until, finally, finally, with one last choking groan, it is over and they are both, man and boy, finally released.

The man in chains kneels silently on the hard, empty floor. His head is bowed, as if in fatigue and satiety. John Wayne Gacy kneels in a bare prison conference room: he kneels like a spent performer, center stage, alone and waiting. Soon the spotlight will shrivel about him until there is only a single ray, like a halo, very bright. And then there will be darkness, and a moment for the audience to absorb the power of his performance. A moment only before they burst into frenzied applause.

But there is no spotlight, and the man kneels silently, in his chains, his head bowed, as if in prayer.

CHAPTER
26

FIRST DAY OF the trial, the prosecution's got Robert Egan, some cocky young lawyer who had never lost a murder trial, standing in front of a jury saying that John Gacy was "rational and evil," a premeditated murderer. John could hardly believe it. What did Egan think? Did he think John said to himself, "Who's next?" The prosecutor showed "how nice and goody-goody" all the little shitheads were and how John sat around and figured, "You're going in this grave, you in that one." Jag-off Egan, the guy "could make a fortune writing fairy tales."

One of John's attorneys, Bob Motta, made the opening statement for the defense. Yeah, he said, Gacy did it. But take a look at his house. Twenty-nine bodies, he sleeps with 'em. That's not evil, that's crazy.

Motta gets into this thing about how John's sick and he oughta be put away in a mental hospital for the rest of his life.

John figured, on that first day of the trial, February 6, 1980, that Motta scored the most points. He wanted to correct the problem, help John. The state was bent on revenge. God didn't put people on earth so they could go around getting revenge. Vengeance is mine, saith the Lord. Revenge don't solve shit.

Then, at recess, eating lunch by himself in the bullpen, the whole thing hit John. Both the prosecution and defense wanted to put him away for life. Sure, John knew that he'd never win on an insanity plea if the jury thought he was going to spend only a month, six months in some hospital, but Motta was so fucking convincing. John's own lawyer really wanted to put him away for life. It was like his attorneys, Sam Amirante and Motta, were on the prosecution's side. There was no one on his side.

John felt dizzy then, and his nose began to bleed. Paramedics rushed him to the hospital, where the doctors said his blood pressure was a little high. They couldn't find anything else wrong with him. They never could.

The next day, it was all parents of these kids. Just mothers, mostly. The state had them on for dramatics and shit. Mothers breaking down on the stand, some of them phony as the day is long. This one who fainted, all they did, they asked her for a death study—When did you see your son last?—basic stuff. Then they showed her this bracelet they found on the kid when they dug him up from under the crawl space. She picks it up, says, "That's Sam's bracelet." She's crying in this phony way, all doubled up, then she sort of falls forward, pretending to faint right there in the courtroom. You could hear her head clunk on the witness stand.

John hoped the jury could pick up on how phony the whole thing was.

There were some sincere ones. John could even get tears in his eyes listening to them. But the honest ones didn't fucking faint and cry. They weren't actors. Why didn't his attorneys bring out that some of them were suing him? He had over fifty-five million dollars in wrongful-death suits on his hands. Phony-ass parents so concerned about their kids they could sue him for money.

The next week, the state had Rossi and Cram describe the trenches John had paid them to dig in the crawl space. Trying to make it look like all the killings were premeditated. John felt like jumping up, yelling at the jury. He'd point to Rossi or Cram and scream, "How do you know he's not involved? Because I don't even know if he was involved, and I was one of the witnesses!"

The jury would have to believe that he was crazy. Or that the state was lying about a conspiracy to kill these kids. And it would get the goddamn families, Piest and them, off his case. They were sitting together in the courtroom, the families, and John could feel the heat of their hatred burning into his back. If he could just get into a room with all of them for fifteen minutes, he could explain himself, let them see his side of the whole deal. Show them that he was a "scapegoat" and a "victim."

Ron Rhode took the stand and testified that John had called him seven months ago and said, "You can take it to the bank. I'm walking at the end of the year. . . ." Rhode said that John "told me he had some doctors. They were on his side."

Then the cops testified about the statements, these confessions John was supposed to have made after he was arrested. Nobody said he was exhausted and hung over and on drugs when he made the statements. Or that on one of them, his own lawyer Sam Amirante had advised John to talk to the investigators so the bodies could get a decent burial. Now the prosecution was using that statement, and all the others, against him. The confessions were all "hearsay." They were "self-serving" on the part of the investigators: "Look what I discovered, look what I uncovered."

Just like investigator Greg Bedoe came on and said that John told him he read the Twenty-third Psalm to one of his victims while twisting the rope tight around his neck. He said John confessed to doing "the ultimate number" on some kid who was into S&M. "For a masochist," John had said, "the ultimate number is death." Then Bedoe made it look as if John started bragging about "doing a double": killing two kids at once. John had said he strangled the second one as they stood over the corpse of the first.

Assistant state's attorney Larry Finder came on and said that in the middle of one confession John showed him the rope trick, using his rosary and a ball-point pen. "Pretend your wrist is a neck," John had said, and he twisted the rosary tight around Finder's arm. Later on, Finder described how John diagramed the graves on a pink sheet of paper, then—like he just woke up or something—asked if Jack Hanley made the diagram.

When chief deputy state's attorney William Kunkle introduced that diagram in an enlarged version, John shouted, "Your Honor, I didn't draw that drawing!" Planting a seed in the jury's mind right there. The judge, Louis B. Garippo, admonished him for the outbreak, but it was a lovely seed to plant. If John didn't draw it, who did? Self-serving cops? Bad Jack?

The state rested right after Finder and the rosary shit. John had to decide whether he would take the stand in his own defense. Sam Amirante told him, "John, it's your decision," which was a whole hell of a lot of help. Sam had a cigar that prosecutor Terry

Sullivan had given him for John. Like this prosecutor wanted to be buddies now. Make John think his pal Terry liked him. Fatten him up for the kill when he took the stand. Fuckhead. Next time John saw Sullivan, John said, "That was a good cigar, Terry. How come it didn't say, 'It's a boy'?"

"Who writes your material, John?" Sullivan asked.

John thought he could handle Sullivan on the stand. *William Kunkle was another matter. The deputy chief state's attorney was a big, chunky guy, and there were articles in the paper about how he rode around on a motorcycle and shit. Like some leather queen. Rough trade. Kunkle could take an argument "and just twist it around like a pretzel." That was a bisexual trait—the trick mind—and John hated Kunkle so bad, he figured he was queer. Bisexual at least. How could you hate a guy so bad if he wasn't queer?*

John had to admit he was "afraid of Kunkle"—big, tough, fairy-ass Kunkle—and put off the decision about taking the stand. He wanted to see what the docs said about Bad Jack. It was like he'd just spent fourteen months taking a test, and now the results were coming in. He didn't want to take on Kunkle until he heard what the docs had to say.

The defense led off with Jeff Rignall, who testified that John Gacy picked him up, chloroformed him, chained him into some sort of restraining device, raped him anally, and generally tortured him all night long. John didn't show any emotion, but he was getting pretty pissed: "This is my defense?" Rignall said he had been receiving psychiatric treatment since the attack.

In answer to Amirante's question, Rignall said that in his opinion John Gacy couldn't conform his behavior to the requirements of the law or appreciate the criminality of his actions "because of the beastly and animalistic ways he attacked me." Gacy was, in other words, legally insane at the time of the attack.

On cross-examination, Kunkle pointed out that Rignall had written a book on his encounter with John Gacy and tried to suggest that Jeff had testified for the defense to promote that book. He began taking Rignall over the various tortures he'd endured. The witness began to weep, softly at first, then he doubled over, sort of half fainting and hitting his head on the witness stand. He vomited—John thought, I got guys puking in my defense?—and then, half hidden by the witness stand, began sobbing loudly.

John wasn't sure the defense had scored any points with Rignall, because he thought the jury might be swayed more by emotion than actual legal argument or justice. John sure hoped the defense docs would be a little more help.

Thomas S. Eliseo was a Rockford, Illinois, clinical psychologist who had published a number of papers on schizophrenics and schizophrenic thinking in various professional journals. Testifying for the defense in the first stage of what was to be the kernel of the trial—the insanity defense—he explained to the jury that a psychologist, and in particular a clinical psychologist, uses "psychological testing, which is our specialty."

Eliseo found that Gacy was "of superior intelligence and about the top ten percent of the population." The neurological testing, where a client is asked to arrange blocks on a board while blindfolded, to copy designs, discriminate rhythms, and perform seven other tasks designed to isolate instances of organic brain damage, indicated that John Gacy did not, in fact, suffer from brain damage.

On the ten-card Rorschach test, Gacy gave only eighteen responses, about half what a psychologist might expect from a man of his age and intelligence. Gacy's interpretation of the inkblots "consisted primarily of animals and flowers, which again is unusual." He gave only one response that included people. Eliseo thought Gacy "seemed to be holding back, a very guarded sort of person" who felt he had to "keep himself in control at all times."

In the draw-a-person test, where a client is given a plain sheet of paper and simply asked to draw a person, Gacy "stated he didn't know how to draw . . . and all he would draw would be the head of one of his attorneys." Gacy refused to draw a picture of a woman. "One of the impressions you can draw from that," Eliseo said, "is that he is being somewhat guarded and evasive, not wanting to show much about himself. . . ." Because Gacy drew only a head and avoided "the rest of the human body from the neck down—and in connection with all the other test material and the clinical interview—you wonder what his idea about the body might be, whether it is something bad or disparaging that you have to avoid."

In the thematic apperception test (TAT), the client is given twenty pictures "and the person has to tell a story . . . just make up a story about who the people are and what they are doing . . . again Mr. Gacy did not reveal much about himself." On one card, number thirteen, Eliseo said Gacy showed "inappropriate feelings." The photo shows a woman lying in bed while a man stands in front of the window with his arm shading his eyes. One popular response to the picture, Eliseo said, is that the man "has gotten up in the morning and opens up the blinds and the light is shining. Mr. Gacy interpreted that: first he said he might have had sex with her. Then he changed it to maybe he killed her. And then he laughed inappropriately, talking about killing her and saying it is too late now and seemed to be upset about it, but trying to cover it up."

The Minnesota multiphasic personality inventory (MMPI), Eliseo said, is "based on five hundred sixty-six statements that somebody answers true or false . . . an example is, 'I like *Mechanic* magazine.'" The basis of the test is that people differ and will respond to the questions differently. A librarian, Eliseo said, probably wouldn't be found sitting at a bar reading *Mechanic* magazine, while a truck driver might. The answers a client gives in the MMPI are compared "with people who are in psychiatric hospitals . . . and a normal group so you come with nine different scales on how you compare with people with different psychiatric disorders."

Gacy's responses to the MMPI, Eliseo said, indicated "that he is an extremely disordered person, that his thinking is confused, that he resembles to a large extent people who would be classified as schizophrenic, classified as paranoid. . . ."

There is a lie scale on the MMPI, a list of a dozen questions designed to indicate whether a person is trying to look good. One of the statements on the lie scale, for instance, reads, "When I was a child I would sometimes try to sneak into a movie theater if I thought I wouldn't get caught." Most people, Eliseo said, answer "true." Those who answer "false" may be "trying to look good." The higher the score on the lie scale, the more indication there is that "someone is trying to look good." John Gacy scored zero on the lie scale: he was, Eliseo said, not lying to look good.

Based on the tests and a clinical interview, Eliseo diagnosed Gacy in two ways. The doctor testified that Gacy was "a borderline personality, a person who on the surface looks normal but has all kinds of neurotic, antisocial, psychotic illnesses." The personality structure underlying Gacy's apparent normality, Eliseo said, was paranoid schizophrenia, which Eliseo described as "the viewpoint of a person who basically sees the world as a place where you have to be constantly careful, very suspicious, very guarded. That there are constant dangers out there and feeling at times people are out to hurt you. And also the feeling that you are better than other people." Eliseo said that the paranoid schizophrenic will exhibit "grandiosity . . . he feels that he can do things and that he is justified in doing these things, and feels they are right. It is in contrast to what he says openly. What he says consciously."

Paranoid people, Eliseo said, "are usually paranoid most of their lives." He thought Gacy had been suffering from the disease since "his midtwenties . . . and I would hypothesize after the death of his father in 1969 is when it began."

John was "on a high." Eliseo great. Paranoid schizophrenic. John felt like he "passed the test."

The prosecution wanted to show that Gacy was never out of touch with reality and did not fit the legal definition of insanity because he was able at all times to appreciate the criminality of his conduct and conform his actions to the requirements of the law. Kunkle, on cross, bore down hard on Eliseo. Kunkle threw his powerful bulk into the questions: an aggressive, angry man who demanded to know how the psychologist could give an opinion as to when the condition started.

"Are you telling this judge, Mr. Eliseo—"

Motta objected. "It is 'Doctor.' "

"It is whatever I choose to call him."

"It is Dr. Eliseo, counsel, and I will ask the court—"

"Mr. Witness—"

"Just one moment. I will ask the court to admonish the state's attorney to give this witness the proper respect."

"Some people don't call me 'Judge,' " Garippo replied. "He may be referred to either way."

"Mr. Witness," Kunkle said, "are you telling this court that an individual could be in a psychotic state, paranoid schizophrenic, as you say—a quite serious mental disease—from his twenties?"

"Yes, sir," Eliseo replied.

"Through the time of this hypothetical person's arrest, which would be almost twenty years later . . . that he would be psychotic for seventeen years and would never be hospitalized, never diagnosed, would never be treated?"

"Yes, sir."

Kunkle seemed to rattle the psychologist with his aggressiveness, his lack of respect. "How many cases like that have you seen?" Kunkle demanded.

"Few."

"Would you name those?"

Eliseo, resonating with Kunkle's palpable anger, replied: "Particularly with paranoid schizophrenia, I don't want to name— Richard M. Nixon."

Kunkle was amazed and impressed. "You have treated President Nixon?"

"No. From what I have read and seen, King George the Third, of England."

On further direct examination by Motta, Eliseo said again that Gacy's paranoia, his schizophrenic condition, started in his twenties and was continuous and uninterrupted from that time. "That does not mean he was psychotic overtly all of the time, but the condition was there, and probably he looked good, like most people do."

"Objection," Kunkle said. "Either it's continuous or it's not."

It was the first of what were to be many similar exchanges. The defense was anxious to show that Gacy was suffering from a mental disease characterized by the appearance of normality—an illness that erupted into full-blown "florid" psychosis at odd intervals.

The prosecution would push the defense doctors, trying to counter their testimony that Gacy was psychotic or mentally ill only at the time of the murders. It was an argument, the prosecution felt, that was offensive to common sense, that seemed a little too convenient for the defendant—he was only legally insane while committing murder. In a related argument, the prosecution wanted to suggest that Gacy feigned mental illness to escape punishment.

Since Dr. Eliseo had based much of his diagnosis on the

results of the MMPI, Kunkle asked if the test couldn't have been faked. Was there a scale that corresponded to the lie scale, only one that measured malingering, one that measured people who wanted to look bad, who were faking illness?

"There is a malingering scale," Eliseo said. "That is a scale developed in the Army, a military situation where they have much more malingering than we have in civilian occupations. . . ."

Kunkle pointed out that when you subtract the MMPI's K scale from its F scale "and get a number of eleven or higher, it gives a high probability of malingering or faking. . . . Do you know what Mr. Gacy's F score was?"

"Twenty."

"And what was his K score?"

"Nine."

"And what is twenty minus nine?"

"Eleven."

Eliseo admitted that if Gacy did malinger, if he had lied to simulate mental disease, it would affect the test.

Kunkle hammered away at the cornerstone of the defense argument, the idea that while Gacy appeared normal, he was psychotic at the times the crimes were committed. "Well, Doctor, after he had killed the first person he had killed and he buried and hid that body underground, is that an indication to you that he did not appreciate that he had committed any criminal act?"

"Afterwards, he would not be aware."

And the second murder, was he not aware of the criminality again?

"At the moment that he did it, he was not aware of the criminality."

"Or the third?"

"Yes, I think all of them he did not."

"Right through thirty-three?"

"Yes, sir, that he was in a state where he was psychotic for that period and all he thought was to kill this person."

"He was psychotic for the whole period and all he could do was kill people?"

"No, not for the whole period, but during the time he actually went around and committed the act, not for the whole eight years. . . ."

William Kunkle, it appeared, was having a hard time believing this testimony. "Was he psychotic for eight years solid, or wasn't he? Yes or no."

"Yes, but."

" 'Yes but'?"

"Yes."

And Kunkle dismissed Dr. Eliseo with a grand gesture of contemptuous disbelief. "But for thirty-three bodies. I have nothing further."

The second doctor to testify in John's defense was Lawrence Z. Freedman, a psychiatrist and psychoanalyst whose accomplishments, honors, and published articles took twenty pages of trial transcript to detail. Freedman was presently chairman of the Institution of Social and Behavioral Pathology, had been chairman at the conference on Rage, Aggression, and Violence at the Center for Advanced Study in Behavioral Sciences at Stanford. He had published many scholarly articles, and he was the author of the chapter on forensic psychiatry in the *Comprehensive Textbook of Psychiatry*.

Freedman testified that he spent "about fifty hours" interviewing John Gacy. It was, the doctor said, an unusually long period of time to spend in direct examination but that "Mr. Gacy is a very complex man." In fact, Freedman testified that "I found Mr. Gacy one of the most complex personalities I have ever tried to study."

During that time, Freedman noticed that Gacy "would contradict himself." He said that "Mr. Gacy is a man who isn't quite sure who he is and from time to time would manifest different aspects of his personality, which sometimes contradicted previous aspects demonstrated in our conversations."

Jack Hanley was not some alternate personality, but Dr. Freedman did think the name had "various levels of significance. It is very common for middle-class men to protect their reputations when they solicit boy prostitutes, to use a false name. In my opinion, however, it goes beyond that. I believe Mr. Gacy is, in fact, troubled, uncertain about the two aspects of his personality: the driven aspects and the one which expresses such extraordinary aggression and sexual perversion."

Gacy, Freedman said, is a man who is psychotic at the core but whose defense mechanisms resemble neurosis. A neurotic,

Freedman said, "is a person who has some kind of incapacity or compulsion which disturbs him or makes him unhappy and offends others but is not serious enough to totally incapacitate him." The neurotic, Freedman said, lies between normalcy and psychosis, which is "the most severe form of mental illness." Schizophrenia is a form of psychosis characterized by distortion in the thinking process and by dissociation, "a separation between ideas and acts and the feeling which would normally accompany them."

Freedman said that Gacy's history showed a pattern of "at least neurotic and psychosomatic illness from very early childhood. And my impression is that the shift from a serious neurosis to the beginnings of psychosis probably occurred about the time of Christmas of 1969, when he was at a very low point in his life, an inmate at Anamosa, a failure as his father had always predicted. His father died on Christmas. He had wanted to present his father with a painting. He asked one of his friends at the prison to make a painting. He was unable to go to the funeral. I think that triggered the difference between serious neurosis to the development of a psychosis."

Freedman said that "Mr. Gacy, from the time of his birth, according to his mother, has always been considered to have had physical problems. I think this preoccupation with physical problems was, in a sense, taught to him. His mother believed that when he was born, he had respiratory distress because of congestion of fecal matter in the womb. Year after year, Mr. Gacy—John, I suppose, as he was called when he was a youngster—would be told that he had heart diseases, so his anxieties, which were very great, tended in part to be translated into physical concern, preoccupation with himself."

Gacy, Freedman said, shows "an extraordinary dissociation. . . . Mr. Gacy described to me, as he did to others, the conditions under which Robert Piest was killed, in great detail. At the same time, his Uncle Harold . . . was dying. In his description of the boy and his strangulation and his death, there was an extraordinary absence of ordinary manifestations of human feeling. There was no feeling for this boy" or for any of the other victims in "his descriptions of other such episodes.

"There was a kind of concern of a sort concerning the death of his uncle, who was his mother's last remaining brother, but in describing these events which resulted in the deaths of the people, it was as though he was describing taking a drink of water. There was a certain amount of pride in his being able to use his cunning to overcome the strength of these muscular youths, whom he called 'dumb and stupid.' "

Freedman described the "remarkable dissociation between emotion . . . between feeling and behavior" as "pathological."

Freedman also described Gacy as compulsive, obsessive. Freedman's books, for instance, were not in order, lying about his office, and that had irritated John. "Similarly, when he would describe cruising, he would want to make sure I knew which street he had gone to and at what time, and he has an extraordinary memory for these details." Considering the "peril" that Gacy was facing, Freedman said the fact that these "obsessive, compulsive preoccupations override his concern" was "abnormal."

Freedman said he "tried to figure out how Mr. Gacy could crowd in all the activities he did: the political activities, the social activities, the organizations of large parties, dressing up as a clown and going to children's wards, his relationship with his wife and friends, his cruising.

"Only a man with profound drive and great organizational abilities could have done this . . . a driven man who is able to accomplish all these different things by extraordinary organization of his time and energy." Freedman said that he believed "this was a more and more frantic effort to obliterate from his consciousness forms of behavior and feeling which he could not stand to face and so he worked harder and harder to relate to his business, to people, to clubs, anything that would keep him from looking into himself and being a lonely person, dumb and stupid, incapable, as his father often called him."

The father, whom Freedman described as "a man's man," was "extremely disappointed in his son. He wanted his son to do the things that he did, and he found him inept. He was very brutal toward him, he gave him the feeling he was dumb and stupid . . . over time, Mr. Gacy developed serious concern, anxiety which he would deny about his sexual identification: how masculine he was, how feminine he was. The pattern of his life revealed that he made serious efforts to establish meaningful relationships with women."

Gacy, Freedman said, "becomes very angry when the term 'homosexuality' is ascribed to him. He insisted that he is not homosexual, that he is bisexual, and that oral sex [with males] was a form of masturbation. He thinks a homosexual is a man who loves other men, and he had no such feelings for these people. They were trash whom he picked up. They were dumb and stupid."

Clearly, Freedman said, Gacy was engaged in homosexual activity, but "by projecting his own homosexual feelings onto the partner whom he paid or tricked or persuaded, he was denying his own homosexual role and projecting it onto the other person."

In describing the process of projection as it related to Gacy, Freedman went back to John's youth, when "a contractor would come by and take John . . . to look at his construction. . . . He would get John to wrestle with him, and John would find himself with his head between the contractor's legs." Freedman thought this was a significant contribution to John's sexual confusion, as was the fact that "every relationship he had with girls during this period was severely punished."

Aside from sexual confusion in his youth, John's family situation resulted in difficult and ambiguous emotional situations. A dramatic example of the mixture of feelings occurred when, as a teenager, John fought with the Old Man. "His father," Freedman said, "began to curse him and say, 'Hit me, hit me, you coward.' And John replied, 'I love you, I won't hit you, I love you, I won't hit you.'"

"This mixture of aggression and love," Freedman said, "indicates an enormous strain on the psychological structure of the individual. The next day, as typically happened in that family, nothing was said . . . it was as though nothing had happened."

As John grew older, "he began having fights about other things . . . for example . . . he borrowed money from his father to buy a car and then his father began to berate him about paying the money back until he finally simply left home, drove the car to Las Vegas, and stayed away for approximately three months, during which time he . . . had a great fright during one night at the mortuary, finally became lonely and came back." Freedman didn't describe the "great fright" John experienced.

The psychiatrist believed that John was one of many homosexuals who "are afraid of . . . a program of public disfavor. . . . This does not necessarily lead to paranoia, but if there is a stronger-than-average trend in that direction which is . . . denied by him, there is projection: I'm not a homosexual, he's a homosexual. And this . . . develops, through a series of psychological maneuvers, to 'He hates me.' And then there is a defensive maneuver to defend one's self against the other, hating person."

Freedman testified that projection is a "psychological defense. It is not something that one decides to do. It happens to you."

Another psychological defense, Freedman said, is repression. "We all have repression. As we mature and develop, there are things which children do which we must not only stop doing but forget we ever did. That's repression, and it occurs normally. Under very tortured circumstances, such as I believe characterized John Gacy's childhood, the repression takes an abnormal turn. . . ."

Gacy repressed his murderous impulses, but when this psychological defense mechanism broke down, "then all the things he fears come out—when the stress is too great, when fatigue becomes overwhelming, depression becomes too great—the things which are being covered by other forms of activity, in a sense, explode."

Alcohol or other drugs, Freedman said, can break down the defense mechanisms, but other things—stress, for example—could trigger a psychotic episode. "At the time of his accosting the Piest boy," Freedman pointed out, "his uncle, who he once slipped and called his father, was dying. This whole relationship with the Piest boy was mixed up with this death in the family, which, perhaps meaningfully, was occurring just as the Christmas season approached, just as his father had died at Christmas. . . ."

The very acts of oral and anal sex that Gacy perpetrated on his victims may have been the causes of John's murderous rage. "I think," Freedman said, "that he projected his own frightened awareness that this was homosexual . . . and he thought of them as trash, to be put out of their misery by these methods: a projection of his own feelings—which might have been turned against himself—turned against them."

Freedman also thought "it was very significant [that] these were muscular teenagers." John had been "a flabby and inadequate teenager, and these boys represented what he had never been able to attain." Freedman said that "the young teenage muscular boys whom he seduced through cunning and allegedly attacked reflected both the hostility he felt toward those who personified what he failed to achieve—at least in his father's eyes—and toward himself."

Only the Piest murder, Freedman said, did not follow a pattern. "In fact, if one views the Piest tragedy in the context of what happened previously, it seemed to have violated all his measures of self-protection." The Piest murder, in Freedman's opinion, was geared toward apprehension.

Freedman testified that "Mr. Gacy suffers serious disturbances in his thinking, his mood, and his behavior. He has displayed severe ambivalence. That means contradictory feelings—love and hate—toward key figures in his family, beginning with his father and including his image of himself. . . . Mr. Gacy demonstrates . . . seemingly neurotic and psychophysiological symptoms. The compulsive work, the obsession with detail, the sexually deviate compulsions, the drug addictions and the antisocial aggressivities, the inappropriateness of his feelings and his actions all subsume a personality which is best described as pseudoneurotic schizophrenic paranoid. The most acute and dangerous paranoia apparently emerges during periods of great tension, often accompanied by a large intake of Valium, alcohol, or marijuana."

The fact that John Gacy instructed employees to dig holes to be used as graves was not inconsistent with Freedman's diagnosis, he said, "because there are numerous examples of paranoidal personalities who prepared for their deadly acts."

In Freedman's opinion, Gacy posed as a police officer for a combination of reasons: manipulation of others, and a kind of self-manipulation that helped "overcome his deep-seated feelings of inferiority."

It was significant and contributed to the diagnosis of paranoid schizophrenia, Freedman said, that Gacy could deny being a violent person one moment and in the next explain the rope trick in detail. The fact that he stored bodies under his bed and in his closets was a "profoundly pathological phenomenon" that further contributed to the diagnosis.

The fucking old man screwed him. John couldn't believe it. Freeedman, who asked to meet Jack Hanley—the one John figured liked him and understood him—said there was no big split, no Bad Jack. He wouldn't even say John was legally insane, that he couldn't appreciate and conform.

"The question," Freedman had said, "goes to the legal and social thresholds of punishability . . . it is not a psychiatric question but a legal question. And I feel these questions are outside my level of competence."

Fairy Kunkle, with his self-satisfied smirk, zeroed in on that right away. Hadn't Freedman testified for the defense in the case of Simon Peter Nelson two years previous, and at that time did he not give such an opinion? Nelson was accused of killing his six children, Freedman said, and he "developed, as is not uncommonly the case, a total amnesia for those events." Freedman examined Nelson during the course of a summer and "one day that amnesia was broken through." Nelson, "in a dissociated state," presented "a definite reenactment of the killings. . . ."

There were some elements in the Nelson case that were similar to the case in question: a complicated relationship with a hated father, a father who committed suicide on his wife's birthday. Freedman, listening to Nelson's reenactment, believed the man "thought he was committing suicide in three different ways." There was "a splitting of his personality, the assumption of the personality of the father."

Freedman testified, right in the middle of all this, that he had never seen John in a dissociated state. Like he didn't believe that John really couldn't remember the killings. The jury didn't know it, but Freedman seemed to be saying that John had lied to him. That Bad Jack didn't exist.

The fucking old man even came up to John afterward and said he was sorry he couldn't help. The man was "a Judas." This was one doc who had actually met Bad Jack. John was sure of it.

John had guys puking in his defense and doctors who were supposed to be on his side hinting that he was a liar. He was "down."

The prosecution knew it, too. They gave him another cigar that day.

CHAPTER

27

So Freedman screwed him. *John wasn't giving up hope. A quitter never wins, a winner never quits. There were more docs ready to testify for the defense.*

Next up was Dr. Robert Traisman, a clinical psychologist specializing in psychodiagnosis, who examined Gacy in 3 North at Cermak for three and half hours on May 10, 1979.

On the Rorschach inkblot test, Traisman testified, Gacy offered only sixteen responses, whereas, Traisman said, "with an individual with his high level of intelligence, one would expect at least double that."

In the draw-a-person test, Gacy first drew Traisman, which the doctor thought was "defensive on his part . . . reflective of his own uncertainty with his own body. I would imagine he needed somebody to play off of or use as a model. . . ." Traisman noticed that Gacy had carefully drawn the left hand and heavily shaded the wedding band there, while the right was "very small, almost mittenlike. . . ." Citing research on the test—"interpretations that have stood up"—Traisman said that the right hand is the power side, the masculine side, while the left "is thought to symbolize the more feminine side." He thought "Mr. Gacy had difficulty in feeling a degree of masculine identity with himself."

The second drawing Gacy identified "as a thirty-four-year-old washerwoman." It was, Traisman said, "anything but a feminine woman. It was a very massive, masculine-appearing woman," a woman with the "arms of a football player." She wore a tight belt with two long loops over the genital area that the doctor thought were very obvious phallic extension symbols, which "certainly suggested strong sexual anxiety . . . within him."

When Gacy was asked to draw anything he liked, he drew his own house and "almost every brick was drawn in detail." He drew in the lamppost, the garden, and the design on the aluminum door. "The drawing," Traisman testified, "reflected a tremendous compulsiveness and perfectionism to him, as did other tests."

Gacy's responses to standardized pictures of the thematic apperception test, Traisman said, "reflected . . . marked feeling of sexual inadequacy, much sexual confusion, a great deal of hostility and rage, and an essential lack of feeling for other individuals."

Based on all the tests, Traisman said he considered Gacy to be "a paranoid schizophrenic . . . an individual who has a great deal of difficulty in integrating his behavior or integrating his emotions or self in normal ways of living. . . ."

It was entirely possible, Traisman said, for a paranoid schizophrenic to appear normal on the surface. Such individuals, Traisman said, are "called ambulatory schizophrenics."

Dr. Richard G. Rappaport, a psychiatrist in private practice with a special interest in forensic psychiatry, testified that he examined Gacy for a total of sixty-five hours over a period of about five months. There was some question in the doctor's mind about whether Gacy was lying; however, he didn't think John was malingering or feigning illness because "the entire picture in this individual is too consistent and too classical to believe he could in any way develop symptoms and signs and a history which would indicate that this illness is really contrived."

Based on the results of a neurological history and examination, Rappaport concluded that there was nothing physiologically wrong with John Gacy that would cause a mental illness. The EEG was within normal limits. The CAT scan was normal. A chromosomal analysis, Rappaport said, indicated that Gacy did have the XXY chromosomal pattern that is thought to indicate an inherited tendency toward violent or criminal acts.

Rappaport studied Gacy's medical records, "which were extensive." But for all the hospitalizations, all the heart problems, "there was . . . nothing diagnosed of a serious or actual existing condition."

The medical records, Rappaport testified, were "significant in understanding his overall personality. I think that they were all what is commonly called hysterical or conversion symptoms. That means that somebody can psychologically induce a condition which appears to be medical. This is to be differentiated from malingering, which is a conscious attempt to produce an illness . . . for example, somebody who is afraid of something—let's say blood—might faint. Well, fainting is a hysterical symptom. Passes out, causes themself to avoid that situation."

Rappaport diagnosed Gacy as "a borderline personality, or personality organization with a subtype of psychopathic personality also manifesting instances of psychotic or paranoid schizophrenic behavior." It was essentially Freedman's diagnosis—pseudoneurotic paranoid schizophrenia—under a newer name.

The borderline personality organization, Rappaport said, is considered to be a serious mental illness, falling somewhere between the neurotic and psychotic diagnoses.

Gacy, Rappaport said, had been cooperative during the interviews. The man was, in fact, a self-confessed "motormouth." In analyzing Gacy's effusive and bewildering stream of talk, Rappaport noticed that "almost invariably, everything he said he would present both sides." The psychiatrist found this significant and thought John "was unable to really feel one way at any time about anything. . . . He was unable to relax in a sense with the existence of any one thought."

Like Freedman, Rappaport found John's relationship to his father to be of seminal importance. "His father," Rappaport said, "would come home from work and be in a good mood and go down in the basement . . . and when he would come up, he would be drunk . . . harsh, punitive, critical, and sometimes in a rage . . . any little incident could be a source of anger." Rappaport mentioned the fishing trip where John was blamed for two weeks of rain, the running enamel on the first window John ever tried to paint. The basement, Rappaport said, "struck me as very important . . . it was always locked up . . . a very prohibited area, and the mystery around the basement seemed to pervade his thinking

. . . the mystery was enhanced by the fact that the father changed his personality . . . from the time he . . . went down into the basement and the time he came up. . . . I think the idea of something prohibitive was crucial in that he was not allowed access to this."

Simultaneously, Gacy's medical problems "affected his ability to participate in sports and to be a part of the gang, part of the peer group and affected his feelings about himself in relationships to other kids and adequacy. . . . I think he felt he was defective."

Gacy, Rappaport said, practiced myriad perversions that the psychiatrist defined as repetitive and persistent forms of behavior that take the place of normal sexual relationship with a mature adult. Perversions are "representations of a block due to fear of castration . . . and the fear is allayed . . . by adoption . . . of the . . . perversions."

Rappaport said the first source of castration fear in the male arises out of the Oedipal situation, the familiar romance in which a young boy may fall in love with his mother. These Oedipal feelings "are usually diminished after the age of six until puberty. . . ."

Another source of castration fear, the doctor said, arises out of homicidal impulses. "The little boy, in wanting to possess his mother, wants to do away with his father. . . . However, in John Gacy, because of the abuse that he received . . . he developed heightened feelings of wanting to get rid of his father, tremendous homicidal feelings with rage."

The third source of "expectation of punishment," Rappaport said, arose out of Gacy's desire to please his father. "He became a very hardworking, very ambitious, industrious individual. He tried intensely to get his father's favor. . . . So he was, in a sense, selling himself . . . and he felt very angry about doing that." It was a form of prostitution that had "something to do with his depreciation of the victims. . . ."

The first of Gacy's psychosexual disorders or perversions to appear during his development was fetishism, which Rappaport said was the "use of an inanimate object to heighten sexual pleasure and take the place of the actual sexual object. . . . The fetish is usually a symbol for the penis which helps the individual deny the expectation of castration. He sees that as an object symbolizing a penis and then can, in his mind, deny the fact that this castration might take place."

Women's underwear, in particular, Rappaport said, "helps the individual to deny the nakedness of the female: the naked female . . . just appears to somebody in this situation as a castrated individual. So rather than being able to view that naked female, he only is willing to view the underwear and to deny to himself that this is a castrated individual. This is one of the reasons he collected the underwear, and I think that it even has something to do with his . . . stuffing them in the victims' mouths."

In collecting these articles, Rappaport said, Gacy was "able to see a representation of a fetish, a penis, and thereafter in his mind" he may have believed that he himself was "not going to be castrated for the things that he has done. He carried it to such an extent that eventually he was able to replace in his mind the female. . . . He is afraid of the female because it reminds him of the fear of castration, so he went so far as to eliminate from his sexual life the female" and to "adopt the role of homosexuality."

Rappaport pointed out that the newest literature from the American Psychiatric Association did not define homosexuality as a perversion or psychosexual dysfunction. The category is now called "ego-dystonic homosexuality" and "just considers those homosexuals who feel uncomfortable with that tendency. Ego-dystonic means it does not feel good or compatible with your self-image." Rappaport thought Gacy's homosexuality was of the ego-dystonic type.

In the male homosexual, the doctor said, "there is the obvious elimination of the castration fear because . . . the sexual partner has a fetish, and you are not threatened by the idea of a penisless object. . . ." In addition, Gacy fit the profile of a "narcissism homosexual," one who is "able to see in the other partner . . . someone like himself . . . to tender, in some way, tenderness to this other individual and then enjoy . . . the tenderness he is imparting. He is able to imagine the person given the tenderness is him. . . ."

Gacy didn't want "to participate with women because they required something of him. . . . Males, as far as he was concerned, he only got from them. And what he was getting . . . was this feeling of admiration. He played the role of father, and he was able to be tender and give them advice . . . point out to them how

. . . dumb it was to go with a stranger and to go into somebody's car. . . . In a sense he was trying to do this at first as a father figure . . . and he was identifying with them as though he was the son getting this advice" that "he was unable to get . . . from his father. So he was able to play several roles."

Gacy also practiced sexual sadism, which Rappaport defined as "the persistent use of psychological or physical means of degrading and punishing and humiliating the sexual object or another person for the purpose of sexual pleasure." In reality, the doctor said, "it is an expression of aggression . . . rather than the sexual drive."

The sadist, Rappaport testified, "identifies with the aggressor. In this particular case, Gacy was identifying with "his father, the person who inflicted all of the pain on him . . . the humiliation. . . . He was able to take out his hostility on helpless victims who were either tied up, who were in some way degraded, humiliated, and this gave him a great deal of relief in feeling this control."

The last of the perversions practiced by John Gacy was necrophilia, which Rappaport said has two forms. Sexual necrophilia "refers to the male having sexual relations with a corpse," while "nonsexual necrophilia is the idea of looking at, being near, gazing at a corpse . . . the idea is again to have a completely helpless victim and to enhance the feelings of power and control to allay the fear of castration."

The necrophiliac "tends to collect corpses as a fetishism expression of necrophilia and as a way of assuring himself of the fact that people love him. He has . . . all these bodies, people who supposedly loved him and cared for him and then he feels better . . . because he has . . . representations of a lot of people that care for him."

Necrophilia, Rappaport said, "is not an isolated perversion" but "a culmination of a series of perversion acts." Taken together, the fetishism, ego-dystonic homosexuality, sadism, and necrophilia constitute "polymorphous perversions" that, Rappaport said, "[are] chief characteristic[s] of the borderline. . . ."

The borderline personality organization, according to Dr. Rappaport, can encompass the narcissistic personality disorder. The narcissistic person, Rappaport said, has an overweening sense of grandiosity: "He is all that exists, everything exists around him,

for him." Another characteristic "is a pervasive sense of power
and brilliance" combined with an exhibitionistic tendency "to
display himself," to "want to be in the limelight . . . have people
looking at him and admiring him. . . ." In Gacy's case, the narcissism could also take "subtle form . . . he would march in parades,
would be a clown . . . a politician. . . ."

The narcissistic person is also characterized by his inability
"to feel empathy for other people. He has no idea what others are
experiencing when they suffer . . . he only knows his own feelings."

A final characteristic of the narcissistic personality, Rappaport
said, is "entitlement, which means he feels he is entitled to have
everything. People are to serve him and do for him."

A second personality disorder that fits into the category of
the borderline personality organization, Rappaport said, is the
antisocial or psychopathic personality. That, Rappaport explained,
is "someone who has all of the characteristics of the narcissistic,
plus . . . a deep problem with the superego," which, Rappaport
said, was one of "three parts of the psychic structure: the id, the
ego, and the superego. Everyone has heard these terms. The id
represents the drives that the newborn child has at birth. The
superego represents the value of the parents and society," which
"is a controlling mechanism over the drives of the id. And the ego
is the personality or culmination of this inner action between the
id and superego. . . ."

Rappaport said that "the word 'conscience' is a common
term which refers to the superego . . . you can say . . . there is a
defect in conscience. . . . They have gaps, spaces in the conscience.
Sometimes they can do what is right . . . and sometimes they
don't."

The inconsistency "comes from the fact that the parental
values were inconsistent. On the one hand, the father might tell
him not to behave badly, but then he himself would behave badly
. . . he himself is violent and disparaging and humiliating and
degrading, so that the child has the conflict in understanding what
is right and wrong . . ." and "develops a conscience or superego
[that] is inconsistent," that has "holes," "gaps."

As a result, the antisocial personality has "repeated conflicts with the law and with society."

In addition, Rappaport said, "the psychopath or antisocial
person seems to have the quality of remorse, sensitivity, feelings,

empathy, sadness . . . but underneath he is cold and ruthless. He does not have these characteristics. They only seem to be there, and that is why, in many cases, people who came in contact with Gacy thought he was a normal guy . . . he pretends to be someone who has all the characteristics of a normal individual, but underneath they don't really exist."

Rappaport thought that the narcissistic and antisocial personality disorders "didn't explain many of the other aspects" of Gacy's behavior, however. A diagnosis of borderline personality organization, however, would encompass these aspects.

The borderline, Rappaport said, is characterized by overwhelming feelings—"intense affect"—of "hostility or depression, and the depression in the borderline" results out of a sense of "loneliness." The borderline "cannot tolerate being alone, tends to seek out crowds . . . he might have parties at his house with four hundred of his closest friends or surround himself with these bodies." Or go cruising at two in the morning.

A second characteristic of the borderline "is the presence of impulsive behavior. . . . It is either . . . episodic in the form of self-mutilation or drug overdoses or otherwise chronic in the form of alcoholism or promiscuity," such as Gacy's "polymorphous perversion sexuality."

The borderline, Dr. Rappaport said, experiences "episodes of psychoses. These are transient in nature, and they often occur as a result of rage. They are sometimes different than the full-blown psychotic paranoid schizophrenia, but there is a great deal of similarity. The chief difference is that they are short. They may last only hours, and at the end of this time, the person reintegrates to a degree." The psychotic experiences can happen as a result of drug and alcohol abuse, or "they come about from stress, fatigue, and internal stress."

Finally, Rappaport said, the borderline will use "three primitive ego defenses: splitting, projective identification, and gross denial." The first of these, splitting, begins in the first few days of life, in the "oceanic feeling" of the newborn who "cannot differentiate himself, his body boundaries . . . where he begins, where his mother begins. After a few days or a few weeks . . . he begins to see . . . that there is a mother or a person out there. He recognizes . . . when he cries that someone either comes or doesn't come. . . . A person brings a bottle or changes his diaper. . . .

"He also begins to recognize that he has feelings which are different. At times he feels at peace . . . and other times he feels distressed. So he's beginning to differentiate himself from the outside world. . . .

"In the normal individual, as he develops, he should have the ability to fuse these concepts. To recognize that mother sometimes answers his needs and sometimes doesn't. It's the same mother."

In borderlines, Rappaport said, "there is a defect at this point. . . . He's unable to recognize and to comprehend and to allow himself to feel hate and anger toward the same person that he loved." The person could be the mother or the father, and, in Gacy's case, Rappaport thought "it was both" but "predominately the father." Young John Gacy "was unable to metabolize the feelings . . . so he split them off and capsulated apart these two feelings. . . . At various times he was in touch with one or the other, but never both at the same time. It would produce too much anxiety. It would be overwhelming and could cause a full-blown psychosis, a personality state [Gacy] could not withdraw from if he had not used this particular defense mechanism."

Gacy, Rappaport said, "could not see himself or another individual as having a combination of qualities." In conversation, Rappaport noticed that John would present one idea followed quickly by the opposite idea and "never put them together. [He] sees himself as a peaceful, calm, easygoing individual. At other times, he sees himself as totally rageful [and has] almost no memory or no realization of the other side of him, and that's where the big split comes in."

Gacy split off "the negative qualities . . . the things he didn't like about himself . . . the incestuous idea . . . homicidal feelings toward his father . . . embarrassment feelings he had about his homosexuality . . . rage toward his parents. These feelings he wants to get out of his self. The recognition internally that these feelings exist built up . . . tremendous rage inside him. He has a need to discharge these feelings, to get them outside himself. So he creates a scenario."

In the scenario, "he brings . . . young boys to his home," where he can star in a play scripted by himself, and the play itself is an example of the second primitive ego defense common to borderlines: projective identification. "First," Rappaport said, "he begins to act as a father to them . . . acts tenderly . . . tries to show them that he has a fatherly instinct and they are boys he can take care of. As I mentioned, these are . . . young men and boys who are at the height of the Oedipal themselves, who have the characteristics of the developed phallus . . . they are boys . . . he can identify with, who he recognizes as having qualities that he feels. . . .

"Now, he'd get these boys and he would begin to project onto them the qualities that he had inside himself and that he didn't like. . . . He could say that they are selling themselves, as he sold himself to try and impress his father. He could say that they were degraded . . . dehumanized as his father made him." He begins to feel it is not himself he is hating, but the young men.

At first, Rappaport said, Gacy would have been at least unconsciously aware that the familiar hatred he sensed in the boys actually existed within him. But "at some point in the scenario that he goes through" Gacy would progress from simple projection to projective identification. "He then feels that these qualities . . . exist in the other person. They are no longer a part of him. They are in this other person and he feels expunged or cleansed. . . . Now he sees these persons as . . . bad . . . homicidal . . . threatening. . . .

"He is then the father in identifying with the aggressor, and these victims, these boys, are then himself. He can . . . kill them . . . and in a way rid himself forever of these qualities that are inside of himself: the hostile threats and frightening figures that pervade his unconscious. He is so convinced that these qualities exist in this other person, he is completely out of touch with reality . . . and he has to get rid of them and save himself . . . he has to kill them."

Gross denial, the third of the primitive ego defenses common to borderlines, according to Rappaport, allowed Gacy to live with the horror of what he had done. "This is a way," the doctor testified, "that the borderline has of disengaging himself from the consistency of what he does. He's able to see the dead body there somewhat as if it were a cocoon, an empty shell from a butterfly. It's only a representation of the bad part of him. It's a shell. It's flimsy. It has nothing to do with humanness. He's able to grossly deny the fact that there is any human quality there, and basically, he has to just get it out of sight and get rid of it so that he has no more connection with that bad quality in himself.

"In another sense, under necrophilia . . . and fetishisms, there's a need to maintain some association with these representations of a once loving animate object.

"The basement plays a part in this because he'd been able to be like his father in making a basement very important. The father . . . stored his junk down there. John was able to . . . identify with his father in throwing his own junk . . . down in the basement. And that's where he buried all those bodies representing himself."

In answer to Amirante's question, Rappaport said that John Gacy did in fact suffer from a mental disease: "I believe," the doctor testified, "that he has a personality disorder called a borderline personality organization with a subtype of antisocial or psychopathic personality manifested by episodes of an underlying condition of paranoid schizophrenia." As a result of that disease, Gacy "did lack substantial capacity to control his behavior at the time of each of those crimes . . . and to conform his conduct to the requirements of the law."

Rappaport thought "the seeds in the source of the borderline condition and the pathological condition . . . started in early childhood. However, typically the borderline doesn't really exist in its full state until sometime during adolescence. I would imagine at the time that he . . . ran away to Las Vegas, worked in a mortuary, I think about that time he was definitely borderline." The level of Gacy's illness was intensified by the crucial happenings of his life, "the loss of his father and loss of his second wife through divorce."

Kunkle, on cross, tried to make the psychiatric testimony look tortured, too complex to explain something very simple. Burying the bodies—"these former love objects," as Kunkle kept referring to them—in the crawl space had been, in fact, a very successful means of concealing evidence. It didn't "require some great psychiatric theory to support it. It would simply be a rational idea."

"It might be irrational, too," Rappaport said.

"But it could be?"

"It could be rational, yes."

Under further questioning, Rappaport admitted that Gacy's

psychosexual disorders—the fetishism, sadism, and necrophilia—exist "separate and apart" from the borderline diagnosis but that "by the time you get to the sadism and necrophilia, it is pretty sure you have a personality disorganization. . . ."

Rappaport, in answer to Kunkle's intense questioning, said Gacy wasn't necessarily psychotic every time he engaged in sadism but that he was psychotic when he was killing.

Kunkle asked the doctor to assume "that lots of people have every bit as tortured . . . a childhood as this defendant, would they all become multiple murderers?"

"No," Rappaport replied.

Kunkle then tried to suggest that Gacy had attempted to fake mental illness, specifically a multiple personality.

"Are you familiar with the police reports . . . wherein the defendant would inject into the conversation . . . the name of Jack or Jack Hanley? . . . Did that indicate to you a multiple personality?"

"At one point I considered that," Rappaport said. "However, he told me so many different stories about it that I didn't believe it existed . . . there was no other evidence that a multiple personality existed."

Rappaport even consulted Dr. Cornelia Wilbur, an authority in the field of multiple personalities, who confirmed Rappaport's conclusion.

"Well," Kunkle demanded, "would the name Jack or Jack Hanley: could that have been inserted into those conversations by the defendant for the purpose of lying to the police officers, just as you felt he might have been lying to you?"

Rappaport didn't think so. Gacy, he said, used the name to disguise himself, to masquerade as a police officer: "He had many ideas as to what the name meant."

Yes, Rappaport said in answer to Kunkle's question, he believed that Gacy was psychotic at the time of each and every one of the thirty-three murders.

"How about specifically Robert Piest?" Kunkle asked.

"Same thing."

"Psychotic?"

"Yes."

"Floridly psychotic?"

"Yes."

"Certainly floridly psychotic when he strangled him to death?"

"Thinking he is the father and Piest the son: it was a psychotic delusion."

"How about when he laid him down on the floor and went on and answered the phone call? . . ."

"I think he was under the same delusion and was able to handle the phone calls, but he was under the delusion."

"And what about when he handled the phone call from the hospital about his uncle: still floridly psychotic?"

"Yes."

"What are the symptoms of psychosis?"

"A person out of touch with reality, a person who has thinking, mood, and behavior disorder. . . ."

". . . And the defendant was in florid psychosis when he was handling his business on the phone with this Piest body in the other room?"

"Yes."

John was "on a high" again. Rappaport was the best yet: he talked about the split, talked in terms the jury could understand, and Kunkle couldn't break him.

The doc even nailed Kunkle: wiped that smug bisexual smile off his face. Reversed the chunky fairy right there on the stand and got everyone— the jury, the judge, even the families—laughing at him. Laughing at Kunkle.

The chief deputy state's attorney was hammering away at his old theme, the idea that if John were psychotic, it should have shown up sometime in a social situation or something and not just when the crimes were committed.

"Schizophrenia is a psychotic disorder, is it not?" Kunkle had demanded. "It is a serious mental illness?"

"Yes," Rappaport had said.

And then Kunkle fucked up. "Every psychiatrist in this country would probably agree that psychiatry is a very serious mental illness?"

For the first time at the trial, there was laughter. The whole courtroom went up for grabs, and they were laughing at Kunkle. John was careful to keep a straight face—"psychiatry is a very serious mental illness"—but he was cracking up inside.

Rappaport, smiling slightly, said, "That's called a Freudian slip, and it comes from the unconscious." The doc was saying that

Kunkle had fucked up, from the unconscious. Just like John fucked up, from the unconscious. It could happen to anyone.

Kunkle was rattled. The prosecution didn't bring him any cigars, and John suddenly knew—it was like a revelation from God—that the jury was going to acquit: not guilty by reason of insanity. The state would have to put John in some institution, okay, but he knew what would happen; he could see it in fantasies bright as sunlight. A mental hospital: you can't keep someone in a mental hospital if he can prove he's sane. They gotta review you every ninety days or something.

After listening to the psychologists, John knew he could "control those tests." In the inkblot, you come up with all kinds of crazy things, not just bees and flowers. You got to say you see at least forty things in there. Include some people in the blots and put a little violence in there, but not too much. The Minnesota multiphasic would be a snap. John took the thing so many times he had a good idea of which questions "I shouldn't answer true to, even if the answer is true in my own mind." He would "fuck up some of the pictures instead of putting them in exact order. And on the drawings: draw two full figures, man and woman, whether they look good or not. And slim down the women so they don't have fat arms. Make sure the women don't have no apron strings hanging down by the crotch. Draw a full body, always a full body, and give it enough room on the paper. And if I make a mistake, don't let the doc see it. Don't change nothing, don't erase nothing."

Of course, John wouldn't depend entirely on the tests. He had committed "the crime of the century" and turned himself into a "multimillion-dollar property." On the opening day of the trial, he counted over seventy reporters. There'd be books and movies. John would control the rights, and he'd "manipulate the docs with money, control the Illinois State Board of Health" with the millions his crimes would earn him.

Jesus, he was so high after Rappaport. Really silly with happiness and plans and jokes. Just like if there were books and movies, well, shit, why not patent the handcuff trick? The rope trick. It was an idea that made him laugh aloud. Sell Pogo the clown suits to kids on Halloween. Make an 8213 Summerdale dollhouse for little girls. Comes complete with twenty-nine bodies. Have a full bathtub in there and a plastic boy doll kneeling on the side with its head in the water. Make more money "on optional bodies."

That was all just joking, but John knew there was money to be made. Joseph Wambaugh could write the book. John respected the guy 'cause he'd been a cop and he had a sense of humor. The movie should be really classy. John didn't know who could play him as a youngster, but as an adult, he was leaning toward Rod Steiger. The guy was a powerful actor who had a lot of John's "colorful charisma," and, like John, he could be really deep at times.

John could just see Steiger dominating the press conference after the trial. Some reporter would ask him how it feels to win, and Rod Steiger would have this really deep, sad expression on his face and he'd say, "I don't think anyone wins when thirty-three die." A great line.

Of course, the end could be Steiger walking out of the mental hospital in ninety days. He'd look into the camera—a real big close-up shot—and say, "Gacy outsmarted you again." And that would be the end of the movie. Fade to black right there.

Or . . . or maybe the movie should end with a close-up of Steiger looking out at the world in complete triumph, and then, slowly, he'd start to laugh. Not say anything. Just laugh. And it wouldn't be any crazy, out-of-control laugh, either.

CHAPTER
28

THE DEFENSE RESTED after Rappaport, and the first witness to testify for the state in rebuttal was Donald Voorhees, then twenty-seven. John could see that the past dozen years hadn't been good to the kid "who blackmailed" him and "fucked over" him, who had "outsmarted" him in Iowa. Voorhees. The kid looked like shit.

He was wearing these little round hippie glasses. Watery eyes swimming around behind the glass: eyes that didn't seem to see what they were looking at. John noticed that the kid was shaking pretty badly. Voorhees. Looking to outsmart him one more time. But—John could see it now—Voorhees was too fucked up to testify. Voorhees: the kid whose blond hair and muscular body and trick innocence were models for each and every one of the thirty-three boys Bad Jack murdered.

The little bastard was so scared he told the defense he felt he was not "competent" to take the stand. He had to be examined outside the presence of the jury.

Judge Garippo asked Voorhees if he had made a statement to the effect "that you felt incompetent to testify."

There was no response, and Egan for the state asked, "Did you say that, Don?"

A minute dragged by. Voorhees wet his lips and looked

about, seeing nothing. "You have to answer the question," Garippo said finally. "What did you mean by that?"

"Let me think," Voorhees said, and the words lay dry as sand on his tongue. What do you mean when you say things? "I am totally bent out of shape," Voorhees said finally. It seemed as if the witness wanted to say more. He mouthed the words once, twice, then whispered brokenly, "You know?"

Motta asked Voorhees if he was seeing a psychiatrist.

"Yes, sir, I am."

"How long have you been seeing him?"

Voorhees couldn't answer that and he stared blankly at the walls, the ceiling, looking for help. "For a while?" Motta prompted.

There was no answer to the question anywhere in the courtroom. The witness's eyes rolled helplessly, pleadingly: please stop this.

"All right," Motta said, "we will . . ."

But Voorhees had finally found the answer—how long had he been seeing a psychiatrist? a psychiatrist? how long?—and he said, "Ever since I heard Gacy was out of prison. Yes, I have had problems."

Garippo ruled that Voorhees could testify, and, in the presence of the jury, he fell completely apart. The witness said that he had worked for Gacy for about a month, spreading gravel on the driveway. The man had given him liquor and "he came on to me sexually." Voorhees couldn't elaborate, couldn't say just what it was that Gacy had done to him.

The answers Voorhees gave were lifeless things, dragged painfully up out of some interior depth, some dark and unhealthy place where there was mud and excrement and a kind of death before death. The witness took a minute or more to respond to each question, and the state finally, mercifully, withdrew him as a witness.

John knew it was important not to show emotion, and so he didn't smile, didn't laugh aloud. A credible witness? Voorhees? He testifies that he wasn't on medication but that he drank beer for breakfast. When John took the stand in his own defense, he'd really destroy Voorhees. Tell the jury "Voorhees didn't want to testify on account of he was involved in blackmail." See who outsmarts who in the end.

The state continued with all these witnesses who testified about the sodomy conviction in Iowa. The last Iowa witness was

Dr. Leonard Heston, a professor of psychiatry who had examined John in 1968. The diagnosis then, Heston said, was "antisocial personality . . . a personality who comes into repeated conflict with society and social norms." Heston testified that the antisocial person is not considered to have a mental disease or defect but a "defect in personality." A character flaw.

Heston agreed in part with Rappaport—the antisocial part— but said that he disagreed with the borderline diagnosis because "it virtually precludes a psychotic condition. Once that is achieved, then you are out of the borderline and then into some other diagnosis, usually schizophrenia."

Right away, John could see how he'd "destroy" Heston on the stand. He'd tell the jury that this was the same "superficial diagnosis" Heston made in Iowa, and if John had gotten the treatment he needed twelve years ago, there wouldn't have been any bodies down there in the crawl space. The first thing John was going to do when he was acquitted, he was going to sue the state of Iowa for what they had done to him. He'd been made "a victim" in Iowa.

He was still soaring on the Rappaport high, but something about the testimony of Donald Voorhees was weighing him down and he didn't know why.

John wasn't sure if he'd done the right thing during Robert Donnelly's testimony. "Just being cool and laughing": it might have been a mistake. "The jury looked over at me and I'm smiling and laughing while this guy is talking about how I supposedly fucked him over. Stuff he was saying was just crazy as shit. Totally unbelievable."

Just like the prosecution tried to make Donnelly look like "another goody-goody": twenty-one years old, scholarship student in law and government at the College of St. Francis. He said John picked him up around midnight on December 30, 1977.

Donnelly had a speech impediment—he stuttered slightly—and words came painfully to him, like razors in his throat. At first John thought he was going to be another Voorhees. The kid could barely look at him long enough to point him out in court.

Donnelly said that Gacy, posing as a police officer, had stopped him on the street, demanded to see some identification, then pulled a gun on him and handcuffed him. Once inside his house, Gacy threw him on a couch. Donnelly testified that Gacy

spoke in an authoritative manner, "like a police officer would talk
. . . he appeared to be quite sober and in control of all his senses."

*In court, John, listening to this bullshit, snorted audibly, as if
smothering a laugh of total disbelief. The kid talked like Elmer Fudd. He
was funny. Real dumb and stupid.*

Donnelly said Gacy "was talking to me and he was mentioning that he was an important person and still he didn't get the
respect he deserved."

Donnelly said that when he refused a drink—he was still
handcuffed—Gacy "came out from behind the bar and he picked
it up and he walked over to me and he just tossed it on my face."

*John, sitting by his lawyers, shook his head, smiling. Like he's
going to throw a drink on somebody and mess up his couch and rug? John
Gacy, Mr. Compulsive Neat, who gets pissed when some doc's books are
out of order? That John Gacy throws a drink? Real believable testimony.*

Donnelly refused a second drink and Gacy said, "You're a
guest, you should accept my hospitality." And then, Donnelly
testified, "he reached down and he took my face and he held my
mouth open and started pouring the drink."

The witness testified that Gacy "took my pants and undid
them. He started pulling down my pants and my underwear. . . ."

Donnelly was having a hard time talking about this, John
could see. The Elmer Fudd voice was cracking, the razors were
ripping the flesh in his throat, and there were tears in Donnelly's
eyes "because," John said later, "he was lying under oath."

Terry Sullivan asked, "What did he do after he pulled your
pants down?"

"He went and he got on top of me and I could tell that he
didn't have any pants on because I could feel his knees and he,
he put his knees between my legs and he grabbed onto my
shoulders. . . ."

Donnelly couldn't go on. Judge Garippo said, "Let's take a
recess." Donnelly, sobbing, said, "This is hell." He was crying so
hard he couldn't catch his breath. "This is hell," he said.

*John laughed aloud so that everyone would know what a phony-ass
actor the kid was. He glanced over at the jury: can you believe this shit?*

*After the recess, Donnelly said that he had gotten the support he
needed from his girlfriend. He was like some football player shaking off an
injury, acting brave for the jury. John nodded to him, but he made the
gesture real sarcastic. Nice act, asshole, but no one here's buying it.*

Donnelly testified that Gacy had raped him. Then "he took me by the arm and led me through the house to the bath- room . . . he turned my face to the wall of the bathroom and . . . pushed my head against the wall. And then he reached around my neck and he pulled something around my neck, and he started twisting it."

Donnelly testified that Gacy had said, "My, aren't we having fun tonight?"

Gacy banged Donnelly's head against the wall several times and "then he tripped me down onto the floor and then he got down and picked me up by what was around my neck. The bathtub was filled with water, and he stuck my head under the bathtub and I started fighting it and I was just squirming and moving and holding my breath and then . . . I passed out."

Sullivan asked, "Now, when you went into that bathroom, was that tub already full with water?"

"It was."

John couldn't help it, he had to laugh again. Crazy, unbelievable shit. Like he's going to fill the tub before he goes out to pick up someone. Like it was all premeditated or something, drowning the little bastard. The kid looked at John then, just once, and there was something different about him. He didn't seem so frightened anymore.

Donnelly testified that when he came to on the bathroom floor Gacy "stuck my head under the bathtub a second time. . . . I was really weak, and I could barely struggle. I just tried to hold my breath . . . and I couldn't and I started breathing water and I passed out again."

The kid was talking about being weak, but his voice was getting stronger.

"What is the next thing you remember?"

"I was awake on the floor again."

"What happened next?"

"He did it again."

John looked over at the jury and shook his head, smiling sadly, the way you smile when somebody real dumb and stupid fucks up in front of everybody. Some of the jurors were looking back—the guy with the moustache, the blond-haired guy John figured was "liberal" because he was blond, the heavy-set woman—and John couldn't read anything in their hard, blank expressions. He wanted to tell them that the John Gacy he knew could never torture anyone. That John Gacy was a "gentle individ-

ual." He tried for a gentle, forgiving smile, to show them that. He felt the grin waver weakly on his face.

"Did you pass out again?" Sullivan asked.

"Yes."

"When you came to the next time, did you see where Gacy was?"

"I looked up and he wasn't in the doorway. . . . I started to look around and he said, 'Are you looking for me? Here I am.' "

Gacy was sitting on the toilet, with the lid down. "He got up, and he"—Donnelly was stuttering again—"he, he unzipped his pants and he started pissing on me."

John laughed too loudly this time—it was more than a gentle man's whispered chuckle—and Garippo glanced over at him. He thought the judge might admonish him. Why the hell would you piss on somebody? John wanted to scream. What sense did that make?

"What happened after that?" Sullivan asked.

Donnelly said Gacy "brought over a magazine, one of those nude magazines, and he showed it to me and he asked me if I liked the girls and I said 'yes' and he said, 'You're sick.' " Then "he punched me and then he grabbed me and he stuck me under the bath water one more time."

When Donnelly came to, "I was on the bathroom floor and he picked me up and he led me into . . . a bedroom and he tripped me onto the floor and then he sat down like he first had on the couch, like sideways on me, and he said, 'You're just in time for *The Late Show.*' And he turned on a projector and I didn't look up and he grabbed me by the hair and he held my head up and made me watch the movie." It was "a gay porno flick."

The movie lasted about ten minutes. Gacy had Donnelly sit against the wall. "I, I, I rolled over and I got myself against the wall." He was still cuffed.

Gacy left the room and came back with a dining-room chair. He sat in the chair, Donnelly said, and "put his foot right in my stomach." Gacy had a gun in his hand and "he told me we were going to play Russian roulette."

Gacy said, " 'Aren't we playing fun games tonight? Aren't these good games?' "

John, sitting at the defense table, looked back into the courtroom and noticed that "Harold Piest was getting hyper." The families were so filled with hate they'd believe anything. God didn't put people on earth to hate one another. John rolled his eyes to the ceiling and sighed audibly. He chuckled a bit, but he really didn't know how to act now. Was it smart, laughing in court? The kid's voice wasn't quavering anymore: it was like he was getting stronger on the stand. Feeding off of John's forced laughter and confusion. The kid could look right at John anytime he wanted.

Donnelly testified that Gacy aimed the gun "at my head . . . and he said, 'Look at me' and he slapped me on the face again and I was looking up there and he pulled the trigger and nothing happened. . . . Most of the time, he just clicked it once. A couple of times he clicked it twice, and then after about ten, fifteen times, it went off. . . . I realized it must have been a blank because I was still alive."

After testifying that the gun went off, Donnelly said, "I was shaking and he reached down and he grabbed my throat with his hands and he just started twisting my head and he was, he was choking me and I passed out because . . . the next thing I realized, I wasn't on the floor anymore, I was on a bed. . . . I was still handcuffed, but there was something around my feet, right above my ankles." Donnelly's legs were spread and he was naked and his hands were cuffed behind his back. "I, I, I had a gag in my mouth and it was like stuffed in my mouth . . . he rolled me over . . . then he took something, I don't know what it was, and he started shoving it inside of me. . . . I was feeling extreme pain and I started to get dizzy and I passed out."

John tried another snorting laugh, because now the guy said he'd passed out, what, five times, six times in one night. It wasn't believable testimony, but John couldn't get the laugh to sound right. The kid looked right at John and he wasn't afraid anymore.

Donnelly testified that when he came to, the object was still in his anus. Gacy started taking the gag off and said, " 'Don't scream,' but as soon as he got it out, I screamed . . . he pushed my head down into the bed and punched me in the side. . . . I was terrified and I said, 'Look, you are going to kill me. Just kill me now. Get it over with.' He told me my time was coming and to shut up and he slapped me and he put the gag back in my mouth."

The kid was talking about wanting to die, but he glanced over at John just then. Like John was the one who was going to die.

Donnelly said that when it started to get light out, Gacy made him take a shower and—John made an effort to laugh at this part—drove him to work.

In the car Donnelly said Gacy asked him, " 'How does it feel knowing that you're going to die?' and I just didn't answer." Gacy pulled up in back of Marshall Field, where Donnelly worked. "He told me that he was going to get me and kill me later and he told me to lean forward and he took off the handcuffs and as he was taking off the handcuffs he told me, he said, 'You're going to die later, but don't tell, don't go to the police or anybody and don't tell them because they are not going to believe you.' "

Donnelly did, in fact, go to the police, and he found that Gacy was right. "They didn't believe me."

John snorted again, real loud, so the jury would know they shouldn't believe Donnelly, either. The kid gave him another one of those death looks and it was very hard for John to force the laugh out of his mouth. Later, walking back through the bullpen, John was pretty sure the smiling and head shaking hadn't been a good idea. He got the feeling that one of the guards assigned to him, Stanley, had suddenly started to hate him. Stanley had acted pretty neutral before. John knew then he shouldn't have laughed. Especially when Donnelly broke down, he shouldn't have laughed. The jury might think that he liked to see young men cry and shit. They might think that suffering amused him.

And then it hit him. Maybe Voorhees had outsmarted him a second time. Fucked him over by making it look like John Gacy had destroyed his entire life. Influencing the jury with emotion instead of the law.

The high—that soaring Rappaport high—collapsed. Suddenly, John was afraid. *If the defense docs were any good at all, he wouldn't testify, because then he wouldn't have anyone to blame for losing. He'd read where you could win a new trial on appeal if you can prove that you didn't agree with the plea. John figured he could say he was against the insanity plea from the first. Say he wanted to go with a straight "not guilty."*

That's the way he'd play it if the defense docs were any good.

A. Arthur Hartman, for twenty-eight years the chief psychologist of the Psychiatric Institute of the Circuit Court of Cook County, conducted about twenty-five hours of interviews with John Wayne Gacy over a period of two months. Testifying for the state, Hartman said he agreed with Dr. Heston: Gacy was "a psychopathic or antisocial personality with sexual deviation" who showed "minor symptoms or characteristics of paranoid hysterical reactions." He thought Gacy was capable of understanding the criminality of his conduct and that there was no evidence that he ever had "a mental breakdown or mental illness of the type that we consider a psychotic condition."

Hartman said that Gacy's statements, in twenty-five hours of interviews, were marked by "contradictions, indications of marked evasiveness, variation in what he would say at one time or another, attempts to rationalize or excuse."

Gacy gave only fourteen responses on the Rorschach, but Hartman saw no indication of bizarre or peculiar responses, "no indication of schizophrenic-type responses. . . ." The doctor thought that Gacy's responses to the inkblots, all those bees and flowers, indicated that "he knew what was appropriate and conventional. . . ."

In the sentence-completion test, Hartman said he was struck by "the general normality and conventionality" of Gacy's responses. "He presents himself . . . in almost an idealistic, altruistic way. For example, a sentence like, 'The happiest time' he answers, 'is when I am helping others.' "

Hartman said that such altruistic responses are typical of antisocial personalities who, classically, "mislead people," lie.

Hartman, in answer to Amirante, said the fact that Gacy was a complex person and a difficult case didn't preclude a diagnosis of antisocial personality. "The antisocial personality can be particularly complex. In fact, one of the frequent definitions is that he presents a complex picture. He may seem . . . bright, even charming, and yet have . . . strong antisocial attitudes, an aggressive lack of feelings, lack of remorse or guilt about acts of aggression against others. . . ."

Hartman suggested that John was a liar. The next expert witness for the state came right out and said it. Dr. Robert A. Reifman, the director of the Psychiatric Institute of the Circuit Court of Cook County, had conferred often with his colleague Dr. Hartman. Both men had experience with prisoners who had tried to cop an insanity plea, who feigned mental illness, who were pulling what the convicts called a "bug stunt."

Reifman spent sixteen hours with John Gacy. "It was my diagnosis," Reifman testified, "that Mr. Gacy suffered from a personality disorder, specifically narcissistic type," which "is not considered a mental disease."

The finding of narcissistic personality did not exclude a

diagnosis of antisocial personality, Reifman said. "Antisocial personality is a subtype of narcissistic personality. I didn't think it would be completely fair to call Mr. Gacy an antisocial personality, because it excludes the other aspects of his personality in which he's well accomplished." The doctor cited Gacy's success in business as one example of those other aspects.

Reifman didn't think Gacy fit the profile of a borderline personality because "in my experience . . . they do not function very well. They are occupationally very poor; they can't hold jobs. Their lives are chaotic." Gacy, on the other hand, was efficient and successful. He ran "a very successful contracting business." He was a "reasonably successful politician . . . a reasonably successful clown. He had lots of friends, and he was, generally speaking, a very efficient, successful person. Even with respect to the crimes, he was extremely efficient."

For the same reason, Reifman disagreed with Dr. Freedman's diagnosis of pseudoneurotic paranoid schizophrenia, because then "it would be impossible for him to function in a socially acceptable . . . way. Mr. Gacy functions extremely well . . . a pseudoneurotic schizophrenic is a frightened, constricted person who is teetering on the brink of psychosis and can't function."

Reifman found "no evidence that Mr. Gacy was psychotic" and "no evidence to support a diagnosis of paranoid schizophrenia." The hallmarks of schizophrenia, Reifman said, are "delusions, hallucinations, and loss of contact with reality." Gacy, Reifman testified, did not exhibit these symptoms.

The murders, Reifman said, were not thirty-three brief psychotic episodes. "I don't believe that you can have thirty-three cases of temporary insanity."

Gacy's descriptions of the murders proved that he was never out of touch with reality. "A person who gets some people to put handcuffs on has to talk to them. First of all, he has to gain their confidence, and he has to talk to them in a calm, rational way.

"Now, Mr. Gacy told me that he would put the handcuffs on himself, show how easy it was to get the handcuffs off . . . he literally conned them into putting the handcuffs on. A person who . . . was out of touch with reality cannot function in that kind of goal-directed behavior. . . . If he is angry or disturbed, I think it would have been unlikely that anybody would have gone along with him.

"Secondly, when he used the rope trick, it's a very intricate operation: You tie knots, you twist. . . . On that basis there's no evidence he was out of contact with reality when he performed these crimes."

Reifman said that while Gacy "seemed to be candid and forthcoming," he was actually "evasive," and, at first, denied any guilt. "He told me," Reifman testified, "that he was four persons: he was John Gacy the clown; John Gacy the politician; John Gacy the contractor; and a fellow named Jack Hanley, who, it was suggested, went ahead and did these crimes." Gacy said he had no memory of the murders and "did not know about Jack Hanley.

"Well, it became very clear that most of the murders were committed with no witness and that the only information we have about the murders is information given us by John Gacy, and the information was considerable. So, therefore, the idea that Jack Hanley was a person who functioned in this way without Mr. Gacy's knowledge was not true. He had very good recall. . . ."

Reifman said he did not find any evidence at all to support a multiple-personality theory and added that "no other psychiatrist or psychologist subsequent to myself did either."

If the murders weren't brief outbreaks of psychotic behavior or the workings of an alternate personality, neither were they the products of irresistible impulse, in Reifman's opinion. As an example of such an impulse, Reifman postulated a "person who has to vomit . . . in front of their family and company . . . the urge to vomit becomes very strong and they struggle with it. Finally . . . they vomit in spite of the social connotations. They cannot resist the urge to vomit . . . it's truly an impulse a person cannot resist."

Reifman didn't think Gacy even struggled against his homicidal impulses. "In fact, if we regard the testimony of Cram and Rossi, who dug graves underneath the crawl space for the purposes of burying bodies: I don't think a person who plans to have an irresistible impulse in the future could be having irresistible impulses."

Under cross-examination by Amirante, Reifman said that "Mr. Gacy likes to talk, and when he talks, he just talks everything. So I felt it was a good source of information."

Amirante asked if Gacy's effusive stream of talk didn't demonstrate loose association, a characteristic of schizophrenia.

"When Mr. Gacy says on one hand . . . he killed somebody and on the next hand he says he didn't do it, is that loose association?"

"I think that's lying," Reifman said flatly. "I think he doesn't remember what he says from one day to the next because he lies."

"You said he was lying," Amirante said. "What was he lying about? That he didn't do it, or that he did do it?"

"My impression," Reifman said, "was that he was lying when he said he didn't do it."

Was that conjunction of truth and falsehood consistent with logical thinking? Amirante asked.

"A person who lies in what . . . is their best interest may be functioning logically."

Amirante asked if there weren't "patchy blocks" in Gacy's recollections of the murders he talked about. "You are assuming patchy blocks," Reifman said. ". . . There were things that he said he didn't remember, and I didn't believe him. I believe he has an excellent memory."

In fact, Gacy's claim that he couldn't recall the moment of the murders, Reifman said, indicated to him that the man was malingering, trying to feign insanity.

Amirante asked if Gacy hadn't told the doctor he thought it was stupid to act crazy and that he was not crazy.

"That's what he said."

"But on the other hand, you are saying that he was trying to fake being crazy."

"That's correct."

Reifman disagreed with his colleague Dr. Hartman, with Dr. Freedman and Dr. Rappaport, who all thought Gacy was not malingering. "He was trying to fake a multiple personality," Reifman said. ". . . There is no doubt in my mind when he came in for the interview he was trying to fake a double personality."

"Isn't it probable," Amirante asked, "that a person who does such a horrible thing would try to blame it on somebody else, or another part of him? Isn't that possible?"

"Oh, I think he would try to blame it on anybody else," Reifman said, "if he were smart, sure."

Gacy was, Reifman said, "explicitly vague . . . he tries to obfuscate, or tries to present a picture that is not clear."

On redirect examination by Kunkle, Reifman said that he

thought Jack Hanley "was an attempt to use an insanity defense to avoid responsibility for the crime." A bug stunt.

The day's headline read, "Gacy Faked Insanity to Win Plea in Court: Doctor." All they had on the television was "Reifman and the bathtub boy." Like they believed that Donnelly's story was true and that Reifman could really tell "when somebody is lying and when he isn't." Nobody can do that.

The prosecution kept giving him cigars, but they had another "ploy" working. They were trying to break him down. Investigator Greg Bedoe had sidled up to him and said, "Just keep laughing, John." Like it was going to be the last time he ever laughed again.

And then prosecutors were putting PDM stickers that they had stolen from his house on their notebooks. There was one stuck on the wall beside the courthouse phone John used to call Ma. Kunkle knew it would piss him off. Maybe make him mad enough to take the stand where Kunkle would tear him apart with bisexual tricks. He couldn't beat Kunkle. If John "cut him up with words" the jury would think he was "too smart to be insane." If he just sat there, acting dumb and stupid, Kunkle would "butcher me for breakfast."

John could see how the state was "building a noose tighter and tighter around my neck." They were "using emotion and not the law." Mothers fainting on the stand. Voorhees. The bathtub boy. Rignall—John's own witness—talking about fireplace pokers and then puking right in front of the jury. Reifman saying that John tried to baffle the docs with bullshit, "obfuscate," "present a picture that is not clear." Like John was trying to outsmart the docs with insanity.

John wasn't going to take the stand, not after Reifman and the bathtub boy. He'd remain a "mystery man." Tell the judge he never agreed with the insanity defense. Get his grounds for appeal on the record, right there in the trial transcript.

The only thing the state had proved is that there were bodies buried in his crawl space. They could give him ten years for "concealing a homicide." Three hundred thirty years served consecutively, but ten years served concurrently. He'd be out in a year and a half, just like Iowa. That's how the trial should have gone; it's how his trial on appeal would go.

If he took the stand now it would look like he agreed with the plea. And if he never took the stand, if he was a "mystery man," he could control the money from the books and films about the "crime of the century" and use it for lawyers and shit on appeal.

Besides, John was "paranoid of Kunkle."

The last expert witness for the state in rebuttal was Dr.
Idiot, James Cavanaugh, the director of the section on the law in
the Department of Psychiatry at St. Luke's Medical Center in
Chicago. He was a little bit of a surprise because John always
figured him for one of the character-flaw, antisocial-personality-
diagnosis docs, but Cavanaugh came in with a combination of
Hartman and Reifman. Cavanaugh said John had "a mixed personality disorder" and that his was both a narcissistic personality and
an antisocial personality. Hitting all the defense bases right there.
   *It was another "superficial diagnosis," especially when you com-
pared it to Rappaport's testimony. But then Dr. Idiot attacked Rappaport
without ever mentioning him by name.*
   Cavanaugh said the major concept behind psychoanalytic
theory "is that human behavior is determined by events that have
gone before. It's a highly deterministic theory of psychology that
says if you experience certain things in the past, then it's possible
to predict or to reconstruct the reason behind why, subsequently,
certain types of behavior patterns, thoughts, feelings, fantasies
occur.
   "In this sense, it is difficult, if you accept the psychoanalytic framework, to assess responsibility because in, for example, a
matter of breaking the law, the analyst will be able to give an
explanation as to why this particular behavior occurred, based on
a reconstruction of events, interactions that particular individual
had in the past. The law is based on the concept that each of us
has a free will. And therefore we are responsible for our behavior
in a sense, irrespective of what has gone before.
   "You therefore have an inherent conflict between a deter-
minant particular psychology that seems to explain everything on
the face of one's earlier development, in conflict with a legal
system that holds everyone responsible in demonstrating a free
will. There's therefore this inherent conflict between the two
positions.
   "Legally, the only one who had been allowed to escape the
judgment of responsibility . . . is when such an extreme situation
arises that questions about one's ability to form an intent to
commit a crime are raised."
   Kunkle, on direct examination, referred to Motta's opening

statement and "his desire that the defendant would be put in some mental institution for the rest of his life . . . is it possible to guarantee a person found not guilty by reason of insanity, and then committed to a mental hospital, Department of Mental Health in Illinois, will remain there for the rest of his life?"

"Absolutely impossible," Cavanaugh said. ". . . We find it very difficult to keep people in hospitals who in fact need to be there because of a concern, which I can understand, that to hospitalize is a deprivation of civil rights. . . ."

Motta and Amirante were objecting, but John knew that it was all over right there. Kunkle was smirking up at Dr. Idiot, who was sitting there like he hadn't just dropped "the biggest bomb of the trial."

On cross by Motta, Cavanaugh restated his position. John Gacy "would not meet the state's involuntary-commitment standards," Dr. Idiot said.

John's letter to Judge Garippo, written in haste and rage, read, in part, "I . . . ask for a mistrial, as never before has this court allowed a professional witness plant a seed in the Jury head like it was done yesterday.

"I think that you can give them instructions until you're blue in the face and you won't take that out of their heads.

"When Cavanaugh said, 'John Gacy would not qualify for commitment to a mental institution and would have to be set free if he were found not guilty by reason of insanity.'

"As you know, other than so-called statements made by me, and given in a self-serving manner by officers for the prosecution, there is only evidence that I owned the house that was used for the bodies, their safekeeping.

"Until something is done to correct this injustice, I will no longer have anything to do with my attorneys. And I am taking back my word in regards to not saying anything in the courtroom. The prosecution continued to tries to make me mad while the trial is going on with the taking of my PDM Contractor labels and putting them all over the place. That's receiving of stolen properties. And yesterday Greg Bedoe came up to me in open court and told me I should stop smiling, and swore at me, I don't have to take that. . . ."

Garippo called John forward. "Are there any tactics your attorneys are using that you don't agree with?" he asked.

"I was against the insanity defense from the beginning," John said for the record.

Tobias Brocher, a psychiatrist associated with the Menninger Foundation, testifying for the defense, said he diagnosed John as a borderline personality tending toward schizophrenia.

Dr. Helen Morrison, a psychiatrist in private practice and the editor of *Handbook of Forensic Psychiatry*, said John suffered from a "mixed psychosis or an atypical psychosis." She talked about splitting and projective identification, all the Rappaport stuff. Jack Hanley, according to Dr. Morrison, was "the policeman, the investigator, the big man, the man who could take care of all sorts of things. He was a protector against . . . inner disorganization. . . . He was a safety mechanism." Hanley was not an alternate personality, however. "That's too advanced."

In cross, Egan asked Morrison if she thought "John Gacy would have killed Robert Piest if there was a uniformed police officer in the home with him at the time."

"Yes, I do," Morrison said.

John felt like screaming at Egan and Kunkle and the jury and all the goddamn families. "There was a police officer there, you assholes! Jack Hanley was there!"

The prosecution brought in Dr. Jan Fawcett, chairman of the Department of Psychiatry at St. Luke's, who said he disagreed with the defense docs and that John was not suffering from a mental disease. Big surprise. Blah, blah. Doctor days.

The prosecution closed by saying John Gacy was evil.

"These murders," Terry Sullivan said, "were carefully planned, they were calculated, and they were carefully covered up. Seldom if ever has anyone been so cold, so calculating, so cunning over such a long period of time as John Gacy."

The defense said he was insane.

John Gacy "tried so hard when he was a little kid," Amirante said. "He tried so hard to be good. But he was caged in his own flesh. He was eaten up by his raging illness."

March 12, 1980:

The jury returned its verdict in less than two hours.

"Gacy Found Guilty," the headlines read. "Jury Rejects Insanity Plea."

March 13, 1980:

They brought back the sentence in two hours, fifteen minutes. "We, the jury, unanimously conclude that the court shall sentence the defendant, John Wayne Gacy, to death."

There was applause in the courtroom, most of it coming from the area where the families had been sitting for the past six weeks.

"I hope he burns in hell," one mother said.

CHAPTER
29

THEY PUT HIM IN the condemned unit at Menard Correctional Center. Condemned prisoner N00921, awaiting execution, worked on his appeal. He was looking hard at the first search warrant. If the high court threw that one out, they'd have to suppress the second search, the one where they found the bodies. No bodies, no evidence. No evidence, no conviction. "It's the theory of fruit from a poisoned tree," John Gacy explained after his conviction. "The first warrant is poisoned. All the fruit they got from that is poisoned." On top of all that inadmissible evidence—all those bodies—there were dozens of reversible errors in his trial. He hadn't even agreed with the insanity plea. His objection is right there, in the trial transcript. And no way those postarrest statements had been voluntary. His lawyers had been incompetent.

It was intricate work, thinking about the appeal. John's fellow convicts on the hill, death row, or in the pit, general population, didn't help. The prison administrators "just bend over backwards to please these guys if they're black. When we had all-white officers, this place was run real tight. Now all they ask for is minority officers. They got 'em coming in drunk, coming in selling pills, selling grass. They're selling sunglasses."

What bothers John the most is "the head honchos of the

black ones. There's about three or four that lead them. Everything to them is racist. And they say they want to get me. Like I'm the one who invented the death penalty. Like if they get rid of me, there'll be no more death penalty. I said to one, I says, 'Don't take kindness for weakness. You're wrong. Just cuz I don't want to fight doesn't mean I won't. You're talking to John Gacy now. You don't want to talk to the other side.' "

Gacy said, "I remember them all. I remember all thirty-three of them."

He said, "I'm the only one who knows everything." That's to the Old Man's credit. Say what you want, John Stanley taught his son something about the world. Life is a contest of wills, of determination and intelligence. The other guy is always bent on outsmarting you. The docs were like that, smart, and John knew they were digging for the root of something they thought grew deep in soul, some dark flower. They were looking to outsmart him with tests, with inkblots, with his own drawings. But John Gacy is not dumb and stupid: he knew that all the psychiatrists— the defense docs included—were actually "witnesses for the state." He didn't tell them everything. He held some things back: he tended the dark flower on his own. There were still some secrets, nice little secrets, and all the smart lawyers and docs and cops would never know. It made John feel good, keeping his secrets. But then, secrets aren't much good unless someone, somewhere knows how you outsmarted them all.

Just like when they searched the house and found the freezer out back, some idiot figured the meat John always bought in bulk might actually be body parts. He could just see these assholes unwrapping a side of pork and waiting around for it to thaw, feeling a little sick to their stomachs.

So they thawed out his whole freezer and never looked twice at the sections of garden hose hanging in the garage. Never figured out that John had a nice little hobby going. "I took a few of them out there," John said once. "Put them on the table and tried embalming them."

It was fascinating, the embalming process, and John had watched it often enough at the mortuary in Las Vegas, where he had once worked. The thing about the bodies, it was okay: they were dead, they didn't care, you could do anything to them. It was like science.

Even when revealing his secrets, John stressed the idea that death and sex had come together in his mind through a series of divine "accidents," acts of God almost. Just like he had been fighting his urges—feelings of tenderness toward his male friends— all of his teenage years. It was a courageous fight, and he had been strong.

Every day he asked himself, "Why was it in me?" Was it something God gave him to overcome, like the trials of Job? Those desires: he'd never done anything to deserve them. He always wondered, when he was young, if people could see it in him. The Old Man could, John knew.

John Stanley had this piercing expression, a look like he could see through his son: see even beyond the urges and night fantasies, see right through to something even darker. The Old Man could look directly into John's soul, and what he saw there were slop and mud and excrement. John knew it, just by the Old Man's expression. When John Stanley looked at him, John felt "transparent." So he had to live with that, and it probably had something to do with the first "accident."

It had happened in Las Vegas, when John "ran away from home" at the age of twenty. In the mortuary, free of the Old Man for the first time in his life, John could "experiment." Maybe just do it once. Get it out of his system. See what it was like. "They were just dead things," John said, "they couldn't tell anybody."

And that might have been it. Just once, twice. But then they brought in some kid—a young boy, seventeen or eighteen— and John couldn't believe it: the dead boy had an erection. Forensic pathologists will tell you certain types of back injuries cause a lingering erection in death. The phenomenon is extremely rare, but the body John remembers did have an erection. Was that John's fault? That God gave him this?

It was late at the mortuary. Lights out: nobody else there. An open coffin, silver-gray with a white interior. John got inside and arranged himself atop the dead boy.

What if he were the dead one? How would that feel? John wrestled with the body until it was on top of him. He lay there for a moment, feeling the weight of death press down on him and listening to the thudding of his bad heart. Had it skipped a beat?

He could feel his diseased heart swelling inside his chest. He didn't know, for a moment, whether death, like a gift of love, was coming to him as he lay gasping in the white interior of that silver-gray coffin.

There was a sudden terror so sublime John couldn't comprehend it. He was up and out of the coffin then, slapping at his body as if it were covered with crawling, slimy things. He could hear himself, hear the half-choked screams of revulsion and fear. At the same time—this was part of the horror—John knew there was nothing on him at all. It was his body that was repulsive. Himself.

The fright sent him back to Illinois the next day, but John knew "it was a seed." Something had been planted in all that muck the Old Man saw at the bottom of his soul. A seed planted by accident.

The prosecutors always insisted that John Gacy had never told them any more than they already knew. He claimed he could recall "patchy blocks" of five of the killings, but Greg Godzik and John Butkovitch had been PDM employees. They could easily be tied to John Gacy. Investigators could connect him to John Szyc through the car. And they knew he'd killed Rob Piest.

But they never could explain why John told them about the first one: the Greyhound bus boy. It was a murder the police knew nothing about. The boy still is unidentified.

John told them about the first one because it was the second important "accident." What happened with the Greyhound bus boy: it was just as John said, with some exceptions.

Sure, he'd picked the kid up at the Greyhound bus station. They'd "got into it, okay." Maybe they did a little S.&M.

It was just after Christmas, the anniversary of John Stanley's death. Funeral services for John's Aunt Pearl would be held the next day, and John could vaguely recall whipping the Greyhound bus boy. They went to sleep then: John in his room, the boy in the guest room.

Something different here, though. In this later version of the murder, John very specifically said that it wasn't four in the morning when he woke to find the boy standing by the bed with a knife in his right hand. It was already light out, morning. Maybe John heard him; maybe the boy actually reached out and touched

John's foot. Could be he actually shook it gently, like he was trying to wake John up.

All John could see was the knife. He lunged at the kid and grabbed for the hand that held the blade. They didn't really fight for the knife, though. Not in this version of the story. The boy seemed surprised, John said, frightened, and he hardly fought at all. He brought the knife up from his side as if to protect himself, just as John reached for his wrist. The knife sliced into the fatty part of John's palm.

"What are you doing?" the kid screamed. Like he couldn't understand why a man would want to protect himself from a kid with a knife. "What's the matter with you?"

John couldn't stop looking at the blood pouring out of his hand. He remembered feeling "a surge of power from my toes to my brain." He was no longer "the sick individual who was physically weak. I felt ten times stronger than I ever was before." The power centered in his hands. The sense that his hands were extremely large and powerful was overwhelming. "I felt that I could grab this son-of-a-bitch and break him in half. I felt all the blood going to my face. It felt like my eyes were bulging out of my head."

There was a kind of one-sided fight then, but John had to admit that the kid didn't actually "fall on the knife and kill himself."

He said he grabbed the boy in his huge hands and flung him hard against the wall. The kid hit his head, dropped the knife, and slid slowly down the wall. When John moved forward, the boy kicked him in the stomach, doubling him over.

"Motherfucker," John heard himself say, "I'll kill you."

He was on him then, straddling the boy's chest. His left hand was tangled in the boy's blond hair, and he was banging the head onto the floor. The knife was in John's right hand, and he saw it plunging into the boy's naked chest. There was blood, hot and slippery, and it felt, to John, like some strange and violent form of sex.

The room, John said, seemed to be whirling. There were some incomprehensible sounds: the splat of the knife, the screams of pain and fear, the awful "guzzling" of open chest wounds. "It was like that *Goodbar* movie," John said, "where he stabs the girl in the end."

When the boy was finally still, John rolled off his body. "I felt exhausted," he said, "just totally drained." He looked down at the wash pants he'd worn to bed. They were covered with blood, of course, but John noticed something else there. "I seen the front of my pants were all wet," John said.

The ejaculation had been an involuntary response, like a sneeze, but the power of that orgasm numbed his mind. "That's when I realized that death was the ultimate thrill," he said.

It was this revelation, as much as the never-ending "gurgulation" from the bedroom, that had him "walking around like a chicken with its head cut off. I was drained, physically and emotionally." John found himself in the bathroom, washing the blood off his body, off the knife he seemed to be carrying. When that was clean, he took it back to the kitchen, "where it belonged."

He noticed, then, that the table was set in two places. John hadn't done that. There was a carton of eggs on the counter and a chunk of bulk bacon on the cutting board. No slices had been cut from the bacon.

The boy had set the table for two, and he'd walked into John's bedroom to wake him, absentmindedly carrying the knife in his right hand. Maybe he was going to ask John if he wanted any bacon.

"See," John explained, "he wasn't trying to outsmart me at all. He was trying to do something nice."

So the first one had been an accident, not John's fault at all. That's why he told the cops about it. Because he was completely innocent.

He didn't tell them about "the ultimate thrill," though. He didn't tell them that the seed planted a dozen years before had taken root when he killed the Greyhound bus boy.

As nearly as John can recall, as closely as police and pathologists can figure, it took another three and a half years for the dark flower to reach full bloom.

John said he buried the bodies in his crawl space because "they were my property." He sometimes referred to them as "my trophies." He liked having them in the crawl space because "sex was always better, just knowing they were down there." And it was smart, storing his trophies in the crawl space. If the police had been finding bodies out in the parks or the rivers all along he never would have been able to talk his way out of the Rignall mess or the Donnelly arrest. But he's outsmarted the police for six years. Because he buried them in the crawl space. It was a stroke of "animal genius," storing his trophies down there.

"I'm in the *Guinness Book of World Records*," John said, and it was a matter of obvious pride to him. You don't get into that book by being dumb and stupid.

"Killing them was almost too easy," John once said. It was no challenge after the first dozen or so. In some of the later ones, John said, he even changed the rules. "Just like, some of them, they weren't even handcuffed. I just used the rope trick." The nights he killed two at once—and John said it happened more than once—were special challenges, like the time "I did a double with only one pair of cuffs."

Those were the best times, John said, fun times when the dark flower was in full bloom.

The bodies, his trophies, were evidence of a brilliance John could barely believe belonged to him. It was like a destiny from God, his brilliance. He felt almost as if it had come from somewhere outside the person he knew as John Gacy.

On February 15, 1983, Henry Brisbon, a black man known as the I-57 killer, was being escorted to the Menard prison law library when he somehow slipped out of his handcuffs, broke away from a guard, and stabbed John Gacy in the arm with a sharpened wire.

Brisbon, the second most notorious killer on Menard's death row, was convicted of murdering two people in a two-dollar robbery along Interstate 57. He received the death sentence after fatally stabbing a fellow inmate at the Stateville Correctional Center in 1978.

Gacy and another man injured in the attack had been out of their cells, sweeping the tier on a voluntary work program. Guards said they were not aware of any feud among the three men.

Gacy was treated for a puncture wound at the prison hospital and released. Officials said Brisbon would be punished for the attack. They said his in-cell television and radio privileges could be revoked.

In the summer of 1984, the Illinois Supreme Court, voting

7 to 0, upheld John Gacy's conviction and death sentence, order-ing that he be executed by lethal injection. The justices found Terry Sullivan's carefully prepared search warrants to be entirely proper and denied claims that Gacy's postarrest statements to various officers violated his constitutional rights in any way.

After studying the transcripts of the trial, the justices concluded that Gacy's attorneys—Sam Amirante and Bob Motta—were not incompetent. On the contrary, Justice Joseph Golden-hersh, writing for the court, said Gacy's attorneys mounted a "vigorous" defense and that "there is no merit to the assertion that their representation was ineffective."

The court also ruled that a statement made by William Kunkle during the penalty phase of the trial did not justify a reversal of the death penalty. Kunkle had said, "As a citizen of Illinois, I don't want to pay this guy's rent for the rest of his life."

Lawyers for the Illinois public defender's office, who rep-resent Gacy, said they expected " to follow the common practice in criminal cases of asking the U.S. Supreme Court to review the decision."

William Kunkle was "very pleased" with the decision. The court set November 14, 1984, as the date for Gacy's execution, but Kunkle said, "We're probably looking at three or four years at a minimum, unfortunately."

On March 4, 1985, the United States Supreme Court denied John Gacy's appeal.

John paints pictures of clowns, but the one he did of the Seven Dwarfs caused a good deal of controversy. When the gover-nor heard that John had made thirty-five dollars for that painting at the Illinois State Fair, he banned any further sales. In the painting—a rendering straight out of Walt Disney— the dwarfs were carrying picks and shovels. Some people thought that the digging implements were references to the crawl space under the house at 8213 Summerdale.

John told one reporter that the painting was designed "to bring joy into people's lives, that's all."

At Menard, John studies the pictures of the victims and wonders "who the hell they were and where they came from." He figures most of them were products of broken homes.

It's the families John thinks of most, though. He "feels sorry for them" because they are "filled with hate." Hate doesn't solve anything. You can't live a life filled with hatred; you can't do anything productive. Hate fills up all your time. John "prays for them." Like him, they've experienced tragedy. Unlike him, they can go on with their lives should they so choose. If he could give them a message, he'd tell them to seek solace in the Bible, in the word of God above. Seek and ye shall find.

John's not asking for forgiveness. "If I did the crimes, then I don't deserve to live," he said. The sad part is, no doc "has been able to prove to me that I did it." That's "the biggest joke": After all this time, after all the docs, John still doesn't know. He swears he doesn't, "with God as my Witness."

He'd like to explain that to the families, especially the Piests. Maybe he should have taken the stand. "If I would have told the truth about Robby, the truth as I know it, how could Kunkle have picked that apart? What could he say if I told the truth—that I might have done it, but if I did, I don't know why?"

It was too bad Kunkle had scared him off the stand, John said. That was where he could have made his statement to the families. He would have said something to help them, to ease their minds. He wanted them to see that John Gacy was every bit as much a victim as their sons. "I would have started with my youth," John said. "I would have shown how I was the first victim. How I was cheated out of my childhood. How I was victimized in Iowa. I would have gone through the ones I remember and explained everything so that the families could see my side of it."

For a time, John wanted to write a book. Not for money. The money would have gone to charity. The book would contain everything he didn't understand and would be addressed to the families. He'd call it "The 34th Victim."

But the state took that away from him, too. Illinois has a civil law that says a criminal can't financially benefit from his crimes. Even if the money is going to charity.

It was another victimization, this denial of his chance to finally explain himself to the families, to present his side. He wanted them to "meet the real John Gacy" and not "a monster the media created."

He wondered if, finally, after his death—after the last

victimization—there would be someone, somewhere who would understand how badly it had hurt to be John Wayne Gacy.

In Illinois, execution by lethal injection involves the administration of three different drugs through intravenous tubes. The first, sodium thiopental, is a surgical anesthetic that causes the loss of consciousness.

When the condemned is asleep, a combination of potassium chloride and Pavunol are pumped through the tubes. Pavunol paralyzes the diaphragm. Potassium chloride stops the heart.

When the drugs are properly administered, lethal injection is an entirely painless way to die. Death comes in about seven minutes, while the condemned sleeps.

The funeral service John says he wants would be a 10:00 A.M. white Mass at St. Francis Borgia. He wants to be dressed in a blue suit, a white shirt, and a red tie with blue stripes. The hands should be folded over his chest, steepled as if in prayer. A black rosary should be fit in under the thumbs.

John would like the congregation to sing his three favorite hymns: "Amazing Grace," "How Great Thou Art," and "Holy God, We Praise Thy Name."

He wants to be buried in Maryhill Cemetery, in the plot at the head of his father's grave.

The coffin should be silver-gray with a white interior.